Literary Disruptions

JEROME KLINKOWITZ

Literary Disruptions

THE MAKING OF A POST-CONTEMPORARY AMERICAN FICTION

Second Edition

UNIVERSITY OF ILLINOIS PRESS
Urbana Chicago London

LIBRARY OF CONGRESS CATALOGING IN PUBLICATION DATA

Klinkowitz, Jerome.
  Literary disruptions.

  Includes bibliographies and index.
  1. American fiction—20th century—History and
criticism. I. Title.
PS379.K55   813'.5'409   75-4806 80-15092
ISBN 0-252-00809-X (cloth)
       0-252-00810-3 (paper)

History of a Minor Maker

His images cohered
no more than
hill-slopes
sun-browned
& slid down
by boys on
cardboard
sleds.

He failed the meaning of feeling.
He suffered the scorn of zebras,
those even
animals.

His music was
tensionless as
the schizophrenic
singing
in his ice-bath.

His lines bent
from sentiment
the way bright
moths veer off
the 70 mile
an hour windshield.

Toward the end he was seen
watering his typewriter,
gluing grass to paper.

And, though warned against wind,
he wandered out, sick,
tearing off bedclothes, bandages—
found later,
perfectly still, all
his wounds calm
as kites.

—DAVID HILTON

Preface to the Second Edition

A decade and a half after their first appearance on the American scene, the literary disruptions of Ronald Sukenick, Raymond Federman, Gilbert Sorrentino, and their colleagues are still matters for controversy. The effect of their work has been considerable, inspiring a wholly new aesthetics for American fiction, but also drawing attacks from critics such as John Gardner (*On Moral Fiction*) and Gerald Graff (*Literature Against Itself*), who seek the standards of an earlier day.

A predictable irony has been that innovations of American art are better appreciated in Europe than at home. At universities in England, France, Germany, Austria, Poland, Hungary, and Yugoslavia, the innovative American fiction of the past fifteen years is a popular subject for study, discussion, and graduate research. Our fictionists are invited there to read and teach, and critical response to their work has been more positively inclined than the ingrained conservatism of American academics might allow. The heart of this activity has been at the Centre de Recherche sur la Littérature Américaine Contemporaine, directed by Professor André Le Vot at the Université de Paris III (Sorbonne Nouvelle). The Centre's two journals, *Revue Française d'Etudes Américaines* and *Trema,* shame our own with their comparative range and vigor.

It has been my pleasure to develop this volume's Postface and update its Bibliography during lectures and discussions at the Sorbonne's Centre; and to André Le Vot, Marc Chenetier, Régis Durand, and their colleagues I am grateful for a stimulating and constructive attitude toward disruptive American fiction. As Joyce, Fitzgerald, and Hemingway found a home in Paris during the Twenties, so may a new fiction be reborn in this still friendly environment.

March/October, 1979

        —Jerome Klinkowitz
        Hotel du Panthéon
        Paris

Preface

"Post-contemporary," someone told me when they read this book in manuscript, means "future," and as applied to fiction would indicate a literature not yet written. In some senses this is the meaning I intend. For even the well and intelligently read, "contemporary American fiction" suggests Ken Kesey, Joseph Heller, John Barth, and Thomas Pynchon at best—and at worst Updike, Roth, Bellow, and Malamud. My thesis is that the most contemporary of this lot, Barth and Pynchon, are in fact regressive parodists, who by the Literature of Exhaustion theory have confused the course of American fiction and held back the critical (although not the popular) appreciation of Kurt Vonnegut, Jr., Donald Barthelme, Jerzy Kosinski, and the other writers surveyed in this book. Vonnegut and company, however, have performed a radical disruption, far different from the ironies and burlesques of Barth and Pynchon and their imitators who follow in such polite thematic (and not formal) revolt from what has gone before. Hence the prologue, "The Death of the Death of the Novel," would sort out the funereal from the re-creative in recent fiction. The writers discussed after Barth and Pynchon are indeed post-contemporary; while their critical appreciation has until just recently lagged behind, their theories and techniques are vivid proof of the direction which fiction will take, and is taking, as the future unfolds before us.

Although the prologue studies fiction of the Sixties in general, my real concern begins with the publishing season of 1967–68, when for the first time in a long time a clear trend in literary history became evident. In that year all the fictionists of the new disruptive school published major works; the public discovered Kurt Vonnegut, Jr., and the publishing industry acknowledged the new movement by giving the National Book Award to Jerzy Kosinski for his extremely disruptive novel, *Steps*. Many other fictionists were writing in 1967–68, of course; but then, in 1916 three generations of novelists—those of James, Dreiser, and Hemingway—were writing in one form or other, so some critical and historical discrimination is appropriate. The authors studied in *Literary Disruptions* are of a definite style and school: given to formal experimentation, a thematic interest in the imaginative transformation of reality, and a sometimes painful but often hilarious self-conscious artistry, they stand apart from the Updike group, and especially from Barth and his circle, as clearly as do Hemingway and Fitzgerald from their two generations of elders writing as they began their own careers.

Several persons share the credit for helping this study to evolve and see light. Foremost to be thanked are the writers themselves. Kurt Vonnegut, Jr., Donald Barthelme, and Jerzy Kosinski each submitted to formal interviews as I was completing this book. Jim Sloan, Ron Sukenick, Raymond Federman, and Gil Sorrentino all contributed an undue amount of time and understanding in their correspondence, conversation, and friendship. My student John O'Brien introduced me to the work of virtually all the writers studied in Chapter Six and thereafter; his book *Interviews with Black Writers* stands as an important part of my own education. The editors of *Partisan Review, Modern Fiction Studies, North American Review, Fiction International,* and *Chicago Review* were kind enough to let me think out loud in the pages of their magazines; for the use of some of my material first printed there, in much different form, I am very grateful. Keith McKean, Joseph Schwartz, Charles Newman, Jonathan Baumbach, and Ann Lowry Weir read the manuscript in its entirety, as did Elaine Klinkowitz; Kathie Hinton, Joe David Bellamy, Loree Rackstraw, Dan Cahill, and John Somer read parts, and for all their help I owe a substantial debt of gratitude. Finally, the Committee on Research of the University of Northern Iowa provided a summer grant and much continuing support, which allowed me to complete this work.

—Jerome Klinkowitz
Cedar Falls, Iowa

Contents

The Death of the Death of the Novel

Fiction breeds its own continuity. Because it is the most public of the literary arts and the most immediately responsive to social life, developments of form in the American novel have been clear-cut and at times even monumental. The year 1851 marked the publication of *The House of the Seven Gables* and *Moby-Dick;* 1885, the ascendancy of Realism with Howells's *The Rise of Silas Lapham,* Twain's *Adventures of Huckleberry Finn,* and the first collected edition of Henry James. The last commonly accepted milestone in the development of American fiction has been 1925, when F. Scott Fitzgerald's *The Great Gatsby* and Ernest Hemingway's *In Our Time* resolved the dichotomy of Romanticism and Realism in favor of well-crafted fiction and the novel of selection.[1]

Since the Twenties there have been variations in theme of course, but for the most part the American novel has been marked by a conservative stability of form. For nearly fifty years, when in other countries such exotic talents as Gide, Hesse, Beckett, Robbe-Grillet, Cortazar, Borges, and Gombrowicz flourished, American fiction rested content with novels of manners or of social politics, while the innovations of a Patchen, a Hawkes, a Miller, or a Burroughs were kept—in some cases by court order—decisively underground.

By the late 1960's an uneasiness had come to the criticism of fiction. "At the moment," Stephen Koch wrote in 1967, "our literature is idling in a period of hiatus: the few important writers of the earlier generations are dead, silent, or in their decline, while the younger generation has not yet produced a writer of unmistakable importance or even of very great interest." [2] Criticism itself fared

---

[1] The best analysis of this last transition is James E. Miller, Jr., *F. Scott Fitzgerald: His Art and His Technique* (New York: New York University Press, 1964), especially the chapters "Saturation" and "Selection."

[2] Stephen Koch, "Premature Speculations on the Perpetual Renaissance," *Tri-Quarterly* #10 (Fall, 1967), p. 5.

no better; by that time no less than four studies of the ranking contemporary novelist, Saul Bellow, had appeared, but a typical review found them "inflated and tiresome exercises in the art of trivia." [3] The novel itself was said to be suffering a "curious death," chroniclers of its demise including Louis Rubin, Leslie Fiedler, Susan Sontag, and Norman Podhoretz. [4] "Even though there is a large body of new work," Koch concluded, "nothing thus far has been heard at the highest levels except an eerie silence."

It must feel strange indeed to be an emerging novelist when the novel has just died. Stranger still to write books which nobody buys, when book companies' stock falls two hundred points in eighteen months; when the returns keep flooding in, when your publisher remainders your first printing. During the 1967–68 publishing season there were many signs to suggest that fiction was in trouble, but Fiedler, Sontag, Podhoretz, and their colleagues were proclaiming the genre's decline even before the review copies were out, which turned out to contain an amazingly rich harvest: Donald Barthelme's *Snow White*, Ronald Sukenick's *Up, In the Heart of the Heart of the Country* by William H. Gass, *Tales* by LeRoi Jones, major novels by Richard Brautigan, Ishmael Reed, Steve Katz, and others—a season climaxing with the belated discovery of Kurt Vonnegut, Jr., through his retrospective collection *Welcome to the Monkey House*, and the National Book Award for Jerzy Kosinski's *Steps*. The point at issue between this critical despair and such a flurry of new, substantial work marks another division in the history of the novel, greater than the ones before because the nature of fiction itself was being challenged in a radical disruption of the genre's development. Ronald Sukenick described the phenomenon in a *Chicago Review* interview with Joe David Bellamy: "One of the reasons people have lost faith in the novel is that they don't believe it tells the truth any more, which is another way of saying that they don't believe in the conventions of the novel. They pick up a novel and they know it's make believe. So,

[3] Robert H. Fossum, "Review Essay: Four Studies of Saul Bellow," *Studies in the Novel*, 1 (Spring, 1970), 104.

[4] Louis Rubin, "The Curious Death of the Novel: Or, What to Do about Tired Literary Critics," in *The Curious Death of the Novel: Essays in American Literature* (Baton Rouge: Louisiana State University Press, 1967); Leslie Fiedler, "Cross the Border, Close the Gap," *Playboy*, 16 (December, 1969), 151, 230, 252, 254, 256–258; Susan Sontag, "Against Interpretation," in *Against Interpretation* (New York: Farrar, Straus & Giroux, 1964), pp. 3–14; Norman Podhoretz, *Doings and Undoings* (New York: Farrar, Straus & Giroux, 1964).

who needs it—go listen to the television news, right? Or read a biography."[5]

"People no longer believe in the novel as a medium that gets at the truth of their lives," Sukenick wrote again in 1973. Conventional novels had presented data, but in terms of fraudulent ideals, and sophisticated readers began despising these works for the lies they presented as real-life stories. Persistent story-tellers would have us believe as fact that life has leading characters, plots, morals to be pointed, lessons to be learned, and most of all beginnings, middles, and ends. In his novel published the same year, *Breakfast of Champions,* Kurt Vonnegut, Jr., played with the cynical farce of all this when he pondered the abominable behavior of his countrymen and concluded that "They were doing their best to live like people invented in story books. This was the reason Americans shot each other so often: It was a convenient literary device for ending short stories and books." [6] Vonnegut added that others suffered disappointing lives which failed to be perfect fictions, as year by year we were learning that still more readers were despairing of the whole mess and abandoning fiction altogether for history, biography, or even television. The more instant and accurate the replay, the more truthful seem the facts, although in the process the organizing and clarifying power of art was forgone, and fiction was at the point of no longer existing.

"The great advantage of fiction over history, journalism, or any supposedly 'factual' kind of writing," Sukenick countered, "is that it is an expressive medium. It transmits feeling, energy, excitement. Television can give us the news, fiction can best express our response to the news. No other medium—especially not film—can so well deal with our strongest and often most intimate responses to the large and small facts of our daily lives. No other medium, in other words, can so well keep track of the reality of our experience." [7]

[5] Joe David Bellamy, "Imagination as Perception: An Interview with Ronald Sukenick," *Chicago Review,* 23 (Winter, 1972), 60. Reprinted in Joe David Bellamy, *The New Fiction: Interviews with Innovative American Writers* (Urbana: University of Illinois Press, 1974).

[6] Kurt Vonnegut, Jr., *Breakfast of Champions* (New York: Delacorte Press/Seymour Lawrence, 1973), pp. 209–210.

[7] Ronald Sukenick, "About Fiction in General and OUT in Particular," publicity release distributed to reviewers by Swallow Press, February, 1973. Expanded as "Innovative Fiction, Innovative Criteria," *Fiction International* #2–3 (Spring/Fall, 1974), p. 133.

Nevertheless, by the 1960's writers had abandoned the Great American Novel, and had turned fiction instead—like poetry before it—into an elitist, academic diversion. Although several critics had comments on the subject, the key document in defining and endorsing this new aesthetic for the novel was John Barth's essay, "The Literature of Exhaustion." Given prominent publication in the *Atlantic Monthly* of August, 1967, following by a year the wide success of Barth's novel *Giles Goat-Boy* and the prestigious republication of his earlier works, it influenced discussion of fiction in much the same way that social and political essays by LeRoi Jones, Eldridge Cleaver, Julius Lester, and others were affecting their own fields about the same time. Barth's seemingly radical aesthetic was that in the novel writers faced "the used-upness of certain forms of exhaustion of certain possibilities." [8] From then on writers could only parody older stories and earlier forms—but at no great loss, since the crucial matter was "the difference between the *fact* of aesthetic ultimacies and their artistic *use*." [9] Barth's discovery and momentary triumph in his fiction was the issue of "how an artist may paradoxically turn the felt ultimacies of our own time into material and means for his own work." [10]

Three months after his seminal essay, one of the few on literary theory the *Atlantic* had published since the editorship of William Dean Howells, the same magazine featured Barth's contribution, "Lost in the Funhouse," a major story from his forthcoming collection of the same name. "So far there's been no real dialogue, very little sensory detail, and nothing in the way of a *theme*," the narrator admits after the piece is well underway. "And a long time has gone by already without anything happening; it makes a person wonder. We haven't even reached Ocean City yet: we will never get out of the funhouse." [11] And so his protagonist Ambrose doesn't, never getting into it in the first place. But in *Lost in the Funhouse* (1968) Barth had pushed on into the realm of fiction which his *Atlantic* essay alleged was "new," the Literature of Exhaustion. "The final possibility," his story "Title" insists, "is to turn ul-

---

[8] John Barth, "The Literature of Exhaustion," *Atlantic Monthly,* 220 (August, 1967), 29.
[9] Ibid., p. 31.
[10] Ibid., p. 32.
[11] John Barth, *Lost in the Funhouse* (Garden City, N.Y.: Doubleday, 1968), p. 77.

timacy, exhaustion, paralyzing self-consciousness and the adjective weight of accumulated history. . . . Go on. Go on. To turn ultimacy against itself to make something new and valid, the essence whereof would be the impossibility of making something new." [12] In some of his stories Barth brought American fiction to the level of innovation and self-conscious artifice practiced by Julio Cortazar in such tales as "Continuity of Parks" and "The Night Face Up" (from *End of the Game and Other Stories*) and by Jorge Luis Borges in "The Circular Ruins" (collected in *Ficciones*). "I try to write simple, straight-forward stories," reported Borges; [13] for his part, Barth confessed to being "less and less interested in working with tapes and graphics and things of that sort—and more and more interested in story telling." [14] Yet, in comparison with his Argentine models, Barth's attempts were hardly sustained; coming when it did (as he finished *Lost in the Funhouse*), "The Literature of Exhaustion" read as a literary suicide note.

Or else as an equivocation, since for the one story about Ambrose which demands a parody of the conventional ("Lost in the Funhouse"), the collection offers two others, "Ambrose His Mark" and "Water Message," which do quite well within the older, apparently unexhausted forms. Moreover, the uses Barth finds in the title story for his new aesthetic are for the most part gratuitous—a musing with italic script, obvious references to unexceptional techniques, and as its principal innovation the simple use of suspense as a structural device: "At this rate our hero, at this rate our protagonist will remain in the funhouse forever." [15] The story's ineffectualness can be seen by contrasting it with Gilbert Sorrentino's "The Moon in Its Flight." In formalistic terms, the latter story is a carefully plotted exercise in literary hysteria, as the author tries to guide his characters through a romance in the historically lost year of 1948, all the time knowing how conventional fiction invites itself to be misread. "Isn't there anyone," he pleads, "any magazine writer or avant-garde filmmaker, any lover of life or dedicated op-

---

[12] Ibid., p. 109.

[13] Norman Thomas di Giovanni et al., eds., *Borges on Writing* (New York: Dutton, 1973), p. 53.

[14] Joe David Bellamy, "Algebra and Fire: An Interview with John Barth," *The Falcon* #4 (Spring, 1972), p. 7.

[15] Barth, *Lost in the Funhouse*, p. 78.

timist out there who will move them toward a cottage, already closed for the season, in whose split log exterior they will find an unlocked door? Inside there will be a bed, whiskey, an electric heater. Or better, a fireplace, white lamps, soft lights. Sweet music." Or, "All you modern lovers, freed by Mick Jagger and the orgasm, give them, for Christ's sake, for an hour, the use of your really terrific little apartment. They won't smoke your marijuana nor disturb your Indiana graphics. They won't borrow your Fanon or Cleaver or Barthelme or Vonnegut. They'll make the bed before they leave. They whisper good night and dance in the dark." [16] But all of that is impossible, for "This was in America, in 1948. Not even fake art or the wearisome tricks of movies can assist them." Even worse, fears the narrator, how can the contemporary reader of his paperback magazine piece appreciate the meaning of this ancient world? "Who remembers the clarity of Claude Thornhill and Sarah Vaughan, their exquisite irrelevance? They are gone where the useless chrome doughnuts on the buick's hood have gone." [17] Sorrentino uses the same correlative in his novel, *Imaginative Qualities of Actual Things* (1971), as itself one of those imaginative qualities of actual things, when "Leo saw her standing in the sun: Just like Dick Haymes in the old movie. She was something to see, etc." Therefore the narrator tells us at once, to keep the experience one of art and not just history, that "The value of the popular song is that it deals in superficialities that release the emotions. Scratch the veneer of those pedestrian lyrics and you look into a crystal ball of the past." [18] Or as we are asked in the story, "She was crying and stroking his hair. Ah God, the leaves of brown came tumbling down, remember?" [19] Gilbert Sorrentino finds by Barth's own definition a point of true exhaustion in narrative art, and seizes it to more effectively tell his story. Here technique is more than simple discovery—it becomes an integral part of the fiction itself.

But the critical reaction to Sorrentino's work—along with that to a whole artistic generation, including Vonnegut, Barthelme, Suken-

[16] Gilbert Sorrentino, "The Moon in Its Flight," *New American Review* #13 (1971), p. 157.

[17] Ibid., p. 153.

[18] Gilbert Sorrentino, *Imaginative Qualities of Actual Things* (New York: Pantheon, 1971), p. 116.

[19] Sorrentino, "Moon in Its Flight," p. 157.

ick, and others—was for a time aborted, because of the depressing effect of Barth's essay and the even greater impression made by his continuing work. That a newer style of fiction did become popular in the late 1960's was beside the point, since anything designed in the wake of Barth's parody and subversion seemed a hopeless or even reprehensible cause. That right within our dispensation of "the death of the novel" tight, snappy little books by Kurt Vonnegut, Jr., and Richard Brautigan were selling like mad, competing with TV and sometimes winning, was irrelevant. Other writers such as Sorrentino, Barthelme, Sukenick, and Rudolph Wurlitzer were extending these forms, finding a new life for fiction, only to be described by Pearl Kazin Bell (in a review typical of the period) as "celebrants of unreason, chaos, and inexorable decay . . . a horde of mini-Jeremiahs crying havoc in the Western world." [20] The more social and cultural issue, as Nathan Scott let slip in his major essay on contemporary fiction, was that the "inward liberation" of the imagination which these writers used as a counter to transcend Barth "offers us an effective release from the bullying of all the vexations of history"—and, incidentally, that this aesthetic had been so demonstrably adopted "by the hordes of those young long-haired, jean-clad, pot-smoking bohemians who have entered the world of psychedelia." [21]

Chimera, John Barth's trilogy of retold classical myths which followed *Lost in the Funhouse* in 1972, stands as an allegory of his own exhaustion. As with "Autobiography: A Self-Recorded Fiction" and the funhouse story in the earlier collection, *Chimera* confuses the product of art with the conditions of its inception, a process which obviously fascinates Barth (leading to such pieces as "Night-Sea Journey") but which often results in simple bad writing, as when the story admits "I must compose myself." [22] *Chimera* is even more indulgent, renaming Dunyazade, sister of Scheherazade, "Doony," and in another place allowing a character on the death of a parent to impel herself "dead dadward." [23] Relocat-

[20] Pearl Kazin Bell, "American Fiction: Forgetting Ordinary Truths," *Dissent,* Winter, 1973, p. 26.

[21] Nathan A. Scott, Jr., " 'New Heav'ns, New Earth'—the Landscape of Contemporary Apocalypse," *Journal of Religion,* 53 (January, 1973), 12–13.

[22] Barth, *Lost in the Funhouse,* p. 36.

[23] John Barth, *Chimera* (New York: Random House, 1972), p. 103.

ing the determinants of race, moment, and milieu from the subject
one is writing about to the writing itself, from topic to technique or
from ethic to aesthetic, is hardly an innovation; evidence suggests
that the same was attempted in the nineteenth century.[24] A figure in
most of Barth's work is the writer seeking immortality. "Fair as the
country was and the goatboy life my fellow's lot," his narrator of
"Anonymiad" confesses, "if I could not've imagined my music's
one day whisking me Orionlike to the stars, I'd have as well flung
myself into the sea." [25] Hence the door closing to new literary activity would be a death sentence: "I had begun to run out of world
and material. . . . I imagined my *opera* sinking." [26]

Despite his recourse to technique (in parody, burlesque, and
ironic commentary) as a way of sustaining his role as fictionist,
Barth has received little attention as a purely formal innovator.
Rather, the major studies of his work prefer to discuss his themes.
Both Charles B. Harris and Raymond Olderman find a complete
explication within myth and draw neat correlations to the work of
Joseph Campbell.[27] Thematically, Barth is read as an example that
"the symbolic affirmation that transcends conflicts without offering
a program of action is just about the only affirmative ending the
novel of the sixties can have without running into sociology or
romanticism." [28] From his own parameters of the decade Olderman
excludes consideration of Barthelme, Kosinski, Sukenick, Sorrentino, and most other fictionists who moved formally beyond Barth.
So does Harris, who prefers to let that decade close with a facile
thematic imperative: "So Barth, like most other absurdist novelists,
sees human commitment to other human beings—in short, love—as
one of the few relative values available in an otherwise valueless
universe." [29]

Barth's narrator in "Title" speaks otherwise: "In this dehuman,

---

[24] Jerome Klinkowitz, "Ethic and Aesthetic: The Basil and Isabel March Stories of
William Dean Howells," *Modern Fiction Studies,* 16 (Autumn, 1970), 303–322.

[25] Barth, *Lost in the Funhouse,* p. 172.

[26] Ibid., p. 194.

[27] Charles B. Harris, *Contemporary American Novelists of the Absurd* (New Haven:
College & University Press, 1971), pp. 110–115; Raymond Olderman, *Beyond the Waste
Land: The American Novel in the Nineteen-Sixties* (New Haven: Yale University Press,
1972), pp. 76–81.

[28] Olderman, *Beyond the Waste Land,* pp. 91–92.

[29] Harris, *Contemporary American Novelists,* p. 120.

exhausted, ultimate adjective hour, when every humane value has become untenable, and not only love, decency, and beauty but even compassion and intelligibility are no more than one or two subjective complements to complete the sentence. . . ." [30] Nor can he complete the sentence. In the "Bellerophoniad" (published almost coincidentally with Harris's and Olderman's theses) Barth speaks more directly:

> *"My general interest in the wandering-hero myth dates from my thirtieth year, when reviewers of my novel* The Sot-Weed Factor *(1960) remarked that the vicissitudes of its hero—Ebenezer Cooke, Gentleman, Poet and Laureate of Maryland—follow in some detail the pattern of mythical heroic adventure as described by Lord Raglan, Joseph Campbell, and other comparative mythologists. The suggestion was that I had used this pattern as the basis for the novel's plot. In fact I had been unaware of the pattern's existence; once appraised of it I was struck enough by the coincidence (which I later came to regard as more inevitable than remarkable) to examine those works by which I'd allegedly been influenced, and my next novel,* Giles Goat-Boy *(1966), was for better or for worse the conscious and ironic orchestration of the Ur-Myth which its predecessor had been represented as being. Several of my subsequent fictions—the long short-story* Menelaid *and the novella* Perseid, *for example—deal directly with particular manifestations of the myth of the wandering hero and address as well a number of their author's more current thematic concerns: the mortal desire for immortality, for instance, and its ironically qualified fulfillment—especially by the mythic hero's transformation, in the latter stages of his career, into the sound of his own voice, or the story of his life, or both. I am forty.* [31]

"He was a writer of tales," a Barth look-alike explains himself to Scheherazade and her sister in the "Dunyazadiad," "anyhow a *former* writer of tales in a land on the other side of the world." He confesses that as a popular vehicle the novel had died, and that

> His own pen (that magic wand, in fact a magic quill with a fountain of ink inside) had just about run dry. . . . His career, too, had reached a hiatus which he would have been pleased to call a turning-point if he could have espied any way to turn: he wished neither

---

[30] Barth, *Lost in the Funhouse*, p. 107.
[31] Barth, *Chimera*, pp. 198–199.

to repudiate nor to repeat his past performances; he aspired to go beyond them toward a future they were not attuned to and, by some magic, at the same time go back to the original springs of narrative.[32]

Measuring Barth's work of this period, Robert Scholes has drawn a comparison with the "aesthetic allegories" of Henry James:

> Barth, in *Lost in the Funhouse,* gave us a volume of aesthetic allegory about the nature of fiction which is fully worthy of comparison with James—and the comparison is instructive. For James, in stories like "The Lesson of the Master" and "The Death of the Lion," the career of a dedicated literary artist could be seen comically and the question could be raised as to whether it indeed might compensate for the sacrifice of "life" that it inevitably entailed. But in general James leaves us feeling that the satisfactions of art are sufficient compensation for the sacrifices. While for Barth, it is clear in the *Funhouse* that being an artist is only a poor substitute for being a lover.[33]

"Imaginative potency is as crucial to the daily life of his spirit as sexual potency," reads the "Bellerophoniad," [34] and it is precisely because Barth has suffered an exhaustion (if not castration) of the imagination that his fiction falters. The last two novellas of *Chimera* are marked with situation-comedy routines of male impotency, as Barth's women shrilly mock his fall from capability. His "own devastating self-analyses in his last two books," concludes Scholes, "say all that can be said" of his successes or failures.[35]

"Nobody had enough imagination," Ambrose muses at the close of "Lost in the Funhouse." He envisions a "truly astonishing funhouse, incredibly complex yet utterly controlled from a great control switchboard like the console of a pipe organ." He would be its operator: "Panel lights would show what was up in every cranny of its cunning of its multifarious vastness; a switch-flick would ease this fellow's way, complicate that's, to balance things out; if anyone seemed lost or frightened, all the operator had to do was." Ambrose decides that "he will construct funhouses for others and be their secret operator—though he would rather be among the

---

[32] Ibid., pp. 9–10.
[33] Robert Scholes, "The Allegory of Exhaustion," *Fiction International* #1 (Fall, 1973), p. 107.
[34] Barth, *Chimera,* p. 202.
[35] Scholes, "Allegory of Exhaustion," p. 110.

lovers for whom funhouses are designed." [36] Barth's metaphor
for the imagination, as the mechanics of a funhouse, emphasizes its
limits above anything else. And there is even less argument for
transcendence when it is such a second-best choice.

Throughout Barth's recent work runs an uncomfortable confes-
sional thread: "Somewhere along that way I'd lost something, took
a wrong turn, forgot some knack, I don't know; it seemed to me that
if I kept going over it carefully enough I might see the pattern, find
the key." [37] Again "he felt that a treasure-house of new fiction lay
vaguely under his hand, if he could find the key to it." The answer
he finds in *Chimera,* however, is no different from and of no greater
effect than his suspicions first voiced in 1967. *"The key to the
treasure is the treasure,"* [38] he writes, and finds himself back with
Dunyazade and her sister, parsing out the thousand and one tales of
the Arabian nights. "The narrator has narrated himself into a corner" *(Lost in the Funhouse),*[39] turning "in ever-diminishing circles
like a moth around a candle, till I feared we must disappear up our
own fundaments" *(Chimera).*[40] Or, "Silence. There's a fourth possibility, I suppose. Silence. General anesthesia. Self-extinction.
Silence." [41] Hence the pity for one who was once our most promising fictionist. "Whether he has painted himself into a corner, or is
banking into the last turn on his flight to disappearance," writes
Robert Scholes, "I want to call out to this great story-teller and say,
'Hey, come out of there. We need you.' But I have neither the right
nor the words to make such a plea." [42]

Even before John Barth came to his present prominence, a
younger novelist, a graduate in engineering from Cornell University, was winning awards for nearly all his literary productions.
Thomas Pynchon's early stories, "Entropy" and "Under the
Rose," were selected as among the year's best by Martha Foley and

[36] Barth, *Lost in the Funhouse,* p. 97.
[37] Barth, *Chimera,* pp. 72–73.
[38] Ibid., p. 4.
[39] Barth, *Lost in the Funhouse,* p. 112.
[40] Barth, *Chimera,* p. 205.
[41] Barth, *Lost in the Funhouse,* p. 110.
[42] Scholes, "Allegory of Exhaustion," p. 110.

the O. Henry Prize committee; his novel *V.* received the Faulkner first novel award in 1963, while a later effort, *The Crying of Lot 49* (1966), won a belated-recognition prize. In 1973 his mammoth *Gravity's Rainbow* merited more media attention than any other such book in recent history, and it was (except for Kurt Vonnegut's novels) the only example of densely experimental fiction to survive on the *New York Times* best-seller list. At a time when other innovative writers were excluding from their works conventional techniques such as extensive characterization and plot, Pynchon directed his art to the opposite extreme: in his first and third novels characters numbered in the hundreds and plots became Byzantine if not fully incomprehensible. *The Crying of Lot 49,* while more economical in its *donnée,* spoke directly to the notion of plot—or conspiracy, as the paranoid delusions of its characters might so interpret.

In this sense Pynchon is a member of the school of Exhaustion. His techniques do not serve an attempt to create stable fictions, but as a commentary on themselves. Rather than be a plotter himself, Pynchon assigns that function to a character—in *V.,* Herbert Stencil. "He is the man," suggests Tony Tanner, "who is trying to make the connections and links, and put together the story which might well have been Pynchon's novel." By standing back from fiction's function, "Pynchon is able to explore the plot-making instinct itself." Hence technique becomes theme: development is suspicion, plot becomes paranoia, and Pynchon is able to exploit the whole theory that "the plots men see may be their own inventions." [43] These interests reflect his times, when, according to Richard Poirier, "The techniques that emerge . . . get to be more interesting than do the characters themselves. Characters become the passive receptors of phenomena from outside; they become all ears, listening to the sounds of voices, noises from the street, literary parodies and emulations, music." [44] As a result, concludes Poirier, "Human beings have lost themselves in the variety and completeness of their own corporate invention." [45] And so as man

[43] Tony Tanner, *City of Words: American Fiction 1950–1970* (New York: Harper & Row, 1971), p. 156.

[44] Richard Poirier, *The Performing Self* (New York: Oxford University Press, 1971), p. 9.

[45] Ibid., p. 12.

traces out the plots of his world, one must ask, with Tanner, "Do we live in fantasy because things have usurped too much of the human domain; or is the visible accumulation of junk around us only the result of our proclivity for fantasy-life?" [46] How much is made up? At the conclusion of *Gravity's Rainbow* Pynchon reveals that the most popular artifact of the space and rocket age, "The countdown as we know it, 10-9-8-U.S.W., was invented by Fritz Lang in 1929 for the Ufa film *Die Frau in Mond*. He put it into the launch scene to heighten the suspense. 'It is another of my damned "touches," ' Fritz Lang said." [47] Or as Richard Poirier anticipates, "The implication is that the human imagination, out of which all of these have issued [the political, physical, and sexual organizations of life], is impossibly entangled in its own creations, and that it would get even more entangled by any further effort on the part of interpretive critics to sort it all out." [48]

It may come to nothing—its own fundament, a painted-in corner. "Stencil sketched the entire history of V. that night and strengthened a long suspicion. That it did add up only to the recurrence of an initial and a few dead objects." [49] The fearful symmetry is synthetic, made by man, as we learn in *Gravity's Rainbow:* "Outside, in the Blitz, the sounds of V-1 and V-2, one the reverse of the other. . . . Pavlov showed how mirror-images Inside could be confused. Ideas of the opposite. But what new pathology lies Outside now? What sickness to events—to History itself—can create symmetrical opposites like those robot weapons?" [50] None, obviously:

> It means this War was never political at all, the politics was all theatre, all just to keep the people distracted . . . secretly, it was being dictated instead by the needs of technology . . . by a conspiracy between human beings and techniques, by something that needed the energy-burst of war, crying, "Money be damned, the way of life of [insert name of Nation] is at stake," but meaning, most likely, *dawn is nearly here, I need my night's blood, my funding, funding, ahh more, more. . . .* The real crises were crises of allocation and priority, not among firms—it was only staged to look that way—but

[46] Tanner, *City of Words,* p. 179.
[47] Thomas Pynchon, *Gravity's Rainbow* (New York: Viking, 1973), p. 753.
[48] Poirier, *Performing Self,* p. 21.
[49] Thomas Pynchon, *V.* (Philadelphia: Lippincott, 1963), p. 445.
[50] Pynchon, *Gravity's Rainbow,* p. 144.

among the different technologies, Plastics, Electronics, Aircraft, and their needs which are understood only by the ruling elite. . . .[51]

Perhaps it is just dream, subjective fantasy, but the effect is the same. "The actual way in which Conspiracy helps us pursue that dream," argues Raymond Olderman, "is not in its real existence, but in our paranoid reactions; we respond to the world as if Conspiracy were true and our response makes its effect as real as if it did exist." [52]

Pynchon thus works it both ways: nihilism on the one hand, conspiracy on the other, both to the same effect. Tony Tanner concludes that

> The blank wall and the encoded wall are both finally disturbing; just so, in the case of a plotted or a plotless universe. By balancing between the two possibilities, it seems . . . that Pynchon does produce a serious study of the state of consciousness in contemporary America, while a writer like Barth, who opts to emphasize his mockery of plots at an extreme, excessively plotted length, seems to . . . fall away from seriousness without discovering any compensating new sources of interest or beguilement.[53]

As Richard Poirier suggests, "What distinguishes Pynchon in *Gravity's Rainbow,* especially from such writers as John Barth and Borges, is that he does not, like them, make use of technology or popular culture or literary convention in an essentially parodistic spirit." Rather, he "respects the imagination imbedded in the instrumentalities of science. . . . He is locating the kinds of human consciousness that have been implanted *in* the instruments of technology and contemporary methods of analysis; not content with recording the historical effect of these, he is anxious to find our history *in* them." [54] *V.* itself sidelights a Barthian artist who produces in acrylics a series of cheese danishes, hardly a viable product: "this technique for the sake of technique—Catatonic Expressionism, or parodies on what someone else had already done." [55] This manner

---

[51] Ibid., p. 521.
[52] Olderman, *Beyond the Waste Land,* p. 138.
[53] Tanner, *City of Words,* p. 180.
[54] Richard Poirier, "Rocket Power," *Saturday Review of the Arts,* 1 (March, 1973), 62.
[55] Pynchon, *V.,* p. 297.

of "Arranging and rearranging was Decadence, but the exhaustion of all possible permutations and combinations was death." [56] Or Barth's fourth possibility, four years before he published this conclusion himself.

Yet for Pynchon silence is not an ultimate horror. Despite its range and density, his own work at times suggests it, and in an early story, "Entropy," he poses his characters in a theoretical discussion of its possibilities. The subject is Gerry Mulligan, the baritone saxophonist who starting in 1952 experimented with the first pianoless jazz quartet. "It occurred to me," offers a musician in the story, "in one of these flashes of insight, that if that first quartet of Mulligan's had no piano, it could only mean one thing." "No chords," suggests the bass player. "What he is trying to say," comes the correction, "is no root chords. Nothing to listen to while you blow a horizontal line. What one does in such a case is, one *thinks* the roots." The logical extension " 'Is to think everything,' Duke announced with simple dignity. 'Roots, line, everything.' " [57] And so the Duke di Angelis Quartet plays on at Pynchon's party, without instruments, in utter silence.

Much has been written about Thomas Pynchon's thematic concern with entropy,[58] but in all cases the phenomenon is understood in a pejorative sense. However, entropy has aesthetically structural properties: thematically it may suggest chaos and disorder, but the more proper connotation is one of equilibrium, the sublime balance toward which all systems tend. "The maximum of entropy," says Rudolf Arnheim in *Entropy and Art*, "is reached when the system is in the best possible order." [59] Yet in none of his three novels does Pynchon propose such a cosmic reordering as an imaginatively entropic system might imply. As author he stands back from his work to make an implicit ironic commentary on plot, but to this point Pynchon has been reluctant to rejoin his work as its self-responsible creator. That task first fell to Robert Coover, whose *The Universal Baseball Association, Inc., J. Henry Waugh, Proprietor* (1968)

---

[56] Ibid., p. 298.

[57] Thomas Pynchon, "Entropy," *Kenyon Review*, 22 (Spring, 1960), 289–290.

[58] Harris, *Contemporary American Novelists*, pp. 76–99; Olderman, *Beyond the Waste Land*, pp. 123–149; Tanner, *City of Words*, pp. 153–180.

[59] Rudolf Arnheim, *Entropy and Art* (Berkeley: University of California Press, 1971), p. 25.

made the great transition from exhausted fiction into an imaginatively transformed genre. It happens on the second page of his book:

> *Rookie pitcher Damon Rutherford, son of the incomparable Brock Rutherford, was two innings—six outs—from a perfect game!* Henry, licking his lips, dry from excitement, squinted at the sun high over the Pioneer Park, then at his watch: nearly eleven, Diskin's closing hours. So he took the occasion of this seventh-inning hometown stretch to hurry downstairs to the delicatessen to get a couple of sandwiches. Might be a long night: the Pioneers hadn't scored off of old Swanee Law yet either.[60]

Henry Waugh isn't a player, or even a spectator to the ball game. He is its creator, by the throw of three dice determining the life of a card-table baseball league.

> You roll, Player A gets a hit or he doesn't, gets his man out or he doesn't. Sounds simple. But call Player A "Sycamore Flynn" or "Melbourne Trench" and something starts to happen. He shrinks or grows, stretches out or puts on muscle. Sprays singles to all fields or belts them over the wall. Throws mostly fastballs like Swanee Law or curves like Mickey Halifax. Choleric like Rag Rooney or slow and smooth like his old first-base rival Mose Stanford. Not easy to tell just how or why.[61]

Nominal prime mover, Proprietor J. Henry Waugh practices a deistic ethic:

> Oh, sure, he was free to throw away the dice, run the game by whim, but then what would be the point of it? Who would Damon Rutherford really be then? Nobody, an empty name, a play actor. Even though he set his own rules, his own limits, and though he could change them whenever he wished, nevertheless he and his players were committed to the turns of the mindless and unpredictable—one might even say irresponsible—dice. That was how it was. He had to accept it, or quit the game altogether.[62]

To this point Coover's career in fiction had been much like Pynchon's. His first novel, *The Origin of the Brunists,* had won the

---

[60] Robert Coover, *The Universal Baseball Association, Inc., J. Henry Waugh, Proprietor* (New York: Random House, 1968), p. 4.

[61] Ibid., p. 47.

[62] Ibid., p. 40.

Faulkner prize in 1966. Like Pynchon's work, it was very long and materially dense, and its innovations were restricted to those of theme. Both authors for a time limited their imaginative indulgence to colorful names and comic songs, but in concluding *The Universal Baseball Association* Coover moved beyond the literature of exhaustion into a new life for fiction. The moment comes when the dice determine that Damon Rutherford be struck and killed by a line drive through the box. The deistic Henry Waugh panics and then despairs, leaving the players, according to one review, to "go their own way after that, found private religions and stage reformations, and proceed to talk like 17th-century parsons and death-of-God theologians. Is there really a Henry Waugh? Who knows?" The team continues its profoundly interesting story, but unlike an overburdened and possibly exhausted fiction, it need not maintain the lie that all this may have happened, since we know Henry Waugh—however mad—looks on from above.

Pricksongs and Descants (1969) is Coover's full exploitation of the new imaginative mode in fiction. In "The Elevator" his protagonist constructs an elaborate fantasy of falling to his death; however, at the last moment he neatly steps out of his imaginative structure, allowing it to move on without him—and the elevator car to plunge down the shaft empty. "The Baby Sitter" is the author's tour de force. The story begins with an unexceptional family scene, with all involved—including the babysitter—going their own ways:

> Mrs. Tucker appears at the Kitchen doorway, holding a rolled-up diaper. "Now, don't just eat potato chips, Jimmy! See that he eats his hamburger, dear." She hurries away to the bathroom. The boy glares sullenly at the babysitter, silently daring her to carry out the order. "How about a little of that good hamburger now, Jimmy?" she says perfunctorily. He lets half of it drop. to the floor. The baby is silent and a man is singing a love song on the TV. The children crunch chips.[63]

As the evening evolves, Coover presents not only what "does happen" (which by itself is in conventional literature a screaming ambiguity, considering that even the most traditional fiction is completely made up) but all the things which *could* happen. As the

---

[63] Robert Coover, *Pricksongs and Descants* (New York: Dutton, 1969), p. 207.

minute-by-minute actions of the characters escalate to include their own fantasies, Coover reports them as dutifully as fact. Intentions vie with other intentions; the imaginative persistently works its way into the actual world, occasionally colliding with reality like an off-cue actor stumbling into the wrong scene. By the story's end everything that might possibly happen has, and Coover has completed the ultimately realistic short tale.

Writing such fiction is by no means just self-indulgence. John Barth at times explored the deeply ethical significance of facing one's art honestly, of continuing to tell stories when one's narrative materials were exhausted. But Barth's considerations have yet to be integrated with his stories themselves—and in his recent works he has told no stories, only speculated on the possibilities and despaired of them. To move beyond this detente, Steve Katz has incorporated this very honesty with the narrative matter at hand. *The Exagggerations of Peter Prince* (1968) speaks to the humor in such situations, but also to the heartbreaking impossibility of narrating certain events—or of making them up, to be more accurate. "Enough! Katz, you're making this all up," he exclaims on the third page of his novel.

> It doesn't make a bit of sense. It's not a promising beginning. Why can't you follow the instructions? You can't write whatever you want: Peter Prince Peter Prince Peter Prince. Where's the story? How are you going to catch us up in it and write a novel so the reader won't be able to put it down, he's so involved. He'll put the book down right now and say, "Who cares?" without even a placemark. What will your friends say? They'll say, "Katz, cut it out, you're making it all up. You're fucking around with boredom in our heads." A reader wants to know what's going on. What's going on? [64]

Katz has taken on a difficult task: "Writing this book is like trying to hug a plastic cleaning sack (beware of that plastic cleaning sack) stuffed with Jello" (p. 66). So at times he skips transitions, as much as thirty pages of his protagonist's travels. He has various reactions to all these places, "a group of impressions, a batch of moods, which were to be described in the thirty pages I decided not

[64] Steve Katz, *The Exagggerations of Peter Prince* (New York: Holt, Rinehart & Winston, 1968), p. 3. Subsequent references follow in parentheses.

to write, all of which could add up to sensitivity galore, but you'll have to take my word for it" (p. 113). Another series of pages he crosses out, except for one where a character is drawn particularly well. Otherwise, it's "Good-by structure. Good-by well-made-book" (p. 132) as Katz faces problems peculiar to the writer of a post-contemporary fiction. These may be closely technical, such as working under flourescent light: "don't think this book isn't influenced by the fact that sixty times each second it gets dark in here, making over the period of years it takes to write a book, no matter how small each instant, an appreciable amount of darkness" (p. 136). Or the problems of describing a pluralistic, relativistic, post-modern world, where "Sometimes it's so hard to tell what has really happened. It's impossible to know. That's why I want to develop multiple possibilities simultaneously" (p. 157). Above all, the author confronts the most immediate problem of writing his book. At one point Katz is delayed waiting for Ronald Sukenick, who has promised him a place in his own novel (Katz later appears, "briefly on a special guest appearance from his own novel," on page 325 of *Up*); at other times he has poets such as Ted Berrigan write him a filler paragraph, and finally he arranges for his protagonist, Peter Prince, to advertise (for promotional consideration) household products as the narrative continues. Katz maintains complete candor through all of this: "I'm just trying these empty spaces with luminous motion, and things. Things, things, things: How a novel can fill with them like a barrel with sponges. They rise like pieces from a sunken ship and lie noiseless on the tide" (p. 165).

Unlike Barth's, Katz's complaints are not gratuitous, for he has more to write about than his own inability to write. *The Exagggerations of Peter Prince* does have a "story": of Thwang-Nuc, adopted child of Peter Prince and his wife Bebo. She is an orphan of the war against Vietnam, and half her body bears the scars of jellied gasoline designed to burn people. The family lives in a garden apartment complex, with all the luxuries of American middle-class life. "For all this Thwang-Nuc had been sacrificed to napalm, for these shoddy apartments, for this desperate communal note, for noise of complaints in housing projects sifting through the apartments like dust through rubble" (p. 81). Beyond these facts the story is untellable:

He loved to see her sleeping. She was silent, she hadn't screamed all night, poor, wounded child. Her burnt side was exposed, the scar tissue shiny and stiff like wrinkled ceramic. Something was different. He could hardly see her breathing. He stared at her blanket to see it move just a little in the blue shadows. The breathing was faint, if at all. He touched her hand that was cold, the joints stiff. Her face was covered by a fine, plastic membrane. Nothing. She didn't breathe at all. Peter Prince turned away. To the window where her room faced the repeated forms of the rest of the Ma-Jo development. "No," he said, and tried to tear the membrane from her face. It stuck to his hands like oil. It was a plastic cleaning bag (I told you to look out for that plastic cleaning bag). It tried to smother his arms. Nothing was there. She had been dead. Right. That was it. Nothing had come in a plastic sack and had roosted on her face. (p. 95)

The story is too pathetic to sustain, and—as did Gilbert Sorrentino with his own fictional material—the writer must break away, and hysterically exhaust a series of forms in the hope of absolving his artistic creative responsibility. "He didn't know how to deal in himself with the discomfort he felt seeing these miserable people through the veils of his own possibilities," so Katz takes his hero "back into the motion of dreams where he could remake Peter Prince as he preferred him, after he knew" (p. 237). The result may be an experimentation in failure, but the form is honest and integral with its story; superior, Katz would argue, to a successful lie.

The Exagggerations of Peter Prince shows that on the level of sentiment, at least, certain stories outstrip formal bounds. Richard Brautigan's fiction demonstrates the same on the level of language and idea. The former can exist in a pure substanceless state, not only in the highest of mathematical abstractions, but more often in the most mundane of common lives. He concludes *Trout Fishing in America* (1967) with one such example, a letter of bereavement which in its very typicality suggests how language can exist purely as itself, with no reference at all to content:

Feb 3-1952

Dearest Florence and Harv.

I just heard from Edith about the passing of Mr. Good. Our heart goes out to you in deepest sympathy Gods will be done. He has lived a good Long life and he has gone to a better place. You were expect-

ing it and it was nice you could see him yesterday even if he did not
know you. You have our prayers and love and we will see you soon.
    God bless you both.

Love Mother and Nancy.

That such lifeless substance can be transformed into something
imaginatively viable is seen by Brautigan's artistic act: he has
always wanted to end a book with the word "mayonnaise," so to
this letter (which forms his last chapter, "The Mayonnaise Chapter"), he adds the P.S.: "Sorry I forgot to give you the mayonnaise." [65] Life can exist in pure forms as well, most often in the
quotidian elements we never question, such as a Deanna Durbin
movie. "She sang a lot. Maybe she was a chorus girl who wanted to
go to college or she was a rich girl or they needed money or something or she did something. Whatever it was about, she sang! and
sang! but I can't remember a God-damn word of it." [66] The narrator, while unable to describe a single Deanna Durbin film, can picture all of them. If content is so facile and even relatively unimpor-
tant, may we not then transform it, reshape it to better suit our
needs? Brautigan does this very thing by drawing on the poetic technique of metaphor. He sees objects more clearly through the magic
of an apt, implied comparison. Each page speaks in images, such as
dust looking "like the light from a Coleman lantern," the smell of
Lysol in a hotel lobby, sitting "like another guest on the stuffed furniture, reading a copy of the *Chronicle,* the Sports Section," or a
character looking up "from underneath a tattered revolution of old
blankets." Perception, for Brautigan, is an act of constant comparison. A ukulele seems "pulled—like a plow through the intestine";
more lyrically, "The water bugs were so small I practically had to
lay my vision like a drowned orange on the mud puddle." His very
title, *Trout Fishing in America,* is pushed to imaginative limits: it
takes place as a life experience, a hotel, or a paraplegic wino crated
and shipped to Nelson Algren in Chicago. The trout stream is finally
sold in foot lengths at the Cleveland Wrecking Yard. Brautigan's
metaphors create a lyrical space, a clarifying distance between object and perceiver so that the former may make some sense. John J.

[65] Richard Brautigan, *Trout Fishing in America* (San Francisco: Four Seasons, 1967), p.
112.
    [66] Ibid., p. 90.

Clayton observes that "the view I'm offered at the Cleveland Wrecking Yard's window is one of bitterness and deadening brick. But Brautigan lets me out of dealing with that desperate reality (and I want to be let out); he snatches me up inside his *process of imagination*—the magazines eroding like the Grand Canyon, the magical perception of the patients' complaints. I am given imaginative magic as a liberation from decay." [67] To create a metaphor is imaginative; to extend it and draw in the readers' participation is an act of magic, a kinesthesis of facts that can more effectively capture and reflect the world. As the narrator of *Trout Fishing in America* remarks of a young doctor out camping, "he was leaving for America, often only a place in the mind." [68] It is Richard Brautigan's genius to have found the imaginative apparatus for telling such otherwise untellable stories.

By 1968 John Barth had claimed the elements of traditional fiction—scene-by-scene construction, realistic dialogue, third-person point of view, and the exploitation of symbolic detail—were exhausted and of no use to the novelist except in parody, burlesque, and ironic commentary. Writers such as Coover, Katz, and Brautigan were moving on to a new aesthetic for fiction, beyond Barth's regressive literature of exhaustion. Yet the tradition itself was not to die; as a second imperative that the novel was not dead, a whole new group of writers appeared to appropriate and revive its discarded techniques. They were the "New Journalists," led by Tom Wolfe, who admitted that "by the Sixties, about the time I came to New York, the most serious, ambitious and, presumably talented novelists had abandoned the richest terrain of the novel: namely, society, the social tableau, manners and morals, the whole business of 'the way we live now,' in Trollope's phrase." Wolfe noticed that "There is no novelist who will be remembered as the novelist who captured the Sixties in America, or even in New York, in the sense that Thackeray was the chronicler of London in the 1840's and Balzac was the chronicler of Paris and all of France after the fall of the

---

[67] John Clayton, "Richard Brautigan: The Politics of Woodstock," *New American Review* #11 (1971), p. 57.

[68] Brautigan, *Trout Fishing*, p. 72.

Empire.'' [69] The new chroniclers were to be Wolfe, Jimmy Breslin, Dan Wakefield, Gay Talese, and the new nonfiction Norman Mailer—journalists who changed their art by appropriating to it the central techniques which had sustained fiction for two centuries. The key shift these journalists undertook was to make us read real-life experiences ''as imaginative literature,'' according to Robert Langbaum; [70] or, as Barry H. Leeds wrote of Mailer's work, to function ''not as journalist, but as narrator-participant,'' recounting ''historical events through the subjective and metaphorically rich voice of the central character who experiences them.'' [71]

Placing oneself as the imaginative center of an otherwise documentary experience is an innovation dating from the late 1960's. The chief examples best known as nonfiction novels are Truman Capote's *In Cold Blood* (1965), Norman Mailer's *Armies of the Night* (1968), and James Simon Kunen's *Strawberry Statement* (1969). The first two were products of established fictionalists whose careers were in decline, who approached the new form as a comeback. But for Kunen the nonfiction novel was neither a retread form nor a literary hybrid—as a sophomore political science major at Columbia, he found it to be the naive and natural form in which to account for another innovation in American life from this same period: the campus disorder. There were far more disruptions in the 1967–68 season than the literary ones in fiction. All literature was enjoying a new freedom of expression implemented by court decisions in favor of works by William S. Burroughs, Henry Miller, and others; the Beatles had revolutionized popular music, the values of a youth culture were first being fanfared, and all literary effort was being affected by the demands and sensibilities of the first entirely television-bred generation. Political disruptions were rampant: opposition to the Vietnam war had solidified, riots and assassinations dominated the news, and for the first time in our history a presidential administration was forced, in European fashion, to abdicate its rule. Black culture was undergoing a transformation to militant self-

[69] Tom Wolfe, ''Why They Aren't Writing the Great American Novel Anymore,'' *Esquire,* 78 (December, 1972), 157.

[70] Robert Langbaum, ''Mailer's New Style,'' in *The Modern Spirit* (New York: Oxford University Press, 1970), p. 163.

[71] Barry H. Leeds, *The Structured Vision of Norman Mailer* (New York: New York University Press, 1969), p. 6. For a complete discussion, see Michael L. Johnson, *The New Journalism* (Lawrence: University of Kansas Press, 1971).

consciousness, and amid all of this nineteen-year-old James Kunen was searching for a form in which to express it. Others with a more explicit knowledge of the past had already tried: Dotson Rader, for example, drew on the same subjects of war resistance and campus disruption for his own work, *I Ain't Marchin' Anymore* (1969), but unlike Kunen he could not find a form to accommodate their lyrical potency. Rader starts with awesome allusions to the genesis of SDS and makes extensive references to the more strident passages of the Port Huron Statement. From this beginning he searches for a conclusive middle and end, but at war with his rational impulse are the idealistic notions of the movement he is trying to describe. Although he recognized the conflict between his methods and their subject, he cannot use it in the strategy of his work, and so both slip out of control. Rader can deftly parody the halls-of-ivy mystique ("The lawns of Columbia are very wide and long and at night the lights filter against the pollution in the air and spread a soft white haze over the grass"), but at the crucial moment of his rebellion he pathetically falls victim to the mystique himself: "There were cops everywhere in sight. The campus was vacant of everyone else. And except for an occasional student shouting an obscenity at the cops from a window it was quiet. I loved the place. Despite all that had happened, I loved Columbia."

When idealism is unsuccessfully forced into a foreign structure, it may easily degenerate according to the classic pattern, from romanticism to sentimentality. The failure of Rader's work is not that he feels such contradictory emotions, which may in themselves be insightful, but that the deliberately rationalistic plan of his book cannot contain them. *I Ain't Marchin' Anymore,* while promising a strict analysis of ideals in conflict with reality, dissipates into an unstructured trauma of the narrator's identity. Although there are hints that the final problem is nonrational, that somehow "war and riots and escalating violence" are interwound "with the attack on manhood," Rader is unable to find an explanation satisfactory to the logical structure of his book. Why should the young white radical be forced "to create personhood while at the same time finding relief from tribal guilt, guilt whose victims clutter the ghettos of urban America"? [72] In this very statement Rader plunges from the lan-

[72] Dotson Rader, *I Ain't Marchin' Anymore* (New York: McKay, 1969), p. 144.

guage of social psychology into the jargon of a pamphleteer. A victim of his own poster art, neither Rader himself nor the structure of his art can *explain* (his intended purpose) why the vain bloodshed of the Columbia bust "was the first event in most of our lives where we felt effective, where what we were doing belonged to us." Instead, we are offered a muddle of sentimentalism and hysteria, plus a weakly existential and most emphatically non-Aristotelian ending, where he admits that his radicals "were unable to concede that the only possible community was in rebellion." [73] Such a conclusion has lyric potential, but it is inorganic to Rader's plan. The author himself is plainly puzzled at the end, and so is the reader.

James Kunen's book is disruptively different. It's the same campus, the same war, and in most cases the same politics, but the work produced from these sources tells quite another story. Kunen is closer to the events by not imposing a rational structure (he can't even decide on his own introduction, so he surrenders and gives us all four drafts), and he lets his book record the most real event of all: the making of the book itself. He is straight-arrow honest about his content, and the form it's put in:

> This book was written on napkins and cigarette packs and hitchiking signs. It was spread all over, but so is my mind. I exhibit a marked tendency to forget things. I can remember only three things at a time. If I think of a fourth thing, I forget the first. Like a cigarette machine. You take one pack out—all the rest fall down a notch. Exactly analogous in every salient detail.
>
> The best, truest way to read this book would be to rip it up and throw the scraps all over the house. Then later, should you come across a piece, read it, or don't read it, depending upon how you feel. Or, better, save it until four o'clock in the morning when you would rather do almost anything else, and read it then. Above all, don't spend too much time reading it because I didn't spend too much time writing it. [74]

The hassle of writing the book becomes "the Book" itself. Selecting a journal form, he can enter for July 7, "At 5:30 the goddam

---

[73] Ibid., p. 41.
[74] James Simon Kunen, *The Strawberry Statement* (New York: Random House, 1969), pp. 6–7.

birds started waking up with their familiar cry of 'Another-day-gone-and-you-haven't-done-shit caw, caw, caw, jweep.' '' In the midst of recounting a problem with Columbia's trustees he interrupts, ''That does it, I can't write,'' and clears his mind with a page of speculations on handwriting, smoking, and southern agrarian interests. On page 145, in mid-paragraph, ''Here, arbitrarily, the Book ends'' . . . but not before three postscripts. Yet Kunen is not at all naive, or derelict in his responsibilities as artist. He mocks the idea that man can be enumerated, listed, or categorized, as when he nonsensically lists his likes and dislikes; and his form makes the same parody, that the events at Columbia in 1968 could be rationally organized. This form in turn facilitates a special view of the world, where logic can logically fracture logic (''I passed a store called 'Hard-to-Get-Records.' I wonder if they have easy-to-get-records. If they don't that makes them hard to get, in which case they should have them''), and a lack of a priori structures can show the world in its own madness.

Kunen's method is honest, organic to the materials of his study, and reveals the ultimate truth of what's *really* going on. On the day of Robert Kennedy's assassination (one of the actual days he is writing ''the Book'')', Kunen considers the nature of death in Vietnamized America: ''people aren't really shot; fire is directed at their positions. And they're not really people; they're troops. There aren't even dead men: only body counts. And the degree of deadness isn't always too bad; sometimes it's light or moderate instead of heavy.'' [75] The basis of Kunen's honest and insightful position is his view of himself. Unlike Rader, described on his book jacket as ''The Eldridge Cleaver of the white new left,'' Kunen insists that ''I am not a leader, you understand. But leaders cannot seize and occupy buildings. It takes great numbers of people to do that. I am one of those great numbers. What follows is the chronicle of a single revolutionary digit.'' He seems at times the nebbish of the student revolution: when challenged by jocks, ''As is my wont in these situations, I begin enumerating all the jocks who are some of my best friends, really.'' Hitchhiking in Connecticut, he has little luck: ''A couple of times guys in cars gave me the finger. My reac-

[75] Ibid., p. 55.

tion to that is generally one of relief that they didn't throw anything at me. Then a car came by and threw a beer can at me.''

But nebbishness conceals a self which unheroically maintains its own identity within a revolution which so easily contained Dotson Rader. During the first occupation Kunen amusingly watches out for the furniture and mops up spills, and ''at four o'clock, like Pavlov's dog, I go to crew, assuring a long-hair at the door that I'll be back.'' Refreshingly, he can be caught in a personal dilemma, far from the Port Huron Statement, but of the nature which vitalizes narrative art: ''God, what was I going to do?'' he confesses. ''I *liked* Dean Deane.'' Because Kunen's unstructured approach has not tried to reshape an unstructured experience, the self that emerges from these incidents is not at all traumatic or hysterical. He is quietly modest, yet his statements have the ring of authenticity, as when he tells his girl friend, ''I look up in my head and there's this great emptiness, a void; there's nothing there. I don't know anything.'' Apart from any rhetorical or heroic posturing, Kunen simply demonstrates that ''I have a mad desire to live.'' And his sense of living in a confusing, absurd world emerges naturally, even spontaneously, from the Columbia experience. The ''strawberry statement'' itself suggests the ontology of Kunen's world. ''Commenting on the importance of student opinion to the administration,'' he tells us, ''Professor Deane declared 'Whether the students vote ''yes'' or ''no'' on an issue is like telling me they like strawberries.' '' Kunen's simple reply, ''I like strawberries,'' draws its power not from any revolutionary rhetoric, and only partially from the narrative of political events preceding the announcement. What Dotson Rader and even such critics as Richard Poirier describe as ''The War Against the Young,'' [76] Kunen sees as a war against the self. He answers a dean and a college who treat him as if he did not exist by responding, as Erich Fromm would have it, by saying I am I. ''I like strawberries.'' I am Spartacus.

Standard Operating Procedure (1971) draws closer to the war—right into it, in fact, with the grisly record of atrocities which may be our most noteworthy accomplishment in Southeast Asia. Artistically, the leap is even more profound, from the ''Notes of a

[76] See Poirier, *Performing Self,* pp. 143–166.

College Revolutionary'' to the ''Notes of a Draft-age American,'' which are, at first glance, the reams of testimony from the Citizens' Commission of Inquiry on U.S. War Crimes in Indochina. How do you write a book about war crimes? The record, already presented in three dozen other historical accounts, should speak for itself. ''This was supposed to be an 'instant' book,'' he admits in its preface, ''to be published shortly after the Veterans' Inquiry. It is late because I had great difficulty with it. I did not see what I could possibly add to the testimony, or what right I had to add anything.'' [77] The record should be able to speak for itself. But it can't—only people can speak. So from the start Kunen has some justification; it takes a human imagination, placed at the center of these experiences, to make them coherent and communicable. But old-fashioned forms pale before the enormity of the events. ''I told my friend,'' says Kunen, ''that book writing is frustrating because you know you are doomed to failure before you even start, because there is a gap between the word symbols and reality—you can only write *about* things, you can't put things in a book'' (p. 173). So how will we get to the true reality of the experience, what's really going on, especially in that most incredible of places, Vietnam?

Kunen's response is the same as for his college book: simple honesty, the reality of writing the book and the plain truth of *his* printed page. As opposed to the speechless record, Kunen is eloquent, but only because he closes the gap between ''word symbols'' and reality by making those symbols his reality. He tries to fool nobody: *Standard Operating Procedure* is not a rational synthesis of the war, but the imaginative and evocative act of an artist coming to personal terms with it. The record itself, collected by scores of GI veterans ''spurred by troubled sleep and indelible stains on their hands,'' was that of ''a collective ineloquent Macbeth.'' Kunen's success is that he articulates the otherwise unspeakable: the horror of the crimes, but also the insane unreality of their commission. Language may be the heart of it, since ''Our whole Vietnam vocabulary is a lexicon of distortion.'' According to the Military Assistance Command, ''South Vietnam'' should always be called ''The Republic of Vietnam,'' whereas ''The Democratic Republic of

[77] James Simon Kunen, *Standard Operating Procedure* (New York: Avon Books, 1971), p. 14. Subsequent references follow in parentheses.

Vietnam'' must always be referred to as ''North Vietnam.'' Troops of the North Vietnamese army and of the National Liberation Front are termed ''Communists.'' (What then are American soldiers: Imperialists? Registered Democrats and Republicans?) There is no real death, as Kunen discovered when trying to comprehend Robert Kennedy's assassination—only casualties, which may with some reasonableness be only light or moderate. ''Cost-of-living index, crime rate, hamlet-pacification rating, fielding average, industrial output, free-throw average, kill ratio—it's all the same,'' observed Kunen, ''all an attempt to get a handle on the world with numbers, and thus make it manageable'' (p. 25). ''It's an unfortunate wrinkle in our conceptual faculties that numbers of human beings killed becomes numbers. 1,000 x apples = 1,000 apples. 1,000 x people killed = 1,000'' (p. 160). Listening to their testimony and talking with them personally, Kunen forever heard what these witnesses thought, never what they felt. ''American males are taught not to pay any attention to feelings, which lead to 'emotionalism' and 'irrationality.' In no instance was a veteran able to describe to me what he felt during atrocities, only what went through his head.'' And that excludes much of the situation's reality.

The first corrective is to *be there*. ''Americans, all of us, pro and anti,'' Kunen argues, ''insist on thinking that Southeast Asia is a far-off corner of the world. When I was there, however, I found that Vietnam is not way off across the ocean. It is right there, right under your feet. The U.S. is across the ocean, in a far-off corner of the world'' (p. 311). It is a great imaginative leap, however, to this ultimate reality, and making it is Kunen's finest achievement. At least one veteran took the leap, too: Gary Battles, who made his separate peace in Vietnam so that he could find out what the war was about. To fully understand, one must create imaginative space. Kunen, twenty-three years old, thinks of his future grandchildren: ''They won't understand why the war did not become the center of our lives, why stopping it did not pre-empt all other concerns, why opposition did not progress far beyond *dissent*. They won't understand how it was possible, that while the war was going on, a new football league grew and merged with the old, hemlines rose and fell amid great controversy, and the nation rediscovered romance'' (p. 365). So James Simon Kunen becomes the imaginative center of this world, testing all possibilities and feeling the full effects. He breaks the structures which facilitate reason yet obscure the truth, and establishes a lyrical distance between judgment and event in which his full human powers can operate..

The Strawberry Statement and Standard Operating Procedure do not succeed by any facile adoption of topic. The subject matter is there; but more important, it has been brought here, to the reader, through Kunen's imaginative, artistic act. His honesty aids him in his politics, and no less in his art. He criticizes the blatant unreality that in war dispatches, political speeches, and popular sentiment passes for the real thing, but he can also spot the problem on his own side of the fence, as when he finds an old leaflet scheduling an emergency conference for Friday to discuss and act upon the imminent invasion of North Veitnam and the threatened Third World genocide, but cannot tell what "Friday" the leaflet may have referred to ("There was no connection between that leaflet and the reality of the war"). Kunen occupied Hamilton Hall at Columbia, but also rowed crew; he sees at once that "it's absurd and probably obscene to be paddling around in something that's worth two years' rent to families down the hill from the campus," but also that "There's no way to convert crew shells into food or to redirect the funds of the people who give them." He has the sense to explain to his movement colleagues and to the readers of Sports Illustrated, where these comments appeared (June 16, 1969): "It's like 'eat your potatoes, Johnny, there are people starving in China.' "

As a first-person journalist, Kunen has emerged with a reputation as the gentle freak, covering such American banalities as the launch of Apollo 11, and making such clear-headed observations as "At T minus 7 the sun came up, an event of considerably greater magnitude than the launching, but no one noticed." (A few other good ones, from the same affair: "I went into a NASA coffee wagon. You come to the cream before the coffee before the cups. All the best minds went into the rockets"; "I considered tripping over a wire, cutting off TV coverage, just to see if they'd postpone the launch until Huntleybrinkley and the Cronk got back on"; "I watched a helicopter take off. It wasn't a rocket, but then it wasn't 3½ miles away, either"; and a query about the real thing, free from restraints of press credentials, anonymous sources, and criminal, cowardly courtesy: " 'James Kunen for the US Quarterly,' I said during the question period. 'I'd like to direct a question to Dr. von Braun. How do working conditions at Cape Kennedy compare to those in Nazi Germany when you developed the V-2 robot bomb for use against the British civilian population?' ") [78] In a series of essays about the war for *True* magazine (the best is "Pieces of War," May, 1971), Kunen sought an answer for Vietnam in the simplest, most mundane places, and found it only by placing himself in the experience. The form of his works exhibits the same honesty: no games, no illusions, no attempt to supply a rational structure, but the presentation of the most immediate reality at hand, the writing of his books, and from these indisputable facts to draw the substance of his art. In this manner Kunen maintains the realest thing around: himself. His contemporaries—Rader, Mark Gerzon, Richard Zorza—are movement journalists. As editor of *Defiance,* Rader reminds his readership of "the essential issues which in point of fact define us: an immediate and unconditional end to the American war of aggression in Southeast Asia; an end to racism; self-determination for colonial peoples within and outside the United States; the abolition of sexual chauvinism." [79] Although James Kunen might sympathize with and even work actively for these causes, his art does not allow him to be *defined* by them. He rather celebrates a self which, in the face of oppression by a university, a government, or the cosmos itself, maintains and revels in its integrity and independence. Writing on the solar eclipse for *Esquire,* Kunen noted why he, and so many others, were drawn to watch it. "Not so much to see the eclipse," he realized, "but to avoid never seeing one." He is most impressed because

> the next total eclipse over a populated area of the United States is going to be in 2024. To watch an eclipse is to see a very common thing, really, a thing which has happened perhaps two billion times and will happen two billion times more, but only one time when you are alive. Eclipse watching tells you that you are going to die. For sure. It's a way of confronting your mortality. It is a very dangerous sport. [80]

[78] James Simon Kunen, "The Great Rocketship," *US: A Paperback Magazine* #1 (June, 1969), pp. 11–20.
[79] Dotson Rader, "Preface," *Defiance* #1 (October, 1970), p. 9.
[80] James Simon Kunen, "Ecliptic Vibrations," *Esquire,* 74 (July, 1970), 34.

Without a radical disruption in its tradition, the novel might have sustained grievous injury in the late 1960's, a universe away from the times in which fiction was first conceived and the rules for it set. Yet despite all the cultural and historical innovations in topic, it was the old-fashioned *form* for this content—in the guise of a mimetic pretense at life—which was the most debilitating thing of all. If the world is absurd, if what passes for reality is distressingly unreal, why spend time representing it? Physical, social, and political conditions may be a mess, and to view them from one perspective, imposing a rational order, is an aesthetic mess; so when everything else has changed, including the very ways we experience our world, should not the novel change too? To John Barth's valid case for the exhaustion of old narrative forms Robert Coover, Steve Katz, and Richard Brautigan added a new aesthetic for the novel: not just the reporting of the world, but the imaginative transformation of it. Even the conventional techniques of fiction could be revitalized in a form more forthrightly in harmony with the world's documentary nature, as James Kunen and others demonstrated in their nonfiction novels. Of everything that died in the years from 1967 through 1969, only one obituary now seems to be false: the death of the novel, which through the continuing innovations and growing popularity of Kurt Vonnegut, Jr., Donald Barthelme, Jerzy Kosinski, Ronald Sukenick, and others was to be the precursor in fact of fiction's greatest renaissance.

ONE

Kurt Vonnegut, Jr.

The poster appears in practically every bookstore window: "Kurt Vonnegut, Jr.," with a picture of the man himself looking (as an early reviewer put it) like a corduroy-covered batwing chair, peering across the list of books he has written. *Cat's Cradle, Slaughter-house-Five,* and his eight other titles are stacked inside, for another million readers to buy this year and almost certainly for many years to come.[1] There is no other living American novelist one could imagine on such a poster—not Saul Bellow, or at the other extreme Harold Robbins. Yet the posters remain, and can be found in head shops, pizzerias, and college bars, stamping those places as the dusty portraits of William Butler Yeats define an Irish pub.

College sales have undoubtedly been the factor which pushed Vonnegut over the top, making him not only one of the largest sellers, but also probably the most talked-about American novelist since Ernest Hemingway.[2] But Kurt Vonnegut, Jr., marked like a painted bird with his self-proclaimed attention-getting name, has been around for two decades, doing stories for the *Saturday Evening Post* and letting three of his books see first light as shoddy drugstore paperbacks [3] while waiting for America to discover him as its great public writer. The country is having its field day now, as the resurrected *Post* digs up Vonnegut's 1950 nostalgia pieces for each quarterly issue, and old paperback bins are riffled for copies of those

[1] There are more than fifty distinct American editions of Vonnegut's novels, story collections, and plays, plus scores of foreign issues. Since January, 1970, his Dell paperback editions have each been reprinted six to eight times per year, in press runs of 25,000 to 50,000 copies each.

[2] Since 1969 over four dozen interviews with Vonnegut have appeared in major magazines and newspapers, and in that same brief time twice that many critical books and articles (and of course hundreds of reviews) have been published. For a complete list, see the bibliography.

[3] Kurt Vonnegut, Jr., *The Sirens of Titan* (New York: Dell, 1959); *Canary in a Cat House* (Greenwich, Conn.: Fawcett, 1961); *Mother Night* (Greenwich, Conn.: Fawcett, 1962).

queer editions: *Utopia-14*,[4] *Canary in a Cat House*, and the totally disreputable first edition of *The Sirens of Titan* with its garish advertisements and sexy come-on cover. Vonnegut served a twenty-year apprenticeship—from 1949, when he left his job as public relations man for General Electric's Research Laboratory to support his growing family by writing stories for the slicks, up to 1969, when *Slaughterhouse-Five* became his first best-seller. Within those years lies the work of a lifetime: six novels, two story collections, and the roots for his plays on Broadway and TV. For an American grappling with some fast, confusing changes, Kurt Vonnegut's newly discovered career was the missing link, spanning the years from today's issues back to the simpler times when the television adaptation he helped write, "Auf Wiedersehen," was the vehicle for Ronald Reagan to introduce Sammy Davis, Jr., in his first dramatic role.[5] General Electric Theatre, *Collier's,* the *Saturday Evening Post*—these were the markets Vonnegut worked, spinning tales of Buick Roadmasters and All Electric Homes that seem, in their almost grandfatherly tone, to have been written for us today.

For twenty years, while Vonnegut wrote his simple stories of the American middle class, his publishers tried frantically to build him a novelist's reputation as exotic as his name. His first novel, *Player Piano* (1952), was given a large book club printing, and a quarter of a million copies were prepared in paperback. But it was a science fiction book club, and a retitled and luridly dressed paperback pitched to the s-f audience; neither succeeded as well as the several hundred copies of the first edition which sold in Schenectady, New York—home of the General Electric Corporation, and of the people who recognized some very down-to-earth things of which their former PR man was making fun. *The Sirens of Titan* followed in 1959: 177,550 paperback copies. Even at thirty-five cents, if each one had sold Vonnegut could have rested from the *Post* for half a year. But the page one blurb proclaimed, "Malachi Constant was the richest man in America. . . . Since attaining manhood, there

---

[4] The retitled paperback of Kurt Vonnegut, Jr., *Player Piano* (New York: Scribners, 1952), prepared by Bantam Books (New York) in 1954.

[5] A television drama by Kurt Vonnegut, Jr., and Valentine Davies, adapted from the story "D. P.," *Ladies Home Journal,* 70 (August, 1953), 42–43, 80–81, 84, by Kurt Vonnegut, Jr., produced by William Frye, directed by John Brahm, and transmitted nationally on "General Electric Theatre" by the Columbia Broadcasting System, October 5, 1958.

was no woman he desired who had not succumbed,'' hardly suggesting that within was a technically challenging and very serious novel. To complicate matters, Vonnegut picked the same time to hit the catastrophe of all serial writers, a slack year when absolutely nothing sold. "In those days," says Vonnegut, "if you had published something you could go to a paperback house and give them one chapter and an outline and they would give you money which would pay your grocery bill anyway." [6] And so his third novel, *Mother Night* (1962), which many critics today call his best, was sacrificed as a pulp paperback. Encountered in this edition it is often mistaken for what it fictionally purports to be, "an American traitor's astonishing confession" of his hideous acts as a Nazi in World War II. *Canary in a Cat House,* a curiously uneven collection of Vonnegut's stories from every which place, died a similar death with the same publisher. In 1963 an editor from one of the paperback houses which printed Vonnegut got a job with Holt, Rinehart and Winston, taking the manuscript of *Cat's Cradle* with him. *God Bless You, Mr. Rosewater* followed in 1965, and for the first time in a decade Vonnegut could boast of original hardbound publication. But only 6,000 copies of each were printed, not many sold, and reviewers and librarians alike followed habit in classifying the books as "science fiction," even though in the presidential election of 1964 seventy million Americans had voted on issues—the reconstitution of society, the possible military destruction of the world—very close to the themes of Vonnegut's two novels. In fifteen years of writing Vonnegut had won success only in the topically familiar but auctorially anonymous field of popular magazine fiction. His career seemed schizophrenic: scores of stories read by a mass popular audience, and a group of curious novels acknowledged by only the smallest of intellectual elites, neither of which appeared to admit the other's existence.

Yet for an ever-increasing paperback market Kurt Vonnegut, Jr., provided fodder. By 1966 all his novels were available in low-priced but quality editions, widely distributed to drugstores and paperback bookstalls. His full canon was for once at hand, and

---

[6] Interviewed by Robert Scholes on the University of Iowa campus and broadcast locally on October 4, 1966. Published in *The Vonnegut Statement,* ed. Jerome Klinkowitz and John Somer (New York: Seymour Lawrence/Delacorte Press, 1973), pp. 90–118.

when personal details about the man started coming out, readers could finally put things in place. His reviews for the *New York Times Book Review,* beginning in late 1965, showed him not as a raving sci-fi lunatic or an anonymous hack writer, but as the guy next door who, faced with the evaluation of a dictionary, could only shrug, "Prescriptive, as nearly as I could tell, was like an honest cop, and descriptive was like a boozed-up war buddy from Mobile, Ala." [7] Other pieces, crafted in the new style of personal journalism which placed the writer himself at the imaginative center of experience, followed in the Sunday magazine sections of the *Times* and other papers, and in such popular journals as *Esquire* and *McCall's.* [8] A reprint of *Mother Night,* [9] where Vonnegut added a preface clarifying his role as author, revealed something which was in fact true: as a twenty-two-year-old prisoner of war he had survived the Allied firebombing of Dresden, Germany, an atrocity killing more people than the atomic bomb at Hiroshima. Readers now knew something about this man, a solidly middle-class kid from Indianapolis who went to Cornell to study chemistry, and who witnessed scientific truth when American and British warplanes dropped it on an open city. And those same readers could now buy all his books in paperback, to discover that the tangled world of middle-class homes, Nazi perversity, and unimaginable machines of destruction was in its cumulative effect their world, too, only glimpsed a few years earlier by this son of an Indiana architect.

When Seymour Lawrence, the independent Boston publisher who had spotted Vonnegut this very way through the *Times* reviews and paperback reprints, published *Slaughterhouse-Five* in 1969, it was almost inevitable that Vonnegut's careful and complete preparation would make the book a best-seller. Swelled by a college underground where the science fiction paperbacks had their best market,

[7] Kurt Vonnegut, Jr., "The Latest Word" (review of *The Random House Dictionary*), *New York Times Book Review,* October 30, 1966, p. 1.

[8] See especially "Excelsior! We're Going to the Moon! Excelsior!" *New York Times Magazine,* July 13, 1969, pp. 9–11; "Physicist, Purge Thyself," *Chicago Tribune Magazine,* June 22, 1969, pp. 44, 48–50, 52, 56; "Yes, We Have No Nirvanas," *Esquire,* 69 (June, 1968), 78–79, 176, 178–179, 182; "Biafra," *McCall's,* 97 (April, 1970), 68–69, 134–138. A full listing of Vonnegut's journalism appears in the bibliography to this volume.

[9] Kurt Vonnegut, Jr., *Mother Night* (New York: Harper & Row, 1966); also included in the second paperback edition of *Mother Night* (New York: Avon, 1967), and all subsequent editions.

people had been "hearing" of Vonnegut for some time. Now he was presentable in a widely distributed hardbound edition, promptly picked up by the Literary Guild and serialized as well. Moreover, the book was a coming to terms with the matter of Dresden, beginning with a first-person chapter locating Vonnegut securely within this book and explaining his work for the past twenty years. "What do you say about a massacre" had been the unsaid premise of his five previous novels. From *Player Piano* through *God Bless You, Mr. Rosewater,* Vonnegut had dealt with an unending series of catastrophes, from social revolutions and a world war through a Martian invasion to the ultimate destruction of the world itself. The short stories, written "to finance the writing of the novels," [10] spoke more directly of Vonnegut's day-to-day life, as a solid ex-Midwesterner trying to support his wife and six children by writing stories of people in similar predicaments, spinning fantasies to take himself and his readers beyond their quotidian lives for a better perspective on them. *Slaughterhouse-Five* traced the two streams back to where they join in a meat locker five stories beneath the city of Dresden, where on February 13, 1945, the young soldier from Indianapolis witnessed the greatest single military destruction of human life in modern times.

Expressing what he saw took Vonnegut five books of trying. To clarify what was really going on, he kept rearranging what we take to be our world. First to be transformed was society, the wrong way in *Player Piano,* where indeed social change could take us if technology were to overrule human value, and later the right way in *God Bless You, Mr. Rosewater,* where our whole social ethic is stood on its head so that there might be some worth for man. The world as first encountered in this novel is a portrait in viciousness, perhaps the most bitter of any of Vonnegut's books. Norman Mushari is the rapacious lawyer out to attach whatever portion of the Rosewater fortune he can; to match his personality, we learn that "He had an enormous ass, which was luminous when bare." [11] The fortune itself is a product of nineteenth-century robber baron tactics, spiced

---

[10] Kurt Vonnegut, Jr., "Preface," *Welcome to the Monkey House* (New York: Seymour Lawrence/Delacorte Press, 1968), p. xiv.

[11] Kurt Vonnegut, Jr., *God Bless You, Mr. Rosewater* (New York: Holt, Rinehart & Winston, 1965), p. 17. Subsequent references follow in parentheses.

with a touch of simple human greed—"Thus the American dream," writes the head of the Rosewater Foundation, "turned belly up, turned green, bobbed to the scummy surface of cupidity unlimited, filled with gas, went *bang* in the noonday sun" (p. 21). To be a true philanthropist Eliot Rosewater would help his fellow man, and for this he is considered insane. " 'The secret is that they're human,' " his wife pleads to his family. "She looked from face to face for some flicker of understanding. There was none. The last face into which she peered was Norman Mushari's. Mushari gave her a hideously inappropriate smile of greed and fornication" (p. 67).

Among the unfortunates of the world are some Rosewaters themselves. A cousin, Fred Rosewater, lives in Rhode Island, sells insurance to a nondescript clientele who can only hope for a substantial fortune through their own deaths, and who as the son of a suicide feels destined for that end himself. For a moment he feels important, when in an old family history he discovers that his line descends from colonial heroes; but turning to subsequent pages, he finds that "The manuscript was hollow. Termites had eaten the heart out of the history. They were still there, maggoty blue-grey, eating away" (p. 167). "Important people" abound in Fred's village; most of them behave according to the same cupidity and lack of intelligence which described the early Rosewaters. "Who really does run this crazy country?" a servant girl asks of them. "These creeps sure don't." Meanwhile, Eliot has moved his Foundation offices from Fifth Avenue out to Rosewater County, Indiana, to a shotgun attic above a lunch room and liquor store, where few outsiders could believe "that land anywhere could be so deathly flat, that people anywhere could be so deathly dull." Eliot's mission: " 'I'm going to love these discarded Americans, even though they're useless and unattractive. *That* is going to be my work of art' " (p. 47).

The program proposed in *God Bless You, Mr. Rosewater* is for all Vonnegut's novels the most immediately practical. Unlike the aesthetics, theologies, and metaphysics of his earlier works, *Rosewater* seeks hard facts. "You can safely ignore the arts and sciences," Eliot advises. "They never helped anybody. Be a sincere, attentive friend of the poor" (p. 23). He does like science fiction—but that has never been regarded as "literature" anyway, certainly not by

Eliot Rosewater. " 'I love you sons of bitches,' " he announces to a convention of s-f hacks. " 'You're the only ones with guts enough to *really* care about the future, who *really* notice what machines do to us, what cities do to us, what big, simple ideas do to us. . . .' " His favorite writer is Kilgore Trout, marketed in dirty bookstores because "what Trout had in common with pornography wasn't sex but fantasies of an impossibly hospitable world." More accurately, s-f writers understand the imaginative possibilities of life. For the convention Eliot demonstrates the totally arbitrary nature of our reality, as he scribbles his name on blank checks and makes them worth just so much money. " 'Think about the silly ways money gets passed around now,' " he tells the writers, " 'and then think up better ways' " (p. 31). Better Living Through Chemistry, Progress Is Our Most Important Product—Kurt Vonnegut, Jr., the public relations man who could easily have written these slogans, took his own advice and wrote novels which effectively created whole new worlds, most practically in his fifth attempt, *God Bless You, Mr. Rosewater.* " 'Americans have long been taught to hate all people who will not or cannot work,' " Kilgore Trout himself explains at the novel's end. So what can one do when automation (the villain in *Player Piano*) denies a job for everybody? " 'The problem is this: How to love people who have no use?' " Trout considers the answer:

> "In time, almost all men and women will become worthless as producers of goods, food, services, and mere machines, as sources of practical ideas in the areas of economics, engineering, and probably medicine, too. So—if we can't find reasons for reassuring human beings because they are *human beings,* then we might as well, as has so often been suggested, rub them out." (p. 210)

In a hypothetical Trout novel about an overpopulated and dying planet, a victim in an "Ethical Suicide Parlor" asks, in his dying words, " 'What in hell are people *for?*' " (p. 30). In the almost identical "Welcome to the Monkey House" written by Vonnegut himself, he poses the same question. But, rather than to accept the present world as it is and depict the miserable fate of humans in it, Vonnegut chooses to show just how arbitrary and conventional the "world" is, and how easily it may be changed for something better.

In *Rosewater* it is just a case of transforming the social ethic (something that happens over a longer period of time anyway), to treasure people for something other than what they can produce.

In an interview given the morning after his play *Happy Birthday, Wanda June* opened off Broadway, Vonnegut described his fascination with the relativity of change. "I'm obsessed with another name now: The Barringafner of Bagnialdo. He's a guy who each day decides what's valuable. One day, it's land, one day it's clothes, etc., so that everybody is wealthy some time or another." [12] Throughout his career Vonnegut has made such reorderings on a cosmic scale. Before *Rosewater* he had considered the larger forces which so construed determine man. How far is he responsible, where does he stand in the universe, and how does that universe relate to him? *The Sirens of Titan, Mother Night,* and *Cat's Cradle,* novels written at the center of Vonnegut's career, try to answer these overwhelming questions. *The Sirens of Titan* takes the form of Eliot Rosewater's favorite genre, science fiction, to trace out the eschatological imperative of human nature. "What mankind hoped to learn in its outward push was who was actually in charge of all creation, and what all creation was all about." [13] Or as the protagonist, Malachi Constant, reads in a letter from his father, *"What I want you to try and find out, is there anything special going on or is it all just as crazy as it looked to me?"* (p. 90). Through this novel Vonnegut attacks the notion of absolutist religion which would claim God's purpose as its own. *"Take Care of the People, and God Almighty Will Take Care of Himself,"* affirms Vonnegut's new faith, "The Church of God the Utterly Indifferent." An infinite amount of evil-doing is abolished, simply by recognizing that "Puny man can do nothing at all to help or please God Almighty, and Luck is not the Hand of God" (p. 180).

Instead, Vonnegut suggests that man construct his own eschatology through the imagination. When Malachi, later known as "Unk," does, Vonnegut praises the work. "It was literature in its finest sense, since it made Unk courageous, watchful, and secretly

[12] Lawrence Mahoney, " 'Poison Their Minds with Humanity,' " *Tropic: The Miami Herald Sunday Magazine,* January 24, 1971, p. 44.

[13] Kurt Vonnegut, Jr., *The Sirens of Titan* (New York: Dell, 1959), p. 7. Subsequent references follow in parentheses.

free. It made him his own hero in very trying times" (p. 132).
When properly understood, religions are imaginative systems too,
capable of changing the world, as is done in *The Sirens of Titan* by
the founding of Vonnegut's new Church. " 'Any man who would
change the World in a significant way must have showmanship, a
genial willingness to shed other people's blood, and a plausible new
religion to introduce during the brief period of repentance and horror that usually follows bloodshed' " (p. 174). And that is the plot
of Vonnegut's novel—again, after demonstrating that the truth of
our existence was not what we absolutistically thought it was anyway. Our whole history, highpointed by Stonehenge, the Great
Wall of China, the Golden House of the Roman Emperor Nero, the
Moscow Kremlin, and the Palace of the League of Nations, has
been just a series of messages to a flying-saucer pilot, stranded for
several hundred thousand years on Titan, a moon of Saturn, and
waiting for a replacement part the size of a can opener. His mission
has been to carry a message across the universe which reads, simply, "Greetings."

Vonnegut followed *The Sirens of Titan* with *Mother Night*,[14] in
which he explores the limits of human responsibility. There is much
fun in the book, and it is one of the ironies of Vonnegut's canon that
while his grimmest material is found in his portraits of south central
Indiana, Germany under the Nazis in World War II provides some
of his greatest hilarity. Rather than show Himmler, Hess, Eich-
mann, and even Hitler as trailing slime, Vonnegut presents them in
their utter banality. *Mother Night* takes a solemn note of the six
million dead, but also reminds us that the Germans of 1933–45 attended dances, patronized the theatre, and played ping-pong. By
1962 there existed a whole library of literature on their atrocities,
including William L. Shirer's mammoth and apparently complete
The Rise and Fall of the Third Reich. But it was a German historian
who in reviewing Shirer's book complained that all English and
American histories failed to consider "the entire domestic history of

---

[14] Robert Scholes, " 'Mithridates, He Died Old': Black Humor and Kurt Vonnegut, Jr.,"
Hollins Critic, 3 (October, 1966), 1–12; Scholes, *The Fabulators* (New York: Oxford Uni-
versity Press, 1967), pp. 35–55; Doris Lessing, "Vonnegut's Responsibility," *New York
Times Book Review,* February 4, 1973, p. 35; Jerome Klinkowitz, "Kurt Vonnegut, Jr., and
the Crime of His Times," *Critique,* 12, #3 (1971), 38–53; Klinkowitz and Somer, eds., *The
Vonnegut Statement,* pp. 158–177.

wartime Germany'' as a clue to understanding the "defiance of self-interest and sanity'' by an entire people for more than a decade.[15] The domestic comedy Vonnegut sketches suggests, in the end, an elaborate absurdity. His protagonist, Howard W. Campbell, Jr., functions as both a Nazi propagandist and an American spy. Practically everyone else in his world has double identities as well: Heinz Schnildknecht, an expert at propagandizing New Zealanders and Australians, who is really an Israeli agent; Lazlo Szombathy, Campbell's suicidal garbageman who is really a veterinarian with a cure for cancer; Private Bodovskov, plagiarist of Campbell's work who is executed for his only original work, a satire of the Red army; and dozens of other persons, places, and in some cases things which manage a schizophrenic identity. Even the Gettysburg Address figures in: Goebbels admires its skillful rhetoric, but the speech brings Adolf Hitler to tears. Meanwhile across the ocean Franklin D. Roosevelt listens nightly as the anti-Semitic Campbell's greatest fan.

One of Howard Campbell's guards in the Tel-Aviv prison is Arpad Kovacs, who spent the war as a Jewish spy among the S. S. in Germany. He boasts to his captive: " 'I was such a pure and terrifying Aryan that they even put me in a special detachment. Its mission was to find out how the Jews always knew what the S. S. was going to do next. There was a leak somewhere, and we were out to stop it.' He looked bitter and affronted, remembering it, even though he himself had been that leak.'' [16] Campbell's double identity is the most ironic, since he was at the very same time the best Nazi propagandist and the best Allied spy. He even knows its clinical name: " 'I've always known what I did. I've always been able to live with what I did. How? Through that simple and widespread boon to modern mankind—schizophrenia' '' (p. 136).

The madness in Vonnegut's cosmos goes beyond the clinical illness. To maintain an integral self in this chaotic world is schizophrenia writ large. Faced with the spectacle of Nazi Germany, Campbell takes solace not unusual in our culture: he retreats first to

[15] Klaus Epstein, "Shirer's History of Nazi Germany," *Review of Politics,* 23 (1961), 230–245. Specific references are to pp. 230 and 236, and were first drawn by Paul Varnell.

[16] Kurt Vonnegut, Jr., *Mother Night* (Greenwich, Conn.: Fawcett, 1962), p. 10. Subsequent references follow in parentheses.

art, then to love. Imperative in this plan is that he have a self to flee to, unabused and secure from the intrusion of others. Like any artist, Campbell presents "lies told for the sake of artistic effect." He knows that deep down his fictions are "the most beguiling forms of truth," but their surface is all fabrication. Hence when put on the air as a vicious propagandist, he seeks refuge in parody and satire. "I had hoped, as a broadcaster," he claims, "to be merely ludicrous" (p. 122). Beyond this he flees to love, where his escapist and schizoid tendencies are even more pronounced. He creates *Das Reich der Zwei:* "It was going to show how a pair of lovers in a world gone mad could survive by being loyal only to a nation composed of themselves—a nation of two" (p. 27). As a narcotic it gets him through the war, "an ability to let my emotions be stirred by only one thing—my love for Helga" (p. 36). Campbell hopes the self—shielded by art and by love—will be inviolate, so there he hides.

It is Vonnegut's argument, however, that in the world so construed the self can be violated at every turn. His love is the first to fall. When Helga is captured on the Russian front, Campbell would respond romantically in grief and melancholy. But modern espionage not only mocks his grief, but even uses him to do the mocking:

> This news, that I had broadcast the coded announcement of my Helga's disappearance, broadcast it without even knowing what I was doing, somehow upset me more than anything in the whole adventure. It upsets me even now. Why, I don't know.
> It represented, I suppose, a wider separation of my several selves than even I can bear to think about.
> At that climactic moment in my life, when I had to suppose that my Helga was dead, I would have liked to mourn as an agonized soul, indivisible. But no. One part of me did not even know that the announcement was being made. (p. 140)

Nor will history spare his love. The intimate diary of his life with Helga is stolen and turned into pornography, complete with color plates. "That's how I feel right now," Campbell tells his spy chief, "like a pig that's been taken apart, who's had experts find a use for my every part. By God—I think they even found a use for my squeal" (pp. 155–156).

Art is no better refuge. To cover his self-respect and perhaps coincidentally topple the Nazi regime by its own absurdity, Howard Campbell had hoped to be satirically ludicrous. "But this is a hard world to be ludicrous in," he learns, "with so many human beings so reluctant to laugh, so incapable of thought, so eager to believe and snarl and hate. So many people wanted to believe me!" (p. 122). His propaganda has instead prolonged the war. "I realize that almost all the ideas that I now hold, that make me unashamed of anything I may have done as a Nazi, came not from Hitler, not from Goebbels, not from Himmler—but from you," a high-ranking German tells him. "You alone kept me from concluding that Germany had gone insane" (p. 75). Vonnegut's protagonist measures the fate of his several selves: "The part of me that wanted to tell the truth got turned into an expert liar! The lover in me got turned into a pornographer! The artist in me got turned into an ugliness such as the world has rarely seen before" (p. 156). The self is not inviolate; there is no place to hide.

And so the confessions of Howard W. Campbell, Jr., end on what might be a note of weak despair. But Vonnegut's novel closes more optimistically, since its author chooses to look beyond Campbell's responsibility and into the whole idea of a world so conceived. Why is it such a horrible world? How has the self been lost? Vonnegut's answer may be found in examining just such a notion of an inviolable self. Because men have abandoned all else and have selfishly fled to their selves, and because they have established their own person as the romantic center of the universe, when the self collapses all quite literally is lost. Campbell learns this, and therefore does not follow through on his offer to surrender to the Israelis and take their punishment for his crimes against humanity. At the last moment—on the eve of his trial, when evidence for his acquittal has come in the mail—he makes his decision. "I think that tonight *I* will hang Howard W. Campbell, Jr., for crimes against *himself*" (p. 202, italics added). In *Mother Night* Vonnegut details once more how the world is something we ourselves create; hence his indictment in his own signed headnote to the story: "This book is rededicated to Howard W. Campbell, Jr., a man who served evil too openly and good too secretly, the crime of his times."

"The world" has ever been for Kurt Vonnegut, Jr., an exquisitely flexible concept. In his seven novels and various short stories he has had it overpopulated, technologically revolutionized, fire-bombed, invaded by zombies from Mars, and—in *Cat's Cradle*—formally destroyed. In this work Vonnegut's protagonist is himself writing a book, *The Day the World Ended,* "an account of what important Americans had done on the day when the first atomic bomb was dropped on Hiroshima, Japan." He begins with routine queries about Dr. Felix Hoenikker, inventor of the bomb; as with his letter to Hoenikker's son Newt, his methods are strictly documentary and without event ("I will, of course, submit the final version to you for your approval prior to publication," etc.). Newt's answer opens a whole can of worms, and soon John, the writer, finds his soul clouded and "as foul as smoke from burning cat fur." [17] And his book is disrupted:

> When we got into Dr. Breed's inner office, I attempted to put my thoughts in order for a sensible interview. I found that my mental health had not improved. And, when I started to ask Dr. Breed questions about the day of the bomb, I found that the public-relations centers of my brain had been suffocated by booze and burning cat fur. Every question I asked implied that the creators of the atomic bomb had been criminal accessories to murder most foul. (p. 41)

From then on his work becomes hopelessly problematic. As with Vonnegut's earlier depiction of Nazi war criminals, there is much mirth to be had with the memory of Dr. Hoenikker. Newt tells of his family life with his sister and older brother Frank and their father, the father of the atomic bomb. Angela "used to talk about how she had three children—me, Frank, and Father. She wasn't exaggerating, either. I can remember cold mornings when Frank, Father, and I would be all in a line in the front hall, and Angela would be bundling us up, treating us exactly the same. Only I was going to kindergarten; Frank was going to junior high; and Father was going to work on the atom bomb" (p. 23). Hoenikker's laboratory was an assemblage of kitchen stuff and toys; here he would play with his gadgets and sometimes hit upon new ideas. For several months his atomic research waited while he played with turtles.

[17] Kurt Vonnegut, Jr., *Cat's Cradle* (New York: Holt, Rinehart & Winston, 1963), p. 33. Subsequent references follow in parentheses.

> Some people from the Manhattan Project finally came out to the
> house to ask Angela what to do. She told them to take away Father's
> turtles. So one night they went into his laboratory and stole the turtles
> and the aquarium. Father never said a word about the disappearance
> of the turtles. He just came to work the next day and looked for things
> to play with and think about, and everything there was to play with
> and think about had something to do with the bomb. (p. 24)

But the hilarity and especially the preciousness is quickly undercut
when the affecting scene of the absent-minded scientist walking
away from his automobile in a traffic jam concludes so: his wife re-
trieves the car, is unused to driving it, and in a resulting accident receives a pelvic injury which subsequently proves fatal during child-
birth.

Vonnegut again relieves his habitual problem of a too sordid
world by reminding us that it is just made up, even what we most
firmly believe to be true. As the action shifts to the Caribbean island
of San Lorenzo, he introduces us to his second major religion, that
of the holy man Bokonon. "Pay no attention to Caesar," reads a
precept of this religion. "Caesar doesn't have the slightest idea
what's *really* going on" (p. 88). Bokononism is a religion which
subverts the lies people tell themselves about existence with better
lies. San Lorenzo is a hopeless pocket of poverty, beyond even the social and political schemes of a Lionel Boyd Johnson (Bokonon's original name). And so "When it became evident that no governmen-
tal or economic reform was going to make the people much less
miserable, the religion became the one real instrument of hope.
Truth was the enemy of the people, because truth was so terrible, so
Bokonon made it his business to provide the people with better and better lies" (p. 143). Bokonon and his partner McCabe devise a system of dynamic tension, of Good and Evil pitted against
each other in a soul-sustaining force:

> McCabe and Bokonon did not succeed in raising what is generally
> thought of as the standard of living. . . . The truth was that life was
> as short and brutish and mean as ever.
> But people didn't have to pay as much attention to the awful truth.
> As the living legend of the cruel tyrant in the city and the gentle holy
> man in the jungle grew, so, too, did the happiness of the people
> grow. They were employed full time as actors in a play they under-

stood, that any human being anywhere could understand and applaud. (p. 144)

When Vonnegut's narrator is chosen President of San Lorenzo, he determines to govern without this fabrication, without "the hook" which was the operative symbol of McCabe's penal authority. But at once he becomes possessive, mean, and sexually dominant—the very qualities Bokononism subverts. And so the holy man's creed prevails.

The only workable answer to life, argues *Cat's Cradle,* is "the whole truth." Nathan Scott, in relating the comic to the religious, has remarked that only comedy can tell the whole truth. When the entire story is not told, when a salient element of reality is denied concrete existence, we have the heresy of Gnosticism, which posits "a God unknowable by nature . . . and utterly incommensurable with the created order." [18] Vonnegut aims in the other direction. He grants the finite a real existence, rather than as the imperfect shadow of some higher ideal. Pushed far enough, such doctrine would constitute the heresy of Manichaeanism. The value of Bokononism, however, is that it allows what Scott terms the "comic *katharsis,*" which involves "such a restoration of our confidence in the realm of finitude as enables us to see the daily occasions of our earth-bound career as being not irrelevant inconveniences but as possible roads into what is ultimately significant in life." [19] A Gnostic approach to the evils of San Lorenzo would indeed encourage a flight from "meaningless" finitude. But such a flight would be hopeless, as Vonnegut demonstrated in *Mother Night.* Modern man, romantically placed at the center of the universe and hence responsible for his own salvation, cannot flee from evil, even into himself; for in himself he will find only evil's deepest source. Vonnegut's alternative in Bokononism is a recognition of the finite for what it is: an external repository of certain elements, some of which may be evil but none of which is egocentrically identified with Man. Wylie Sypher, whose discussion in *The Loss of the Self* coincides with the theme of *Mother Night,* makes a plea for a new fiction which is answered in *Cat's Cradle.* Sypher speaks of "our need for

[18] Nathan Scott, "The Bias of Comedy and the Narrow Escape into Faith," *Christian Scholar,* 44 (Spring, 1961), 13.
[19] Ibid., p. 32.

an unheroic heroism'' or ''anonymous humanism'' [20] which will relieve man of his untenable position as the center of the universe.

There is a ''cruel paradox'' of Bokononist thought: the heartbreaking necessity of lying about reality, and the heartbreaking impossibility of lying about it. And also this ''calypso'' of the native religion:

> Tiger got to hunt,
> Bird got to fly;
> Man got to sit and wonder, ''Why, why, why?''
> Tiger got to sleep,
> Bird got to land;
> Man got to tell himself he understand. (p. 150)

Of greatest importance is the disclaimer printed on the first page of *The Books of Bokonon:*

> In the beginning, God created the earth, and he looked upon it in His cosmic loneliness.
>
> And God said, ''Let Us make living creatures out of mud, so the mud can see what We have done.'' And God created every living creature that now moveth, and one was man. Mud as man alone could speak. God leaned close as mud as man sat up, looked around, and spoke. Man blinked. ''What is the *purpose* of all this?'' he asked politely.
>
> ''Everything must have a purpose?'' asked God.
>
> ''Certainly,'' said man.
>
> ''Then I leave it to you to think of one for all this,'' said God. And He went away. (pp. 214–215)

The meaning of the world remains man's invention, as it is in each of Vonnegut's novels.

Slaughterhouse-Five is a triumph of Vonnegut's imagination, a product of twenty years of prototypes where at last the author has found a way to emphasize benign constructions of the world, and forget about the bad. The firebombing of Dresden was, throughout Vonnegut's career, never far beneath the surface. With his growing prominence he became explicit, adding to a 1966 reissue of *Mother Night* a revealing introduction, detailing the extent of his own ''per-

---

[20] Wylie Sypher, *The Loss of the Self in Modern Art and Literature* (New York: Random House, 1962), pp. 147–165.

sonal experience with Nazi monkey business.'' [21] Two years in residence at the University of Iowa Writers Workshop gave him the financial support and free mornings to complete his ''Dresden book.'' The firebombing itself would prove to be his block: in one draft Vonnegut envisioned the typography becoming darker and darker, running together as the date of the bombing—February 13, 1945—drew near, until at that narrative point the pages would be entirely black, then slowly clearing away into legibility as the event receded into history. What Vonnegut did send to his publisher (and to *Ramparts* magazine, who politely inquired if this was all there was to the manuscript) was a strange, apparently disjointed account, beginning with Vonnegut himself and ranging on to include the lifetime adventures of one Billy Pilgrim, ''a novel somewhat in the telegraphic schizophrenic manner of tales of the planet Tralfamadore, where the flying saucers come from.'' [22] In the first chapter Vonnegut spoke directly to his publisher and editor, Seymour Lawrence. ''It is so short and jumbled and jangled, Sam, because there is nothing intelligent to say about a massacre'' (p. 17).

Slaughterhouse-Five is a book about many difficult things to say. Billy Pilgrim faces death in Dresden and is asked to articulate it. He is also at the bedside of his dying mother; '' 'How did I get so *old?*' '' is her unanswerable question. But Vonnegut, with his customary hilarity in the face of the unspeakable, offers a parable for Billy's aphasia. He's drunk, trying to start his car and drive home after a party:

> The main thing now was to find the steering wheel. First, Billy windmilled his arms, hoping to find it by luck. When that didn't work, he became methodical, working in such a way that the wheel could not possibly escape him. He placed himself hard against the left hand door, searched every square inch of the area before him. When he failed to find the wheel, he moved over six inches and searched again. Amazingly, he was eventually hard against the right-hand door, without having found the wheel. He concluded that somebody had stolen it. This angered him as he passed out. (pp. 40–41)

[21] Kurt Vonnegut, Jr., *Mother Night* (New York: Harper & Row, 1966), p. v.
[22] Kurt Vonnegut, Jr., *Slaughterhouse-Five* (New York: Seymour Lawrence/Delacorte Press, 1969), title page. Subsequent references follow in parentheses.

What the eminently logical Billy doesn't know is that "He was in the back seat of his car, which was why he couldn't find the steering wheel."

Vonnegut delights in such challenges to our smug knowledge "of what's *really* going on." In *Breakfast of Champions* (1973) he describes a work of science fiction, of sorts: "Kilgore Trout once wrote a short story which was a dialogue between two pieces of yeast. They were discussing the possible purposes of life as they ate sugar and suffocated in their own excrement. Because of their limited intelligence, they never came close to realizing that they were making champagne." [23] Vonnegut's credo is never to be the victim of such short-sightedness himself. But the matter of Dresden presents a special problem. After a plane crash Billy is hospitalized with the official Air Force historian of World War II, who is revising his work into a single-volume edition. "The thing was, though, there was almost nothing in the [original] twenty-seven volumes about the Dresden raid, even though it had been such a howling success. The extent of the success had been kept a secret for many years after the war—a secret from the American people. It was no secret from the Germans, of course, or from the Russians, who occupied Dresden after the war, who are in Dresden still." To this Billy can only say, "I was there" (p. 165), and try to avoid the stylization and phoniness which characterize war stories, be they the Frank Sinatra–John Wayne heroics which Vonnegut's war buddy's wife Mary O'Hare detests, or the British prisoners who turn their captivity into *The Pirates of Penzance*. Either way is a hopelessly bad lie, especially for the otherwise admirable British—"They could tunnel all they pleased. They would inevitably surface within a rectangle of barbed wire, would find themselves greeted listlessly by dying Russians" (p. 80).

Slaughterhouse-Five is most notable for bringing up the question of what surely is—according to Vonnegut—the greatest lie of all, dwarfing Dresden with its cosmic implications. "If I hadn't spent so much time studying Earthlings," remarks a Tralfamadorian to Billy Pilgrim, "I wouldn't have any idea of what was meant by 'free

[23] Kurt Vonnegut, Jr., *Breakfast of Champions* (New York: Seymour Lawrence/Delacorte Press, 1973), pp. 208–209.

will.' I've visited thirty-one inhabited planets in the universe, and I have studied reports on one hundred more. Only on Earth is there any talk of free will'' (p. 74). What possibilities there are for ''better lies'' beyond free will are considered by Vonnegut through his metaphor of ''time travel,'' which serves both as a resolution of the story's theme and as a technique for expressing the truth of these facts within the structure of a novel. In his fifth chapter Vonnegut has described a Tralfamadorian novel, and the scheme is familiar of recent innovative works on our own planet, including those of Brautigan, Katz, Barthelme, Kosinski, Coover, and Vonnegut himself:

> each clump of symbols is a brief, urgent message—describing a situation, a scene. We Tralfamadorians read them all at once, not one after the other. There isn't any particular relationship between all the messages, except that the author has chosen them carefully, so that, when seen all at once, they produce an image of life that is beautiful and surprising and deep. There is no beginning, no middle, no end, no moral, no causes, no effects. What we love in our books are the depths of many marvelous moments seen all at one time. (p. 76)

Such experiences are not at all unearthly; Billy practices spatial juxtapositions even when he is not time-traveling, as when a drive through the gutted Ilium ghetto reminds him of Dresden in ruins. Throughout the book (and in all his works) Vonnegut plays with such hop-scotching images: a radium watch dial in Mammoth Cave, a few pages later the faces of Russian prisoners described the same way, and so forth.

In previous novels Vonnegut reorganized human ethics, history, and theology; *Slaughterhouse-Five* presents his greatest restructuring, that of time and space. The Tralfamadorians (Vonnegut's creation) have spatialized time, balancing a horizontal or linear determinism with a vertical, modal freedom. As Billy Pilgrim recounts:

> ''The most important thing I learned on Tralfamadore was that when a person dies he only *appears* to die. He is still very much alive in the past, so it is very silly for people to cry at his funeral. All moments, past, present, and future, always have existed, always will exist. The Tralfamadorians can look at all the different moments just the way we can look at a stretch of the Rocky Mountains, for instance. They can see how permanent all the moments are, and they

can look at any moment that interests them. It's just an illusion we have here on Earth that one moment follows another one, like beads on a string, and that once a moment is gone it is gone forever.

"When a Tralfamadorian sees a corpse, all he thinks is that the dead person is in a bad condition in that particular moment, but that the same person is just fine in plenty of other moments. Now, when I myself hear that somebody is dead, I simply shrug and say what the Tralfamadorians say about dead people, which is 'So it goes.' " (p. 23)

The justification for such restructuring is the bad experience Vonnegut's characters have had with life so far. Of Eliot Rosewater and Billy Pilgrim, Vonnegut says, "They had both found life meaningless, partly because of what they had seen in the war. Rosewater, for instance, had shot a fourteen-year-old fireman, mistaking him for a German soldier. So it goes. And Billy had seen the greatest massacre in European history, which was the firebombing of Dresden. So it goes." Therefore "they were trying to re-invent themselves and their universe. Science fiction was a big help" (p. 87).

To make it meaningful, the world must be reinvented. Science fiction time-travel is Vonnegut's metaphor, but behind this device stands man's greatest power, what separates him from other living creatures—the ability to imagine that anything, even he himself, is different from what is. Turn things around, make them different. Overcome the trouble, in one's mind to start with, but, when you have the technology, that way too. The horrors of war, our complex machines of destruction: why not reinvent them, as they would be reinvented when we take a war movie and run it backward:

American planes, full of holes and wounded men and corpses, took off backwards from an airfield in England. Over France, a few German fighter planes flew at them backwards, sucked bullets and shell fragments from some of the planes and crewmen. They did the same for wrecked American bombers on the ground, and those planes flew up backwards to join the formation.

The formation flew backwards over a German city that was in flames. The bombers opened their bomb bay doors, exerted a miraculous magnetism which shrunk the fires, gathered them into cylindrical steel containers, and lifted the containers into the bellies of the planes. The containers were stored neatly in racks. The Germans below had miraculous devices of their own, which were long steel tubes. They used them to suck more fragments from the crewmen and planes. But there were still a few wounded Americans, though, and some of the bombers were in bad repair. Over France, though, German fighters came up again, made everything and everybody as good as new.

When the bombers got back to their base, the steel cylinders were taken from the racks and shipped back to the United States of America, where factories were operating night and day, dismantling the cylinders, separating the dangerous contents into minerals. Touchingly, it was mainly women who did this work. The minerals were then shipped to specialists in remote areas. It was their business to put them into the ground, to hide them cleverly, so they would never hurt anybody ever again. (p. 63)

And so Vonnegut turns to a reconstruction of reality, to the human imagination, to art. In Chapter One of *Slaughterhouse-Five* he recalls his Guggenheim trip to Dresden and a book he took along, *Celine and His Vision* by Erika Ostrovsky. "Time obsessed him," Vonnegut noted of Celine. "Miss Ostrovsky reminded me of the amazing scene in *Death on the Installment Plan* where Celine wants to stop the bustling of a street crowd. He screams on paper, *Make them stop . . . don't let them move at all . . . There, make them freeze . . . once and for all! . . . So that they won't disappear any more!"* (p. 19).

Such radical use of the imagination to build a new freedom and dignity for man is part of Vonnegut's appeal to youth. In this respect his great following may seem to have run after a prophet, but there has been precious little guru-making of the man, certainly less than for Salinger and his Zen wisdom a decade ago, and nothing resembling the cult surrounding Tolkien. Rather, there is a great correspondence between what Vonnegut says when he appears at colleges, and what he wrote for the same students' parents in the days of the *Saturday Evening Post*. "We're not too young for love," a teenage runaway admits to her boyfriend in an early story.[24] "Just too young for about everything else there is that goes with love." A decade later, in his Bennington commencement speech, Vonnegut was saying the same thing: that young people

[24] Kurt Vonnegut, Jr., "Runaways," *Saturday Evening Post*, 234 (April 15, 1961), 26–27, 52, 54, 56.

should not accept responsibility for reforming the world. In practical terms, that is an impossible duty for any human being to bear. The answer lies rather in our attitudes, our philosophies—in short, what comes from our imagination. Vonnegut's beliefs in human decency are perhaps the most consistent thing about his writing, whether it be the occasional stories in the *Post,* where basically good and simple people—storm window salesmen, small town businessmen—triumph over far more imposing people and ideas,[25] or in the novels, where with much more artistic apparatus he sets about redefining our universe, which is, as he establishes, nothing more than a dominant state of mind.

The years Vonnegut spent conceiving and writing his Dresden book, 1965–69, have proved to be the watershed of his career. His five previous novels hovered about its theme of artistic re-creation, but the author always held back from such a complete fusion of personal fantasy with the apparently "real." And for all the years previous he'd had to severely discipline his imagination to keep within the money-making formula of stories for *Collier's* and the *Saturday Evening Post* which were supporting his family. But for several personal and professional reasons, by 1966 this world was coming apart, and his published work began a much more obvious flirtation with the realm of fantasy, particularly as it impinges upon and influences our mundane lives. Vonnegut's radical experiments with his fantasy world are best signaled by his curiously unconventional story, "Brief Encounters on the Inland Waterway." Written for *Venture: Traveler's World,*[26] the piece is a brilliant spoof of travel literature, even concluding with instructions from the author on how to acquire guidebooks to the waterway. Its expository style blends fancy and fact, creating an artful reality that is further heightened because of the imposing presence of the actual Kennedy yacht. The Kennedys, of course, especially the late president in 1966, were emblematic to the American public of all the glory and majesty ever hinted at in *Collier's.* What emerged, then, from Vonnegut's tour of duty as a writer of so-called slick fiction is a man keenly at-

[25] See especially Vonnegut's uncollected stories "Poor Little Rich Town," *Collier's,* 130 (October 25, 1952), 90–95; "Bagombo Snuff Box," *Cosmopolitan,* 137 (October, 1954), 34–39; "A Present for Big Nick," *Argosy,* December, 1954, pp. 42–45, 72–73.

[26] Kurt Vonnegut, Jr., "Brief Encounters on the Inland Waterway," *Venture: Traveler's World,* 3 (October/November, 1966), 135–138, 140, 142.

tuned to the cultural tensions of the popular literature and imagination of his time, a writer astutely capable of working within the popular conventions of his day, transcending them and maturing as an artist.

Kurt Vonnegut, Jr.'s last conventional stories appeared in *Redbook,* the *Saturday Evening Post,* and *Ladies' Home Journal* in 1962–63.[27] Thereafter his bills were paid by more public activity: teaching in the University of Iowa Writers' Workshop, reviewing for *Life,* and doing feature essays for the *New York Times Book Review.* It was a very evident shift. As a writer he was more prominent even in his own fiction, including the hybrid Kennedy story and the new introduction to *Mother Night,* both published in 1966. Vonnegut's time at Iowa included work on *Slaughterhouse-Five;* he begins, "All this happened, more or less," and proceeds to involve himself at the center of his story. In following years he became a spokesman on personal, national, and human events, until by June 29, 1970, *Time* could report his commencement address at Bennington College, "Up Is Better Than Down," as the week's top event.[28] The writer of stories had become a story himself.

Most of Vonnegut's essays revolve around himself. Recognizing his own emergence from the forms of fantasy, he began his new career with a piece on science fiction for the *New York Times.* His efforts in fantasy, including the early novel *Player Piano,* were in fact "about life, about things I could not avoid seeing and hearing in Schenectady, a very real town, awkwardly set in the gruesome now," [29] where he worked for General Electric. Two decades later he would reconsider the craft of fantasy, whether expertly written by Hermann Hesse,[30] taught with great futility at writers' conferences,[31] or slickly popularized by that phenomenon of the later 1960's, Maharishi Mahesh Yogi. The latter brought Vonnegut full

---

[27] Kurt Vonnegut, Jr., "The Lie," *Saturday Evening Post,* 235 (February 24, 1962), 46–47, 51, 56; "Go Back to Your Precious Wife and Son," *Ladies Home Journal,* 79 (July, 1962), 54–55, 108, 110; "Lovers Anonymous," *Redbook,* 121 (October, 1963), 70–71, 146–148.

[28] "Vonnegut's Gospel," *Time,* 95 (June 29, 1970), 8.

[29] Kurt Vonnegut, Jr., "Science Fiction," *New York Times Book Review,* September 5, 1965, p. 2.

[30] Kurt Vonnegut, Jr., "Why They Read Hesse," *Horizon,* 12 (Spring, 1970), 28–31.

[31] Kurt Vonnegut, Jr., "Teaching the Unteachable," *New York Times Book Review,* August 6, 1967, pp. 1, 20.

circle, back to himself: "Maharishi had come all the way from India to speak to the American people like a General Electric engineer." [32] Kurt Vonnegut, Jr., became his own measure in confronting problems, including "the narrowness and dimness of many lives out that way" in Middle America, but also questions of peace and war facing the whole nation. "Excelsior! We're Going to the Moon! Excelsior!" Vonnegut half-heartedly exclaims, and responds to the fantasy-like statistics of outer space: "If I were drunk, I might cry about that." [33] "War" he translates as a "Series of Collisions," reminiscent of when "collisions between steam locomotives were arranged at the Indiana State Fairgrounds—to cheer up the folks," emerging from Depression doldrums to gasp, "My God—looky there." [34] War research, counterinsurgency, cold and hot war diplomacy—all are taken in Vonnegut's view as manifestations of childish behavior, since "When you get to be our age, you all of a sudden realize that you are being ruled by people you went to high school with. You all of a sudden catch on that life is nothing *but* high school." [35]

Free of the need to write formula fantasy and equipped with the innovative tools of the New Journalism, Vonnegut could project himself in the equivalent of his famous chrono-synclastic infundibulum, stretching from murders in Provincetown, Mass., to the dying nation of Biafra, all the time measuring himself against these horrors of life. "Joking was my response to misery I couldn't do anything about," reads a lesson confirmed by this trip. [36] Once an optimist, training to be a scientist, Vonnegut could look for the best. "I fully expected," he told the graduating class at Bennington, "that by the time I was twenty-one, some scientist, maybe my brother [Bernard], would have taken a colour photograph of God

[32] Vonnegut, "Yes, We Have No Nirvanas."

[33] Vonnegut, "Excelsior! We're Going to the Moon! Excelsior!"

[34] Kurt Vonnegut, Jr., "War as a Series of Collisions" (review of *Bomber* by Len Deighton), *Life*, 69 (October 2, 1970), 10.

[35] Kurt Vonnegut, Jr., "Times Change," *Esquire*, 73 (February, 1970), 60; also see "Topics: Good Missiles, Good Manners, Good Night," *New York Times*, September 13, 1969, p. 26; "The Scientific Goblins Are Gonna Git Us" (review of *Unless Peace Comes* by Nigel Calder), *Life*, 65 (July 26, 1968), 8; and "Torture and Blubber," *New York Times*, June 30, 1971, p. 41.

[36] Kurt Vonnegut, Jr., " 'There's a Maniac Loose Out There,' " *Life*, 67 (July 25, 1969), 53–56; "Biafra."

Almighty—and sold it to *Popular Mechanics* magazine. Scientific truth was going to make us *so* happy and comfortable.'' But Dresden, Dachau, and Hiroshima intervened, making Vonnegut ''a consistent pessimist'' and writer of stories instead. Quoting Shakespeare, he justified fantasy's humor: ''To weep is to make less the depth of grief.'' [37] But standing before the American Academy of Arts and Letters, Vonnegut spoke as a man transcending fantasy. He had to, for in the two decades of his writing career science had eclipsed the more simple formulae. By 1971, perhaps, biochemistry could be everything; but man's ultimate needs remain, and the writer's vision becomes a simple plea for community.[38]

In the four years between his sudden fame and the publication of *Breakfast of Champions,* Vonnegut was a man without a genre. In the first chapter of *Slaughterhouse-Five* he declared that, after twenty years and six novels, he had come to terms with (and apparently exhausted) the substance of his fiction. ''I've finished my war book now,'' he proclaimed. ''The next one I write is going to be fun.'' [39] But the new novel was soon abandoned—publicly recalled and suppressed, in fact [40]—while he scripted the Broadway production of *Happy Birthday, Wanda June,*[41] an entirely new vision wherein society favorably transformed itself and left its reactionary central character behind, quite the opposite of Vonnegut's mode in fiction. Following that were ambitious plans for more plays, musicals, and films, but the only concrete issue of 1971–72 turned out to be his redrafting of a committee-written script, *Be-*

[37] Kurt Vonnegut, Jr., ''Up Is Better Than Down,'' *Vogue,* August 1, 1970, pp. 54, 144–145.

[38] Kurt Vonnegut, Jr., ''The Happiest Day in the Life of My Father,'' 50th Address on the Evangeline Wilbour Blashfield Foundation, Ceremonial of the American Academy of Arts and Letters and the National Institute of Arts and Letters, May 26, 1971, *Proceedings.* Reprinted as ''What Women Really Want Is . . . '', *Vogue,* 160 (August 15, 1972), 56–57, 93.

[39] Vonnegut, *Slaughterhouse-Five,* p. 19.

[40] Bruce Cook, ''When Kurt Vonnegut Talks—and He Does—the Young All Tune In,'' *National Observer,* October 12, 1970, p. 21; Carol Kramer, ''Kurt's College Cult Adopts Him as Literary Guru at 48,'' *Chicago Tribune,* November 15, 1970, sec. 5, p. 1; Richard Todd, ''The Masks of Kurt Vonnegut, Jr.,'' *New York Times Magazine,* January 24, 1971, p. 19.

[41] Kurt Vonnegut, Jr., *Happy Birthday, Wanda June* (New York: Seymour Lawrence/Delacorte Press, 1971). The author's typescript of the preface to this volume in the Swen Franklin Parson Library, Northern Illinois University, indicates that on p. 4 Vonnegut at first included a paragraph synopsis of his forthcoming novel, but crossed it out.

tween Time and Timbuktu, broadcast as a ninety-minute special on National Educational Television.[42] As if in celebration of the feat of *Slaughterhouse-Five,* the NET production gathered the bits and pieces of Vonnegut's twenty-year world and presented them as a cosmic Yoknapatawpha: the chrono-synclastic infundibulum of pure imaginative freedom when a poet is launched into space and his responses measured back on earth. "What does the show mean?" Vonnegut considered, having the record of his literary career placed so handily before him. "Well—it means, for one thing, that we will never get very far from this planet, no matter how much money we spend. So we had better stop treating the planet as though it were a disposable item to be used up and thrown away. It means, too, that, no matter how far we may travel, we can never get out of our heads." [43]

Breakfast of Champions brought Vonnegut back to fiction, building on the years of self-imposed retrospective study since *Slaughterhouse-Five.* "I have become an enthusiast for the printed word again," he announced in 1972. "I have to be that, I now understand, because I want to be a character in all of my works. I can do that in print. In a movie, somehow, the author always vanishes. Everything of mine which has been filmed so far has been one character short, and the character is me." [44] The subsequent novel deals with something before and beyond Dresden: the "great depression," which can be a reference to what happened in America during the 1930's, what is happening to the ecology and survival-potential of our planet now, and to the very personal effect both these events (and the years in between) have had upon the psyche of a literary artist. Vonnegut remembers the 1930's as a time when jocular impoliteness got one through the day, when his own childhood models (cited elsewhere as Jack Benny, Fred Allen, and Henry Morgan, and incorporated into *Breakfast of Champions* as a wildly irreverent columnist for the *Indianapolis Times*) survived the decade-long "Blue Monday" by their black humor, a term some

[42] March 13, 1972. Published in book form as Kurt Vonnegut, Jr., *Between Time and Timbuktu* (New York: Seymour Lawrence/Delacorte Press, 1972).

[43] MS comments on production by Kurt Vonnegut, Jr., owned by the author. Quoted with the permission of Mr. Vonnegut. (Original draft of a preface for *Between Time and Timbuktu* which was dropped in favor of the version cited below.)

[44] "Preface," Vonnegut, *Between Time and Timbuktu,* p. xv.

contemporary critics use to define such works as Terry Southern's *Magic Christian,* Bruce Jay Friedman's *Stern,* John Barth's earlier books, and Vonnegut's novels. But our own times of corruption, pollution, overpopulation, and decay are a far different matter, for no one can hope, as forty years ago, "that the nation would be happy and just and rational when prosperity came."

To write a novel adequate to our present reality, Vonnegut synthesizes not just the themes, but also the techniques of his literary career which spans America's change. Kilgore Trout, the prolific science fiction hack from Vonnegut's own previous novels who seems to epitomize the wildest flights of fantasy, is brought to meet the most thoroughly middle-class character Vonnegut ever created: Dwayne Hoover, proprietor of Dwayne Hoover's Exit Eleven Pontiac Village and owner of a share in the Holiday Inn and a string of Burger Chefs in Midland City, Indiana. Like Vonnegut, Trout creates fantasies of impossibly hospitable worlds, which, as in *God Bless You, Mr. Rosewater,* are marketed as pornography. At the same time Hoover has been learning the relative and totally conventional nature of reality, as by amassing economic power he can increasingly effect changes in the world around him. The state of our planet, however, has by the time of *Breakfast of Champions* outstripped the limits of conventional middle-class control. Ice cream, aluminum siding, and even the martini euphemized in the book's title pale before the new synthesis needed to keep our dying world in order. Trout, arguing the transformative power of ideas, of the imagination, writes a book explaining to any reader why things are so bad: every person and thing in the universe is a robot, existing simply for the test of one human being as a free-will prototype. That prototype, of course, is Dwayne Hoover, the reader.

The crazy events of life have been, in the jargon of the Detroit of Dwayne Hoover's Pontiacs, "destructive testing" of the one person with free will. In Trout's novel that person is Dwayne; in *Breakfast of Champions* it is Kilgore Trout, and in the Vonnegut canon—novels, plays, a hundred stories and essays—it is Kurt Vonnegut, Jr., himself, since he is the only real person in his self-contained, imaginatively created universe. And at the end of this most recent novel Vonnegut performs the supremely creative act by setting his characters free: " 'I am approaching my fiftieth birthday, Mr.

Trout,' I said. 'I am cleansing and renewing myself for the very different sorts of years to come. Under similar spiritual conditions, Count Tolstoi freed his serfs. Thomas Jefferson freed his slaves. I am going to set at liberty all the literary characters who have served me so loyally during my writing career.' '' [45]

In a copy of his manuscript which was circulated to a few reviewers in September, 1972, Vonnegut concluded *Breakfast of Champions* on an uncertain note. ''And I am now in that wing of the Midland County Hospital which houses the mentally disturbed,'' he advised. ''Dwayne Hoover is my friend.'' He added that he was not surprised. ''I always knew that sooner or later I would write myself into a loony bin. The big trick now is to write myself out again.'' [46] Vonnegut accomplished just this by the time bound galleys were released two months later. At the novel's publication an interviewer asked him what the title meant. ''It has to do to a certain extent with the early part of my life,'' Vonnegut answered, ''with my making peace with certain things that happened to me during the breakfast of my life. And now here I am, well past lunch now, and have made my peace with something that happened at breakfast.'' [47] In interviews several years before Vonnegut had remarked that his father's death in 1957 had driven him into a writer's block for some time, and that his next book would be about that death. [48] The revised ending of *Breakfast of Champions* was to make it that book, as several false starts in manuscript dating from 1957 imply. At that time Vonnegut was working on a piece of fiction titled *Upstairs and Downstairs*. In it we see the genesis of Fred T. Barry, inventor of the Robo-Magic washing machine and sponsor of the Midland City Festival of the Arts which brings together Dwayne Hoover and Kilgore Trout. Fred has moved into the narrator's home—he's twelve years old and his mother needs money, because his father is dying. The several manuscript versions describe these facts, and toy with Fred Barry's transforming power of money. But as the father's death approaches, the rest of the story blurs, almost like the Dresden

[45] Vonnegut, *Breakfast of Champions*, p. 293.

[46] MS owned by the author, pp. 357–360. These pages were subsequently rewritten and numbered 358–360. MS also indicates that the preface was expanded at a very late date.

[47] Frank McLaughlin, ''An Interview with Kurt Vonnegut, Jr.,'' *Media & Methods*, May, 1973, p. 45.

[48] ''We Talk to . . . Kurt Vonnegut,'' *Mademoiselle*, August, 1970, p. 296.

pages of the early *Slaughterhouse-Five* draft.[49] Only with the revised ending of *Breakfast of Champions* does Vonnegut find a way to confront this second great trauma in his life. With his characters freed, he dematerializes and somersaults lazily through the emptiness left by his departed characters. Kilgore Trout still cries out to him, but in the voice of Vonnegut's father, who has appeared to fill the void. And the novel ends with "what Kilgore Trout cried to me in my father's voice: *'Make me young, make me young, make me young.'* " [50]

It has been an irony in the history of contemporary fiction that Kurt Vonnegut, Jr., now our most popular and one of our most respected writers, remained virtually unknown for the first twenty years of his writing career. That it took the pressure of the first generation bred in the somewhat surreal presence of our times to make him famous speaks for the radical disruption which occurred in American fiction. Vonnegut's rise to eminence coincides precisely with the shift in taste which brought a whole new reading public—and eventually critical appreciation—to the works of Richard Brautigan, Donald Barthelme, Jerzy Kosinski, and others. Ten years and several books their elder, Vonnegut by his long exile underground was well prepared to be the senior member of the new disruptive group, and the first of its numbers to be seriously considered for the Nobel Prize. By 1973, when *Breakfast of Champions* appeared in a hardbound first printing of 100,000 copies and as the major selection of four book clubs, there was little doubt that a fiction widely scorned only six years before was now a dominant mode in serious contemporary literature.

[49] MSS owned by the author.
[50] Vonnegut, *Breakfast of Champions,* p. 295.

TWO

Donald Barthelme

"What we love in our books are the depths of many marvelous moments seen all at one time," Vonnegut's Tralfamadorian critic remarks of the novels on that distant planet. The Tralfamadorian novel, with its "urgent messages" read "all at once, not one after the other" to "produce an image of life that is beautiful and surprising and deep" [1] is an apt description of Donald Barthelme's fiction which since 1963 has been appearing with great regularity in the *New Yorker* and from time to time in other magazines as well. Considering innovations in fiction, Vonnegut has observed that "the limiting factor is the reader. No other art requires the audience to be a performer. You have to count on the reader's being a good performer and you may write music which he absolutely can't perform, in which case it's a bust." The innovators must teach their audience how to read their works: "it's a learning process and *The New Yorker* has been a very good institution of that sort, they have a captive audience and they come out every week and people finally catch on to Barthelme, for instance, and are able to perform that sort of thing in their heads and enjoy it." [2] For his own part Barthelme has acknowledged that "I wish I could write something that would adequately satisfy Kurt's definition." [3] His over one hundred stories, collected in five volumes and supplemented by his novels *Snow White* and *The Slightly Irregular Fire Engine,* have made him not only one of the more prolific but also "the most imitated fictionist writing in America today," [4] and the obvious model for Vonnegut's complete Tralfamadorian novelist.

[1] Kurt Vonnegut, Jr., *Slaughterhouse-Five* (New York: Seymour Lawrence/Delacorte Press, 1969), p. 76.

[2] Jerome Klinkowitz, unpublished interview with Kurt Vonnegut, Jr.

[3] Jerome Klinkowitz, "Donald Barthelme," in Joe David Bellamy, *The New Fiction: Interviews with Innovative American Writers* (Urbana: University of Illinois Press, 1974), p. 51.

[4] Charles Newman, "The Uses and Abuses of Death: A Little Rumble through the Remnants of Literary Culture," *Tri-Quarterly* #26 (Winter, 1973), p. 38.

Like Vonnegut, Barthelme is the son of an architect, Donald Barthelme, Sr., designer of several imaginative structures in Houston. "My father was a 'modern' architect in the sense that he was an advocate of Mies and Corbu, et al.," the younger Barthelme has remarked. "He was something of an anomaly in Texas in the thirties. The atmosphere of the house was peculiar in that there were very large architectural books around and the considerations were: What was Mies doing, what was Aalto doing, what was Neutra up to, what about Wright? My father's concerns, in other words, were to say the least somewhat different from those of the other people we knew. His mind was elsewhere." Of his childhood Barthelme adds,

> In the late thirties my father built a house for us, something not too dissimilar to Mies's Tugendhat house. It was wonderful to live in but strange to see, on the Texas prairie. On Sundays people used to park their cars out on the street and stare. We had a routine, the family, on Sundays. We used to get up from Sunday dinner, if enough cars had parked, and run out in front of the house in a sort of chorus line, doing high kicks.[5]

Donald Barthelme attended the University of Houston; after army service he returned to work as a reporter on the *Post* and, in 1957, to become founding editor of the University of Houston *Forum,* a handsomely produced literary and intellectual quarterly which—with its early publication of Walker Percy, William H. Gass, Joseph Lyons, Roger Callois, Alain Robbe-Grillet, and Leslie Fiedler—was for a time as much a local anomaly as the Barthelme Tugendhat home. In 1961 he moved to New York, where he was managing editor of the art and opinion journal *Location;* when this magazine folded in 1964, Barthelme devoted his full time to fiction. Since then he has averaged eight stories per year in the *New Yorker*.

For most of his career Barthelme has been a controversial writer, often attacked as a figure for less imaginative people's discomfort with the times. A character's statement, "Fragments are the only form I trust," is forever attributed as Barthelme's own quotation and taken as his aesthetic, most lately by Joyce Carol Oates:

> "Fragments are the only form I trust." This from a writer of arguable genius, whose works reflect the anxiety he himself must feel, in book

[5]. Klinkowitz, "Donald Barthelme," pp. 46–47.

after book, that his brain is all fragments . . . just like everything else. Passive, drifting, witty, melancholy-hilarious, surrealist (though nearly seven decades have passed since Alfred Jarry wrote "Ubu Roi") . . . even the construction of his sentence is symptomatic of his role: It begins with "fragments," the stern healthy noun, and concludes with the weak "I." But there is a point in history at which Wilde's remark comes horribly true, that life will imitate art. And then who is in charge, who believed himself cleverly impotent, who supposed he had abdicated all conscious design . . . ? [6]

Aside from the elemental concern that the "I" of the story is not necessarily the author, Barthelme's aesthetic is much more complex than the structural device of nonstructure. Structure, the stronger the better, is his chief concern. The roots for it may be found in his interest with the forms of language and even the sounds of words. At times he simply puns, but always within imaginative structures: " 'If we can just cross that spit of land there,' " says a bishop to his flock "(gesture with fingers, glitter of episcopal rings) 'and get to that harlot over there' (sweep of arm in white lacy alb) 'pardon, I mean hamlet. . . .' " [7] Barthelme's modifications of language are usually clever and sometimes suggestively disconcerting, as when he pictures a group of engineers who boast, "We have rots, blights, and rusts capable of attacking [the enemy's] alphabet," plus "the deadly testicle-destroying telegram." [8] They are also studying "the area of real-time online computer-controlled wish evaporation," because "Wish evaporation is going to be crucial in meeting the rising expectations of the world's peoples, which are as you know rising entirely too fast." [9] Into the phraseological structures of technocrats and politicians Barthelme has put his own absurdity, and the form is none the worse for the insertion. Some would say Barthelme has redeemed it and made it better. The revitalizing force of his fiction is evident in some of his earliest pieces, never collected, such as "Snap, Snap," "L'lapse," "Man's Face," and "Down the Line with the Annual." [10] The first story is an expanded New Yorker col-

[6] Joyce Carol Oates, "Whose Side Are You On," New York Times Book Review, June 4, 1972, p. 63.

[7] Donald Barthelme, "Several Garlic Tales," Paris Review #37 (Spring, 1966), p. 65.

[8] "Report," in Donald Barthelme, Unspeakable Practices, Unnatural Acts (New York: Farrar, Straus & Giroux, 1968), p. 55.

[9] Ibid., p. 54.

[10] New Yorker, 41 (August 28, 1965), 108, 110–111; New Yorker, 39 (March 2, 1963), 29–31; New Yorker, 40 (May 30, 1964), 29; New Yorker, 40 (March 21, 1964), 34–35. In

umn filler, which lists *Time*'s and *Newsweek*'s compulsive use of the verb "snapped" (instead of "said"), while the second is a parody of an Antonioni script which makes such directions as "Shabby pigeons whirl about meaningfully." "Man's Face" is in fact a whole novel, "Forty Coaxial Chapters" in the form of program notes from *TV Guide* (samples: Chapter XXXII—"on a field trip, Timmy finds a rock"; Chapter XXXVIII—"Sandy Koufax and Sen. Hubert H. Humphrey discuss ambergris"). "Down the Line with the Annual," however, is Barthelme's most mature experiment of the four. Here he uses the peculiar language and form of the *Consumer Bulletin Annual* as an index to universal angst. Reading the year's reports, the narrator is convinced that "We are adrift in a tense and joyless world that is falling apart at an accelerated rate." The *Bulletin*'s language, he finds, is an apt description of life itself:

> The world is sagging, snagging, scaling, spalling, pilling, pinging, pitting, warping, checking, fading, chipping, cracking, yellowing, leaking, staling, shrinking, and in dynamic unbalance, and there is mildew to think about, and ruptures, and fractures of internal organs from lap belts, and substandard brake fluids, and plastic pipes alluring to rats, and transistor radios whose estimated battery life, like the life of man, is nasty, brutish, and short.

One of Barthelme's favorite forms is the list. He lists doctors ("Dr. Caligari / Dr. Frank / Dr. Pepper / Dr. Scholl . . ."), knights, magazine ads, "Eddie and Debbie" fan magazine headlines, and, in the form's source, litanies of Catholic doctrines, dogmas, and sins. Within such forms as the list and the litany Barthelme has exercised his greatest talent, that of revitalizing language by carefully selecting it and placing it in strange and insightful forms. A barricade in "The Indian Uprising" is constructed of "window dummies, silk, thoughtfully planned job descriptions (including scales for the orderly progress of other colors), wine in demijohns, and robes." [11] He places an alien word within an otherwise predictable sentence: "In the so-called 'silver cities' there is a particular scale—66, 67, 68, 69 degrees—at which intercourse occurs." [12] Barthelme has a sense of the shape of words them-

June, 1974, Farrar, Straus & Giroux announced that these and the subsequent pieces referred to would be published in a volume titled *Guilty Pleasures*.

[11] "The Indian Uprising," in Barthelme, *Unspeakable Practices*, p. 5.

[12] "Paraguay," in Donald Barthelme, *City Life* (New York: Farrar, Straus & Giroux, 1970), p. 21.

selves, a talent going beyond the simple writing of nonsense sylla-
bles. For instance, he describes "the exotic instruments of Cleveland" as "the dolor, the mangle, the bim"; [13] a card hand reads
"The four of fans, the twelve of wands, the deuce of kidneys, the
Jack of Brutes"; [14] and in his novel, *Snow White,* the breakfast
table is set "with its big boxes of 'Fear,' 'Chix,' and 'Rats.' " [15]
Barthelme presents, within the outward shapes of familiar words,
bold, strange, and terrifying ones, which shock us into a new awareness of his fictional world. In "The President," when the chief executive speaks, "One hears only cadences." Saying in fact nothing,
he simply makes the accepted gestures and repeats empty phrases,
so that "Newspaper accounts of his speeches always say only that
he 'touched on a number of matters in the realm of. . . .' " [16]
Barthelme's genius is not only in noticing the empty phrases, as
George Orwell did twenty-five years ago in "Politics and the English Language," but also in infusing those empty forms with the
work of vivid imagination—a process beneficial to both form and
content.

The novel *Snow White* (1967) is Barthelme's major thematic
exploitation of language and the forms it takes. There is much running and playing with the shapes of language (such as "The President's War on Poetry") (p. 55). The ghost of George Orwell once
again hovers near, as an electric wastebasket destroys paper by
means of "An intimidation followed by a demoralization eventuat-
ing in a disintegration" (p. 129). Barthelme comically makes language live when he confesses that "I wanted to make a far-reaching
reevaluation. I had in mind launching a three-pronged assault, but
the prongs wandered off seduced by fires and clowns" (p. 53).
Words themselves are the theme of the book, for Snow White's
lament is "OH I wish there were some words in the world that were
not the words I always hear!" (p. 6). But she hears the same old
words, in the same empty forms, unvitalized by imagination:
" 'Snow White,' we said, 'why do you remain with us? here? in

---

[13] "Up, Aloft in the Air," in Donald Barthelme, *Come Back, Dr. Caligari* (Boston:
Little, Brown, 1964), p. 129.

[14] "A Picture History of the War," in Barthelme, *Unspeakable Practices,* p. 143.

[15] Donald Barthelme, *Snow White* (New York: Atheneum, 1967), p. 6. Subsequent references follow in parentheses.

[16] "The President," in Barthelme, *Unspeakable Practices,* p. 149.

this house?' There was a silence. Then she said: 'It must be laid, I suppose, to a failure of the imagination. I have not been able to imagine anything better.' *I have not been able to imagine anything better''* (p. 59). She needs, of course, her prince. "By this Snow White means that she lives her own being as incomplete, pending the arrival of one who will 'complete' her'' (p. 70). She expects any of a long list of princes, but a world so devoid of imagination is also princeless. " 'What is troubling me,' '' complains the dwarf Clem, " 'is the quality of life in our great country, America. It seems to me to be deprived.' '' He is most worried " 'that no one responded to Snow White's hair initiative,' '' that her invitation to climb her tower went unheeded because " 'Americans will not or cannot see themselves as princely' '' (pp. 140–141). It was only by chance that the Seven Dwarfs escaped the fate of the country:

> Before we found Snow White wandering in the forest we lived lives stuffed with equanimity. There was equanimity for all. We washed the buildings, tended the vats, wended our way to the county cat-house once a week (Heigh-ho). Like everybody else. We were simple bourgeois. We knew what to do. When we found Snow White wandering in the forest, hungry and distraught, we said: "Would you like something to eat?" Now we do not know what to do. Snow White has added a dimension of confusion and misery to our lives. Whereas once we were simple bourgeois who knew what to do, now we are complex bourgeois who are at a loss. We do not like this complexity. We circle it wearily, prodding it from time to time with a shop-keeper's forefinger: What is it? Is it, perhaps, *bad for business?* Equanimity has leaked away. There was a moment, however, when equanimity was not the chief consideration. That moment in which we looked at Snow White and understood for the first time that we were fond of her. That was a moment. (pp. 87–88)

One dwarf, Edward, retreats beneath the boardwalk, "blowing his mind" with "nine mantras and three bottles of insect repellent" so that he might "stop being a filthy bourgeois for a space, even a short space" (p. 142). But the world at large remains bland and unimaginative. To quest for the princess " 'You need a Paul or Paul-figure for that sort of activity,' '' but Paul, the apparent prince, is " *'pure frog . . .* frog through and through.' '' He misreads his cue and drinks the poisoned cup himself, leaving Snow White to blame

" 'the very world itself, for not being able to supply a prince. For not being able to at least be civilized enough to supply the correct ending to the story' " (p. 132). The ending in fact supplied is a return to equanimity. "We prize equanimity," concludes the dwarf-narrator. "It means things are going well" (p. 180).

Language, with and without the revivifying force of imagination, is the chief concern of *Snow White,* as it is in most of Barthelme's fiction. It includes discussions of " 'the "blanketing" effect of ordinary language,' " the part of language which "fills in" between the other parts. " 'That part,' " we are told, " 'the "filling" you might say, of which the expression "you might say" is a good example, is to me the most interesting part' " (p. 96). It is particularly interesting because " ' the per-capita production of trash in this country is up from 2.75 pounds per day in 1920 to 4.5 pounds per day in 1965 . . . and is increasing at the rate of about four percent a year. Now that rate will probably go up, because it's *been* going up, and I hazard that we may very well soon reach a point where it's 100 percent.' " At that point, "The question turns from a question of disposing of this 'trash' to a question of appreciating its qualities, because, after all, it's 100 percent, right? And there can no longer be any question of 'disposing' of it, because it's all there is, and we will simply have to learn how to 'dig' it—that's slang, but peculiarly appropriate here" (p. 97). Hence Barthelme's characters strive "to be on the leading edge of this phenomenon," and "that's why we pay particular attention, too, to those aspects of language that may be seen as a model of the trash phenomenon" (p. 98). That is why Barthelme pays particular attention to language; it would be hard to find a statement more central to the method of his fiction.

In a world of 100 percent trash, its imagination dead and its language simply "blanketing," being bored (as was Snow White) is only an index to larger problems. How does one effectively "know" this world? One can study the trash, as Barthelme's heroes do; they "like books that have a lot of *dreck* in them, matter which presents itself as not wholly relevant (or indeed, at all relevant) but which, carefully attended to, can supply a kind of 'sense' of what is going on." Barthelme's world is phenomenological rather than Jamesian, for his characters vainly ask, " 'Where is the figure in the carpet?' " The dwarfs try to comprehend Snow White:

"Now, what do we apprehend when we apprehend Snow White? We apprehend, first, two three-quarter scale breasts floating towards us wrapped, typically, in a red towel. Or, if we are apprehending her from the other direction, we apprehend a beautiful snow-white arse floating away from us wrapped in a red towel. Now I ask you: What, in these two quite distinct apprehensions, is the constant? The factor that remains the same? Why, quite simply, the red towel. I submit that, rightly understood, the problem of Snow White has to do at its center with nothing else but *red towels*. Seen in this way, it immediately becomes a non-problem. We can easily dispense with the slippery and untrustworthy and expensive effluvia that is Snow White, and cleave instead to the towel." (pp. 100–101)

To break through the *dreck,* trash, and blanketing into a true knowledge of person and event leads Barthelme to experiments in epistemology. His two best-known stories, "Views of My Father Weeping" and "Robert Kennedy Saved from Drowning," are written in this mode. The Kennedy story has a fame of its own because it first appeared in the *New American Review* just two months before the assassination, and was collected in the widely noticed *Unspeakable Practices, Unnatural Acts* (1968) almost simultaneously with the event. It is, despite its experimental form, a conventional epistemology. Gathering together notes from various sources, the story attempts to tell what the man was, to put down on paper the meaning of his life. K. (for Kennedy) is observed at his desk, but the conclusions are ambiguous: "He is neither abrupt with nor excessively kind to associates, or he is both abrupt and kind." Of the messages he sends, " 'Some . . . are important. Others are not.' " [17] Reports are taken from others, as K. is described by secretaries, an administrative assistant, a former teacher, and a friend. But they are simply glimpses, hard to pin down, and sometimes ambiguous. Reading a newspaper, he is amused by anecdotes, depressed by tragedy; but, "On the other hand, these two kinds of responses may be, on a given day, inexplicably reversed" (p. 37). On the lawns of Hickory Hill, he is awkward and uncomfortable with his children; the scene has the quality of a bad snapshot, and the effort to know Kennedy is weak and inconclusive. When K.

[17] "Robert Kennedy Saved from Drowning," ibid., pp. 35–36. Subsequent references follow in parentheses.

himself speaks, we hear only *dreck* (" 'It's an expedient in terms of how not to destroy a situation which has been a long time gestating, or again how to break it up if it appears that the situation has changed, during the gestation period, into one whose implications are not quite what they were at the beginning''), or else loaded comments defused at the last moment, which come to nothing. *"Speaking to No One but Waiters,"* he recites a bland litany of courses, again offering no clues. Caught in moments of reflection, he is no more helpful: he speaks vaguely of "an insurmountable obstacle," hurling himself "into the midst of it," and proceeding "mechanically." He has his "dream," composed of lyrical orange trees and a farm in the hills, but also with "a steady stream of strange aircraft which resemble kitchen implements, bread boards, cookie sheets, colanders . . . on their way to complete the bombing of Sidi-Madani" (p. 42). *"He discusses the French Writer, Poulet,"* but the effect is all blanketing: " 'What Poulet is describing is neither an ethic nor a prescription but rather what he has discovered in the work of Marivaux. Poulet has taken up the Marivaudian canon and squeezed it with both hands to discover the essence of what may be called the Marivaudian being, what Poulet in fact calls Marivaudian being.' " (p. 46).

The writer turns to K.'s largest following, youth, but they are as enigmatic as their hero. "They sit on the sidewalks, back to back, heads turned to stare," and "stand implacably on street corners. . . ." They "say nothing, reveal only a limited interest, refuse to declare themselves." Their numbers range into the distance, "staring" (p. 45). Finally the writer performs the act of an actual reporter on a California beach during the primary campaign—he saves Kennedy from drowning. For once, "His flat black hat, his black cape, his sword are on the shore"; but the modern Ahab cannot strike through, for Kennedy "retains his mask." K.'s ultimate words, on so crucial an occasion, are a simple " 'Thank you' " (p. 47), less even than was expressed to the waiters who brought him his lunch. Although Barthelme has assembled all varieties of reports, including considerations of the *dreck* he claims is so revealing, the point of "Robert Kennedy Saved from Drowning" is that the conventional epistemology fails. Unlike *"Karsh of Ottawa,"* we are unable to get the "one shot in each sitting that was, you know, the key shot, the right one'' (p. 40). And the spirit of Kennedy, unlike Churchill or Hemingway, is never captured—unless that spirit be the enigma itself.

''Views of My Father Weeping'' is by design a more successful attempt to know persons and events. The event of the story is stated simply in its first section: ''An aristocrat was riding down the street in his carriage. He ran over my father.'' [18] The narrator seeks to discover the identity of the aristocrat, but also to understand the loss of his father, and it is for this latter endeavor that Barthelme constructs his radical epistemology. Like ''Robert Kennedy Saved from Drowning,'' ''Views of My Father Weeping'' is constructed of several disjunctive, aphoristic paragraphs which suggest the meaning of the father and his death. Some carry the simple narrative plot, tracking down the culprit, and others are vignettes from the past: pictures of the father frozen in memory (''My father throws his ball of knitting up in the air. The orange wool hangs there''). At the heart of the story, however, are the several ratiocinative passages where the narrator, in the process of unpuzzling the crime, becomes a detective of the knowing process itself. He ponders:

> Yet it is possible that it is not my father who sits there in the center of the bed weeping. It may be someone else, the mailman, the man who delivers the groceries, an insurance salesman or the tax collector, who knows. However, I must say, it resembles my father. The resemblance is very strong. He is not smiling through his tears but frowning through them. I remember once we were out on the ranch shooting peccadillos (result of a meeting, on the plains of the West, of the collared peccary and the nine-banded armadillo). My father shot and missed. He wept. This weeping resembles that weeping. (pp. 3–4)

To find out, he must ''apply some sort of test, voiceprint reading,'' or study further the memories which present themselves. The recurring pattern is weeping. ''But why watch it. Why tarry? Why not fly? Why subject myself? I could be somewhere else, reading a book, watching the telly, stuffing a big ship into a little bottle, dancing the Pig. I could be out in the streets feeling up eleven-year-old

---

[18] ''Views of My Father Weeping,'' in Barthelme, *City Life*, p. 3. Subsequent references follow in parentheses.

girls in their soldier drag." "But," he continues, "if it is not my father sitting there in the bed weeping, why am I standing before this
bed, in an attitude of supplication? Why do I desire with all my
heart that this man, my father, cease what he is doing, which is so
painful to me?" In the midst of this process the narrator momentarily breaks down: "Why! . . . there's my father! . . . sitting in
the bed there! . . . and he's weeping! . . . [. . .] Father, please!
. . . who has insulted you? . . . [. . .] 's death . . . I won't per-
mit it! . . . I won't abide it! . . . I'll . . . move every mountain
. . . climb . . . every river . . . etc." (ellipses Barthelme's). Although the plot is put back in order, it comes to nothing. Lars Bang,
the coachman with the final clue, is revealed as "an absolute bloody
liar," and on a note of unresolved complication ("Etc.") the story
ends. But if we think back we see that as an epistemology the story
has been a success. Although the murderer is never discovered, and
the narrator, in the act of learning, often fails, the process of knowledge has been made very clear. Process is the story itself, and by
means of it the image of the father has been sustained and studied
more effectively than the conventional epistemology of "Robert
Kennedy Saved from Drowning" would allow. The father is not understood rationally, nor is his memory presented in linear fashion.
Instead, we know him as a supra-rational, emotional complex: the
process by which he is known to his son.

Knowing the world is, for Barthelme, ultimately an achievement
of the imagination. His stories are often formed by startling concep-
tions. "Me and Miss Mandible" is the journal record of a thirty-
five-year-old man confusingly returned to the sixth grade: "Plucked
from my unexamined life among other pleasant, desperate, money-
making young Americans, thrown backward in space and time, I am
beginning to understand how I went wrong, how we all go
wrong." [19] Barthelme also offers "The Balloon," which, "beginning at a point on Fourteenth Street, the exact location of which I
cannot reveal, expanded northward all one night, while people were
sleeping, until it reached the Park. There, I stopped it; at dawn the
northernmost edges lay over the Plaza; the free-hanging motion was
frivolous and gentle." [20] "That was the situation, then," we are

[19] "Me and Miss Mandible," in Barthelme, *Come Back, Dr. Caligari*, p. 108.
[20] "The Balloon," in Barthelme, *Unspeakable Practices*, p. 15.

told, but we are immediately warned that "it is wrong to speak of 'situations,' implying sets of circumstances leading to some resolution, some escape of tension; there were no situations, simply the balloon hanging there—muted heavy grays and browns for the most part, contrasting with walnut and soft yellows." People did not successfully learn the "meaning" of the balloon; instead, they hung "green and blue paper lanterns from the warm gray underside, in certain streets, or seized the occasion to write messages on the surface, announcing their availability for the performance of unnatural acts, or the availability of acquaintances." The people conclude "that what was admired about the balloon was finally this: that it was not limited, or defined." Barthelme appreciates form, but he never allows it to define the content. Or if it does, that very definition is made to appear ludicrous. His story "Porcupines at the University" [21] is written in a very conventional form; but the contents run amok, at once mocking the form and drawing their own imaginative life from it. Porcupines threaten to invade the university; the dean tries to hold them off, pleading " 'We don't have *facilities* for four or five thousand porcupines.' " The animals themselves are contained in an absurd form, "wrangling . . . across the dusty and overbuilt West" with a porcupine wrangler: "Dust clouds. Yips. The lowing of porcupines. 'Git along theah li'l porcupines.' " The wrangler himself hopes soon to " 'sit on the front porch of the Muehlebach Hotel in New York City and smoke me a big seegar. Then, the fancy women.' " The Muehlebach Hotel is amusing only because Barthelme puts it in New York; the porcupines are interesting and imaginative only because of the form Barthelme places them in.

In an early essay, "The Case of the Vanishing Product," [22] Barthelme announced his fascination with the subject of form and content. Reviewing an art design annual, he noted that "a remarkable number of the advertisements give not so much as a clue to what is being advertised." The true content of the ad remains invisible, and of the items visible, such as keys, clocks, corkscrews, and kiosks, "None . . . is being offered for sale. Instead, they are the means by which we are to conceive of other things which *are* being

[21] *New Yorker*, 46 (April 25, 1970), 32–33.
[22] *Harper's*, 223 (October, 1961), 30–32.

offered for sale—typically nowhere in sight." It is fascinating to watch Barthelme at this point in his career, in transition from his roles as editor, art director, and public relations man to that of a fictionist, analyze the techniques of modern advertising, which in its very novelty of presentation effaces the product itself. Hence the *New York Times* is advertised by children playing in the park, with no newspapers in sight, and some of the most successful and appealing ads are for General Dynamics, "which in a few short years has built an enviable reputation in a field that, I suspect, few readers of its advertisements could define. What does General Dynamics *do?*" Modern advertising, which first drew its imaginative substance from the experiments of Joyce, Eliot, and Faulkner, here turns about to nourish literary art itself, as Barthelme's fictions rejuvenate the presentation of content. In this respect one notes that Barthelme's harshest critique of a fellow novelist is that he is "tired," that "the feeling of terror Mr. Greene could once produce from these materials has leaked away," and that "we are left with the manner." It is a case of "exhaustion at the deepest level, at the level of feeling." [23] Barthelme's own " 'central obsession is not to be boring, because he is so easily bored himself,' " his literary agent has reported; [24] his measure against boredom is a revitalization of his material by imaginatively exploiting content within contrasting forms. One of Barthelme's most delightful experiments in this mode, a piece somewhere between fiction and essay, remains uncollected. "And Now Let's Hear It for the Ed Sullivan Show!" [25] is an almost documentary report of an average Sunday night performance, except that the narrator seems more pleased with the form than the content. Although his lines are wearing out, "Still, Pigmeat [Markham] looks good," and "[George] Carlin is great, terrific, but his material is not so funny." Helen Hayes is inspiring, even though the narrator knows her misty eyes are looking up only "into the lighting grid." But when a song by Ed Ames becomes "sub-memorable," Barthelme quickly substitutes (as the medium itself might) "Something memorable: early on Sunday

---

[23] Donald Barthelme, "The Tired Terror of Graham Greene," *Holiday,* 39 (April, 1966), 146.

[24] Richard Schickel, "Freaked Out on Barthelme," *New York Times Magazine,* August 16, 1970, p. 15.

[25] *Esquire,* 71 (April, 1969), 126, 54, 56. Later collected in *Guilty Pleasures.*

morning a pornographic exhibition appeared mysteriously for eight minutes on television station KPLM, Palm Springs, California. A naked man and woman did vile and imaginative things to each other for that length of time, then disappeared into the history of electricity. Unfortunately, the exhibition wasn't on a network. What we really want in this world, we can't have.'' From this point on Barthelme embellishes the show's standard form with great imagination: "Ed enters from left (what's over there? a bar? a Barcalounger? a book? stock ticker? model railroad?)''—and concludes only after all the credits have rolled.

Barthelme will not bore us. He dismisses old and irrelevant forms which no longer conform to the reality we experience. Part of his technique is contrariness: if the predictable form is fast-moving excitement, as in a Batman story, he excites us with absurd delays and digressions.[26] He approves of the litany as "the only form of discourse'' [27] because it can be so ludicrously violated by substitutions in content. And he admires "a long sentence moving at a certain pace down the page aiming for the bottom'' precisely because it is "still a construction of man, a structure to be treasured for its weakness, as opposed to the strength of stones.'' [28] Occasionally form itself will carry, as when a publisher remarks that "Sometimes on dull days the compositors play which makes paragraphs like

(!) (!) (!) (!) (!) (!) (!) (!) (!) (!) (!) (!) (!) (!) (!)
* *
? / ? / ? / ? / ? / ? / ? / ? / ? / ? / ? / ? / ? / ? / ? /
0: 0: 0: 0: 0: 0: 0: 0: 0: 0: 0: 0: 0: 0: 0: 0: 0: 0: 0: 0: 0: 0: 0:
? / ? / ? / ? / ? / ? / ? / ? / ? / ? / ? / ? / ? / ? / ? /
* *
(!) (!) (!) (!) (!) (!) (!) (!) (!) (!) (!) (!) (!) (!) (!)

refreshing as rocks in this newspaper here.'' [29] Barthelme's own collage stories delight in superimposing objects on architectural forms ("At the Tolstoy Museum'' [30]). In "The Show,'' [31] Bar-

[26] "The Joker's Greatest Triumph,'' in Barthelme, *Come Back, Dr. Caligari,* p. 152.
[27] Barthelme, "The Indian Uprising,'' *Unspeakable Practices,* p. 8.
[28] "Sentence,'' in Barthelme, *City Life,* pp. 107, 114.
[29] "This Newspaper Here,'' in Barthelme, *Unspeakable Practices,* p. 28.
[30] Barthelme, *City Life,* pp. 48, 50.
[31] *New Yorker,* 46 (August 8, 1970), 26–29.

thelme has organized his talents of form and content, collage and prose, to make a statement on the demands of his own art:

> It is difficult to keep the public interested. The public demands new wonders piled on new wonders. Often we don't know where our next marvel is coming from. The supply of strange ideas is not endless. The development of new wonders is not like the production of canned goods. Some things appear to be wonders in the beginning, but when you become familiar with them, are not wonderful at all. Sometimes a seventy-five foot highly paid monster will raise only the tiniest *frisson*. Some of us have even thought of folding the show—closing it down. That thought has been gliding through the hallways and rehearsal rooms of the show.

Nevertheless, Barthelme concludes, "The new volcano we have just placed under contract seems very promising. . . ."

Barthelme's vignettes are, then, not conventional arguments in the dialectics of form, but imaginative volcanoes, radical stopgap measures to save experiences which might otherwise be eroded with our loss of traditional standards. In this sense he is a counterrevolutionary, opposing the new language of technology and manipulation with pleas for old-fashioned interest and imagination. In a new world, old values must be expressed in new form. For irrational, inconsecutive times, Barthelme's forms revive the values of imagination; the rescue is performed with the finest attentions to art. Not just a juggler of fragments, Barthelme is an assembler and constructor of objects. "The principle of collage," he told Richard Schickel, "is the central principle of all art in the twentieth century in all media." [32] More recently, and with specific reference to fiction, Barthelme has said that "The point of collage is that unlike things are stuck together to make, in the best case, a new reality. This new reality, in the best case, may be or imply a comment on the other reality from which it came, and may also be much else. It's an *itself,* if it's successful." [33] The resulting art can be figurative without yielding to a one-to-one reference. He cites the work of San Francisco artist James Weeks, who "proposes a kind of painting in which the organization of structural elements is not placed at the service of some kind of literary 'meaning' but is, rather,

[32] Schickel, "Freaked Out," p. 15.
[33] Klinkowitz, "Donald Barthelme," pp. 51–52.

enriched by anonymous human presences: people in the service of painting. Pamela Bianco and Robert Levers make paintings that seem to mean, but have recognized that the issue of figurative reference or the lack of it is not after all crucial." Above all, Barthelme argues, "The direct, unmistakable and unclouded recapitulation of some aspect of human experience ('LOOK MA, I'M DANCING!') is today self-defeating," [34] because "art is not about something but *is* something." Only in this way may the writer become a true artist and remove himself from the work: "The reader is not listening to an authoritative account of the world delivered by an expert (Faulkner on Mississippi, Hemingway on the corrida) but bumping into something that is *there,* like a rock or a refrigerator." [35] More actively,

> The reader reconstitutes the work by his active participation, by approaching the object, tapping it, shaking it, holding it to his ear to hear the roaring within. It is characteristic of the object that it does not declare itself all at once, in a rush of pleasant naivete. Joyce enforces the way in which *Finnegans Wake* is to be read. He conceived the reading to be a lifetime project, the book remaining always *there,* like the landscape surrounding the reader's home or the buildings bounding the reader's apartment. The book remains problematic, unexhausted.[36]

In much the same way Barthelme's continuing fiction is an ever-present object, delivered in the weekly *New Yorker* and environmentally landscaped with the coffee table or easy chair.

Because fiction conventionally tends to the opposite extreme, Barthelme often compensates with his close attention to writing as object. "I enjoy editing and enjoy doing layout—problems of design," he has remarked. "I could very cheerfully be a typographer," [37] and his story "Our Work and Why We Do It" [38] details the joys of a shop of printers. Because of this infatuation Barthelme has berated himself, and been berated by critics, for not writing more novels; feeling that he is unable to sustain works, his critics cite him as a craftsman of fragments. But although his books are ar-

[34] Donald Barthelme, "The Emerging Figure," *Forum,* 3 (Summer, 1961), 24.
[35] Donald Barthelme, "After Joyce," *Location,* 1 (Summer, 1964), 15.
[36] Ibid., p. 14.
[37] Klinkowitz, "Donald Barthelme," p. 48.
[38] *New Yorker,* 49 (May 5, 1973), 39–41.

ranged as collections of short stories, they have with increasing
strength boasted the consistency of novels. *Sadness* (1972), his best
collection, follows out the implications of its lead story, "Critique
de la Vie Quotidienne." Cushioned in his easy chair with nine
drinks ranked on the side table, Barthelme's protagonist bravely
faces his daily life, but the memories are catastrophic:

> I remember once we were sleeping in a narrow bed, Wanda and I, in
> a hotel, on a holiday, and the child crept into bed with us.
>
> "If you insist on overburdening the bed," we said, "you must
> sleep at the bottom, with the feet." "But I don't want to sleep with
> the feet," the child said. "Sleep with the feet," we said, "they won't
> hurt you." "The feet kick," the child said, "in the middle of the
> night." "The feet or the floor," we said. "Take your choice."
> "Why can't I sleep with the heads," the child asked, "like every-
> body else?" "Because you are a child," we said, and the child sub-
> sided, whimpering, the final arguments in the case having been pre-
> sented and the verdict in. But in truth the child was not without
> recourse; it urinated in the bed, in the vicinity of the feet. "God damn
> it," I said, inventing this formulation at the instant of need. "What
> the devil is happening, at the bottom of the bed?" "I couldn't help
> it," the child said. "It just came out." "I forgot to bring the plastic
> sheet," Wanda said. "Holy hell," I said. "Is there to be no end to
> this *family life?*" [39]

"Critique," "Perpetua," "Flying to America," and "Daumier,"
together with the uncollected "Alexandria and Henrietta," [40] were
originally "part of a novel, more or less," as Barthelme described
them in his contributor's note for the latter story. These chapters indicate the author's synthetic rather than fragmentary disposition, as
they combine in *Sadness* to capture the state of our daily life and
consider what can be done about it. Our evenings do lack promise;
beyond his nine drinks (or in really bad times ten or eleven) Barthelme's protagonist finds a lurking insatiability, a need for something better with which succeeding stories will cope.

Throughout the fictions of *Sadness* are various palliatives: hy-
potheses in the *Journal of Sensory Deprivation,* experiments with

---

[39] "Critique de la Vie Quotidienne," in Donald Barthelme, *Sadness* (New York: Farrar,
Straus & Giroux, 1972), p. 7.

[40] *New American Review* #12 (1971), pp. 82–87.

an understanding robot companion ('' 'Crushed in an elevator at the welfare hotel!' someone would say. 'It's a very serious problem,' Charles would answer''), and the practical expression of ideal systems, including inspiration-building cathedrals and sense-taming religions. In *Sadness* churches, catechists, and Jesuits outnumber even the serial shots of J & B; but with ''forty-five adulteries in the average Saturday'' of confessions, ''One wonders: Perhaps there should be a redefinition?'' '' 'I can will my dreams,' '' argues a girl being shoved out of life in a literal ''City of Churches,'' and for much of the volume Barthelme plays with those options. In ''Engineer-Private Paul Klee Misplaces an Aircraft between Milbertshofen and Cambrai, March 1916,'' the artist confronts the ever-present secret police; fearing ''damage potential to the theory of omniscience,'' they try to know everything to the last centimeter. Klee's interest is elsewhere, in '' 'The shape of the collapsed canvas, under which the aircraft had rested, together with the loose ropes—the canvas forming hills and valleys, seductive folds, the ropes the very essence of looseness, lapsing,' '' [41] which he sketches. As for the missing aircraft, he diddles the manifest, '' 'With my painter's skill which is after all not so different from a forger's.' '' Once the papers are in order (all that matters), the police leave Klee to his art and a comfortable snack. '' 'I am sorry about the lost aircraft,' '' he admits, '' 'but not overmuch. The war is temporary. But drawings and chocolate go on forever.' '' [42]

Barthelme's insatiable artists make ''A Film,'' photographing such things as the author himself wrote about in earlier stories, and produce ''The Show,'' which includes ''a troupe of agoutis'' who ''performed tax evasion atop tall, swaying yellow poles. Before your eyes.'' Of course these abstractions fail; but as another protagonist says, arguing for art and against analysis, ''what an artist does, is fail. . . . the paradigmatic artistic experience is that of failure. The actualization fails to meet, equal, the intuition. There is something 'out there' which cannot be brought 'here.' '' [43] The unreachable other resists the insatiable self, both in art and in the

---

[41] ''Engineer-Private Paul Klee Misplaces an Aircraft between Milbertshofen and Cambrai, March 1916,'' in Barthelme, *Sadness,* p. 68.
[42] Ibid., p. 70.
[43] ''The Sandman,'' ibid., p. 93.

world, but through the imagination one can resist "The Temptations of St. Anthony," the greatest of which, we learn, is "ordinary life." [44] Imaginative freedom is an option, and fit matter for artistic speculation and even for what Robert Scholes calls aesthetic allegory; but in *Sadness* it is always under the constraint of the real world, a context Barthelme's fiction will not ignore.

The key to Barthelme's new aesthetic for fiction is that the work may stand for itself, that it need not yield to complete explication of something else in the world but may exist as an individual object, something beautiful and surprising and deep. His innovation is peculiarly American. "The new French novelists, Butor, Sarraute, Robbe-Grillet, Claude Simon, Philippe Sollers," Barthelme notes, "have on the other hand succeeded in making objects of their books without reaping any of the strategic benefits of the maneuver—a triumph of misplaced intelligence. Their work seems leaden, self-conscious in the wrong way. Painfully slow-paced, with no leaps of the imagination, concentrating on the minutiae of consciousness, these novels scrupulously, in deadly earnest, parse out what can safely be said." [45] Barthelme dares, like Vonnegut, to say the unspeakable, the vile and imaginative things which lie beneath the surface of our mundane, anesthetizing forms. More abstract writers such as William S. Burroughs make "cut-ups" of these forms, taking words and rearranging them so that new images form from the old constituents. But Barthelme is more the contextualist, closer to our actual society and its *dreck;* "To steal is to proclaim the value of what is stolen," [46] he has written, and what he steals from contemporary America—its junk, its blanketing—is recycled and given immense value in his artistic act. Burroughs works with words alone; Barthelme takes the forms in which we kill them and brings them back to life, as in his Bobbsey Twins revival, "Then":

> Astonishment, surprise and disappointment were so great for a few seconds after the discovery that the best part of the party—the ice cream—was gone, that no one knew what to say. Then Flossie burst out with:
> Then the feast began, and such a feast it was! Mrs. Bobbsey,

[44] Ibid., p. 154.
[45] Barthelme, "After Joyce," p. 16.
[46] Barthelme, "The Emerging Figure," p. 23.

knowing how easily the delicate stomachs of the children can be upset, had wisely selected the foods and sweets, and she saw to it that no one ate too much, though she was gently suggestive about it instead of ordering.

Then a chair would be taken away, so as always to have one less than the number of players, and the game went on. It was great fun, scrambling to see who would get a seat, and not be left without one, and finally there was but one chair left, while Grace Lavine and John Blake marched about.

Then Freddie, anxious as to what would become of Snap if he fought a snake, looked back. He saw a strange sight.

"Then don't you come any nearer if you don't want to get wet," said Bert. "This hose might sprinkle you by accident, the same as it did when Freddie had it," he added.

Then came all sorts of games, from tag and jumping rope, to blindman's bluff and hide-and-seek. . . .[47]

And foremost in art is the imagination, regardless of its subject matter. Indeed, its content is most clearly seen when removed from the world of immediate reference, as Barthelme described when he prefaced an exhibition of women in art, from 2500 B.C. to the present, for the Cordier & Ekstrom Galleries.[48] "Woman is an imaginary being," he wrote, "a fabulous animal kin to the manticore, the hippogriff, the ant-lion. Woman does not exist. What exists in the space 'woman' would occupy, if she existed, is a concatenation of ideas about woman." To capture the animal, the content, we throw out a hopeless net; the animal itself escapes, we are left holding the net, and "The net becomes the animal." But

Art, touching mysteries, tends to darken rather than illuminate them. Artists enrich and complicate (whatever else they may also be doing). In terms of sexual politics, this means adding to the mystification. But more than politics is involved. Woman as a subject, a pretext, for art, becomes momentarily free. Art's resolute refusal to explain itself translates into a refusal to explain women. They are, for a moment, surrounded by a blessed silence.

[47] Donald Barthelme, "Then," *Mother* #3 (November–December, 1964), p. 22.
[48] *she,* Cordier & Eckstrom exhibit catalogue, December 3, 1970, to January 16, 1971, unpaged.

THREE

Jerzy Kosinski

"His art has dealt with the fangs and colors of dream and of daily life among the violations of the spirit and body of human beings." So read the statement of the National Institute of Arts and Letters when it granted Jerzy Kosinski an award "for creative work in literature" just before the publication of his third novel, *Being There,* in 1970. Kosinski is among the more widely honored Americans writing today, winning the Prix du Meilleur Livre Etranger for his first work in fiction, *The Painted Bird* (1965), and the National Book Award for his second novel, *Steps,* in 1968.

We cannot know how close Kosinski was to the wartime horrors of *The Painted Bird* or the transitional agonies of *Steps,* although the themes of those novels, of *Being There,* and of his latest work, *The Devil Tree* (1973), center philosophically on "the self." Reviewers sense the problem and make the most of it, as when John Updike, careful as always about a book's design, noted that the typography of *Being There* "suggests that Kosinski's biography is the last chapter." [1] His life does present a high profile: the professorships, awards, and degrees, but also the exposure as a talk show personality, world traveler while the husband of a steel heiress (now deceased), and even as a latecomer to a party he could not have regretted missing, at the home of his close friends Roman Polanski and Sharon Tate on August 8, 1969. But besides the public record of his own self, Kosinski has studied the role of selves in modern life, not only as a novelist but originally as a professor of sociology. It was to have been his career in Poland, where after a chaotic and catastrophic childhood (which left him mute and illiterate into his teens) he quickly approached the top levels of academia, earning graduate degrees in history and political science (sociology depart-

[1] John Updike, "Books: Bombs Made out of Letters," *New Yorker,* 47 (September 21, 1971), 133.

ments at Polish universities were closed in the early 1950's for political reasons) and undertaking as his special interest the self in
collectivized society. Two of his scholarly works were published in
Poland,[2] and after his dramatic emigration to America in 1957 at the
age of twenty-four he drew on notes for a third to produce *The Future Is Ours, Comrade* (1960) and *No Third Path* (1962), both written under the pseudonym of Joseph Novak.

Despite his wide experience, Kosinski's aim was always to be a
fictionist. "First, when I saw myself as a sociologist, as a social scientist," he has said, "I assumed that I was already operating on a
high level of abstraction. Indeed, equal to that of fiction; after all, a
sociologist abstracts certain social forms into meaningful formulas
which could be perceived by others in an act of self-recognition."
But during the Stalinization of Poland Kosinski perceived that his
art was being corrupted, "That the 'plot' of my 'fiction' was given
to me by the very forces which I resented and abhorred and was terrified by—the Communist Party, and its totalitarian system." [3]
Hence he moved to a new field, photographic chemistry, and then
photography itself; by 1957 his works were featured in more international exhibitions than anyone else's in Eastern Europe. But his
interest was still in fiction: "The photographic darkroom became a
symbol of my life. Only in the darkroom could I function without
being watched. While safely locked inside there, I would turn the
lights on; then I could read from time to time some of the forbidden
literary works." [4]

Photography, however, was a poor substitute for the imaginative

[2] Jerzy Kosinski, *Dokumenty walki o Czlowieka: Wspomnienia Proletariatczykow* [Docu-
ments Concerning the Struggle of Man: Reminiscences of the Members of "The Proletariat"], *Przeglad Nauk Historycznych i Spolecznych,* IV (1954); University of Lodz, Zaklad
Historii Mysli Spolecznej [*The Review of Social and Historical Sciences,* IV (1954); Institute
of Historical and Social Science of the University of Lodz]; published separately as a booklet
by Lodzkie Towarzystwo Naukowe, Lodz, 1955 [Scientific Society of Lodz, 1955]. Jerzy
Kosinski, *Program Rewolucji Ludowej Jakoba Jaworskiego* [The Program of the People's
Revolution of Jakob Jaworski], *Przeglad Nauk Historycznych i Spolecznych,* IV (1954); Uni-
versity of Lodz, Zaklad Historii Mysli Spolecznej [*The Review of History and Historical
Sciences,* V (1954); Institute of Historical and Social Science of the University of Lodz];
published separately as a booklet by Lodzkie Towarzystwo Naukowe, Lodz, 1955 [Scientific
Society of Lodz, 1955].

[3] Jerome Klinkowitz, "Jerzy Kosinski: An Interview," *Fiction International* #1 (Fall,
1973), p. 33. Reprinted in Joe David Bellamy, *The New Fiction: Interviews with Innovative
American Writers* (Urbana: University of Illinois Press, 1974).

[4] Ibid., p. 34.

act Kosinski preferred. "Now a darkroom became a writing desk and paper remained sensitive to light but in a different way. I, not the manufacturer, would make it sensitive, but I would make it sensitive by the inking I would place on its surface. As a photographer I knew that the basic purpose of the photographic process was to reproduce the reality, and that photography would actually accomplish it. If there was a tree in the field and I photographed and developed it in my darkroom, I actually could do this so it would match exactly the imaginary photograph in my mind. Well, I found this profoundly distressing. If my imagination was able to conceive of the images which could be so easily reproduced in the Soviet darkroom—in any darkroom—then clearly there was not much to my imagination. I found it very humiliating that in a photograph I actually could produce what I thought." [5]

Hence the young Polish student used his mastered art of photography to transpose himself to a place where he would be free to write. On a forged "Chase Manhattan Bank Fellowship" and with a cyanide capsule under his tongue should he fail, Kosinski left Poland in 1957 for New York, where he arrived as a penniless immigrant, unable to read or speak English. For several months he lived close to starvation, taking menial jobs while developing a facility with his adopted language, in order to write sociology and fiction about his former experiences. But a close autobiographical reading of these works disregards Kosinski's warning in *Notes of the Author* that "the whole journey could actually have taken place in the mind." [6] Kosinski argues that "The most essential stage of the writing process . . . is the process whereby the writer comes to stand outside the experience he intends to mirror in his book" (p. 9), and it is this act of separation, rather than the clues to identity, which is most interesting to discuss. If the experience itself could be fully known, any artist would argue, there would be no need for the art. Kosinski quotes from Proust that "The grandeur of real art . . .

[5] Ibid., p. 35.

[6] Jerzy Kosinski, *Notes of the Author* (New York: Scientia-Factum, 1965), p. 13. This booklet, and its subsequent companion for *Steps*, were originally appendices which Kosinski wrote to be translated for the German-language editions of his novels, and have been published in English, in booklet form, to establish the author's American copyright. The appendices were designed to clarify the novels' themes for countries which had had fascist histories. Subsequent references follow in parentheses.

is to rediscover, grasp again and put before us that reality from which we live so far removed and from which we become more and more separated as the formal knowledge which we substitute for it grows in thickness and imperviousness—the reality which there is grave danger we might die without ever having known and yet which is simply our life'' (pp. 9–10). Because Kosinski is the consummate artist, he deserves our attention. *"The remembered event,"* he emphasizes, *"becomes a fiction: a structure made to accommodate certain feelings"* (p. 11), and by creatively editing, adding, and shaping his material, Kosinski produces art more lifelike than life itself. Moreover, he writes in English, a language only recently acquired. ''A writer who writes in an accepted language which he has learned as an adult,'' Kosinski says in a passage added to the Dutch edition of his *Notes,* ''has in that language *one more curtain* that separates him from spontaneous expression,'' [7] and hence forces him more directly into the role of artist. *The Painted Bird, Steps, Being There,* and *The Devil Tree* are Kosinski's life in art, and are best read in that way.

The common theme to all of Kosinski's writing is the survival of the self, and is most personally evident not in his novels but in his master's theses and in his two books of nonfiction, *The Future Is Ours, Comrade* and *No Third Path. Dokumenty Walki o Czlowieka: Wspomnienia Proletariatczykow* (Documents Concerning the Struggle of Man: Reminiscences of the Members of "The Proletariat") contrasts the socialist revolution with the prevailing nineteenth-century "Bourgeois philosophies, for which the most important dogma was individualism, the cult of the individual," [8] which the young Polish scholar covertly favored. Even in the heavy rhetoric of the Stalinist period Kosinski manages to express his belief in the self's power: "The true apotheosis of man, the fight for humanity and the respect for human rights, was not created in the fervor of academic and philosophical discussions, the subject of which was the abstract analysis of Nirvana, phenomenalism, voluntaristic metaphysics of Schopenhauer, the classics of pessimism, or the inductive-naturalis-

---

[7] Jerzy Kosinski, *Tijd van leven—tijd van kunst* [*The time of life—the time of art*], (Amsterdam: Uitgeverij de Bezige Bij, 1970), p. 11, my translation. This work combines Kosinski's booklets on his first two novels, and interpolates several paragraphs of new material.

[8] Kosinski, *Dokumenty Walki,* p. 1 in the booklet, p. 411 in the journal.

tic method of Hartmann. It was born in the places of execution, in the prison cells, in the dungeons and casements, in the torture chambers, and amidst the ice of Siberia.'' [9] The czarist prisons tried foremost to destroy the self; but even if only by suicide, the self protested its final triumph. Kosinski's aim in the latter works was to understand the "whole new sociopsychological entity" [10] of man in the Soviet Union, where he found the individual self being all but completely effaced in a new *"collective way of being."* [11] These two volumes are supposedly sociological field research, but again and again Kosinski's own person intrudes. As he admits to a Russian friend, " 'I—I would like to depend on nobody. You know, to tailor my life to my own yardstick, and not to riffle around in ready-made-clothes stores' " (p. 53), and throughout both books we are aware of Kosinski's emotional and psychological distance from the collective system. In the epilogue to *No Third Path* he admits his intentions, that "The greater part of the interview material found in this book was collected at a time when the writer still was intensively seeking a place for himself in the socialist society" (p. 358). Sensing his uneasiness with "that collectivized new world," he notes that "His subconscious came into conflict with his conscious self, his former self rebelled against his new self." As a result he began to " 'separate himself from his own ego' and to work out a method of becoming a 'detached observer of himself,' of observing himself in the most objective and critical manner, in the same manner in which he observed those whom he distrusted" (p. 357). The self described in *The Future Is Ours, Comrade* and *No Third Path* is one deeply alienated from society, and finally from even itself. A Russian colleague accuses Kosinski that " 'your naturalistic remembrances of childhood and the war, your hatred of village life and primitive conditions, your "exercise of intimacy"—all this causes the world of today to reach you in a *distorted image*. You refract it, as it were, in a prism' " (pp. 58–59).

The interpretation of this vision, his notion of the self, becomes the artistic task of *The Painted Bird*. "Fact and memory," Kosinski

[9] Ibid., p. 12 in the booklet, p. 422 in the journal.

[10] Jerzy Kosinski [Joseph Novak], *No Third Path* (New York: Doubleday, 1962), p. 172.

[11] Jerzy Kosinski [Joseph Novak], *The Future Is Ours, Comrade* (New York: Doubleday, 1960), p. 44. Subsequent references follow in parentheses.

queries in *Notes of the Author,* "Is the book simply the product of these two faculties?" He answers, *"The Painted Bird* is rather the result of the slow unfreezing of a mind long gripped by fear, of isolated facts that have become interwoven into a tapestry" (p. 14). The literary device of the child recounting his past is critical; with explicit reference to Jung's *Psychology of the Child Archetype,* Kosinski chooses a narrator who "draws up not simply an adult's catalogue of tidy facts, but spills out the involved, pain-wracked, fear-heightened memories, impressions and feelings of the child" (p. 15). Moreover, the memory itself constructs an artifice, as noted before: *"The remembered event becomes a fiction, a structure made to accommodate certain feelings."* Kosinski's first novel is the artistic probing of ideas not completely expressed in his social studies. The same elements are present: the individual and the group, often mutually hostile, and the problems of communication between the two. In a concluding passage removed from later editions of *The Painted Bird,* Kosinski completes the transition from his earlier works. *"The story of the boy, the Painted Bird of this book, does not end with his regaining the power of speech. He had become part of the society in which he found himself."* [12] Postwar life for the boy becomes the life of the sociologist detailed in Kosinski's first books:

> *Involvement in collective society became more and more forced. Coercive measures trimmed away the vestigial edges of personal freedom. Relentless supervision curtailed away every individual action. This placed a double burden on the youth. During the war years his powers of self-dependence had increased enormously, and the maintenance of personal freedom had been the goal to which he had given all his intelligence and energy.*
>
> *Previously, while living in the forest villages, the boy had been set apart from others by his physical dissimilarity; now, as a young man in collective society, he was set apart by differences of his way of thinking. The experiences of the war years made him unable to con-*

---

[12] Jerzy Kosinski, *The Painted Bird* (Boston: Houghton Mifflin, 1965), p. 269. This passage constitutes a corruption of Kosinski's text, as it was extracted from one of his personal letters and added to the novel without his permission. Kosinski has removed it from all subsequent editions. He discusses this matter in the *Fiction International* interview, p. 33, which is quoted in the epilogue to this volume.

*form to the patterns of thought and behavior demanded by collective
society. Again he was the outsider, the Painted Bird.*[13]

The Painted Bird, of course, tells its own story, but survival is its
recurrent theme. The adventures of the Boy narrator span World
War II, most of it spent wandering from village to village as a
"Gypsy-Jewish" outcast. The result is a fable of existence, as the
six-year-old child learns the expectable lessons of life, such as the
hatching of baby chicks and the taming of a pet squirrel, and the inevitable horrors of death. Almost at once the latter predominate: his
squirrel is tortured and burned alive, and his aged guardian dies and
is grotesquely consumed in a fire. Helplessly abandoned, the Boy is
taken into the shadow world which comes to dominate his life.
Cared for by a witch, he himself becomes "the Black One,"
demonized by his regionally unique black hair and eyes. He learns
the darker side of existence not only through the practice of magic,
but by rehearsing fables of cruelty and sorrow, including that of the
painted bird, who soars "happy and free" to rejoin its flock, only to
be mercilessly pecked to death.[14] The same lessons apply to human
endeavor, as people are brutalized in all manners by their fellows.
Life becomes a Boschean nightmare, and the Boy threatens to be
swallowed up within it.

It is the Boy's strategy of survival, however, that is the darkest element in the book, because of what it suggests about the self in the
world. As the story progresses, death and destruction come to have
their own lyricism, as the most poetic events in life:

> I recalled well the time, in the first days of the war, when a bomb
> hit a house across the street from my parents' home. Our windows
> were blown out. We were assaulted by falling walls, the tremor of the
> shaken earth, the screams of unknown dying people. I saw the brown
> surfaces of doors, ceilings, walls with the pictures still clinging des-
> perately to them, all falling into the void. Like an avalanche rushing
> to the street came majestic grand pianos opening and closing their lids
> in flight, obese, clumsy armchairs, skittering stools and hassocks.

[13] Kosinski, *The Painted Bird,* Houghton Mifflin ed., p. 271.

[14] Jerzy Kosinski, *The Painted Bird* (New York: Pocket Books, 1966), p. 44. Subsequent
references will be made to this text, since it is Kosinski's restoration of his own original version. The later Modern Library (1970) and Bantam (1972) editions incorporate slight stylistic
modifications by Kosinski; only the Pocket Books edition prints the novel as Kosinski wrote it
in 1965. Subsequent references follow in parentheses.

They were chased by chandeliers that were falling apart with shrill cries, by polished kitchen pots, kettles, and sparkling aluminum chamber pots. Pages torn out of gutted books fell down, flapping like flocks of scared birds. Bath-tubs tore themselves away slowly and deliberately from their pipes, entwining themselves magically in the knots and scrolls of banisters and railings and rain gutters.

As the dust settled, the split house timidly bared its entrails. Limp human bodies lay tossed over the jagged edges of the broken floors and ceilings like rags covering the break. They were just beginning to soak in the red dye. Tiny particles of torn paper, plaster, and paint clung to the sticky red rags like hungry flies. Everything around was still in motion; only the bodies seemed relaxed and at peace. (p. 64)

To save himself, the Boy must learn the same grace. His first hero is a Nazi S.S. officer: "In the presence of such a resplendent being, armed in all the symbols of might and majesty, I was genuinely ashamed of my appearance. I had nothing against his killing me. I gazed at the ornate clasp of his officer's belt that was exactly at the level of my eyes, and waited his wise decision" (pp. 100–101). And when he discovers a cistern full of voracious rats, the Boy half-willingly throws his cruel peasant master to a ghastly death, and in so doing learns to control death's lovely horror:

The massive body of the carpenter was only partly visible. His face and half of his arms were lost under the surface of the sea of rats, and wave after wave of rats was scrambling over his belly and legs. The man completely disappeared, and the sea of rats churned even more violently. The moving rumps of the rats became stained with brownish red blood. The animals now fought for access to the body—panting, twitching their tails, their teeth gleaming under their half-opened snouts, their eyes reflecting the daylight as if they were the beads of a rosary.

I observed this spectacle as if paralyzed, unable to tear myself away from the edge of the opening, lacking sufficient will power to cover it with the tin panel. Suddenly the shifting sea of rats parted and slowly, unhurrying, with the stroke of a swimmer, a bony hand with bony spread-eagled fingers rose, followed by the man's entire arm. For a moment it stood immobile above the rats scuttling about below; but suddenly the momentum of the surging animals thrust to the surface the entire bluish-white skeleton of the carpenter, partly defleshed and partly covered with shreds of reddish skin and gray clothing. In between the ribs, under the armpits, and in the place where the belly was, gaunt rodents fiercely struggled for the remaining scraps of dangling muscle and intestine. Mad with greed, they tore from one another scraps of clothing, skin, and formless chunks of the trunk. They dived into the center of the man's body only to jump out through another chewed opening. The corpse sank under renewed thrusts. When it next came to the surface of the bloody writhing sludge, it was a completely bare skeleton. (pp. 55–56)

Thus initiated, he is never far from revenge. Darkness is all; if the lighter side of life should surface, such as in the Boy's idyllic love for the pastoral Ewka, it is quickly blasted away by such sights as her forced copulation with a goat. Hence the climax comes when the barbarian Kalmuks ravage the village. "For a moment, as I looked at them," confesses the Boy, "I felt great pride and satisfaction. After all, these proud horsemen were black-haired, black-eyed, and black-skinned. They differed from the people of the village as night from day. The arrival of these dark Kalmuks drove the fair-haired village people almost insane with fear" (pp. 157–158). There follows the most extravagant cruelty and horror in this already horror-filled book (most of it censored out of the first edition): men are not only slaughtered, but castrated in front of their wives and daughters, who in turn are forced to eat the bloody parts. Girls are multiple-raped in bizarre fashion, and the entire village is destroyed in a frenzy of hate.

From this madness the Boy is redeemed by the conquering Red army. Adopted by the soldiers, he is both pampered and strengthened, taught to read, write, and study the principles of collective society. Of the peasants' wild rumors, the Boy constructs a pleasing vision: "If it was true that women and children might become communal property, then every child would have many fathers and mothers, innumerable brothers and sisters. It seemed to be too much to hope for" (p. 155). But collective behavior is not the topic of *The Painted Bird,* except for a notation that "In the world into which Gavrila was initiating me, human aspirations and expectations were entangled with each other like the roots and branches of great trees in a thick forest, each tree struggling for more moisture from the soil and more sunshine from the sky" (p. 175). These themes, even the real person Gavrila, were treated in *No Third Path* (p. 70), and, in terms of Kosinski's artistic development, were dispatched much earlier than *The Painted Bird*. The author's point here is that the self, in any society, must resort to hate and revenge to survive. Even within his beloved Red army the Boy's hero is not Stalin or Lenin, or even Gavrila, who teaches him politics and art, but the sharp-shooter Mitka, who calmly takes his revenge upon a town of offending peasants. After the war the Boy continues his lifestyle of revenge, to the point of derailing a train to punish a rude market-keeper. Even after reunion with his parents, he seeks the night and low life of the city. If there has been any doubt about the reality of life, *The Painted Bird* resolves it on the side of darkness. The simple act of existence as one's self puts one at odds with society, and even one's fellows are safest when kept at bay. The Boy does survive, but at great price. After being muted by the horrors of life, he does speak again; but, as noted before, his story "does not end with his regaining the power of speech." By dropping this closing frame from the later editions of *The Painted Bird,* Kosinski suggests (like another writer of blackness, Herman Melville) that "Something further may follow of this Masquerade."

The perils of the self, and the artistic exploitation of that peril, continue through Kosinski's second novel, *Steps*. He titles his critical essay on this volume *The Art of the Self,* where "those formerly protective agencies like society and religion" are described as enemies which prevent "the self from functioning freely." [15] The protagonist of *Steps* is aware of collective values, but "to him the most meaningful and fulfilling gesture is negative: it is aimed against the collective and is a movement towards the solitude within which the self can display its reality" (p. 40). The action of *Steps* is "to reach back through a particularly painful past for an age of innocence, for the self which, he feels, is waiting for discovery behind the blocked memories preceding his traumas"; and its method is an immersion "in the heart of the trauma itself" (pp. 35–36). Hence many scenes from *The Painted Bird*—copulation with beasts, castration, the cool revenge of homocide—are revisited and rehearsed in passage after passage of absolute stylistic control. But *Steps,* like its predecessor, tells its own story, too. Through

[15] Jerzy Kosinski, *The Art of the Self* (New York: Scientia-Factum, 1968), p. 22. Subsequent references follow in parentheses.

forty apparently disconnected episodes (structured in the manner of Vonnegut's Tralfamadorian novel) Kosinski describes a hero exploring his own reality and ability to relate to others. Unity is ultimately derived from the same source as *The Future Is Ours, Comrade* and *No Third Path:* a young man, "at the university," who journeys out to villages, other cities, and finally to the United States, relentlessly investigating the substance of human behavior. He gives lessons in the power of credit cards and learns the vulnerability of poverty. He suffers under cruel masters and becomes a master himself. Power and powerlessness, notions derived from the two worlds of *The Painted Bird* and *No Third Path,* are the tensions which create *Steps*. Several incidents are repeated from these books, and their ideas are further developed; but foremost is the character of the vagrant boy, "everybody's victim," and the university student, powerless to change the collective "climate." [16] As in the earlier novel, he seeks revenge and control. He poisons the villagers' children, and "From then on I gazed boldly into my persecutors' eyes, provoking their assault and maltreatment. I felt no pain. For each lash I received my tormentors were condemned to pain a hundred times greater than mine. Now I was no longer their victim; I had become their judge and executioner" (p. 36). At school, he uses the collective's standards against itself, ruining the career of an enemy and improving his own position.

Steps moves from these formulae of Kosinski's earlier work to the philosophy behind them. A parallel series of events and dialogues describes the self in action and analyzes its behavior. In a passing love affair the protagonist learns that "It was almost as though my thinking had to subside before my body could perform" (p. 22). But his thinking cannot subside, and he finds satisfaction only with a prostitute who turns out to be a man. His lesson in love: "All we could do was to exist for each other solely as a reminder of the self." He hears from another girl her story of a satisfactory relationship, where "she could never be so free, or so much herself, with any other person"; her lover is her almost identical brother. Hence the protagonist comes to conduct his own affairs in a way that reverts more to himself than to his partner. On assignment pho-

---

[16] Jerzy Kosinski, *Steps* (New York: Random House, 1968), pp. 36–37. Subsequent references follow in parentheses.

tographing grotesque patients in an old age home, he seduces a young nurse "to reassure myself that I had nothing in common with the inmates" (p. 48). In an affair with another girl he finds that "the consciousness of my role prevailed over my desire to possess her" (p. 101), but such personal detachment has advantages, as when he conquers his repulsion for his gang-raped mistress by making her "an object which I could control or pair with other objects" (p. 57). He salvages this affair, as all others, by removing any chance of human communication. Secure within himself, he is invulnerable to external threat or stimulus. The paradigm of all his love relations is the situation he encounters with the caged, demented woman used as sexual object by countless villagers and farmers. "I thought there was something very tempting in this situation," he considers, "where one could become completely oneself with another human being" (p. 87).

Spaced among these episodes are italicized dialogues, apparently between the protagonist and his present mistress, which probe the intricacies of their relationship. A discussion which begins randomly with the topics of circumcision and sensitivity leads to an exploration of the ideas of unfaithfulness and murder. "Suppose he would become my lover?" she asks. "To kill that thought you'd have to destroy him, wouldn't you?" Juxtaposed are episodes of murder and revenge, apparently from the protagonist's earlier life. In their next conversation each admits to an experiment: he has deviously sent her to a male masseur, "to know what you would do: how you would behave in that sort of situation," while she has arranged another affair because "I felt I had an obligation to know myself better—apart from the self you have brought me to know." A curious notion of the self develops. She argues that "I chose that part of me which wants you over and above the self I would become with him" (p. 44), while he explains his relationship with a prostitute as "When I leave her, the awareness of what has happened leaves with me: that awareness is mine, not hers" (p. 61). The mistress knows "one side" of him only; just as he tells her, "You also offer only the side of yourself which you think is most acceptable to me." The implications are ominous: their relationship is not between complete human selves, but is an exchange of self-reflective postures and modes. Their talk turns almost immediately to the phenomenon of concentration camps, where "the victims never remained individuals" and were not treated as humans by their masters. The mistress, real to her lover only when she is immediately present, understands their relationship. "All you need me for," she admits, "is to provide a stage on which you can project and view yourself, and see how your discarded experiences become alive again when they affect me. Am I right? You don't want me to love you; all you want is for me to abandon myself to the dreams and fantasies which you inspire in me. All you want is to prolong this impulse, this moment" (pp. 132–133). Such is the configuration of the self's survival, in love as well as in other areas of life. The protagonist handles his own affairs in this manner, and also provides for the successful affairs of others, as he pretends to be a deaf mute so that another woman can forget herself and "relate" to him. As Kosinski observes in a passage added to the Dutch edition of his *Notes,* because the protagonist's experience precedes the woman's, he must himself disappear before she can exist as a self, as he has existed with her.[17] Once again, survival is a solitary experience, and acting is possible only when one does not have to feel.

Being There, Kosinski's third novel, finds its roots in the closing chapters of *Steps,* where several episodes form by their close consecutiveness a coherent story, the protagonist's journey to the United States. It is an important transition as he leaves behind "twenty-four years of my life," wishing "to fix the plane permanently in the sky . . . timeless, unmeasured, unjudged, bothering no one, suspended forever between my past and my future." Such suspension may be attractive, and the protagonist lingers much as the Boy of *The Painted Bird* lingered on the threshold of death before his passage into the new collective world of the Red army. But time must go on, and the adjustment must be made to life in America. Two fable-like episodes express the change. The protagonist's "splendid coat, made of Siberian wolf fur," becomes, in the new climate, a positive hindrance, and must be painfully abandoned. And after a time of penury and near-starvation, he must also learn the structures of power; hired by a man in his "luxurious foreign car," the protagonist is introduced to the American un-

---

[17] Kosinski, *Tijd van leven–tijd van kunst,* p. 60.

derworld of intimidation, violence, and control. Within a short time
he too learns how to survive and flourish.

Being There moves the action above ground, to the very heights
of public attention and importance. Here the form of control is television, and the form of the novel is an extended metaphor of its
power. Kosinski's first book of sociology was subtitled "Conversations with the Russians"; it and *No Third Path* drew their form from
the author's admittedly subjective and impressionistic "sketches"
of "the style of Soviet life." [18] The memories of *The Painted Bird*
were recounted in an episodic, picaresque form which reflected their
apparent substance as childhood adventure. With *Steps* Kosinski
made his first formalistic experiment, remarking that "In the light
of the modern understanding of perception and consciousness, the
forms of art based on a conception of time as objective and chronological (in which all events were of equal importance because they
imitate a real temporal sequence which existed above the individual
consciousness) may no longer apply." Accordingly, he tries "to
show time as we perceive it, and show experience as we absorb
it," [19] presenting the drama of a self probing into the nature of its
own existence. In *Being There* collective behavior returns as a
topic, but also to influence the novel's form. Kosinski believes
American society is, in its own way, as collective as that of the Soviet Union; in this country collective rites (such as rock music) and
collective media (such as television) make us "victims of a collective image which . . . engulfs us." [20] His central figure for *Being
There* is a person entirely defined by TV. Named, as if by chance,
Chance, he has spent his entire life secluded in a rich man's garden,
where "all that mattered was moving in his own time, like the
growing plants." [21] His sole device of communication is a television set, which also "created its own light, its own color, its own
time." By changing channels, Chance finds, "he could change
himself," and "Thus he came to believe that it was he, Chance, and
no one else, who made himself be" (pp. 5–6). But Chance is the

[18] Kosinski, *No Third Path*, pp. 20–21.

[19] Kosinski, *The Art of the Self*, p. 18.

[20] Quoted in R. Z. Sheppard, "Playing It by Eye," *Time*, 97 (April 26, 1971), 93; also in
Jerzy Kosinski, transcript of NBC News broadcast, *Comment* (February 28, 1971), pp. 6–7.

[21] Jerzy Kosinski, *Being There* (New York: Harcourt Brace Jovanovich, 1971), p. 4.
Subsequent references follow in parentheses.

farthest thing from a personally created self, the dominating creature we saw described in *Steps*. Rather, he is an absolute blank,
drawing his reality from the forms he sees on TV. Once he enters
the world his lack of substance is made clear to the reader. Perusing
a lawyer's document, he does not know how to read, and so simply
stares at it as long as an actor would on television. But the result is
impressive: the lawyer receives his " 'I can't sign it' " as a carefully weighed answer. Television continues to form the reality of
Being There, as Chance, in utter naivete, manages to deal successfully with all ranks of people by simply mimicking what he has seen
on the screen. But the most fundamental fact, that of his own existence, he cannot prove. At the death of his keeper he can provide no
record of employment; indeed, with no identification of any sort he
is turned out, almost as a nonentity.

How does he succeed? Chance soon learns that "When one was
addressed and viewed by others, one was safe. Whatever one did
would then be interpreted by the others in the same way that one interpreted what they did" (p. 34). As in *Steps,* other selves exist as
screens for one's own projections, and Chance is the quintessential
screen. Hence he is secure when existing as the object of others'
relationships, and triumphs by his great ability to be quite literally
nobody. After mere chance brings him into the home of Benjamin
Rand, a powerful financier, he wins the close friendship of Rand's
wife by "repeating to her parts of her own sentences, a practice he
had observed on TV" (p. 37), and he gains the admiration and respect of Rand himself by offering simple garden metaphors which
are received as profound insights. Almost at once the peculiar mania
of the American collective takes over. After the President visits
Rand and borrows one of the metaphors for a speech, Chance is
thrown up as a national figure, an "adviser to the President," and is
lionized by the press, radio, and television itself. On TV he becomes even more clearly a screen for people's projections, when for
each of his totally bland statements "Part of the audience inter-
rupted to applaud and part booed" (p. 66). At home, Chance
becomes Mrs. Rand's lover, not because of anything he can do ("on
TV what happened next was always obscured" [p. 76]), but because, as she sees it, " 'you want to conquer the woman from
within her very own self . . . you want to infuse in her the need and

the desire and the longing for your love' " (p. 79). What actually
has happened is reminiscent of *Steps*. " 'I am so free with you,' "
she tells him. " 'Up until the time I met you, every man I knew
barely acknowledged me. I was a vessel that he could take hold of,
pierce, and pollute. I was merely an aspect of somebody's lovemaking' " (p. 116). Chance, the nonexistent self, is now an aspect of
hers. Politically, Chance becomes a giant overnight, known by his
assumed name of Chauncey Gardiner. " 'I have read a lot about
you,' " a French diplomat boasts, even though Chance has been in
the news for less than two days. The stock market fluctuates with
every Chance pronouncement. " 'People like Gardiner decide the
fate of millions every day!' " claims the Russian ambassador. As
Kosinski's *reductio ad absurdum* finale, Chance is named vice-
presidential candidate, precisely because "A man's past cripples
him" and Chance has no past. By having no self to conflict with the
projected images of others, he has proven himself to be everyone's
favorite person.

The Boy of *The Painted Bird* and the protagonist of *Steps* survive the world's oppression by implementing their own great lyric
power; Chauncey Gardiner of *Being There* is conversely an absolute
blank of a person who is elevated to power by the narcissistically
reflected dead souls around him. To those who would posit the self
as a simple, ideal creator, Kosinski's fiction (like Barthelme's)
argues a more problematic case of the individual and the world,
especially in *The Devil Tree,* which presents an American character's struggle with his country's unique existence. Jonathan James
Whalen is determined by a past become suddenly pertinent with his
inheritance of the family trust; like Barthelme's characters, he lives
a schizoid life, seeking personal meaning in a world which external
forces won't allow him to create. His father, last of the great American industrial barons, did shape his own world, advising Presidents
and crushing other business enterprises which ran contrary to his
design, or to his self-imposed calling. Living is creating, but in
Jonathan's life second-hand structures allow as little imaginative
space as do the banalities cluttering Barthelme's landscape.

Like Barthelme's artists, Jonathan would hope to transform this
world; he is characterized as young, hip, collegiate, and freaky
enough that hostile critics might suppose he's an avid reader of

Vonnegut, Brautigan, and perhaps even Barthelme's *Snow White*. Heir to a gargantuan business and industrial complex, he cannot escape being "a factor in other people's plans," [22] no matter how imaginatively superior he would wish to be. Kosinski's protagonists are either aspirant live souls who manipulate the dead, or dead souls who passively reflect the rigor mortis around them. Jonathan would prove his awareness in gripping incidents which have become Kosinski's trademark. Some charm us:

> On the crossroads outside Bangkok I used to wait for the villagers driving their carts home from the market.
> The drivers, who smoked opium all day, trusted their donkeys to find their way home, so that by the time the carts reached the place where I waited, the men were asleep. I would leap out of the bushes, approach each patiently trotting donkey and turn him around. The cart drivers never wakened. One day I turned twenty carts around. (p. 15)

Others are fascinating in their horror:

> One morning she recalled a story I had told her before we met Mrs. Llewellyn: I was in a bordello on the outskirts of the city. The madam noticed me looking at a ravaged old woman and offered her to me. When I objected, the madam said that for a hundred dollars I could do anything I wished to her. If I wanted, I could kill her, "with that," she said, pointing to my loins. The madam explained that the old woman had been a prostitute all her life, that she was almost eighty years old now and would soon die. She had no relatives; if I agreed, at least her funeral would be paid for. When Barbara asked if I had killed the woman, I said nothing. (p. 19)

But despite his apparent freedom to do these things, Jonathan is not transforming his world. Other spatial juxtapositions find the younger Whalen in love affairs, on drug trips, and finally in group therapy. The latter he almost at once dismisses; as a friend tells him, "All therapy, from individual analysis to group encounters, is designed to make disturbed patients conform, rather than allow them to discover and live by their emotional truths" (p. 62). The point is well taken, and Jonathan is anxious to shun such cooption,

---

[22] Jerzy Kosinski, *The Devil Tree* (New York: Harcourt Brace Jovanovich, 1973), p. 34. Subsequent references follow in parentheses.

to avoid becoming a surrogate person. To be human, an individual, the only living creature who can "imagine itself apart from the herd" (p. 193) is his aim. But such licit imaginative powers are denied him, since his roots are other people's branches. His condition, of course, is imposed, but in a few days of his life he does his own to sustain it; in matters of pressure (with a pilot, a policeman, a mechanic) or need (particularly with a ski instructor at the end) he habitually relies on his family name and his family money to avail himself, if by now "self " can be said to exist. "What I want is tangible proof that I matter" (p. 39), he claims; as the story closes, we see him beating his lover, running through a multitude of poses, doing anything "to make her react" (p. 206). His behavior recalls an earlier statement: "I live only for other people, for looking good and keeping healthy. I do everything to get a reaction" (p. 72). The words are spoken by a prostitute, a dead self, which Jonathan has been and now becomes.

"All you need me for is to provide a stage on which you can project and view yourself, and see how your discarded experiences become alive again when they affect me. Am I right? You don't want me to love you; all you want is for me to abandon myself to the dreams and fantasies which you inspire in me. All you want is to prolong this impulse, this moment," claims the protagonist's lover in *Steps.* But if her complaint discredits what the imaginative may be, the protagonist's argument suggests more optimistically what it may do: *"Then simply give yourself up to what you feel; enjoy that awareness. Lovers are not snails; they don't have to protrude from their shells and meet each other half way. Meet me within your own self"* (pp. 130–131). Only two whole selves can completely reciprocate, and give the insatiable self the satisfaction that it needs. As long as one remains other, the self resists, and it is not surprising that so much of Kosinski's and Barthelme's work confronts the problems of heterosexual love. Barthelme's fiction has been more obviously aware of everyday concerns, but Kosinski's work has shown a steady progress toward more commonly experiential themes. "There is a place beyond words where experience first occurs to which I always want to return," the latter's protagonist admits. "Instead of expressing myself, I produce a neatly ordered document about someone else's state of mind" (pp. 32–33). At

their best Donald Barthelme and Jerzy Kosinski meet the double challenges to theme and technique in post-Barthian fiction: to squarely confront the great American existence without being overwhelmed by it, and to find the words that lead us not to a state of frustrated inarticulation but to a satisfied quiet.

Kosinski has argued that the subjects of his Polish dissertations—Jakob Jaworski and an anti-czarist revolutionary group of the 1880's—were literary, even fictional artists who abandoned the realm of the imagination to effect more immediately practical ends, and that Stalin, Hitler, and Mao should definitely be listed among the major writers of fiction in the twentieth century.[23] But Kosinski regards pure fiction as superior, as he contrasts his sociological writings to his own novels, which from time to time repeat the same incident: "The difference is that my nonfiction grounds it in a specific place—the U.S.S.R.—and by doing it torpedoes its immediacy, its proximity to the reader. On the other hand, the fiction invokes the reader directly. He cannot discard it by saying, 'It already happened to someone else, hence it won't happen to me. I'm excluded; I'm a bystander.' Perhaps the 'nonfiction as literature' aims at non-evoking; it aims at reassuring the reader that the event had taken place or that it's a large historical process, hence that there's no direct threat to the reader. Fiction assaults the reader directly as if saying: It is about you. You are actually creating this situation when you are reading about it; in a way you are staging it as an event in your own life." [24] Imagination is the superior mode, because "such a vision is total. It encompasses any aspect of our temporality, of our empirical presence. Hence our tangible confinement in time and space is inferior to the play of our imagination. In the moment of this interview you can see yourself conducting the interview with me, but nothing prevents you from 'departing' (while you are still bodily here), to another presence. In other words, the vision is always greater and truer, since a vision encompasses both the actual, 'horizontal' condition and the transcendence into a new 'vertical' mode, self-generating within its own confinement." [25] His method may be misconstrued, as it was by the Polish journalists Hanna Wydzga and

[23] Klinkowitz, "Kosinski: Interview," pp. 41–42.
[24] Ibid., p. 36.
[25] Ibid., p. 42.

Jan Zaborowski, who in their essay "Gry i zabawy ludu polskiego podczas drugiej wojny swiatowej" (Fun and Games of the Polish People during the Second World War) claimed that "The strongest point of Kosinski's work is the creation of the pretense of authenticity," reinforced by what they termed "the autobiographical beginning and end of the book." [26] By the comparison of several passages it is claimed that Kosinski plagiarized his accounts of peasant superstitions and behavior from "a 400-page work of Professor Biegeleisen, published in Cracow in 1929 under the title *The Healing Practices of the Polish Peasantry* (Series: "Works of the Ethnographic Committee of the Polish Academy of Letters and Sciences").[27] But questions about the historical nature of *The Painted Bird*, whether of its relevance as autobiography or its indebtedness to factual sources, are less important than the imaginative effectiveness of the work, since Kosinski sees the best fiction as autobiographical and experiential not of the author, but of the reader.

By his belief in the imagination, Kosinski makes possible a fiction beyond the exhausted subjects and methods of a writer like John Barth. The modern "self," which critics such as Wylie Sypher, Charles Fair, and William Barrett have seen as lost, dying, or hopelessly oppressed, becomes in Kosinski's hands the triumphant power, more to be feared than to be feared for. And, like Barthelme, Kosinski demonstrates the structural art of handling the fragments of contemporary life in a sublimely synthetic way—in a manner which will soon be heralded as organic when the post-contemporary fictionists establish their work as the major literary mode.

[26] Hanna Wydzga and Jan Zaborowski, "Gry i zabawy ludu polskiego podczas drugiej wojny swiatowej" [Fun and Games of the Polish People during the Second World War], *ODRA—Miesiecznik spoleczno-kulturalny* [ODRA—Social and Political Monthly], June, 1966, pp. 20–21.

[27] Ibid., p. 21.

FOUR

LeRoi Jones / Imamu Baraka & James Park Sloan

Just about every contemporary novelist of the disruptivist school did something else before receiving acclaim for his fiction. Jerzy Kosinski wrote sociology; Donald Barthelme edited trade journals; Ronald Sukenick was a literary critic; William H. Gass, a teacher of philosophy. Even Kurt Vonnegut, Jr., the most popular of the lot, supported himself for twenty years by selling stories and essays to the slick magazines, a job at once more professional and less literary than the writing of serious novels. LeRoi Jones, who in 1968 changed his name to Imamu Amiri Baraka,[1] was first and best known as a musicologist and jazz critic, contributing regular columns to *Down Beat* and *Metronome* and writing two major books on the history of the blues and the experimentation in contemporary jazz music. James Park Sloan planned to use his service as a paratrooper in Vietnam and his Harvard honors thesis on Richard Nixon as an entry into politics; instead he wrote one of the first novels of the Vietnam experience, *War Games* (1971), and followed it with the first disruptivist political fiction, *The Case History of Comrade V* (1972). Jones has subsequently written both poetry and drama, but his novel *The System of Dante's Hell* (1965) and his well-integrated story collection *Tales* (1967) are two of the most important works in contemporary fiction.

LeRoi Jones's study of black music led him directly to his own expression in fiction. The years of literary disruption in fiction coincide with radical shifts in black culture—to a more militant, nationalistic, and self-expressive posture—and most noticeably in jazz, where the "cool," progressive style of the 1950's yielded to a massive disruption of the form by Ornette Coleman, Archie Shepp,

---

[1] Because all of his publications cited in this chapter were written under Baraka's previous name, LeRoi Jones, and remain in print with this name, his new name has not been substituted.

Pharaoh Sanders, and others in the mid-1960's. Jones was one of the first critics to accept and understand this music, which is very similar to the innovations in fiction which followed shortly. "Music is for the senses," he wrote in a liner note to Archie Shepp's album, *Four for Trane.* "Music should make you *feel.* But, finally, unless you strip yourself of outside interference, almost all your reactions will be *social.* (Like a man who digs Mozart because it is 'high class,' dig it?) But the point of living seems to be to get to your actual feelings, as, say, these musicians want always to get to theirs. If you can find out who you are (you're no thing) then we can find out what you feel. Because we *are* our feelings, or our lack of them." [2]

To know one's feelings, to recognize one's self in an imaginative act, is the sociological and musicological substance of Jones's early studies. "When black people got to this country, they were Africans, a foreign people," he noted in his first book, *Blues People.* The difference was not slavery, for that was widely practiced in West Africa. "But to be brought to a country, a culture, a society, that was, and is, in terms of purely philosophical correlatives, a complete antithesis of one's version of man's life on earth—that is the cruelest aspect of this particular enslavement." [3] The blues, as Jones established in this work and continues in *Home: Social Essays,* was the vehicle by which the blacks could find out who they were, what they "felt." "The development of the Negro's music was . . . direct and instinctive. It was the one vector out of African culture impossible to eradicate completely. The appearance of blues as a native *American* music was colored by the emergence of an American Negro culture." Of importance to a sense of the larger tradition, "The 'Coon Shout' proposed one version of the American Negro—and of America; Ornette Coleman proposes another. But the point is that both these versions are accurate and informed with a legitimacy of emotional concern, nowhere available in what is called 'Negro Literature,' and certainly not in the middlebrow literature of the white American." [4] Hence Jones's concern with "The

[2] LeRoi Jones, liner notes to *Four for Trane,* recorded by Archie Shepp (Impulse AS-71), August 10, 1964.

[3] LeRoi Jones, *Blues People* (New York: William Morrow, 1963), p. 1.

[4] LeRoi Jones, *Home: Social Essays* (New York: William Morrow, 1966), p. 110.

blues impulse transferred . . . containing a race, and its expression. *Primal* (mixtures . . . transfers and imitations). Through its many changes, it remained the exact replication of The Black Man In The West.'' [5] It is an authentic voice, transferable to a new fiction. ''For an American, black or white, to say that some hideous imitation of Alexander Pope means more to him, emotionally, than the blues of Ray Charles or Lightnin' Hopkins, it would be required for him to have completely disappeared into the American Academy's vision of a Europeanized and colonial American culture, or to be lying. In the end, the same emotional sterility results. It is somehow much more tragic for the black man.'' [6] Jazz, the new fiction, poetry, drama, have this in common: ''The Black Artist's role in America is to aid in the destruction of America as he knows it.'' [7] ''What's needed now for 'the arts,' '' Jones claims in his most recent book of essays, ''is to get them away from white people, as example of their 'culture' (of their life, finally, and all its uses, e.g., art) and back where such strivings belong, as strong thrusts of a healthy people.'' [8] On a literary level, this is the thrust of Jones's own fiction, and of the literary disruption in general.

''We *are* our feelings, or the lack of them''—the same year LeRoi Jones made this judgment of Archie Shepp's music, he was completing his own reorganization of ''the system'' of Dante's Hell. ''I put The Heretics in the deepest part of hell,'' Jones described, ''though Dante had them spared, on higher ground.'' Jones's justification was that ''It is heresy, against one's own sources, running in terror, from one's deepest responses and insights . . . the denial of feeling . . . that I see as basest evil.'' [9] *The System of Dante's Hell* is written with the force of a gathering storm, to be unleashed in *Tales* but here given fuller expression than when recapitulated in the first half of Jones's story collection. The first circle of hell, that of the ''virtuous heathen,'' Jones reserves for the assimilated blacks: ''You've done everything you said you

[5] LeRoi Jones, *Black Music* (New York: William Morrow, 1967), p. 180.

[6] Jones, *Home*, p. 113.

[7] Ibid., p. 251.

[8] Imamu Amiri Baraka (LeRoi Jones), *Raise Race Rays Raze* (New York: Random House, 1971), p. 33.

[9] LeRoi Jones, *The System of Dante's Hell* (New York: Grove Press, 1965), p. 7. Subsequent references follow in parentheses.

won't. Everything you said you despised. A fat mind, lying to itself. Unmoving like some lump in front of a window. Wife, child,
house, city, clawing at your gentlest parts'' (p. 13). Cultural accommodation is self-corruption, such as '' 'The Modern Jazz Blues.'
Bigot blues. Yourself, my man . . . your stone self. Talkin bout
blues. There's a bunch. I mean, the 3 button suit blues. White buck
blues'' (p. 86). From this the narrator goes back to his own beginnings, on Central Avenue in Newark (''This is the center I mean.
Where it all, came on. The rest is suburb. The rest is outside this
hole. Snakes die past this block. Flames subside'' [p. 76]). There
even ''The sun itself was grey'' (p. 30).

As he does again in *Tales,* Jones's protagonist experiences an
alienation from his native world. '' 'You are a young man and soon
will be off to college.' They knew then, and walked around me for
it'' (p. 41). His circle is bohemian, including girl friends—''I never
got to fuck her either, just slick stammerings about the world and
Dylan Thomas and never got the Baudelaire book back either'' (p.
94). He enters the air force, whitest of the military services, and as
an ''imitation white boy'' ventures into the black quarter of Shreve-
port, Louisiana. His terrifying experiences here are only resolved in
his dream-hallucination after a beating by local toughs: ''I sat reading from a book aloud and they danced to my reading'' (p. 152).
The novel ends with a search for a usable resolution in ''Sound and
Image,'' that ''Hell in this book which moves from sound and
image ('association complexes') into fast narrative is what vision I
had of it around 1960–61 and that fix on my life, and my interpretation of my earlier life.'' The problem is that ''God is simply a white
man, a white 'idea,' in this society, unless we have made some
other image which is stronger, and can deliver us from the salvation
of our enemies'' (p. 153).

This stronger image, this knowledge and expression of the self in
literary terms analogous to blues or jazz, is found only in the latter
stories of *Tales. The System of Dante's Hell,* structured according to
the poet's nine circles (and subdivisions thereof), was an imitation
of musical improvisations; with no explicit development from one
short chapter to the next, the work made its statement through almost sensually cumulative successions of tones, moods, and colors,
until the last two sections (about a first experience with a prostitute,

and then the journey into the black section of the southern town) were presented as relatively conventional stories—but influenced by all the modal touches preceding. In *Tales,* the word itself is rejected as a medium for artistic expression; perhaps, as John O'Brien speculates, "because it lacks immediacy." Jones chooses instead "the activity of jazz, making his novel read and sound like a John Coltrane composition." [10] He uses language "less as a medium for rational communication than as a way of mesmerizing readers by sounds and rhythms. The meanings are there, but we are led into them not by the traditional devices of plot and character, but through episodes that are held together by recurring images," [11] as Jones builds his vehicle for authentic cultural expression.

The stories of *Tales* have the consistency of a novel, and Jones establishes the continuity with his previous work by beginning with "A Chase (Alighieri's Dream)." Its metaphor is running; as Claude Brown has observed of the history of the northern urban black community, "Where do you run to when you're already in the promised land," [12] and Jones tries to answer. His scene:

> Place broken: their faces sat and broke each other. As suns, Sons gone tired in the heart and left the south. The North, years later she'd wept for him drunk and a man finally they must have thought. In the dark, he was even darker. Wooden fingers running. Wind so sweet it drank him.
>
> Faces broke. Charts of age. Worn thru, to see black years. Bones in iron faces. Steel bones. Cages of decay. Cobblestones are wet near the army stores. Beer smells, Saturday. To now, they have passed so few lovely things.
>
> Newsreel chickens. Browned in the street. I was carrying groceries back across the manicured past. Back, in a coat. Sunk, screaming at my fingers. Faces broken, hair waved, simple false elegance. I must tell someone I love you. Them. In a line near the fence. She sucked my tongue. Red, actual red, but colored hair. Soft thin voice, and red freckles. A servant.

Through this landscape his protagonist runs. "Get out of the dance, down the back stairs, the street, and across in the car. Run past it,

---

[10] John O'Brien, *Interviews with Black Writers* (New York: Liveright, 1973), p. vii.
[11] Ibid., p. xi.
[12] Claude Brown, *Manchild in the Promised Land* (New York: Macmillan, 1965), p. 8.

around the high building. Court Street, past the Y, harder, buttoning a cardigan, to Morton Street. Duck down, behind the car. Let Apple pass; a few others.'' [13] He dashes to a sexual encounter, then back on the street, where his passage down the sidewalk becomes broken field running in a football game:

> Their arms waving from the stand. Sun and gravel or the 3 hole opens and it's more beautiful than Satie. A hip, change speeds, head fake, stop, cut back, a hip, head fake . . . then only one man coming from the side . . . it went thru my head a million times, the years it took, seeing him there, with a good angle, shooting in, with 3 yards to the sidelines, about ten home. I watched him all my life close in, and thot to cut, stop or bear down and pray I had speed. Answers shot up, but my head was full of blood and it moved me without talk. I stopped still the ball held almost like a basketball, wheeled and moved in to score untouched. (p. 3)

As the tale ends we don't know whether football has been a metaphor for the chase, the chase a metaphor for sex, or sex a metaphor for either of the two. All merge into one suprarational, poetic kaleidoscope, with no tenor to the metaphor at all. It is all vehicle, the stuff of pure improvisation.

In the following stories—more properly ''chapters''—Jones's protagonist assumes several different identities as he searches for his own. In college he measures the distance from his former friends: ''Jimmy Lassiter, first looie. A vector. What is the angle made if a straight line is drawn from the chapel, across to Jimmy Lassiter, first looie. A vector. What is the angle made if a straight line is drawn from the chapel, across to Jimmy, and connected there, to me, and back up the hill again? The angle of progress.'' The line is ''for Jimmy's sad and useless horn. And they tell me (via phone, letter, accidental meetings in the Village) 'Oh he's in med school and married and lost to you, hombre' '' (p. 8). And he makes a portrait of his college roommates, alienated even from them ('' 'That cat's nuts. He was sittin' up in that room last night with dark glasses on . . . with a yellow bulb . . . pretendin' to read some abstract shit' '' [p. 9]). And counterpointed to their own collegiate activity:

[13] LeRoi Jones, *Tales* (New York: Grove Press, 1967), pp. 1–2. Subsequent references follow in parentheses.

"No, no, the utmost share/Of my desire shall be/Only to kiss that
air/That lately kissed thee."

"Uhh! What's trumps, dammit!"

As, "Tell me not, Sweet, I am
unkind,/That from the nunnery/Of thy chaste breast and quiet mind/
To war and arms I fly."

"You talking about a lightweight mammy-
tapper, boy, you really king."

To this he cries, "Lucasta, find me here on the bed, with a hard
pecker and dirty feet. Oh, I suffer, in my green glasses, under the
canopy of my loves. Oh, I am drunk and vomity in my room, with
only Charley Ventura to understand my grace."

Far from the blues, "The Leader" and his classmates are taking
the Howard University curriculum, "Primers for dogs who are
learning to read. Tinkle of European teacups" (p. 18). For all it
means to them "It could be Shostakovich in Charleston, South
Carolina. Or in the dull windows of Chicago, an unread volume of
Joyce. Some black woman who will never hear the word *Negress* or
remember your name. Or a thin preacher who thinks your name is
Stephen. A wall, Oh, Lucasta" (p. 20). The protagonist is torn between two worlds:

> Leader, the paratroopers will come for you at noon. A helicop-
> ter low over the monastery. To get you out.
>
> But my country. My
> people. These dead souls, I call my people. Flesh of my flesh. (p. 22)

The gang soon rushes upstairs to expose a colleague and his homo-
sexual lover. "Doctors, judges, first negro directors of welfare
chain, morticians, chemists, ad men, fighters for civil rights, all admirable, useful men. 'BREAK THE FUCKIN' DOOR OPEN,
RICK! YEH!' "

> A wall. Against it, from where you stand, the sea stretches smooth
> for miles out. Their voices distant thuds of meat against the sand.
> Murmurs of insects. Hideous singers against your pillow every night
> of your life. They are there now, screaming at you.
>
> More prints in the sand, away, or toward some name. I am a poet. I
> am a rich famous butcher. I am the man who paints the gold balls on
> the tops of flagpoles. I am, no matter, more beautiful than anyone

else. And I have come a long way to say this. Here. In the long hall, shadows across my hands. My face pushed hard against the floor. And the wood, old, and protestant. And their voices, all these other selves screaming for blood. For blood, or whatever it is fills their noble lives. (p. 29)

Even apart from college, Jones's protagonist is alienated from his world. As when on a trip to a suburban high school he sees, "in the auditorium, young American girls, for the first time. And have loved them as flesh things emanating from real life, that is, in contrast to my own." "Negroes and Italians beat and shaped me," he admits, "and my allegiance is there. But the triumph of romanticism was parquet floors, yellow dresses, gardens and sandy hair. I must have felt the loss and could not rise against a cardboard world of dark hair and linoleum. Reality was something I was convinced I could not have" (p. 45). He moves into writing, only to become almost hopelessly ofay. "I am Lew Crosby, a writer. I want to write what I'm about, which is profound shit." As such, he is petty and affected ("How can you read *Pierre* if you think your wife's doing something weird? Then you got to take time out to think about *her*" [p. 54]). When she starts an affair behind his back, he is livid because she lacks taste; he calls her a middle-class wreck. The scene where he kills the lover is deliberate in its flatness; but when he drops in on some friends afterwards, a "soft benevolence" comes into their voices as they invite him to "Come on and get high with us." The story ends, like "A Chase," with a run—this time for heroin.

The first half of *Tales* is a carefully orchestrated series of improvisations on the theme of alienated identity, a counterpoint of reflection and expression. In "Heroes Are Gang Leaders" the protagonist is in a hospital ward, eating candy and paging through books about heroism which the charity ladies, surprised that he can read, have given him. Two police officers come in to interrogate and then slap around a helpless, mute wardmate:

And here is the essay part of the story. Like they say, my *point of view*. I had the book, *No More Parades,* all about the pursuit of heroism. About the death and execution of a skyman, or at least the execution, and the airless social compromise that keeps us alive past any use to ourselves. Chewing on some rich lady's candy, holding on

to my ego, there among the elves, for dear god given sanctified life.
Big Man In The Derelict Ward. The book held up in front of my eyes,
to shield what was going on from slopping over into my life. (p. 68)

In "The Screamers" he returns from college (and his books) to a
black dance hall, "Willing for any experience, any image, any further separation from where my good grades were sure to lead.
Frightened of post offices, lawyer's offices, doctor's cars, the
deaths of clean politicians. Or of the imaginary fat man, advertising
cemeteries to his 'good colored friends.' " Instead he joins the band
and the boogalooing crowd which spills out into the street, as "We
screamed and screamed at the clear image of ourselves as we should
always be" (pp. 74, 79). The climactic moment comes in "Salute";
like the hero of *The System of Dante's Hell,* he is in the air force,
being chided by a white officer for failing to salute. He has a retort:
" 'Well, if the airplanes blow up, Chinese with huge habits will
drop out of the sky, riding motorized niggers.' " But that isn't what
he says. "You know I didn't say that. But I said something, you
know, the kind of shit you'd say, you know" (p. 87).

   The LeRoi Jones protagonist finds his own language only in the
second half of *Tales,* beginning with "The Words" and getting full
expression in "New-Sense." He is back from the service, "Now
that the old world has crashed around me, and it's raining in early
summer. I live in Harlem with a baby shrew and suffer for my
decadence which kept me away so long. When I walk the streets,
the streets don't yet claim me, and people look at me, knowing the
strangeness of my manner, and the objective stance from which I attempt to 'love' them." He wants to say something, "But don't
know what it is, except words" (pp. 89–90). The words come in
"New-Sense." He rejects "the Hamlet burden, which is white
bullshit, to always be weighing and measuring and analyzing, and
reflecting. The reflective vs. the expressive. Mahler vs. Martha and
The Vandellas. It's not even an interesting battle." The development of Jones's protagonist, through his novel and this carefully
organized collection of short stories, has been to the point where he
can see the same argument that LeRoi Jones himself made in *Blues
People* and *Black Music.* In *Tales* it is stated in this manner:

                     Except we black people
caught up in Western values. So deeply. Having understood the most

noble attempts of white men to make admirable sense of the world,
now, reject them, along with any of them. And the mozarts are as
childish as the hitlers.

Because reflect never did
shit for any of us. Express would. Express. NOW NOW NOW NOW
NOW NOW.

Blood Everywhere.
And heroes march thru
smiling. (pp. 96–97)

Jones's drama and poetry have argued the same theme as his most
sustained works of prose: that authentic existence is possible only in
the vital act of warring against its challenges. His theatre is now
proclaimed as "Black Arts" and, by necessity, "Revolutionary."
White men are taken by the "Experimental Death Unit #1" and
shot; "J-E-L-L-O," a drama "about Jack Benny and Rochester,
and what happens when Rochester diggs hisself," ends with
Benny's murder.[14] The play *Dutchman* is the major statement of
Jones's radical aesthetic, where a protagonist goes through a change
similar to the one in *Tales*. But LeRoi Jones/Imamu Baraka is mis-
understood if his aesthetic is thought to be simply anti-white, part of
what David Littlejohn calls "the undeclared race war in which all
Americans are, by definition, involved." [15] His careful work on sociology and musicology establishes the need for a unique cultural
expression, and the state of the times demands that this expression
stand in opposition to the more dominant modes. That his fiction
produced as the end product of this new aesthetic matches so closely
the work of other American innovators, such as Barthelme (in form)
and Kosinski (in theme), suggests that his argument against European determinations applies to all American, noncolonial work. His
writing is far more than just politically disruptive.

In 1962, about the same time that LeRoi Jones as musicologist
was making his claims for the legitimacy of native black American
ideas, Daniel Bell published his book, *The End of Ideology*, subtitled "On the Exhaustion of Political Ideas in the Fifties." Claim-

---

[14] LeRoi Jones, "Why No J-E-L-L-O?", *Four Black Revolutionary Plays* (Indianapolis:
Bobbs-Merrill, 1969), p. 89.
[15] David Littlejohn, *Black on White* (New York: Grossman, 1966), p. 4.

ing that all the classic formulae for action had been played out, having "lost their 'truth' and their power to persuade,'' [16] Bell presented an argument as airtight (and as self-accusatory) as John Barth's thesis on the Literature of Exhaustion. This same year, James Park Sloan began the research for his Harvard honors thesis on Richard Nixon, the political figure who had been at the center of American life for the entire period discussed by Bell, 1946–62. Sloan was drawn by several problems with regard to Nixon; he defined his subject as "Nixon and the Liberals: The Response of the Liberal Intellectuals to the Career of Richard M. Nixon, 1946–1962,'' and began with several incongruities. First, Sloan noted that for all the acerbic and personal attacks on Nixon during his career, there was no corresponding enthusiasm among any interests or groups which might conceivably be his partisans. And for all the opposition, Nixon was never clearly described by any consistent ideology. Sloan's conclusion was that he had none, because the age had none, and that Nixon was the man of the age. "There had not been a fundamental issue since Franklin D. Roosevelt,'' Sloan reasoned, "and Nixon was the child of F.D.R. and his New Deal as surely as John Kennedy or Lyndon Johnson.'' [17]

Sloan draws a careful picture of the "Class of 1946,'' Nixon's first year in Washington. He contrasts the young men of this time with their seniors: "between 1930 and 1937, as a generation of American intellectuals were taking a troubled, but receptive look at alien, apocalyptic ideologies, Richard Nixon was receiving a traditional grounding in the small-town, rural American ethic.'' [18] Hence when he himself came to power, it would be with an "emptiness'' characteristic of his California upbringing and suggestive of the decade to come. The study ends with the California gubernatorial campaign of 1962; but in 1968, when Sloan submitted his thesis to the history department at Harvard after spending three years as a paratrooper in Vietnam, Richard Nixon was elected President and accepting responsibility for what was becoming the longest and pos-

[16] Daniel Bell, *The End of Ideology: On the Exhaustion of Political Ideas in the Fifties* (New York: Collier, 1961), p. 397.

[17] James Park Sloan, "Nixon and the Liberals: The Response of the Liberal Intellectuals to the Career of Richard M. Nixon, 1946–1962,'' B.A. honors thesis in history, Harvard College, Cambridge, Mass., March 29, 1968, p. 77.

[18] Ibid., p. 12.

sibly strangest war in American history. Instead of turning directly to politics, James Park Sloan wrote a war novel—the first significant novel about the Vietnam experience, by necessity an exercise in innovative fiction.

For *War Games* Sloan must find a pertinent structuring device. The literary past is of no more use to him than it was to Jones, since the military itself was encountering a type of war in Vietnam which it had never seen before. Sloan had two theories to test, one of which he hoped to use for his book:

THEORY ONE

The timid hero goes to Vietnam like a sissy dipping his toe in the pool. Suddenly he realizes that he can be a cold-water swimmer. This happens because Vietnam provides him with a character-molding experience. It is both purposeful and earthshaking. There is a flash of insight. He realizes that he is now fully mature. He has become a soldier and a man.

This is only a hypothesis. Then there is Theory Two.

THEORY TWO

A tough-minded young man, who unsuspectingly has above-average sensitivity, goes to Vietnam. For the first time in his life he encounters genuine brutality and tragedy—perhaps his first tragic love affair. This experience shocks him into his own humanity. There is a flash of insight. He comes home in total revulsion at war and probably writes a book.[19]

The story of his book becomes the story of his attempts to write "the definitive novel of Vietnam," and its structure becomes one natural and unique to the young college drop-out ripping off the army in Vietnam. Discovering that if the service does dental work on any tooth it is responsible for the care of that tooth and the two adjacent for the rest of the soldier's life, Sloan's protagonist begins a program of systematically complaining about every third tooth. The organization of his dental chart becomes the structure of his novel.

The chart is the realest thing in the book. Much like James Kunen in *Standard Operating Procedure,* Sloan finds that there are many

---

[19] James Park Sloan, *War Games* (Boston: Houghton Mifflin, 1971), p. 4. Subsequent references follow in parentheses.

unreal things in this new war: airliners which race the sun across the Pacific, serving breakfast every hour; APO mail which sends the same letter back and forth across the world twenty-seven times; a peacetime army staffed by uniformed civil servants who must suddenly fight for their careers; and dozens of other incongruities which suggest that Vietnam and its war are a world apart from anything America has previously known. Officially, the army contrives its own unreality to match it. As Kunen noted, it is a nonlinear war, with no objectives to seize and no end date in sight:

> Each departure is festive in its own way. Since there has been no mass homecoming, it seems that each individual's leaving must represent a victory in miniature. Since the rotations after one-year tours are staggered, victory is a continuous process. It is thus more sustained than the sword tendering, paper signing, and ticker-tape marching of previous wars. On the other hand, it is followed by an equally continuous reappraisal. Newcomers are always groaning that "that bastard has left me in a bind." (p. 40)

A matter of duration and simple modal exercise, the service treats it as a game: "I have standardized the statistics as well. Ours. Theirs. We lead by a steady three-to-one. Which is good, but not good enough. Any worse and there would be alarm. Any better and the statistics would be checked. No one really reads the reports. I never bother with the facts. When a town comes up on my roster, I put the monthly battle there. That's the way it is with this war" (p. 87). Despite the battles and very real deaths, it does not seem like a real *war,* as a German construction worker, a veteran of World War II, makes evident with his memories: "Warsaw, Paris, Tobruk, El Alamein, Stalingrad, Siberia . . . Duc Hoa, Tuy Hoa, My Tho, Dong Tam, Cai Be, Nam Can, Cai Cai, Bac Lieu . . ." (p. 109). Why not make them up?

Sloan's protagonist quickly learns that if he is to have a real war, he must make it up himself. "The hero must not merely thrash the villains, but create them. Set them up for the kill like the matador his bull. Lay hold to a portion of the banal, flog it to life, and from it fashion an adversary worthy of his steel. I shall remember to cite Hamlet: devise the play, then act in it!" (p. 9). Others had to make a separate peace, Sloan observes; "I had to find a separate war." As he makes progress through his war, which has become his novel, he wonders, "Have I begun inventing things? A man who goes to war should return with tales to tell. God knows, I would like to take part in tellable stories. Is my life merging with my imagination?" (p. 128). He fears that he is "tramping, step by step, in the direction of the implausible. Was it possible that my life was becoming like that of a literary device?" On patrol with a group of ARVN rangers, his dream catches up with him: sickened by his allies' torture of villagers and disgusting acts with animals, he sets his rifle on automatic fire and destroys them all. For this he expects court-martial and execution, but at least he has performed a significant act in this otherwise insignificant war.

Sloan's protagonist and his "separate war" are saved by his new boss, Col. Rachow, who has authored the army manual, CREATIVE LEADERSHIP AND COLLECTIVE TUNNEL VISION, and who "would have been magnificent . . . as a papal lawyer in the twelfth century. Or perhaps as the head of a noble family encroaching on its vassals" (p. 89). Rachow sympathizes with the protagonist's behavior because he can articulate many of the young soldier's feelings about the unreal war against Vietnam:

> War, said Rachow, has ceased to be tied down by facts. It has become metaphysical; one might say a platonic form. He asked me to picture an amphibious landing across Lake Michigan. Then imagine, he said, such things as landings by Martians; invaders from liquid planets formed of molten lava, surprised and threatened by our explorations. This is the future of military planning. War is no longer waged merely to achieve ends; it is waged as proof of its own possibility. (p. 144)

Moreover, technologically "war had come to a state of entropy! It was more and more complex, but in the process its energy was spent. If he had known sooner, he might have quit the army and written a book—on the war which had made his profession obsolete" (p. 154). And so Sloan's protagonist ends his tour with the creation of his small novel about a small war, *War Games*.

The Case History of Comrade V, while maintaining Sloan's political interest, takes his theories of fiction and self-created realities and transfers them from war to peace, where an intellectual, detained in a medical-security facility, experiments with the definition of his own life. The novel is repeated thrice, in different sections: the "case history" as it is reported in a computer printout read each day for therapy by Comrade V; a diary he is allowed to keep, which often speaks in opposition to the printout; and "The Case History of Comrade V" itself, a paper written by V's psychoanalyst explaining the patient's deviations from the real world. The printout purports to be "his case history, in other words, himself," and must be read by Comrade V as fast as it is printed, as part of his therapy. It describes his extreme withdrawal into the world of mathematics, even as a child: "the boy used his peculiar gifts to create artificial bridges from himself to others, at the same time maintaining the inviolability of his overdeveloped solitary world." [20] Thereby "his psyche, throughout the years, had slyly and tragically refused to make genuine steps of progress in coming to terms with the surrounding realities" (p. 25). His scholarly work becomes the making of "a mathematical model and critique of the entirety of life in the fatherland," "an accurate statistical picture of the knowable universive" which would be "a sort of medieval summa in modern form" (p. 47).

His diary confirms the printout's basic facts but debates their interpretation. At a loss because his therapists have insisted that the diary is to contain no mathematics, he relies on pure logic to prove himself sane. In this way human relations become simple forms:

> She may be a figment or not. What matters (in logical syntax) is the recognition by my mind of the necessity of a certain grammatical form. Not "I am sane," but "You are sane." They missed the point. It is not the good feeling of a friend, but the logic of grammar that matters. No man is permitted the logical outrage of claiming sanity. The very grammar of such a claim is nonsense. It is only necessary to contrive a device for saying it in another person. It thereby follows: the girl need not be real at all. (p. 51).

Thus logical syntax becomes his "Maginot Line of sanity. Ill-chosen word. I mean only a vital line of defense. It is not destined to be outflanked."

Section three, the case history itself, presents the thesis that "cer-

---

[20] James Park Sloan, *The Case History of Comrade V* (Boston: Houghton Mifflin, 1972), p. 10. Subsequent references follow in parentheses.

tain monomaniacal syndromes are endemic to our age—and should be treated as such'' (p. 104). Comrade V has been creating a false universe, but the therapist must ask ''when does the creation of a world, by means of some obsessive crutch, have validity? For both Galileo and Newton created such worlds and were seen in their time as monomaniacs. Freud himself did no less, his crutch being human libido. His universe: human depth psychology. But in modern times the case is different: ''It is rather the utter psychic defeat of self: the plight of an ordinary man too small to cope with contemporary life'' (p. 118). Which would seal the matter tight, except that the author of the paper is, practically speaking, the Comrade V as profiled in the previous sections. ''Empathy is the ability to assume the point of view of someone else while stealthily keeping one foot in the door of objective reality'' (p. 143), the therapist reports, and reveals that he has written the printout himself as a ''fiction'' capable of establishing an ''identification without identification, namely third-person narrative with access to the consciousness of a single character'' (p. 144). As the author leaves the medical-security establishment in which all this has taken place, he reflects, ''what a large part of one's being may come to reside in such a structure'' (p. 147). The word ''structure'' is as ambiguous and suggestive as Sloan's use of it in *War Games,* and as multiform as *The Case History of Comrade V* in its possibilities.

The genius of James Park Sloan is that he has found a way to combine the most sophisticated techniques of innovation in fiction with a structure at once as fascinating and as surprising as that of the best popular suspense fiction. Central to his fiction is the belief that the human imagination is a superman, an effective creator of its own world, even of its own being. ''Raskolnikov, Creator of Dostoyevsky'' is Sloan's theoretical exercise on this subject, a compelling speculation that the justification for the great transition in Dostoyevsky's fiction after his last-minute reprieve on the Semyonovsky Parade Ground was that he was indeed killed that day, to be replaced by an actual double, Raskolnikov:

> Perhaps as the messenger came into view bearing the reprieve (foredestined to be an instant late), the formal solution had yet to be fleshed out. Only later would he realize the possibilities of the false ending, the implausible confession, the conversion in a page of an

eternal demon, the sudden suicide of the nihilist. In time he would realize that the very flaws of his style might be strewn before the future
superman as clues. It would be years before he realized that he had
stumbled that day on a code which would ever afterward confound all
censors and inquisitors, the simple device of making the triumph of
good unconvincing and unappealing. In time, too, he would realize
the perfect clarity of this device, a dialectical story with the demon so
clearly superior to the author that only vulgar, soft-headed fools, the
religionists and patriots, could take the side of the narrator. With the
realization of these facts, only one other creation remained, the invention of an author whose carping narrowness would be believable.
What would have happened, in twenty years, to the young socialist
today being (accidentally) executed for a (nonexistent) plot? Unknown to himself, Raskolnikov had already begun to extrapolate this,
his consummate creation, when he heard the lieutenant issue the
order, "Fire!" [21]

[21] James Park Sloan, "Raskolnikov, Creator of Dostoyevsky," *Modern Occasions* #2
(1974), p. 110.

FIVE

Ronald Sukenick & Raymond Federman

The disruption of American fiction is substantial: Donald Barthelme's comic disabuse has made it uneasy for writers to write, or readers to read, in the insipid forms of the past; and Jerzy Kosinski and others have discredited that noble theme, the loss of the self, which had fueled so many novels before. Moving ahead, LeRoi Jones demonstrated the legitimacy of an indigenous American aesthetic, and James Park Sloan has tested the implications of a totally self-created world. But the most complete disruption goes beyond theme or form: as practiced by such writers as Steve Katz (*The Exagggerations of Peter Prince*), Eugene Wildman (*Montezuma's Ball*), and of late by William H. Gass (*Willie Master's Lonesome Wife*), it questions the entire premise of traditional fiction. All are writers with academic backgrounds, but two new novelists, Ronald Sukenick and Raymond Federman, have published the most straight academic writing and so offer the highest profile of theory behind such works.

The questions asked by fictionists of their style—"with what tenable attitude may one confront the difficult circumstances of contemporary American secular life and avail oneself of the good possible in it? How, in short, does one get along?"—were the subject of Sukenick's study in graduate school, which produced his first book, *Wallace Stevens: Musing the Obscure* (1967).[1] Federman's UCLA dissertation was on Samuel Beckett's early fiction, and he has followed Beckett's career with *Journey to Chaos* (1965) and several other studies. Both novelists are aware of the limits of fiction and how they must be overcome: Sukenick traversing the ground of familiar schools—Jewish-American, bohemian, arty experimentalist—and transcending their techniques, Federman striving

[1] Ronald Sukenick, *Wallace Stevens: Musing the Obscure* (New York: New York University Press, 1967). Subsequent references follow in parentheses.

beyond the final banalities Beckett has destroyed to create something new. What unites them is their distaste for the literature which suspends disbelief, and their search for a new form which can adequately handle the reality of twentieth-century life. As Sukenick told interviewer Joe David Bellamy for the *Chicago Review,* readers no longer believed that novels told the truth; they felt that the shabbily concealed make-believe of fiction was a poor substitute for the more immediate truth of biography, newsprint, and television. "Nobody is willing to suspend disbelief in that particular way anymore, including me," Sukenick complained; [2] hence in his fiction he turned to the theories which originally attracted him to Stevens. "Adequate adjustment to the present can only be achieved through ever fresh perception of it, and this is the effort of his poetry," states Sukenick in his book. "A fiction is not an ideological formulation of belief but a statement of a favorable rapport with reality" (p. 3); through the imagination, our most personally human faculty, we can organize external chaos into something fresh, perceptive, and palatable to author and reader alike. This is not idealism, for "The mind orders reality not by imposing ideas on it but by discovering significant relations within it" (p. 12). Finding the significant is the role of both poet and novelist: "When, through the imagination, the ego manages to reconcile reality with its own needs, the formerly insipid landscape is infused with the ego's emotion, and reality, since it now seems intensely relevant to the ego, suddenly seems more real" (pp. 14–15). There is a role for the fictionist even when, as Sukenick describes in the opening paragraph of his story "The Death of the Novel," "Reality doesn't exist. . . . Time is reduced to presence. . . . Personality has become, quite minimally, a mere locus for our experience." [3]

Sukenick's first novel, *Up* (1968), is a virtual rewrite of American fiction since World War II. His hero, named Ronald Sukenick, is a walking casebook on American fiction since the war, having the intellect of a Glass child, the paranoia of an Alexander Portnoy, the academic hassles of an S. Levin, and all the self-apparent persecu-

[2] Joe David Bellamy, "Imagination as Perception: An Interview with Ronald Sukenick," *Chicago Review,* 23 (Winter, 1972), 60. Reprinted in Joe David Bellamy, *The New Fiction: Interviews with Innovative American Writers* (Urbana: University of Illinois Press, 1974).

[3] Ronald Sukenick, *The Death of the Novel and Other Stories* (New York: Dial Press, 1969), p. 41.

tion of a Wallant or Bellow hero as he tries, moreover, to make it from Brooklyn to Manhattan. Sukenick also goes to the roots, using Orwell ("The worst thing is the cold. I've always hated being cold—maybe they know that. Outrage, humiliation and dread have all been absorbed into this one, final, petty discomfort") and Kafka ("At first I guessed the police wagon was bringing me, in the incidental company of a few routine suspects, to some garage where, perhaps, my car had been towed in consequence of a minor violation") [4] as examples of outdated creativity, mere fantasy reactions to a world demanding a new approach. War movies, television adventure, even the sexploitation book written by his own character are insufficient responses to the real world at hand. The new novel must do something else.

Up recounts the fictive progress of "Ronald Sukenick" toward a supreme fiction which adequately handles the real. As a critic, the actual Sukenick sees the same plot in Wallace Stevens's work, a sustained attempt at a "favorable rapport with reality." Stevens is not simply an idealist, and neither is Sukenick; finding the significant is the role of both poet and novelist. *Up* continues in this direction, seeking rapport with the real as a way of making it through life. Sitting alone yields only paranoid fantasies of secret police and prisons, so Sukenick's figure tries another approach. "On with the radio. Contra solipsism. Retreat from the ivory tower so baleful and maladive. Contact with Outside essential to nerves—if there is an Outside and if this is a contact." But the radio says merely, "The administration categorically denies Moscow's charge that the American delegation is trying to systematically wreck the tentative negotiations for a preliminary meeting to discuss the possibility of top level talks on a temporary cessation of the bilateral boycott of the conference to probe resumption of the nuclear moratorium" (p. 3), leaving Sukenick with little that is palpable. So he turns to his writing desk to create Strop Banally, a combination James Bond and the Marquis de Sade who is apparently on top of the world. Controlling money, women, and consummate power, Banally is familiar but dimensionless, like "somebody seen in a tabloid, on a screen, in a cigarette ad." "The fact is," Sukenick must admit, "that Strop

---

[4] Ronald Sukenick, *Up* (New York: Dial Press, 1968), pp. 1–2. Subsequent references follow in parentheses.

made up his past as he went along, so that by now it was impossible to separate the truth from the fiction'' (p. 4). He is credible only because he himself is an incredible cliché. Without a firm connection to reality, events run off into impossible fantasy, even those Sukenick faces in daily life. ''TEEN PUNKS TERRORIZE STRAPHANGERS'' reads a predictable headline, but as the elements themselves become all too predictable, with greasy, pimpled hoods stomping and raping innocent riders to the tune of transistorized rock and roll, fantasy fills the vacuum and takes control:

> They made her lie down on the table and were having a great time getting her to utter wanton obscenities, when a mounted policeman clattered up shouting, ''I'll teach you young punks. The law is officers first—and then their horses.'' With that he ripped open his fly whence burst a titanic cock erect that he grasped with his strong right hand and, plying it like a billy club, scattered the Gents hither and yon. As they ran to and fro in confusion, an immense woman in blackface and bandanna appeared on the scene and, to whines and plaints of ''Mammy,'' and ''We wuz only havin' fun,'' hauled them off harum-scarum while chanting in a fine and emphatic contralto, ''Mah o *mah,* but you evah-lovin boll weevils gonna *ketch* it.'' (pp. 32–33)

Young Dr. Sukenick's English department gives him no better grasp. Called by his chairman to discuss a case of cheating, he winds up being fired; yet ''We parted on the best terms, he cordial, me smiling—you would have thought he'd just given me tenure.'' Unreal. There has to be a better way.

Considered a failure by his friends, Sukenick examines their own approaches to life. Bernie Marsh is the successful assistant professor, an academic firebrand who advises, ''Make a mint and subscribe to *Dissent*. It's ridiculous. But essentially it's the only realistic point of view.'' Their mutual friend Finch has a different slant on reality, borrowing from one party to pay another. ''My life is nothing but a series of loans,'' he admits, yet he manages not only to survive but to turn a neat profit at the same time. Most apparently successful, however, is Ernie Slade, a real-life Strop Banally who edits ''an action-minded pacifist-anarchist quarterly,'' bankrolled by his heiress girlfriend. Like Banally, Slade is a master of women; but his way is not for Sukenick, who spends much of the book, including flashbacks to his adolescence, unsuccessfully trying to complete the sexual act. Even the one girl he patiently and painstakingly seduces turns out to have been sleeping with Slade all along. But Finch and Marsh are ultimately no more successful, the former locked into a life writing dog food copy while the latter's *Greening of America*-style essay appears in print typographically framed by advertisements of hopelessly Consciousness II America, one written by Finch himself. Early in the book Sukenick reviews his own would-be novel, *The Adventures of Strop Banally,* and remarks that "the author's compelling drive is to feel at home somewhere," to emulate "the mindless gusto with which Strop sails through life" (p. 40).

What young Dr. Sukenick teaches, however, slowly emerges as a more pertinent solution. "It would be hard," he tells his class, "to overestimate the importance of the imagination in confronting and even creating the world in which we live." Stevens, and before him Wordsworth, knew that art was "the invention of reality," seeking "a vital connection with the world that, to stay alive, must be constantly reinvented to correspond with our truest feelings" (p. 217). And so with his fictive art Sukenick slowly comes to terms with reality. His life in *Up* becomes the writing of *Up*. The job is not without its hassles—as on page 222, when he shows the manuscript (finished to that point) to his character Bernie Marsh, who complains of a missing scene. "Well I lost that scene actually," Sukenick admits. "I wrote a long elaborate Cloisters scene and then I left it in a book I returned to the library. I tried lost and found, everything, but I couldn't get it back." Sukenick the character finally succeeds when Sukenick the novelist completes his book. The climaxes are simultaneous: after years and chapters of fantasies and failures, Sukenick is invited to take both his girls to bed at once. " 'Why not? That would be a great scene. That's the scene that sells a novel you know.' " Once his unreal fantasies have been purged, Sukenick can call a party to celebrate (and complete) the last pages, to introduce his real friends ("Steve Katz here briefly on a special guest appearance from his own novel") and his real wife, Lynn, who when presented with her husband's sex fantasy replies, " 'Anyway I thought she'd be prettier.' "

Sukenick's triumph has drawn on Stevens and Wordsworth for

theoretic support, but his final product is simply unadulterated fiction. He has captured reality, not just presenting it but evoking it for the reader, as in descriptions of speeding through Brooklyn or simply killing a water bug. The last scene is lyrical in the finest, most responsible way; clearing his desk as the novel closes and the last partygoers leave, Sukenick looks across the tenement roofs to see a young boy, among the television aerials, making movements with a long, bare pole:

> He holds it above his head, moves it in a slow circle, and lowers it again. No sequel in the vacant air, no signal comes. He raises the pole, moves it in a circle, and lowers it again. The light is emptying from the sky. He raises the pole, moves it in a circle, lowers it. He raises the pole, moves it in a circle, lowers it. He raises the pole, moves it in a circle, lowers it. Again. Again. Again. The light empties from the sky. (p. 330)

He has not made the sun go down; the fact is that the sun will set anyway. But what a wonderful way to make the sun go down.

In *Up,* Ronald Sukenick has written a novel which is relevant, both in theme and technique, to our times. *The Death of the Novel and Other Stories* (1969), however, finds him refining his techniques and extending his themes toward not only the creation of reality, but also the communication of it. Technically more diffuse and inventive, *Death of the Novel* is an exceptionally well structured collection, recalling William Faulkner's dictum that such a volume should have the "form and integration" of a novel, being "an entity of its own, single, set for one pitch, contrapuntal in integration, toward one end, one finale." One need only read the stories Sukenick did not include, "One Every Minute" (*Carolina Quarterly,* Spring, 1961) and "The Sleeping Gypsy" (*Epoch,* Spring, 1959), to sense the delicate balance he has achieved. The former is a well-written but routine episode about buying a car. The latter, while not part of the careful progression of *Death of the Novel,* serves as a prolegomena to the volume. It is the story of a young man, Simon Lode, who chooses *not* to create a relevant world—who remains utterly passive through a series of adventures which determine his life. Whenever his inconvenient habit of self-analysis enters in, it reveals him headed "toward the blank center of a vortex"; yet he is constitutionally unable to help himself, missing job interviews and turning up in the wrong places at the worst times, and so he resigns himself to total passivity. He leaves his job and all affairs in favor of a cheap hotel and piles of pulp magazines; when these run out, he turns to TV and sits before it mesmerized until he dies. His last words are "I am no longer interested, nor do I care, to understand what happens to me." [5]

Unwilling to relate to reality, he dies. Rousseau's painting, "The Sleeping Gypsy," figures as a parable. " 'The Gypsy,' " his fiancee asks, " 'Does the lion eat him?' " " 'He picks up the mandolin and he plays to the lion,' " Simon replies. " 'And if the lion likes the music he becomes enthralled. If he doesn't like the music he eats the gypsy. But he might be dead. He might never wake up.' " [6] To survive in life, one must create successfully. Otherwise one dies, or never lives. *Death of the Novel* features six stories built around this theme. The husband in "The Permanent Crisis" can't relate to the world, having passively stumbled through life, even falling by chance into his marriage. "Something had always turned up," but now his life is at the crisis point and will remain there unless he can put things together. He finally does so as an artist, "listening to himself because there was nothing else to listen to and it sounded right and he wondered why, as if he were some kind of artist and knew he was right but didn't know how he knew." "All he could do was listen to and improvise, he would have to write that down on his page"; but as soon as he has a vital experience, it immediately threatens to outstrip language. "To have at least the words to repeat and understand swept him beyond his words of it." [7]

The technical process of capturing reality is where the stories of *Death of the Novel* take us. "Momentum" begins with the writer's overt statements about his goal, using a tape recorder so that "the speed of the tape is my form," real time and its artistic presentation being one. In one of the many glosses appended to his column of dictation, Sukenick describes the story's theme: "Real means locating the present in terms of the past / locating the self in terms of the present. Wordsworth, Proust" (p. 13). The occasion is a trip to

---

[5] Ronald Sukenick, "The Sleeping Gypsy," *Epoch,* 9 (Spring, 1959), 249.

[6] Ibid., p. 235.

[7] Sukenick, *The Death of the Novel,* p. 7. Subsequent references follow in parentheses.

Ithaca to find lodgings for a summer's residence at Cornell; the plot involves Sukenick's brief affair with a coed; and the resolution comes when he finds her as the person "to whom I could react both as what I was then [a student] and what I am now [a teacher]: unity of experience = reality of self" (p. 38). The mood carries over into the whole event; "i felt wonderful in fact the last time i felt just this way was when i finally left cornell both times singing like a maniac both times total enjoyment of driving a big american car on a smooth american highway with jazzy american music" (p. 39). Past and present are one integral Ronald Sukenick. Like the writer at the end of the previous story, "i had hold of myself had hold of my experience no had hold of a level of experience that i mustn't ever lose sight of again." What else is he writing for, he asks, but "to capture those moments in their crudeness" (p. 40).

"The Permanent Crisis" and "Momentum" are Sukenick's experiments with the theme and technique of capturing reality. "The Death of the Novel," a sixty-page story from which the collection draws its title, is the justification of Sukenick's work in the face of modern life's most severe problems. "Fiction constitutes a way of looking at the world," he begins; but since the world has gone relativistic, godless, and essentially inhumane, how is the writer to view it? Sukenick experiences this problem on many levels, thematic and technical, but emphasizes it all in the very act of writing the story:

> Meanwhile my chief concern is whether I'm going to be able to sell this unprecedented example of formlessness. How can you sell a current in a river? Maybe I better put my editor into it, he's a terrific editor, maybe that'll do the trick. A few more plugs like that and he won't be able to afford not to publish it. Or how about a little sex, that's the ticket. That's what this needs. A little sex. Okay, a little sex. (p. 49)

He tries many of the same ploys from *Up:* acting like Strop Banally with his fifteen-year-old girlfriend, being fellated by his mistress as he sits in his car, midday, at the busiest spot on campus. But the sexual escalation is to no point; as in *Up,* he proves irresponsible to his fantasies, and must come to terms with the real. "Lynn says she'll be in my story soon, but is getting impatient because, as she points out, she has her own interests. Isn't that a quote from my novel?'' (p. 82). Things are settling down for the close. He starts the countdown (''Here begins the last hour that I allow myself to finish this performance. Go'') and runs through a series of parables regarding time and self-identity. But the story will not hold together in any coherent form. ''Everything's blowing up, falling to pieces. Art dissolves back into life. Chaos. It's not the way I planned it'' (p. 100). All the illusions, of sex but also of time and place, dissolve. He puts on his boots and walks out the door, and we learn that Sukenick is not at Cornell with his mistress, or in the East Village with his girlfriend, but in the Connecticut woods with his wife. It's ''Saturday, January 20, 1968,'' the favorable notice of his Stevens book from the February 1 *New York Review* has just appeared, and ''I'm happy folks, and I wish you luck. I disappear around the bend. So Long. End of story'' (p. 102). Sukenick would be merely ingenuous were we to assume that he writes a formless story simply to reflect the formlessness of modern life. What he has done is *not* write a conventional story, to willingly fail in recapturing a reality. As his opening lecture notes stated, ''Reality doesn't exist. . . . Time is reduced to presence,'' and where art cannot discover significant relationships, the best thing to do is grab hold of the present experience and call it quits. What he *can* relate to now are Lynn and the woods. The writing of stories will have to wait until conditions are more favorable (the ultimate reality for any writer).

The stories following are imperatives to write, climaxed by the achievement of a viable form. ''Roast Beef—A Slice of Life'' is pure playfulness, understandable after the debacle of ''The Death of the Novel'' but simply there to prove a point. Leaving a tape recorder on at dinner produces a documentary record of reality, but does not create any significant relationship with it, as the characters themselves admit. ''What's Your Story'' presents the case more clearly: pursued by fantasies of a gangster (Ruby Geranium) and a police detective (Sgt. GunCannon), Sukenick is driven to the point where he must ''tell his story.'' Like the sleeping gypsy, he must wake, face the lion, and pick up his lute. Survival depends upon finding significant relationships with reality, and ''The communication of our experience to others is the elemental act of civilization.'' From these corollaries Sukenick is driven in search of a usable form, and almost at the last minute he finds it. "Start with immediate situation. One scene after another, disparate, opaque, absolutely concrete. Later, a fable, a gloss, begins to develop, abstractions appear. End with illuminating formulation. Simple, direct utterance" (p. 154). We see examples of these techniques in the earlier stories: the writer at his desk, the trip to Ithaca, the marginal notations, the several abortive fables from "The Death of the Novel." That story took Sukenick to the real, artless, yet uncommunicable woods ("So long, folks . . . I disappear around the bend"); he now is able to write "The Birds," an artistic formulation of his Connecticut experience. All aforesaid technical elements are present, helping Sukenick to write "the New American Poetry, the poetry of pure fact." No more sex, no more comedy; "I want to write a story that does a lot of infolding and outfolding. Majestic infolding and outfolding. No petty invective and venom. No comic bits, no noodgy satire like Shawanga Lodge casino. Calm, slow exfoliations. The life cycle of Whistling Swans. Inexorable curves of passion. Rise and fall of continents. Concrete. Innocent. Beautiful. No Meaning" (p. 157). The story even ends with an illuminating formulation, a simple, direct utterance:

birds

the

Were not the term abused beyond any form of recognition, one might term Ronald Sukenick a Realist. The heart of the battle in the last century was where one found reality, on the photographic surface or in the psychological depths below, or whether one went all the way into boundless Romanticism. Sukenick finds reality not by projecting subjective ideals, but by "discovering significant relations" with what is really out there. "This vivid sense of reality," Sukenick has observed with regard to Wallace Stevens, "is produced by the imagination and captured in some metaphor or description." [8] But the key remains finding, within the insipid landscape, something relevant; once that landscape is "infused with the ego's emotion," reality "suddenly seems more real." For Sukenick as re-

---

[8] Sukenick, *Wallace Stevens*, p. 14.

alist, the function of the imagination is not fabricating, or even in the closest sense creating (although both Sukenick and Stevens use that term in its broadest meaning). Its purpose is epistemological, to help man know—and to know in the sense of conviction, not rational proof. In a review of Robert Coover's *The Universal Baseball Association,* Sukenick objected to "what I would call pseudo-myth, an attempt to synthesize one's own version of traditional myth and impose it on contemporary experience as if it explained something." [9] The proper Realist does not want ideas about life; for experiential times, he seeks the experience itself, and prefers to live in agreement with existence rather than counterposed to it. That's real.

Raymond Federman, joining Sukenick in a search for viable forms of fiction, brings with him the authority of recent French fiction. "The Marquise went out at five o'clock"; because he couldn't bring himself to write that line, Paul Valery never became a fictionist, and Federman feels the same unease with such flat, prosaic forms. He left France for America in 1947, the year Camus was depicting Joseph Grand's novel-length effort to write a single opening sentence and discovering how inadequate was any language at all: "the attempt to communicate had to be given up. This was true of those at least for whom silence was unbearable, and since the others could not find the truly expressive word, they resigned themselves to using the current coin of language, the commonplaces of plain narrative, of anecdote, and of their daily paper. So in these cases, too, even the sincerest grief had to make do with the set phrases of ordinary conversation." [10] Federman will not settle for the set phrases or stock forms of ordinary fiction. His scholarship has traced the works of Samuel Beckett to their final destruction of these inadequacies, in drama and film as well as fiction: "The novel cannot truly pass for reality, the theatre is unable to create believable illusion, and the cinema, which essentially should communicate with the viewer simply through a series of moving images,

[9] Ronald Sukenick, "Not My Bag" (review of *The Bag* by Sol Yurick and *The Universal Baseball Association* by Robert Coover), *New York Review of Books,* 12 (March 13, 1969), 41.
[10] Albert Camus, *The Plague* (New York: Modern Library, 1948), p. 69.

must rely on sound or other devices to achieve its primary goal.'' [11]

Unlike the French New Novelists, who write at least in part from the philosophical imperative of phenomenology, Federman is closer to his fellow Americans—Sukenick, Barthelme, and even Richard Brautigan—who face the concretely social problem of an unreal reality and the irrelevancy of forms which depict it. Thematically, his novel *Double or Nothing* (1972) handles the now familiar story of adjusting to the incredible presence of contemporary American life. The solution, however, is in his technique, which foregoes the French approach of describing a phenomenologically real world in favor of making a reality more real: that of the book itself. Federman's peculiarly American disruption is that he works through the problems of French experimentation in his dissertation and academic publications, rather than in an indigenous artistic form himself. Hence when he concludes in *Journey to Chaos* (1965) that Beckett ''shows how the novel form is inadequate to gain an understanding of reality,'' [12] Federman is ready to leap into fiction himself, fully armed, with a new form which *is* adequate. ''Most works of fiction,'' he says verbatim in *Journey to Chaos* (p. 4), in his textbook-reader *Cinq Nouvelles Nouvelles* (1970, p. 4), and in *Double or Nothing* (1972, p. 150), ''achieve coherence through a logical accumulation of facts about specific situations and more or less credible characters. In the process of recording, or gradually revealing mental and physical experiences organized into aesthetic and ethical form, these works progress toward a definite goal: the discovery of knowledge.''

But Beckett's world, the modern world, resists such order; his heroes ''stand as witness for the failure of logic, reason, or whatever mental process man utilizes for the discovery and understanding of the external world'' (p. 47). Fiction cannot represent reality: this is what Beckett's novels prove. *Watt, Molloy,* and the rest are illusions which cannot reach the real, or vice versa; ''like incurable poker players,'' the characters ''are committed to their *mise en jeu,* and, win or lose, they cannot withdraw from the game until all cards are played, all the while knowing that the deck of fictional

[11] Raymond Federman, *"Film," Film Quarterly,* 20 (Winter, 1966–67), 51.

[12] Raymond Federman, *Journey to Chaos: Samuel Beckett's Early Fiction* (Berkeley: University of California Press, 1965), p. 132. Subsequent references follow in parentheses.

cards can be dealt and redealt endlessly'' (p. 202). Beckett's works are indeed stories and texts for nothing. Federman, however, would rather gamble, double or nothing. Hence in Melvin Friedman's *Samuel Beckett Now* (1970) he critically establishes that "the truth is that fiction is not reality, it is simply a language which tells its own story, its own true story," [13] and in his article "The Impossibility of Saying the Same Old Thing the Same Old Way" (*L'Esprit Createur,* Fall, 1971) that "All great fiction, to a large extent, is a reflection on itself rather than a reflection of reality." [14] By the time of *Ping* and *Sans* Federman finds that Beckett has removed fiction from its negative mistakes back to "degree zero," the ultimate situation, "the ultimate reduction and deprivation of fictional, human, and linguistic possibilities. And indeed one can wonder where Beckett can go from there. Beyond this total reduction of fiction, beyond this linguistic purification and designification, how can he possibly move any farther?" (pp. 38–39). *Le Depeupleur* is Beckett's answer, a cylinder of characters which are *seen*, rather than described or told: "A pre-historic condition of man and of fiction." Again, degree zero.

"I am not one of those who believe—and would have us believe—that the ultimate goal of Beckett's writing is silence, that his works propose only the extinction of the human race, and that everything he has written up to now was an effort on his part to reach silence and oblivion" (p. 43). As Federman ends his analysis of Beckett, he begins his own fiction. His critical lessons have taught him the futility of representing reality: logic, order, reason—indeed, anything placed upon the page—stand little chance of sustaining a counterfeit illusion. The novel has outlived its historical function as "news"; disbelief will simply not stand so much suspension. Stories and texts are for nothing, so with nothing to lose Federman can double his bet, that his "real fictitious discourse" (the book's subtitle) is not a sham illusion of some other life but just what it says, so many words on so many pages, bound together as a book the reader holds. Federman's bet is a sure thing; of all possibil-

---

[13] Raymond Federman, "Beckettian Paradox: Who Is Telling the Truth?" in *Samuel Beckett Now,* ed. Melvin J. Friedman (Chicago: University of Chicago Press, 1970), p. 114.

[14] Raymond Federman, "The Impossibility of Saying the Same Old Thing the Same Old Way—Samuel Beckett's Fiction since *Comment c'est," L'Esprit Createur,* 11 (Fall, 1971), 21. Subsequent references follow in parentheses.

ities, the book is certainly the most immediately real thing at hand, and from this point reader and author may together move in the positive direction from degree zero.

The writer, who through fictional persona or third-person omniscience makes a representation of the outside world, has been degraded by the New Novelists back to point zero. To reestablish a fictional voice, Federman divides its role into thirds: a third person, the protagonist, whose life becomes the accumulation of historical data in the usual sense; but also second and first persons—respectively the "inventor," who quite honestly creates these fake historical events, and the "recorder," who transcribes the inventor inventing. "Imagine the imagination imagining," as William H. Gass would say. Or look at these *three* things happening, which according to Federman together make a real story. The story: a protagonist, occasionally named Boris, emigrates to America and is through great labor initiated into a strange new world, simultaneously with the inventor's creation of these "events"—a very immediate task, attended by concrete preparations for writing (so many days alone for work, so many boxes of noodles for food, so many squeezes of toothpaste), all watched over by the recorder, who gives us the complete, eminently real fiction. As we learn from the preface (or, rather, from the "THIS IS NOT THE BEGINNING"):

> this is then how it all started at the beginning just like that once upon a time two or three weeks ago with the first person recording what the second person was doing as he planned the way he was going to lock himself for one year in a room to write the story of the third person all of them ready anxious to be to go to exist to invent to write to record to survive to become [15]

Two hundred and two pages of concrete typescript, the book is its own becoming, and hence claims legitimacy. Federman is covered: no shoddy tricks or trumped up illusions of reality; just so much writing, the book itself. But as he redeems the method of fiction, he also saves its substance. Granted that fiction is not history, but something made up; what then is more real: one phony "thing" the writer decides has "happened," or all the possibilities he *could* contrive, given his situation?

[15] Raymond Federman, *Double or Nothing* (Chicago: Swallow Press, 1971), p. 000000000 [Federman numbers the opening section with an accumulating series of zeroes]. Subsequent references follow in parentheses.

When you read a conventional story, says Federman the recorder, "what you are really reading are the answers to unformulated questions"—the story of the protagonist. But the inventor is as much a part of the action, so the recorder must note the "questions" as well, "To give the questions as the substance of his fiction rather than give the answers." The bet is double or nothing, since "If the questions are given first on paper then the reader can formulate the answers in his mind" (p. 150). The full reality of the writer's fictional construct is effectively transcribed, and the reader is given the chance to receive a truly unexpurgated text. Federman weighs the possibilities, shares them with the reader, and occasionally adds extra pages (p. 63, p. 63.0, etc.) to accommodate variations as he runs through Boris's life: coming to America at nineteen, a concentration camp refugee, to learn of subways, Negroes, jazz, sex, and other items of initiation. "Ahead of him like a huge hole (an enormous hollow sphere) lies his future" (p. 156), a void to be filled by the inventor, busily at work budgeting rent and stocking provisions, mostly noodles, for a year's hard writing. Such a novel can never die; another two hundred pages can be sustained any time, if you wish to refigure on the basis of a dollar a week (more or less) for the room. "IMAGINE THAT!"

Phenomenologists, including Maurice Merleau-Ponty, and many critics of the French structuralists as well, have regretted that we must deal with a second-order language, divorced from the thing signified but living only inasmuch as it points back to that thing. System replaces essence, which can be bad if the latter is what one searches for. From his studies of Beckett, Federman knows that literature fails when it claims to represent the other, so in his own novel he simply lets it represent itself. As such it is a system, an aesthetic one, but by claiming to be nothing else it becomes a real entity. Its substance is more vital because it reflects man's imagination, instead of a secondhand lie about what in a whole other world is real. The experience of life can of course be selected, shaped, and organized by art, and so may be best known; that was the battle fought over half a century ago by James and Wells. But once it is shaped by the imagination, the product is no longer life, nor even a sham representation. It is simply itself—and that recognition may be as great an advance as were Henry James's principles of selection so many years ago.

LITERARY DISRUPTIONS 134

Ronald Sukenick's novel *Out* (1973) may have been the climax of the disruptive phenomenon, as the new methods of fiction finally established themselves in a tradition and cleared the way for spatial experimentation on the American novel. "It is a curious anomaly," Anaïs Nin wrote in 1968, "that we listen to jazz, we look at modern paintings, we live in modern houses of modern design, we travel in jet planes, yet we continue to read novels written in a tempo and style which is not of our time and not related to any of these influences." [16] Despite the American novel's conservative stability of form since the experiments of the 1920's which followed James's theories of selection, Sukenick hopes to fulfill Nin's expectations. His story "The Birds" is, as we have seen and as Sukenick admits, " 'entirely without design precedent or orderly planning, created bit by bit on sheer impulse, a natural artist's instinct, and the fantasy of the moment' " (p. 163). That is part of his essay question which helps conclude the story: "Why do you think the police don't like that? Discuss." The critics don't like it for the same reason: such ruptures of convention thwart our desire to know real things in a calm and rational manner. Law and order must govern life, and anything that imitates it, too:

The police want an end to this disorder and that depends on one question and one question only: What is "ear-tree"? This in turn leads us to the matter of the identity of the man called "Ero." Destroy this as you read. It is printed in a soluble ink which you can lick off the page sentence by sentence. The ink has various flavors depending on the parts of speech to make this easier to understand and swallow.

To get to the point, the police suspect a plot, yet all they see is disorder. They suspect that disorder is part of the plot, if not the point of it. They imagine that they merely have to figure out the plot to put an end to the disorder. But they don't understand the plot and believe the explanation lies with the meaning of the word "ear-tree." In turn they believe that this meaning will lead them to a man called Ero. In real life Ero is an eminent ornithologist, but the police believe that he is the leader of an international liberation conspiracy, and that only in his mind are all the connections coherently held together, the whole matter fully understood. To make matters worse, they aren't even

[16] Anaïs Nin, *The Novel of the Future* (New York: Macmillan, 1968), p. 29.

sure whether Ero is dead or alive, or for that matter whether that is his right name. (pp. 168–169)

Sukenick, again a character, uses his head to decode an explanation, but "Unfortunately, when I showed this interpretation to Ero, he got very angry and tore it up. When I asked what his system of bird symbolism meant to him he replied: 'Nothing. A feather here and there, a color, a squawk, disconnected, opaque, totally self-contained, ending in a triumph of birdness, a song and soar, itself opaque and without equivalent, but the feelings ordered and defined—like that of a bird's song, or of its flight.' " So much for the police, reactionary critics, and the side of Sukenick which seek such forms. The true answer, found in a fortune cookie, reads, "Connections proliferate, meanings are dispelled. The traveler studies out his map" (p. 172).

Out is a study of connections, resolved not in any rational solution but as a spatial entity; only the feelings are "ordered and refined." Experience can be known only by recounting it, but the recounting can never be the experience itself. Raymond Federman took fiction to the crossroads where Sukenick now begins, writing a detective novel of sorts: "Hi. Experience is a code to be broken by the intelligence. I'm from the intelligence. Get your hands up." [17] The resulting fiction will not be a rational pretense of life, but a product of second sight, of the third ear: the total vision of imagination, ordering the real through transcendence, not representation. Sukenick's object of art replaces "abstraction, reduction, essentials, separation, and stillness" with "inclusion, addition, the random, union, and movement." Halfway from the Lower East Side of New York to Laguna Beach, California, his protagonist meets a Sioux medicine man, Empty Fox. "I want to write a book like a cloud that changes as it goes," he tells the Indian when asked his ambition. "I want to erase all the books," Empty Fox replies. "My ambition is to unlearn everything I can't read or write that's a start. I want to unlearn and unlearn till I get to the place where the ocean of the unknown begins where my fathers live. Then I want to go back and bring my people to live beside that ocean where they can be

[17] Ronald Sukenick, *Out* (Chicago: Swallow Press, 1973), p. 122. Subsequent references follow in parentheses.

whole again as they were before the Wasichus came" (p. 136).
Wasichus—"fat takers"—are what the Sioux call white men, despoilers of the continent and disgusting examples of the wrong way to live. The Indian people see the land as a community to which they belong rather than as a commodity to exploit, and are ideals of ecological balance who will neither exhaust the earth nor overload themselves to the point of death. But Empty Fox does more than show a white man how to live; he points a way of life for something else that's dying—fiction—and provides Sukenick with a model for sustaining his novel, which is what the book is all about.

Since 1968, when John Barth declared that literature was "exhausted" and Leslie Fiedler, Susan Sontag, Norman Mailer, and other critics cheered along that the novel at least was dead, Ronald Sukenick had been proving that there is a great deal of life to be rediscovered in the form. *Up* followed Barth with a generous indulgence in aesthetic allegory, but instead of painting itself into a corner or disappearing up its own fundament, *Up* pointed a way out. Is the real world too ponderous and depressingly dull to be captured in interesting fiction? Is it indeed a problem for art? " 'Sure,' " agrees Sukenick's aesthetic-allegorist character, who's involved with living the novel, writing it, and teaching literature at the same time. " 'That's what Wordsworth is talking about. He tells how as a kid he had to grab hold of a wall to make sure the world was really there, but when he grew up the dead weight of reality almost crushed the sense of his own existence. It's when the world seems oppressive, dead, or to put it another way, unreal, that I get the feeling I'm walking around like a zombie.' " To be of help, art must not describe but create reality, seeking " 'a vital connection with the world that, to stay alive, must be constantly reinvented to correspond with our own truest feelings' " (p. 217). Again, from the Stevens book, "When, through the imagination, the ego manages to reconcile reality with its own needs, the formerly insipid landscape is infused with the ego's emotion, and reality, since it now seems intensely relevant to the ego, suddenly seems more real." Insipid reality has been the downfall of many novelists of Barth's generation, who abandoned it entirely for self-indulgent aestheticism. But Sukenick applies to the novel what he sensed about art in general, and revitalizes fiction by having it do what it should: to make reality seem less unreal.

Out moves from the clutter and hassle of the East to the pure space of an empty California beach, leaving behind much of Sukenick's Brooklyn–Greenwich Village–Lower East Side material, and also his forms, which served as parodies of themselves and were— for the Sixties—the style of the time. "It's easier and sociabler to talk technique than it is to make art," Barth admitted in his Literature of Exhaustion essay, but as a form—*Lost in the Funhouse* in fiction, Warhol's soup cans in painting—the result was an apparent dead end.[18] "In the late 60's innovation in general was good, now innovation in general is bad," Sukenick complained recently in the *Village Voice.* "The Pop movement, though it had its moments, was a disaster for the arts. It introduced a confusion of criteria that has yet to be straightened out. Meantime Poppers and Nonpoppers alike pay for their exploitation of the artmart in the name of avant-garde." [19] Or as Gilbert Sorrentino explains in *Imaginative Qualities of Actual Things,* in a passage Sukenick is fond of quoting:

> Art is the undoing of many a hick. I think of those twangy painters slaughtered in the floods of coin the pop art machine produced. Only people like the Pope can engage pop art and survive. I remember having lunch with one of these painters once, in McSorley's. Something about painting the pickle on my plate, my ale, etc. My face was stiff with my polite smile. I can hear that flat Nebraska speech right now. Or take the New York School. Joy of decadence. Wait till the folks in Terre Haute see this! How to put it? That New York becomes a chocolate bunny, and that they print their work, in teams. You see them together, nice young men and women, looking at that bunny. They are amusing, glib articulators of arrested development. Their noses are pointed toward the Iowa Writers' Workshop, or some other Workshop, some Seminar on Contemporary Poetry. Safe in hamburger heaven. Back home again in Indiana.[20]

A few years before, Sukenick had reported the similar destruction of a geographical avant-garde, the Lower East Side of New York, which as the East Village did as much harm as Pop and despoiled a necessary haven, making the survival of serious American art all the less likely. His essay "Live & Let Alone on the Lower East Side"

---

[18] John Barth, "The Literature of Exhaustion," *Atlantic Monthly,* 220 (August, 1967), 29.

[19] Ronald Sukenick, "The Ecology of Literature," *Village Voice,* 18 (April 5, 1973), 26.

[20] Gilbert Sorrentino, *Imaginative Qualities of Actual Things* (New York: Pantheon, 1971), pp. 233–234.

ran in the *Village Voice* during the week of Robert Kennedy's assassination, and was typographically framed by memoria to the slain
candidate.[21]

Yet Sukenick is no writer of obituaries for a dead tradition, nor is
he a New York snob resenting the midwestern tourists invading (and
taking over) his home. His art moves west, toward a California
emptiness, which he sees as anything but derogatory since it is first
established in Empty Fox's South Dakota—a tremendous, surging
sensation of freedom, of liberation from space, even from sound, so
that a resolution seems for once possible. There's always the danger
of an ersatz California clutter, which can happen even in the Black
Hills. "The Wasichus make Disneyland of all this so they can sell
it," accuses Empty Fox; "they get the Indians to pretend they're Indians they make believe these beautiful mountains are beautiful they
pretend magic is magic they make believe the truth is the truth
otherwise they can't believe anything. There is a place with a bill-
board of a mountain in front of the mountain you Wasichus can't see
anything without pretending to see anyway you don't believe it" (p.
141). For Sukenick imagination is an essential faculty of the perception, but through Disneyland it becomes a cheap version of the
willing suspension of disbelief. "Is Disneyland really necessary?"
he asks in his contribution to Raymond Federman's book, *Surfiction.* "It's as if we have to make believe before we can work up the
confidence to believe, as if belief in good conscience were the privi-
lege of primitives or maybe Europeans." [22]

What the primitives have is a better hold on reality, not just
because they are "in closer touch" but because of their ability to
sense the totality of what's going on in the world. "We Sioux are
not a simple people," writes the old medicine man Lame Deer in his
book *Lame Deer, Seeker of Visions.* "We are very complicated. We
are forever looking at things from different angles." [23] Empty Fox
is a man in Lame Deer's tradition, and so is Juan Matus, through
whom Carlos Castaneda learned ways of approaching the world
which Sukenick was at the same time finding appropriate for fiction.

[21] Ronald Sukenick, "Live & Let Alone on the Lower East Side," *Village Voice,* 13
(June 13, 1968), 6–7, 17–18.

[22] Ronald Sukenick, "The New Tradition in Fiction," in *Surfiction,* ed. Raymond Federman (Chicago: Swallow Press, 1974), p. 40.

[23] John (Fire) Lame Deer and Richard Erdoes, *Lame Deer, Seeker of Visions* (New York:
Simon and Schuster, 1972), p. 201.

"For a sorcerer, reality, or the world we all know, is only a description," and in *Journey to Ixtlan* Castaneda tells of Don Juan's "efforts into leading me to a genuine conviction that what I held in mind as the world at hand was merely a description of the world: a description that had been pounded into me from the moment I was born." [24] Castaneda's "mistakes" sound strikingly similar to the failures of modern fictionists to keep up with their world. " 'Your problem,' " says Don Juan in *A Separate Reality*, " 'is that you confuse the world with what people do. . . . The things people do are shields against the forces that surround us; what we do as people gives us comfort and makes us feel safe; what people do is rightfully very important, but only as a shield. We never learn that the things we do as people are only shields and we let them dominate and topple our lives' " [25]—and also our fiction.

Ronald Sukenick would revalidate our imaginations so that we can look at our environment in a real way. For Don Juan, it's a question of two distinct manners of perceiving. " 'Looking' referred to the ordinary way in which we are accustomed to perceive the world, while 'seeing' entailed a very complex process by virtue of which a man of knowledge allegedly perceives the 'essence' of the things of the world." [26] For fiction, it is the ability to transcend a mere describing of life (always a danger in this most mimetic of forms) to a revelation of the truth of experience, which may be at odds with the popular consensus. To stop the world—to call a halt to having one's personal, provisional view of things as absolute— may be a key to the cultural turnabout so apparent around us, reflected in Sukenick's new style of fiction and Castaneda's great popularity. It is echoed in the appeal environmentalist Aldo Leopold has for such a broad intellectual audience as biologist Paul Shepard responding in the *North American Review* and philosopher of ethics John J. McMahon, commenting in the *New Republic:* "Leopold has learned that to absolutize our narrow wavelength of perception is sheer arrogance," and a sure way to extinction. [27]

[24] Carlos Castaneda, *Journey to Ixtlan: The Lessons of Don Juan* (New York: Simon and Schuster, 1972), pp. 8–9.

[25] Carlos Castaneda, *A Separate Reality: Further Conversations with Don Juan* (New York: Simon and Schuster, 1971), p. 264.

[26] Ibid., pp. 16–17.

[27] Paul Shepard, "Hunting for a Better Ecology," *North American Review,* 258 (Summer, 1973), 11–15; John J. McMahon, "Reconsideration: *A Sand County Almanac,*" *New Republic,* 168 (March 31, 1973), 30.

To arrive at "seeing," Castaneda learned in *Ixtlan*, one must stop the world. " 'Stopping the world' was indeed an appropriate rendition of certain states of awareness in which the reality of everyday life is altered because the flow of interpretation, which ordinarily runs uninterruptedly, has been stopped by a set of circumstances alien to that flow." [28] Don Juan's task, as exercised in *A Separate Reality*, "was to disarrange a particular certainty which I shared with everyone else, the certainty that our 'common-sense' views of the world are final." [29] The imagination, Sukenick has said, makes reality seem more real—and Don Juan's methods are a paradigm for liberating oneself from the obstructed, unimaginative view. " 'The little smoke removes the body and one is free, like the wind,' " and the metaphor of bodily flight becomes "the sorcerer's capacity to move through nonordinary reality and then to return at will to ordinary reality." [30] The fullest possibilities of vision—not just the documentary records of what historically occurred—are what Sukenick wants for his fiction, and Don Juan is the master who can show how " 'There are worlds, right here in front of us.' " [31] As Walter Goldschmidt wrote in the foreword to the first Castaneda volume, *The Teachings of Don Juan: A Yaqui Way of Knowledge*, "By experiencing other worlds . . . we see our own for what it is and are thereby enabled also to see fleetingly what the real world, the one between our own cultural construct and those other worlds, must in fact be like." [32]

Although such wonderful revelations of the world are the goal of art, and certainly proper business for the novel, the vitality of Sukenick's theories have made them controversial. Tom Wolfe, who asked "Why aren't they writing the Great American Novel anymore?" and answered "because the new journalists were doing it better," granted Sukenick "a curious ground in between, part fiction and part nonfiction." [33] But other critics—notably Pearl K. Bell in *Dissent*—have cast him among "such celebrants of unrea-

[28] Castaneda, *Journey to Ixtlan*, p. 14.
[29] Castaneda, *A Separate Reality*, p. 19.
[30] Carlos Castaneda, *The Teachings of Don Juan: A Yaqui Way of Knowledge* (Berkeley: University of California Press, 1968), p. 161.
[31] Castaneda, *Journey to Ixtlan*, p. 165.
[32] Castaneda, *The Teachings of Don Juan*, p. viii.
[33] Tom Wolfe, "Why They Aren't Writing the Great American Novel Anymore," *Esquire*, 78 (December, 1972), 272.

son, chaos, and inexorable decay as Kurt Vonnegut, Jr., John Barth, Rudolph Wurlitzer, Donald Barthelme, and a horde of mini-Jeremiahs crying havoc in the Western world.'' [34] The real issue, as Nathan Scott revealed, is that the ''inward liberation'' of the imagination ''offers us an effective release from the bullying of all the vexations of history''—and, incidentally, that this aesthetic has been so demonstrably adopted ''by the hordes of those young long-haired, jean-clad, pot-smoking Bohemians who have entered the world of psychedelia.'' [35] But Sukenick had critically covered himself since 1967, in his *Wallace Stevens: Musing the Obscure*. ''The mind orders reality not by imposing ideas on it but by discovering significant relations within it,'' and even freaky old Don Juan agrees that '' 'Things don't change. You change your way of looking, that's all.' '' [36] If the teachings of Don Juan offer one cumulative lesson, it is that the ''other realities'' bear just as much objective weight as the provisional realities we live day to day, and that the only responsible way out is ''in.'' ''Our particular moment and place is located in our heads and our bodies,'' Sukenick wrote for the *Partisan Review* symposium on the New Cultural Conservativism, ''and at the risk of solipsism we must start there and push outward.'' [37] As he told interviewer Joe David Bellamy in the *Chicago Review*, ''I don't want to present people with illusions, and I don't want to let them off cheaply by releasing their fantasies in an easy way. If the stuff has done that, okay. It's probably inevitable in any case, but it's not really the kind of thing I'm trying to do. . . . Because what that does is allow people to escape, obviously, from reality, and I want to bang them with it.'' [38] Or, as he's said in casual conversation, part of the Disneyland rap, ''the less we use our imagination the more somebody else is going to use it for us—by manipulating us.''

Fiction plays its tricks, but in his own *Village Voice* essay on Castaneda's work Sukenick insists that ''All art deconditions us so that

[34] Pearl Kazin Bell, ''American Fiction: Forgetting Ordinary Truths,'' *Dissent*, Winter, 1973, p. 26.

[35] Nathan A. Scott, Jr., '' 'New Heav'ns, New Earth'—the Landscape of Contemporary Apocalypse,'' *Journal of Religion*, 53 (January, 1973), 12–13.

[36] Castaneda, *A Separate Reality*, p. 50.

[37] Ronald Sukenick, ''On the New Cultural Conservatism,'' *Partisan Review*, 39 (Summer, 1972), 450.

[38] Bellamy, ''Imagination as Perception: Interview,'' p. 70.

we may respond more fully to experience.'' The wealth of that response has been his aim since *Up,* through the efforts to capture the truth of experience in *The Death of the Novel and Other Stories,* and most recently *Out.* While others would let fiction die, Sukenick argues that its great advantage ''over history, journalism, or any other supposedly 'factual' kind of writing is that it is an expressive medium. It transmits feeling, energy, excitement. Television can give us the news, fiction can best express our response to the news. . . . No other medium, in other words, can so well keep track of the reality of our experience.'' [39] Technically, his novel *Out* proves that a novel can be a concrete as well as an imaginative structure, and offers art for the eye and the page-turning hand as well as for the mind. But ultimately Sukenick's genius rests with his discovery that the reality we know is only a description, and that ''The power of a sorcerer is the power of the feeling he can invest in his description so it is felt as a persuasive account of the world.'' [40] This same persuasiveness is the measure of good fiction, which Ronald Sukenick brings to life, proving what an unexhausted novel- ist can do.

In 1973 Sukenick and Federman each completed new novels. Proving that fiction was not at all exhausted, both *98.6* and *Take It or Leave It* [41] were the most sustained, discursive works the authors had yet written. *98.6* was literally a coming ''in'' after the last pages of *Out.* R's companion, Sailor, begins the novel by bringing his boat back to shore—where America has been transformed into a living metaphor for what our life has become. The place is called Frankenstein. This first section of the novel is recounted in the form of dreams; each is dated, the first on Sukenick's birthday, July 14. ''People who grow out of the earth and never get too far away from it never forget they're going back into it. Lesson of the pyramids pressing down. Death is power. Only those who know it can survive and then only for a while no escape.'' This is Frankenstein. It was

---

[39] Ronald Sukenick, ''About Fiction in General and OUT in Particular,'' publicity release from Swallow Press enclosed with review copies of *Out,* p. 2. Expanded as ''Innovative Fiction, Innovative Criteria,'' *Fiction International* #2–3 (Spring/Fall, 1974), p. 133.

[40] Ronald Sukenick, ''Upward & Juanward: The Possible Dream,'' *Village Voice,* 18 (January 25, 1973), 31.

[41] Both novels were in manuscript at this writing. *98.6* is scheduled for spring, 1975, publication by the Fiction Collective, New York.

also the time of the Aztecs, " 'A civilization so deadened by its own proliferation that only death can renew its commitment to life.' " For these circumstances the author dreams a formula: love ÷ power = sadism + masochism. In his dreams he is trapped in a sacrifice: "Now he wonders if there might be some way out through magic. Or through dream. Or acceptance. Or withdrawal. He decides the best thing would be to play his role through."

There is little difference between these nightmares and the world he lives in. "7/14 he puts a dime in a slot and gets a newspaper. The series of murders that turned out to be part of another mass murder now turns out to be part of a series of mass murders." He knows that "the country is racing like a wheel out of contact with the ground a loose flywheel spinning faster and faster till it tears the whole machine apart," but cannot slow down himself. Cultivating his dreams may not be an answer, but at least it provides a passage, suspending things in contemplation:

> 10/13 he has a thing and that is that he's only interested in the extraordinary. He thinks that the extraordinary is the answer to The Problem. For example he'd rather sit home and watch the hummingbird at the feeder outside his window than go through the motions of a common seduction with nothing special about it. Hummingbirds are special birds the way dolphins are special animals they have a certain perspective a kind of openendedness about their intelligence that makes him feel kin. Ariel was a hummingbird. He believes in powers meaning the extension of the ordinary to the point of the incredible and he believes that these powers are real though they can't be willed and they belong to everyone who isn't blinded by the negative hallucination of our culture. A negative hallucination is when you don't see something that's really there.

He wants his life to be extraordinary. "His way of doing this is by falling in love all the time," the metaphor of establishing a relevant relationship from *Wallace Stevens: Musing the Obscure.* But even more than resolution in his personal life, the author seeks an articulation. He makes pangrams (sentences using each letter of the alphabet only once) and is fascinated with the letters left over, since they are pure of any previous meaning. "He believes that one day he's going to find a word this way that will be the key to The Problem a word that didn't exist before." For now he's left with a collage of our culture: newspaper clippings of mass murder, torture, and genocide which are the extraordinary become the mean in a country beyond his nightmares.

"Frankenstein" is composed of a group of semi-documentary accounts of the monstrous conditions of our life. Section Two, "The Children of Frankenstein," is a narrative account of a West Coast commune's attempt to transcend this actuality. Sukenick draws on the tradition of several books popular in the late 1960's and early 1970's—Ray Mungo's *Total Loss Farm,* Alicia Bay Laurel's *Living on the Earth,* and others—to explore a level of truth beyond their surface details of alternative lifestyles and countercultures. Departing from Frankenstein, "The only rule they have is not to talk about the past and that's not a rule it's just everyone seems to feel that way." What the children hope to leave behind is the Great Depression: "It was the kind of trauma that can only happen when you wake up from a dream you think is the real thing." But the children are in fact building their own monster, which is what they playfully call the communal yurt which they are constructing from society's cast-off material ("The house begins to look like a collage made from the wreckage of a supermarket"). The commune develops the same diseases as Frankenstein:

> In his previous life Paul was involved in politics. He used to be a civil rights lawyer but gave it up as futile at least during what he calls the Dynasty of the Million Lies. That's why Altair always comes to him with Krypton's problems. They are usually of a quasi-legal kind having to do with Earthmen like the grocer and the county clerk and the sheriff. There's nothing that Paul wants to do less than anything connected with his work in his previous life. In his new life he's a handyman or rather he's learning how to be a handyman. There seems to Paul nothing better in life that you could do than to be able to work with your hands repairing things patching things together making useful things out of whatever happens to be at hand old wood discarded bottles tin cans rusty machine parts the detritus of the culture. If he can help it with Altair he tries to get away with explaining to him some basic principles and letting Altair go on from there. Like that Earthmen deal in a unit of exchange called money and a set of rules called law and above all an intangible difficult to explain to Altair called power that has nothing to do with the power of cosmic energy and in fact tends to work against it. Do you realize says Altair after Paul gets done explaining why they won't give him his food

stamps that if the Sun were hollow over a million Earths would fit inside?

No.

Do you know that our galaxy has millions probably billions of stars
like the sun and a lot bigger?

Yes.

Can you grasp the fact that beyond our galaxy millions and millions of other galaxies can be seen by telescope? Can you grasp that?

No.

And you talk to me about money and shit like that I mean all I want
is our food stamps.

Worse threats come from the outside, particularly from a paranoia-
inspiring cycle gang. On the inside, the children are no longer able
to live and work together. Energy is misdirected and escapes. The
children of Frankenstein have established only a false normalcy, as
misleading as the constant temperature—98.6—of the girl who
loses her child in a miscarriage.

In the commune is a novelist—Ron, who changes his name to
Cloud, who has chosen these children to be his characters and will
simply describe what they do for his book. But he is also examining
his own way of life, and that's as much a subject of the novel as the
commune's narrative. "Cloud has tried up and he has tried out. Neither of them works. Maybe nothing works. That's possible. They'll
take you part of the way but they won't take you where you want to
go. That's because you don't want to go there." He's tried speeding
up, the method of *Out,* but rejected it, since speeding is unsatisfac-
tory. That's what he discovered in "Frankenstein." Here it has a
name: Skimming. "Cloud doesn't want to be a Skimmer. Skimming is part of The Problem maybe it is The Problem at least that's
what he thinks now."

Instead of speed, the resolution in *98.6* will be one of ideal synthesis. The answer is found in the State of Israel. "This novel is
based on the Mosaic Law the law of mosaics or how to deal with
parts in the absence of wholes," we learn at the beginning of Section Three, "Palestine." This part of *98.6* is hypothetical, based in
part on an implied "if":

I wouldn't go on this way if that Arab wasn't such a lousy shot.
They wouldn't tolerate this kind of writing under a Nixon administration. What Arab. The one where Rosy Greer broke his neck when he

tried to assassinate Kennedy after the California primary two shots
and all he could do was nick an ear lobe. Sirwhat. That's why Robert
favors high collars and wears his overcoat turned up. Yes Robert
that's how he's known to his intimates Bobby's only for the press.

The entire life of Israel is an ideal, just the opposite of what was suffered in Frankenstein:

> Here in Israel we have no need of cars. . . . Automobiles have long
> been exiled from the cities and towns where transportation depends
> on various beasts of burden camels burros oxen. There are even a few
> llamas to be seen and modern experiments are underway with giraffes
> and zebras which in fact antedate the use of the horse in Africa and
> the Middle East. We have an extensive intercity monorail system and
> colorful barges make their way among the canals. Environmental
> planning is largely given over to the artists with the result that the na-
> tive beauty of the Holy Land has been preserved and even height-
> ened. The prestige of novelists along with other artists is such that no
> intermediaries are needed between ourselves and the public and we
> have the means to produce and distribute our own work which is in
> constant demand. Artists are recognized as the creators not only of
> esthetic works but of reality itself all scholars scientists and rabbis are
> acknowledged as artists each working in his appropriate sphere
> even politics is considered to be a certain kind of art. I live in a kib-
> butz called The Wave. The Wave is situated beside the sea and our
> main ritual activity is surfing.

Waves are continuous, filling the gaps so apparent in Frankenstein.
"The waves are the improbabilities of the unknown that one perceives through intuition. Introspection. Empathy. A sense of
beauty. Through imagination." It is the missing dimension which
the author tried to bridge through love in Section One, through
searching for the Missing Lunk in the wilderness of Section Two.
Surfing is only a lighthearted external manifestation, something like
the sufi dancing of William Irwin Thompson's ideal community.
"Perhaps the material of the body is quite incidental to the rhythms
of the body the rhythms of life which may move through the body
then leave it behind. If consciousness affects matter by regulating
entropy, then the State of Israel is a crucial factor." Above all, it is
a product of the imagination, the same force Sukenick argues for in
all his work. It is like a state of consciousness: the State of Israel.

The way to enter it is through imagination, expressed by the fictionist's language, for "language is the connection between spirit and matter after all."

The climax of the State of Israel is the Moment of Luminous Coincidence. It has its sexual equivalence, but in its purest form it is the happening of art, the moment reached as Ronald Sukenick completes his third novel, *98.6:*

Walkin with ma baby on the side of San Francisco Bay I'm listening to the blues I'm about to have A Moment of Luminous Coincidence I feel it coming on it's coming together JESSELONECATFULLER JESSE'SEARLYLIFEWASSPENTRAMBLINGBETWEENGEOR GIATEXASANDCALIFORNIAWHEREHEEVENTUALLYSETT LEDALONGTHEWAYHELEARNEDSPIRITUALSBLUESRAGS ANDHILLBILLYSONGSHEADAPTEDTHEMALLTOHISTWEL VESTRINGGUITARSTYLEBUTITWASNOTUNTIL1950THATH EDECIDEDTOSEEKOUTWORKASAMUSICIANHEHADTROU BLEFINDINGRELIABLESIDEMENSOHEBECAMEAONEMAN BAND playing all the instruments AT THE SAME TIME I'm sitting in Laguna Beach with the cat on my lap listening to the San Franscisco Blues by Lone Cat Fuller AT THE SAME TIME trying to finish my novel AT THE SAME TIME trying to forget about it I pick and open a book at random Fuller Buckminster quotes Fuller Margaret all attempts to construct a national literature must end in abortions like the monster of Frankenstein things with forms but soulless and therefore revolting we cannot have expression till there is something to be expressed AT THE SAME TIME trying to forget about it a trip to a bar in a distant city turns out to be called Frankenstein franks and steins AT THE SAME TIME this morning's mail with an article by Ihab Hassan on Prometheus Frankenstein Orpheus AT THE SAME TIME thinking when you try to sew Orpheus back together what you get is Frankenstein AT THE SAME TIME hearing on the radio Lon Chaney died a few miles away from here in San Clemente AT THE SAME TIME reading this record jacket thinking yes ramble around settle in California pick up this and that adapt it to your own style without sidemen the novelist is a one man band playing all the instruments AT THE SAME TIME playing along on a kazoo AT THE SAME TIME entering The State of Israel AT THE SAME TIME orchestrating the whole thing toward those Moments of Luminous Coincidence when everything comes together AT THE SAME TIME sorry to leave Southern California the sun

the waves the mother tongue another bungled paradise AT THE
SAME TIME happy to be heading for San Francisco another chance
AT THE SAME TIME tieing up my novel AT THE SAME TIME
my life is unravelling AT THE SAME TIME the novel is bungled
fragments stitched together AT THE SAME TIME everything is
seamless perfect not because because because but AT THE SAME
TIME playing the blues letting it go it is as it is. Another failure.

98.6 has proposed not an ideal, but an ideal of an ideal, where the
work of art holds the beauty in suspension so that it might be sustained. As Sukenick describes it, "*98.6* attempts the impossible and
fails, but it fails with a verve, depth of feeling and balance that
renders failure, as the human condition, of greater value than success." And the ideal is no less urgently perceived.

Raymond Federman's *Take It or Leave It* proposes another ideal
state: the Etats-Unis, America, to be discovered by a recently im-
migrated GI (the same protagonist as in *Double or Nothing*) on a
thirty-day leave from the army. Federman uses a similar typograph-
ical play and sexual thematics to plot his character's ideal:

AMERICA—I was going to cross it from one end to the other
from right to left
from New York to San Francisco
going right through the middle
I was going to plunge into it—enter into it
the way you plunge into a big fat women—legs $s p_{r e a d} p_{a r t}$

The army has provided his invitation in the form of a draft notice.
But once inducted, the protagonist suffers. Ridiculed for his French
accent and heritage, he is even more the buffoon for having wanted
to join the navy as a frogman. Instead, he is sentenced to a banal existence among the illiterate, hillbilly paratroopers of the 82nd Air-
borne Division at Fort Bragg, North Carolina.

Take It or Leave It has more of a narrative than *Double or
Nothing,* but only as a frame for the author's linguistic play. The
form of Federman's novel is much like the phony love letters his
protagonist, the Cyrano of the regiment, writes for five dollars
apiece:

I simply piled the words in any old way
up and down
and sideways
metaphors
upon metaphors
contradictions
on top of
contradictions
I exaggerated full blast
I played with words
with double meaning and
triple meaning
without any respect (I must confess) for grammar
syntax   style   spelling
logic
disposition   punctuation
it was just a matter of filling up space
PAGES
and
PAGES
approximately a bucka page I kept telling myself
so!   when I ran out of stuff to say
I would simply copy   borrow   steal
plagiarize   all
over
I would simply open   the place
a book
any   book
(usually romantic novels
or classical tragedies)
and copy whole passages
verbatim et litteratim
throwing in a few foreign words here and there
(usually French words)
those guys didn't know the difference
that's for sure   and the more I gave them the more they loved it
what creativity   what spirit of creativity I was in   Ah
in those days

At a conference held by the Center for Twentieth Century Studies
at the University of Wisconsin-Milwaukee titled "Imagination

Dead Imagine: The Self-Reflective Artwork in Contemporary Literature and Art,'' which brought together for the first time Federman, Sukenick, Sorrentino, and others, Federman argued for a new criteria for art. His topic was "Imagination as Plagiarism," and he proposed that "both these MYTHS—that of the sacred creator, and that of originality—in much of recent art and literature have reached their end." As literature begins to reflect upon itself and turn inward, mocking itself, questioning, examining, undermining, challenging itself, it demolishes "its purpose, its intentionality, and even its own means of production and communication." Having cut itself away from "its sacred source (from the authority of its creator and his precious imagination)," literature stepped out of its frame— which had limited its scope for so long. Freed from such confining seriousness, literature could make the most of its prime constituent, language. With its frame acknowledged as the arbitrariness of convention, the author could choose any form he wished. In the love letters written by the Cyrano of the regiment, Federman picked the simple discipline of making all his lines the same length, changing words until all the characters lined up. In the process he was forced to produce language we might not have otherwise read:

> Fort Bragg, Fayetteville, N.C.
> (Let us say), January 15, 1951

> *My Darling, My Treasure, My Lovely Adorable Juicy Peach, My Dear M******,*

> *You cannot imagine how much I thought of you, last night, under my lonely khaki blankets, alone, in my narrow military bed, surrounded by the heavy oppressive solitude of life in the army. I felt, in me, through my flesh torn by the pain of your absence, a suffering of indefinable nature. The inner emptiness of my soul rang with shrieks and groans: it was as though needles and knives of fire were piercing my body.*

> *Unable to endure this atrocious suffering, I took my private member in my hands, and feeling it palpitating savagely like a lost animal, no a giant fruit rather, an enormous banana which was pulsating there outside my own body, I began to shake it, to handle it, to squeeze it with all the furor of my desire, and suddenly I felt flowing, full blast, Woosh! a delicious juice that I wanted to transmit immediately to your essential organs. Ah! my dearest reservoir, how much I wanted to feel, at that moment, the wild sugars of my fruit flow in you like a torrent. How I wanted to hear them burst inside of you like a gun, like a cannon (a 75 millimeters), no, like a volcano, in the deepest parts of you, in your most secret, tender, wild and unexplored regions.*

> *Ah! if only you knew, my golden treasure, how much I missed you, how much we missed each other, last night, when, alone, naked and vibrant under my*

military blankets, at the most solitary moment of night in North Carolina my eyes closed, I saw the image of your sweet and soft body sneak next to mine inside my bed. Ah! dear feathery chicken, adorable pitless peach of tender flesh, smooth and rosy body of such lovely round contours, velvety like a mushroom without tail, little sugared snail, landscape of my inner dreams, if I could only make you feel, YES, how much I wanted (last night but also every night) to penetrate you, with what endless passion, what a huge desire I wanted to rush towards you beyond the mountains, beyond the valleys, beyond the rivers and the canals from under my khaki blankets of loneliness, then you would have known the dimensions of my love, depth of my pool of pleasure, despair of my trembling hands, sources of my loneliness and frustration. I see in my dreams your voluptuous and greedy hips and your adventurous thighs, hardly ripe, avidly opened to receive, there in that moist furry triangle of yours, the harvest of my nocturnal cultivation.

Federman's fiction is of course influenced by his scholarship on Beckett, and on those New Novelists who followed. But in *Take It or Leave It* he has managed to combine the best features of both worlds: the linguistic play of the New Novelists, plus the narrative joy so common to recent American works. There is a story to Federman's novel, and although it exists for the sole purpose of providing an excuse for the author's imaginative and linguistic pyrotechnics, it is sufficient to provide interest far beyond the boredom Donald Barthelme complained of in the works of Robbe-Grillet, Ricardou, and Sollers.

Liberated from contextual seriousness, Federman's work can at one and the same time hold us with the story and delight us with how it is told. As a narrative complication, Federman's outfit departs for snowjumps at Camp Drum in upstate New York, taking with it the young corporal's travel pay. In pursuit of the regiment, Federman's Buick Special leaves the highway and plunges into a ravine, saved only by being caught in the branches of a giant pine tree. The protagonist finds his way back to the freezing highway:

AN AUTOMOBILE! I jump in the middle of the road wave to that monster gesticulate shout scream stamp my feet rage raise my arms and legs (in spite of the pain and the fatigue) hop leap rear roll myself on the ground crawl climb on top of a snow pile fall on my ass pull out my handkerchief (full of blood) wave it furiously cuff my trembling hands around my mouth to shout louder
stick out my thumb!

He is rescued by a beautiful young woman, who takes him off for a night of sexual and linguistic abandon. But when he rejoins his regiment, the captain says he must make a jump—which he does, breaking both arms and both legs, sending him to the hospital for the balance of his leave, which is cancelled. His trip across the country? Cancelled. America? Cancelled. As the French edition concludes, with its appropriate colloquialism:

> FOUTU! C'était foutu l'Amérique . . . Foutu le grand voyage . . . et la grande découverte . . . et la traversée . . . les montagnes les plaines les plateaux à perte de vue . . . les beaux paysages . . . les rivières . . . le Mississippi . . . le Missouri aussi tout là-bas . . . Les grandes auto-routes . . . les routes non pavées . . . FOUTUS . . . les indiens et les cowboys . . . FOUTUS . . . et aussi le désert rouge . . . les serpents à sonnettes . . . les animaux sauvages . . . tout le barda . . . les grosses usines dans le midouest avec les gadgets . . . et le saucisson . . . les gangsters à Chicago . . . la roulette à Las Vegas . . . et le pétrole au Texas . . . tous les beaux rêves. . . . les movie stars à Hollywood à moitié à poil . . . FOUTU tout ça . . . et la grande virée dans le nord dans le sud en passant par le milieu . . . à travers tous ces états unis . . . FOUTU le grand voyage . . . et Los Angeles . . . et Frisco . . . FOUTU . . . [42]

Writing on fictionist Paul Metcalf, Ronald Sukenick praises what is the form of Federman's fiction as well, the "novel as a concrete artifact like a painting or a sculpture, a worked object in three dimensions." Like *Double or Nothing, Take It or Leave It* is essentially the author's own experience. "Again we get a collage of fact and experience," Sukenick writes, "but what excites me here—what I feel most energy flowing from—is that the experience is direct experience, the author's presumably factual experience interacting with the fact of history." [43] In *Double or Nothing* Federman told two of his stories: the first of immigration to America, the second of *writing* about that immigration. The artistic triumph is the second, for that very self-reflection is the hardest aspect of the story to capture. *Take It or Leave It* has a similar quality, as its narrator tells a second-hand story (told to him long ago) to a group of critics, who often comment, question, or interrupt with their complaints. "And admittedly," Federman said in Milwaukee, "there is nothing

---

[42] Raymond Federman, *Amer Eldorado* (Paris: Editions Stock, 1974), pp. 176–177.
[43] Ronald Sukenick, "On Paul Metcalf," *Lillubulero* #12 (Winter, 1973), p. 49.

more absurd, more nightmarish, more laughable than to sit in a room—within four walls—day after day, month after month, year after year, to create an imaginary situation and fictitious characters ('that nightmare thingness' of which Beckett speaks) by the mere process of lining up words on pieces of paper.'' With John Barth's literature of exhaustion, Federman has agreed that writing can be tedium; but against it he argues for a revival in writing, which in turn most actively engages the reader in a revival of reading, all by simply recognizing the frame of the story for the arbitrary device that it is. And by not taking itself so seriously:

> Perhaps the only way for the writer to escape the tedium and the anguish of such a self-imposed torture is to LAUGH at his own activity. And it is well known, in fact, that many writers, even those whose fiction depicts the most oppressive, most horrendous, the most tragic situations (and this was the case with Proust, Kafka, Celine, and many others I am sure) could be heard laughing within the walls of the chambers where fiction was being shaped. Only laughter, indeed, can save the writer from jumping out the window, from blowing his brains out, or from simply walking away from his absurd undertaking.

SIX

Gilbert Sorrentino

Gilbert Sorrentino is a veteran poet who began publishing fiction just about when critics were announcing its demise. *The Sky Changes* (1966), *Steelwork* (1970), *Imaginative Qualities of Actual Things* (1971), *Splendide-Hotel* (1973), and his massive work in progress are examples of the novel's renaissance, as it turns from an attempt to capture life through belief-suspending conventions back toward the truths which those conventions slight. Sorrentino is of the same generation and of similar influences as the poet Robert Creeley, whose descriptions of his own innovations in fiction are a good introduction to Sorrentino's work. In the preface to his first novel, *The Island* (1963), Creeley describes how people "want an island in which the world will be at last a place circumscribed by visible horizons." A conventional novel would make such a structure of life, but "This island is, finally, not real, however tangible it once seemed to me. I have found that time, even if it will not offer much more than a place to die in, nonetheless carries one on, away from this or any other island." [1] Creeley finds his own solution in the form of the short story, since "The story has no time finally," as he continues in the preface to his story collection, *The Gold Diggers* (1965); "Or it hasn't here. Its shape, if form can be so thought of, is a sphere, an egg of obdurate kind. The only possible reason for its existence is that it has, in itself, the fact of reality and the pressure. . . . The old assumptions of beginning and end—those very neat assertions—have fallen away completely in a place where the only actuality is life, the only end (never realized) death, and the only value, what love can manage." [2]

Sorrentino sees time as the enemy too, and seeks the same actuality beyond it, but without abandoning the novel. Revealing images

[1] Robert Creeley, *The Island* (New York: Scribner's, 1963), p. 5.
[2] Robert Creeley, *The Gold Diggers* (New York: Scribner's, 1965), p. 7.

are well expressed in shorter forms, but life is large, its truths are larger still, and it would be a shame to sacrifice the novel's great scope simply because its methods have been abused. "In the mind there is a continual play of obscure images which coming between the eyes and their prey seem pictures on the screen at the movies," Sorrentino quotes from William Carlos Williams as the epigraph to *Imaginative Qualities*. "The wish would be to see not floating visions of unknown purport but the imaginative qualities of the actual things." To keep hold of these qualities within the novel's broad expanse is Sorrentino's aim. His work has characters who refuse to be drawn, action which will not be resolved, and a theme which resists statement—instead, his novels are rich in the materials of life which will not let themselves be perverted into the mistruths of conventional signals, those instructions to the reader which lead to a presupposed meaning and hence obscure the writer's truth. Sorrentino tells us constantly that it is all made up, that his truth resides not in some moral we draw from the life he has imitated but rather from his invention before us on the page:

> Bunny Lewis, Christian name Joanne, nee Joanne Ward. This is going to be a tough one, because there is something of the archetypal about her. Which is to say, what I have in my hands here is a cliche—before I start. This will not relieve me of the necessity of presenting this woman to you, of course. I could leave her out of the book, but there is much of interest here, she at least will illuminate something of our friend Guy. . . .
>
> She was born in a little town in New Jersey named Boonton. I know this town, it's very grim. It will be better to have her born in a Long Island town, for our purposes, which will soon become dazzlingly clear. Frightfully clear. So, she's in Long Island, you can pick your town, let's put her on the North Shore. Her mother was the kind of woman who served all her meals off unmatched tableware. "Each piece chosen separately, and with love." You know what I mean. . . .[3]

Throughout *Imaginative Qualities* the author comes at us, raging at the restraints of his art yet breaking them hilariously at will. God save the character he comes to dislike. *It's only a story,* he keeps

---

[3] Gilbert Sorrentino, *Imaginative Qualities of Actual Things* (New York: Pantheon, 1971), pp. 89–90.

reminding us, to counter fiction's congenital defect of the illusion becoming real.

No art can succeed when it is willingly mistaken for reality, as the strategy of Sorrentino's story, "The Moon in Its Flight," demonstrates.[4] Therefore in his novels truth lies not in the facts of life, but in the author's design from them. Against the novel's habitual limitation to the linear and domination by time, his innovations offer the possibilities of space, where meanings—and not merely our suppositions of meaning—may at times reside. Sorrentino's first novel, *The Sky Changes,* is the emotional record of a several weeks' trip from Brooklyn to San Francisco, culminating in the separation of the protagonist from his wife and children. "To discover, after 7 years, that he doesn't know her, his wife. And money available, to leave with, to go to Mexico? And why not, to face her there, break out of that cocoon that he has carefully wrapped himself in, the mummy. . . . Perhaps again to find her, have her come to him again, once, in the night, turn quietly toward him in the bed, and not in desperation, nor out of pity, God. To be able to say again 'I love you' and not with his tongue full of dust, filth of the words, the lie, and her lie returned. . . ." [5] The protagonist would "hide from the time that crushes him" (p. 21), taking the cross-country trip "to repair an event, a congeries of events, with the useless aid of space" (p. 123). But there is no change; "He had left a stable misery, a possible misery, to find the same misery on the road" (p. 39), mistaking the occasional peace and joy he finds from time to time "with a peace that he could only have made solid through his own manufacture, his own mind" (p. 74). He assumes that "the future journey would be a constant spiral upward, upward, until, in Mexico, they would all find themselves perfectly happy, perfectly reconciled. . . . And how he wanted to salvage his life" (p. 70). But they never reach Mexico, and there is no reconciliation.

Time would thwart him, the conquerer, but instead space oppresses them. "The Midwest is made up of police and drive-ins," the South of Confederate soldiers who "glared out over the har-

---

[4] Gilbert Sorrentino, "The Moon in Its Flight," *New American Review* #13 (1971), pp. 153–163. This story is discussed at length in the prologue to this volume.

[5] Gilbert Sorrentino, *The Sky Changes* (New York: Hill & Wang, 1966), p. 11. Subsequent references follow in parentheses.

vested cotton fields with the identical eyes of the state trooper at the picnic grove.'' Las Vegas is more appalling, for there is "at each end of the town, blackness, death, the howling wind off the Mojave bringing tons of red dust into the street.'' Even the Southwest threatens with "a treacherous sort of cold, flat and primeval as the earth, a being of enormous power and one which held sway along with the space it filled.'' And nowhere is there an answer. "Wherever they drive, in whatever direction (now toward the south), they seem to head into clouds, into rain, as if even the weather is trying to tell him that the whole thing is stupid. The one thing he did not really know is that it would be stupid. He expected nothing in particular to change on the road, but he did not expect it to be stupid'' (p. 36).

The protagonist's answer, and Sorrentino's meaning, will not be found in the linear structure. Such familiar signals of conventional fiction obscure the writer's truth, or, as Sorrentino says in his essay on William Carlos Williams's fiction, "allow the writer to slip out from under the problems that only confrontation with his materials can solve.'' [6] That the separation comes at the end of the line does not imply that the truth resides there; although *The Sky Changes* establishes a chronology, it does not hesitate to jump ahead and back in "the story" if that is where meaning leads, and the last of the sections (all of which are set up in travel-note form) comes not in the separation at the end of the road, but back several weeks and several hundred miles:

Albuquerque, New Mexico

Before making the move to Taos, he and the driver and M drove to Albuquerque to get a used refrigerator from a man well set up in business there. He was a heroin addict, but wealthy, and so his habit interfered with nothing, his wife was an alcoholic, spending her life in bed, propped up on pillows reading mystery novels and drinking a couple of fifths of brandy a day. They got the refrigerator on the trailer and went back in to have a drink before they started the long trip back to Sante Fe. The man sat in the living-room, his eyes clouded, smiling secretly. His wife weaved around the room unsteadily, making a pitcher of Martinis, getting ice and whisky, laying

[6] Gilbert Sorrentino, "The Various Isolated: W. C. Williams' Prose," *New American Review* #15 (1972), p. 196.

out cheeses and crackers. They sat in the twilight, fast moving into the room, a great rhomboid of crimson sunlight fixed on the wall behind the man and his wife, who now sat together, hand in hand. He was eating eclairs and drinking coffee and she gulped at her Martini, then poured another. There was a momentary lull in the conversation, and he gazed at the couple. They were looking at the three guests, smiling, their eyes calm and blank, their fingers intertwined. They sat, decorous and serene, staring into the gentle sunlight, blunted, secure from each other, and from everything else.

Sorrentino's second novel, *Steelwork,* is a spatial portrait of a South Brooklyn neighborhood during 1935–51. The subject is change, and the book's form comes to terms with this reality, grasped imaginatively. Sorrentino is taken with the imaginative possibility of things, as he describes a group of "Ghost Ships" awash half a mile out from the ferry slips:

They were to be destroyed as targets by the Navy. They were to be repaired and used as ferry boats. They were to be sunk as breakwaters up at Hell Gate. They were to rot forever.

The rats were bigger than dogs and could chew your arm off. They'd killed at least two kids who went swimming years ago. They spoke in tongues. The gypsies caught them and ate them. They were what they made bubble gum from, and glue. They came on shore all together once every ten years. Don't go near the water's edge at night. At full moon.   .   .   .

There were men, alive, in the neighborhood, married, with children, who had been scheduled to sail into death on these ships. They didn't know who they were. At sunset they would glow red in the last pink rays from Jersey. Ghosts and rats.[7]

For his imaginative possibilities, Sorrentino draws upon the imaginative substance of a childhood and adolescence in the neighborhood, such as for "Sexology: 100 Facts" ("45. You can get stuck in a girl's asshole. 46. You can get stuck in a girl's cunt and they have to operate on you. 47. You get the clap easiest from toilet seats in the subway" [p. 47]). But foremost is the sense of loss, the feeling of missing an empty lot or of seeing one there where something else used to be: "They walked slowly to Triangle Park, past

[7] Gilbert Sorrentino, *Steelwork* (New York: Pantheon, 1970), pp. 85–86. Subsequent references follow in parentheses.

the new extension on the Cities Service lot, the holy coalbox gone, past the new A & P on the old tennis court, past the new Baptist church, the doorway right where they used to roast mickeys'' (p. 59). Although they are dated, the sections are not arranged in chronological order, for, as in *The Sky Changes,* true emotion follows space more accurately than time. Hence the book ends not in 1951, when the neighborhood has been destroyed, but back in 1939, on a cold night when the protagonist has a sense of what is to happen:

It was bitter cold, the light was dying fast over the bay to the boy's left, and he hunched closer to the fire, stirring and poking at the mickeys black and charred in the center of the roaring embers. The lot was empty, all the other kids gone home long ago—his mother would kill him when he got in, but he had to eat these mickeys, even if he had to eat them alone. Across the street, the entrance to the park was choked with bulldozers, cranes, heaps of rock and brick and soil, where they were tearing out a gigantic strip of grass and trees to make a highway to connect with the new parkway going through along the bay, and then out the length of Long Island. It was sad to see the park going like that, the tunnels would soon have highway streaking under them, instead of the old, cobbled walks he knew. One crane stood harsh silhouetted against the sky, and he stretched his hands out toward the fire. It was almost completely dark now, and he looked behind him, across the lot, to see if anyway someone was there. But there was nobody. The wind blew the dust up in swirls and then straight across the lot at him. He turned his back to it and listened to the fire scream and sing as the blast hit it, the mickeys split in two now, snow-white meat bursting out from the thick char of the skin. He pushed his stick into them, one after the other, and lofted them from the fire smoking. It began to snow. (p. 177)

Steelwork is a collage of moments, of no time because they are all past. As Sorrentino concludes with an after-epigram, '' 'They are all gone into the world of light.' ''

Imaginative Qualities of Actual Things is Sorrentino's most fully realized expression of the novelist's proper role. Thoughout he fights against the poor writing and misguided aesthetic that characterizes so much of recent conventional fiction. ''Television and the film are by some thought to be more subtle and sophisticated than prose," he claims, "because they can register [the] cliche in one swift image, that is, the cliche is somehow ameliorated because it passes swiftly. One bad still worth a bad short story." [8] All Sorrentino as novelist can do is constantly remind the reader that these are not scenes from real life, that he is constantly making them up before one's very eyes. For this his techniques are various: when a character mentions in a letter that "I don't want to hurt Lou any more than I've already hurt him" the author responds with a footnote—"*This sentence is an example of automatic writing" (p. 10). Other times he speaks directly. "These people aren't real. I'm making them up as I go along, any section that threatens to flesh them out, or make them 'walk off the page,' will be excised. They should, rather, walk into the page, and break up, disappear: the subtlest tone or aroma (no cracks, please) is all that should be left of them. I want you to remember this book the way you remember a drawing" (p. 27). Most of all, he tells the reader, "you don't need to know anything—see a movie" (p. 34), or "If you're interested in the kind of bag Dick would carry, check it in O'Hara—he'll tell you unerringly" (p. 228). As for what happens to his characters in time, "it is all mixed up, how can I tell you what I don't really know?" Sorrentino's aesthetic for fiction is different: "In this book, I'll muddle around, flashes, glints, are what I want. It's when one is not staring that art works. In the middle of all the lists and facts, all the lies and borrowings, there will sometimes be a perfect revelation. These curious essences. The shape and weight of a sentence that lances you" (p. 34). These are the heart of Sorrentino's fiction, "because these things themselves are the plot. They carry all the meaning. Isolate flecks" (p. 124).

Above all Sorrentino is painfully honest about his work and what he is doing with it. The sense of the book itself—as it was for James Kunen, Raymond Federman, and so many other disruptive fictionists—is the most real quality of his writing. "It must be obvious by now," Sorrentino confesses on page 79, "that I'm having a great deal of trouble making up things about [Guy Lewis]. (I feel as if I've been looking out the window at Stuyvesant Town for fifty years.) What I'd really like to do right now is read *Tristram*

---

[8] Sorrentino, *Imaginative Qualities of Actual Things,* p. 12. Subsequent references follow in parentheses.

Shandy—but with this fifty-thousand-dollar advance half spent, it's write, write, write." Again, "I'm getting into trouble with these people, as soon as I stop watching them, they start moving around on me, and acting in an utterly uncharacteristic way. . . . The prose obeys me, but these people that hide behind the letters are doing God knows what" (p. 79). Therefore he rivets his meaning in the prose, and not in the real-life people. As for anything else—hair color, luggage style, who's really sleeping with whom—Sorrentino could care less. "In other words, the reader is asked to write the book that I have no interest in writing" (p. 122).

The irony, and success, of Sorrentino's method is that in the process of his anti-illusionistic, self-consciously artistic writing, brilliantly conceived persons, places, and things are brought before the reader's eyes. Especially when Sorrentino dislikes a character, his prose is superb. "I've got some stories to tell you about this lame," he begins his chapter on Anton Harley, "they'll make you throw tacks and broken glass in front of his bike" (p. 159). He hates him so much that "I'll do my best to make him totally unbelievable" (p. 160), and it thereby follows according to the axioms of Sorrentino's fiction that Harley will be one of his best-drawn people. "Greed was Anton's problem," we learn, and what's interesting is not how he got that way, but how he looks now, "let's say with three cheeseburgers in each hand" (p. 155). He visits friends in the evening, and soon "becomes distracted, passes his hand through his hair. Anton hungry is like a heroin addict who is just feeling the beginnings of junk need. He must eat. He *must* eat! HE MUST EAT! Eat, eat, eat, eat!! His eyes glaze over just a little. If you're a woman, close your legs. Or open them, if that's your pleasure. Anton eats anything. But there was nothing to give him. And, you will recall that I said his host had not cashed his paycheck. An interesting situation. Let's observe Anton in action here" (p. 161). His friends will not play baseball with him for fear "that he might eat the bats." Later, at a party, we peripherally observe Anton, eating paper napkins. Sparked by his hate for this purely literary character, Sorrentino runs him through scene after scene to his detriment, and the result is wonderful, unexhausted fiction:

> With one hand, Anton is reading *Serenade,* with the other, he is
> pushing three slices of pizza into his mouth, there is pizza all over the

floor, and from the looks of things, it seems as if Anton has been—
fucking—some of the pizza. There is a banging from the bathroom,
and muffled shouts. That is his latest girl, whom he has locked in so
that she can't share any of the pie. He'll let her out soon and let her
eat the pizza that he came over, if she wants it. (p. 167)

"If this were only a novel," Sorrentino concludes, "I could really
explore him for you," but it is to the reader's benefit that in conventional terms—luggage, etc.—Sorrentino hasn't. Instead we have the
random, isolate flecks which make *Imaginative Qualities* a brilliant
work of art.

Sorrentino will not tell stories. "Prose will kill you if you give it
an inch, i.e., if you try and substitute it for the world. What I am
trying to do, through all this murk, is to define certain areas of destruction" (p. 112). Pictures, music, sculpture, practically anything
made by the imagination can tell stories, but in conventional terms
only fiction *must,* and Sorrentino finds that unfair. His most recent
work of fiction, *Splendide-Hotel,* demonstrates how the novel may
transcend story—how it may exist outside the world it pretends to
deal with. The day-to-day passings of life provide the easiest structure for fiction, but as a form it can become so self-effacing that the
sense of art may disappear. In order that a day in the life, or a
slice of it, may not become confused with the work itself, Sorrentino chooses for *Splendide-Hotel* a completely artificial structure, the twenty-six letters of the alphabet. Like a baseball game, his
fiction seeks play and virtuosity within well-defined limits: "The
excellent pitcher," he tells us, "mixes up his deliveries, all of
which, however, travel sixty feet, six inches." And like a game of
baseball, the work of fiction "does not stand for anything else. It
exists outside of metaphor and symbol," [9] which explicitly disrupts
the tradition of Malamud and Roth, who would have the baseball
game—and ultimately their novels about it—carry mythical significance, along with lessons for living in our daily world.

"The poet is not an interpreter but a revealer," Sorrentino has
written of Jack Spicer, in whose works things do not connect but
"correspond"; and in his own *Splendide-Hotel* he shows that "that
minuscule flash, that occasion, has more value than the most

[9] Gilbert Sorrentino, *Splendide-Hotel* (New York: New Directions, 1973), p. 16. Subsequent references follow in parentheses.

staggering evasion by explanation of the real. Who will believe it?'' [10] Sorrentino's aesthetic is built around language itself, ''divorced from the image'' and disavowing objective as well as subjective connections, since he will not allow his egoism to impose a lie on what is ''true chaos.'' Beware those who do. Motion exists to be frozen, time to be stopped. ''One would almost think that in this peace there is some sort of truth'' (p. 49).

Through the employment of the imagination the proper artist lays bare the mundane. ''The writer,'' we learn, ''wishes to make this sense exact, or why bother? Precise registrations are beautiful, indeed. The popular novelist deals with feathery edges, one gets a 'tone.' One gets a 'feeling,' '' but at worst it degenerates into a ''story.'' '''I know a writer,'' Sorrentino continues, ''who wished his prose to be transparent so that only the growth of his story would be in evidence. What I mean by 'story' I leave up to you. Perhaps it is the story that the unemployed auto worker tells his friend over red beer. The juke box is playing 'Your Cheating Heart,' another story. . . . The story ends with a quiet grace and one of the men gets up, spits phlegm on the floor, and plays Hank Williams again. They are totally unaware that they are in fashion'' (p. 13). Real-life stories, the kind that prompt reviewers to say the paranovelist ''has created a character who can stand alongside Raskolnikov, Flem Snopes, and Yossarian. He lives, he breathes, he walks off the pages!'' (p. 42). Sorrentino keeps us on the pages, like a painter keeps us on the canvas, to have us sense ''Movement of the line, its quantity, the sifting of the vowels, the A's breeding in decay'' (p. 8). There are phrases that will change your life, whether by Lester Young or by novelists like Gilbert Sorrentino.

Splendide-Hotel, like all of Sorrentino's work, refuses to be a bland metafiction, recounting in second-order terms a story about another reality. It is, as the author once wrote of Hubert Selby's work, something made—''it won't go away, a new thing has been made in the world.'' [11] He achieves this result by closing directly with his material, not allowing any of the ''conventions'' of the novel—originally designed as aids—to stand in the way. In poetry,

---

[10] Gilbert Sorrentino, ''Jack Spicer: Language as Image,'' *For Now* #5 (1966), pp. 28–29; Sorrentino, *Splendide-Hotel,* pp. 16–17.

[11] Gilbert Sorrentino, ''The Art of Hubert Selby,'' *Kulchur,* 4 (Spring, 1964), 29.

and in the poetic techniques which spill over into fiction ("They're married," Sorrentino told interviewer Jack O'Brien),[12] the image "is unfortunately more a concomitant of artifact than it is a way of employing the poem as a lever whereby the mind may be moved to apprehend the real." [13] Fictional conventions are even more likely to efface rather than communicate true meaning, and to become almost Pop Art objects in themselves:

> [John] O'Hara will use a description of a vulgar character's tasteless clothes as an indication of that character's inherent vulgarity: the reader is clued as to what to think. Occasionally, as if to show you that it's nothing but a gimmick, he'll write a story like *Exactly Eight Thousand Dollars Exactly:* one character is held against another, the reader is given over to the movement of the story in terms of these characters' appurtenances and acts, and at the end, he turns the tables on you, a writer's joke. Which certainly indicates that he knows that these tricks are simply that, no more.[14]

But the reader does not always know, and that is how the story may be lost. As Sorrentino argues in his essay on Williams's fiction:

> The novel must exist outside of the life it deals with; it is not an imitation. The novel is an invention, something that is made; it is not the expression of "self"; it does not mirror reality. If it is any good at all it mirrors the process of the real, but, being selective, makes a form that allows us to see these processes with clarity. Signals in novels obscure the actual—these signals are disguised as conversation, physiognomy, clothing, accoutrements, possessions, social graces—they satisfy the desire that we be told what we already know, they enable the writer to manipulate his book so that it seems as if life really has form and meaning, while it is, of course, the writer who has given it these qualities.
>
> It is the novel, of itself, that must have form, and if it be honestly made we find, not the meaning of life, but a revelation of its actuality. We are not told what to think, but are instead directed to an essence, the observation of which leads to the freeing of our own imagination and to our arrival at the only "truth" fiction possesses. The

---

[12] John O'Brien, "Imaginative Qualities of Gilbert Sorrentino: An Interview," *Grosseteste Review,* 6 (1973), 70.

[13] Sorrentino, "Jack Spicer," p. 31.

[14] Sorrentino, "The Art of Hubert Selby," p. 38.

flash, the instant or cluster of meaning must be extrapolated from "the pageless actual" and presented in its imaginative qualities. The achievement of this makes a novel which is art: the rest is pastime.[15]

As Sorrentino's four novels argue themselves, "The invented character can only reveal the actual if he is the creature of the novelist's *invention*, not a signal whom we stupidly think is doing something 'believable.' " [16]

William Carlos Williams was for years Sorrentino's mentor, and the two sides of their correspondence are well documented in each author's papers.[17] "Williams once wrote me that he was glad that I was working steadily again," Sorrentino remarked when he began a five-year period as an editor at Grove Press, "because, he said, that was good for my art; that some of the energy needed to sustain one's self on the job slopped over into the writing, and made one steadily industrious." Hence Sorrentino admires the seventeenth-century metaphysical poets because "they were so involved in the world as men of the Church, commerce, etc. etc., that all of it slopped over into their art, their images were strong and connected with their own steady pushing through the years." [18] The highest praise he has for a poet, for a novelist, is that he "has given us the world back, not distorted, but made realer by his vision." [19]

Gilbert Sorrentino has strong affinities with the disruptivist group, in method (moving it even further away from "story") but also in background. His essay, "Remembrances of Bop in New York, 1945–1950," is an intellectual parallel to LeRoi Jones's work in *Blues People* and *Black Music*. For the generation emerging just after World War II, so radically estranged from everything past, the bop jazz of Charlie Parker and Dizzy Gillespie offered the same sense of identification, expression, and style that the blues provided for an entire culture. Moreover, it was a disruptive musical style in itself, and it is no surprise that practically every innovative fictionist writing today has strong roots in this jazz of the late Forties and early Fifties—John Barth as a jazz drummer; Raymond Federman as

[15] Sorrentino, "The Various Isolated," pp. 196–197.
[16] Ibid., p. 198.
[17] Sorrentino's papers were acquired in 1974 by the University of Delaware.
[18] Gilbert Sorrentino, review of *Watermelons* by Ron Loewinsohn, *Kulchur* #2 (1961), p. 91.
[19] Ibid., p. 92.

a tenor saxophonist who played with Parker; [20] Kosinski as a member of the Iron Curtain youth whose first contact with the West came through Willis Conover's jazz broadcasts on the Voice of America; LeRoi Jones as a jazz critic; and Barthelme, Sukenick, and Sorrentino as aficionados. The move to innovative literature was obvious: "Certainly," argues Sorrentino, "the chances are that a young man, who in 1945 didn't 'dig Dizzy,' would never in 1955 read Charles Olson." [21]

And like Ronald Sukenick, Sorrentino suffered through the "floods of coin" generated by the Pop Art movement in the 1960's, which almost slaughtered a whole generation of artists and critics. "Kitsch into 'Art': The New Realism" is his argument against this style, where "The packaged food, ill-baked cakes, comic strips, etc., are not in any way the *causes* of the tawdry and vulgar in America," which might be suitable matter for art, "but they are the *effects.*" [22] Sorrentino's deepest affinity with Sukenick, however, goes beyond their common Brooklyn birthplaces (68th Street, Avenue I) and young manhood in Greenwich Village. In his study of Wallace Stevens, Sukenick was careful to warn against the dangers of uncontrolled subjectivism, that the proper artist "orders reality not by imposing ideas on it but by discovering significant relations within it." [23] This is the very argument Sorrentino uses against the image, or even more against the Deep Image. "What Deep Image seems to be," he reports, "is a contempt for the thing which is given, a contempt for things as they are as merely crust, or surface, or shell. This must inevitably lead the poet away from his task of interpreting the world *qua* world, into a position from which he imposes his *will* upon the things of the world." This Sorrentino sees as old-fashioned romanticism, even platonism. "It is the *creation* of seemingly intelligible forms, but the avoidance of *extracting* intelligible forms from seemingly unintelligible things (which I see as

[20] Federman's story, "On Jazz," *Partisan Review*, 40 (Winter, 1973), 65–73, is subtitled "remembering Charlie Parker or how to get it out of your system," and draws upon his associations with these jazzmen.

[21] Gilbert Sorrentino, "Remembrances of Bop in New York, 1945–1950," *Kulchur*, 3 (Summer, 1963), 70.

[22] Gilbert Sorrentino, "Kitsch into 'Art': The New Realism," *Kulchur*, 2 (Winter, 1962), 23.

[23] Ronald Sukenick, *Wallace Stevens: Musing the Obscure* (New York: New York University Press, 1967), p. 12.

the artist's main function)." [24] Hence the worthlessness of deliberately obscure poetry: "None of these images reanimate the world in any useful way; on the contrary, the world becomes, through them, a place which is absolutely unintelligible, a chaos whose only order exists in the artist's insistence upon his 'interpretation' " (p. 81). The best praise Sorrentino finds for the poet he is reviewing is to compare him to Sukenick's model, Wallace Stevens: "There is the same penchant in both for the treatment of the two opposites of imagination and reality, the same understanding in both that one is not 'better' than the other but that the poet must make reality useful through the employment of the imagination, and conversely, imagination, to be legitimate, must be inseparably linked to reality" (p. 82). At worst, "once a writer accepts the validity of this [totally subjective] inward world business, he can grind out poems on an assembly line," products of a lazy sensibility which fails to do the essential job of the artist: to make reality more, and not less, real.

The genius of Gilbert Sorrentino's fiction is that while drawing out reality it ultimately stands for itself, and is therefore rich in the materials of life which will not allow themselves to be perverted into the mistruths of conventional "novelistic" signals. His work succeeds because its method controls its substance, instead of the other way around—which for all the forms of art is surprising and innovative only in the novel. A study not of things that happen but of how things happen, his fiction avoids the bland business of parahistorical reporting and instead represents the imaginative qualities of actual things, the totally artificial place where meanings reside.

---

[24] Gilbert Sorrentino, "Poetry Chronicle," *Kulchur,* 3 (Spring, 1963), 80. Subsequent references follow in parentheses.

The Life of Fiction

In 1967 and 1968 it was "the death of the novel." By 1974, with relatively little critical progress made in coping with the new fiction, the topic had escalated to the death of publishing. Even more than in the first days of McLuhan, the technicians of print believed their days were numbered, not because of a change in readers' sensibilities, but because the technological revolution itself was demanding a growth and acceleration which publishing could not match. Even with 350,000 books in print and 35,000 more added each year, bookstores could not possibly stock more than a minuscule percentage; fewer readers could be expected to pay $6.95, $8.95, and finally $15 (for Pynchon's *Gravity's Rainbow*) when the prices of records, FM radios, and color TVs had been held stable or even forced down. Literature was not a mass market commodity, and in 1974 the only markets were mass.

About this time the *New York Times Book Review* added a somewhat regular section, often by Victor Navasky or Wilfrid Sheed, about the death of publishing; suddenly the common reader was treated to an inside glance at the depressing world of publishing—such as nine editors, up to their ears in sirloin and martinis, discussing for an hour and a half whether to give a starving poet $1,000 as an advance on his first book, or $750. When the bill comes it's half the difference. Publishers and authors fought each other over the demise of the popular short story: with *Collier's* and the *Post* dead, *Holiday, Harper's Bazaar,* and many others either cut fiction or reduced it substantially as a gambit to survive. "My God," exclaimed Charles Newman, "the power of literature! All those little stories dragging entire corporations to fiscal ruin." [1] The novel,

---

[1] Charles Newman, "The Uses and Abuses of Death: A Little Rumble through the Remnants of Literary Culture," *Tri-Quarterly* #26 (Winter, 1973), p. 11.

especially the innovative novel, suffered the worst. As Ronald Sukenick reported in the *Village Voice:*

> Publishers, for example, may still publish you, but at the slightest indication that your book won't have a quick-buck success they may not even bother sending it to the stores. They will probably pulp it as fast as they can without telling you—the thing isn't worth even the storage space. Books disappear as effectively these days as works by deviationists in Russia. I know a book dealer who has accumulated a collection of the significant novels of the '60s that is literally worth a fortune because these books have become so rare. Novels in the '70s become rare in a matter of months. Poets have always had marginal institutions, tiny presses, local and/or highly specialized distribution, but for the novel this particular situation is crucial. The novel is the child of mass printing to the point where it is inseparable from it. I noticed a while back that a bunch of novelists went out into the streets of their publishing district to vend their books from a pushcart. Bravo. But are there less quixotic measures that might be taken? [2]

Even the academic and literary quarterlies were slow to acknowledge and then understand the new fiction, although they have recently taken steps to do so. For years *Panache* (Princeton) was the only journal consistently publishing experimental work; under the executive editorship of Carolyn Rand Herron, *Partisan Review* opened its pages to challenging works by Ronald Sukenick, Raymond Federman, Jonathan Baumbach, Leonard Michaels, and several others, at the same time printing critical explorations of these authors. In 1972 Mark Mirsky and Donald Barthelme founded their own tabloid, *Fiction,* as the organ of a writers' cooperative which for fifty cents an issue would bring the new fiction to a wider audience. *Tri-Quarterly* began a series of issues on "Ongoing American Fiction" in the winter of 1973, and in the spring of the same year *Modern Fiction Studies* published a special number on recent American fiction: the authors represented were with only two exceptions "disruptionists," including Vonnegut, Brautigan, Gass, and others. The two-decade-long dominance by Bellow-Updike-Malamud seemed over.

---

[2] Ronald Sukenick, "The Ecology of Literature," *Village Voice,* 18 (April 5, 1973), 26. The collection Sukenick mentions was assembled by Peter Howard of Serendipity Books and purchased by the University of Northern Iowa.

But not for the major, entrenched critics of American fiction—commentators who had built their reputations on the ascendancy of the dense, intellectual fiction of Bellow and his contemporaries, and who were not about to forfeit their positions as arbiters of our funereal taste in fiction. Pearl Kazin Bell recalls the "death of the novel" talk in her 1973 *Dissent* essay, and argues that "for a time Fiedler's prophecy did not seem dismayingly close to the truth, as Heller and Burroughs and Pynchon were joined in the critical limelight by such celebrants of unreason, chaos, and inexorable decay as Kurt Vonnegut, Jr., John Barth, Rudolph Wurlitzer, Donald Barthelme, and a horde of mini-Jeremiahs crying havoc in the Western world." [3] Her association of such a differing, wide-ranging crew of fictionists indicates the lack of discrimination regarding the disruptionists (as opposed to any new author of the late Sixties or early Seventies); one might as easily have lumped together Henry James, Theodore Dreiser, Gertrude Stein, and Ernest Hemingway as fictionists in 1917. In her close analyses Bell is no less unappreciative of the new fiction, especially of Donald Barthelme's:

> He is a perversely dedicated student of the contemporary junkheap, and his tin-can-and-broken-bottle collages attempt a frontal assault on language that seems extraordinarily attuned to the kind of radical sensibility that strains against the "repression" of words as it gropes for "consciousness," nonverbal sensitivities, and the psychedelic innocence of the full-blown mind. Barthelme's writing consistently reduces language—and the things that language names and identifies—to a kitchen midden of dehumanized potsherds that no literary archeologist in his right mind would ever try to piece together. (p. 27)

Her favorite remains Saul Bellow: "What will probably be remembered of American writing in the 1960s and '70s, long after Barthelme and Pynchon have been declared passe, is being written by novelists who care more for people than their garbage, and for words—precise and suggestive—more than *dreck*. Saul Bellow is still, as he has been for almost 20 years, the most inventive, intelligent, and genuinely surprising novelist in America, and *Mr. Sammler's Planet* is one of the few contemporary books that engage the mind and heart as one reads" (p. 31).

[3] Pearl Kazin Bell, "American Fiction: Forgetting the Ordinary Truths," *Dissent*, Winter, 1973, 26. Subsequent references follow in parentheses.

With few exceptions mainstream critics object to the themes expressed in the works of Vonnegut, Barthelme, and their companions, without making a study of the techniques—which often justify these very themes. Nathan A. Scott, Jr., finds amid "the clatter and din of the New Sensibility" the "hope that we may somehow find a way of releasing ourselves altogether from the duties and contingencies of our life in history." [4] He sees our latest fiction as describing "that late stage of things where there is no bang but only a whimper and a sense of the historical process being at an end. Which is to say that we are by way of being seduced by the expensive emotions of Apocalypse" (p. 5). These writings lack "the potency of Relevance. For none of those who seem to carry the period-style—whether it be William Burroughs or Thomas Pynchon or Kurt Vonnegut or Joseph Heller or John Barth or Donald Barthelme or the Norman Mailer of *An American Dream*—strike us as writers who 'believe in "history" as a form of truth' " (p. 24). In another essay Scott describes these same writers, those "who now carry 'the tone of the center,' " as sensing their literary vocation "as *game*," [5] that "the world of the literary imagination is something absolutely figurative and metaphorical" (p. 587). Scott deplores what he considers this literary retreat from the "fact-world," and, using John Barth's first novel as an example, exclaims,

> And so it might be said of the sorts of books being produced today by such writers as Pynchon and Vonnegut and Barthelme and Barth himself: they're all "floating operas" in which, since everything is ambiguous and evanescent, the writer as impresario undertakes not so much to release the mimetic powers of his form as to fashion a prose whose snap and buoyancy and analogical inventiveness will hint at what Todd Andrews takes the world to present—namely, an "infinity of possible direction." (pp. 589–590)

This literature, Scott charges, evades the responsibilities of the modern world; it "is not grappling directly with the difficult issues of history and hope, and it yields no consolations of the sort for

---

[4] Nathan A. Scott, Jr., " 'New Heav'ns, New Earth'—the Landscape of Contemporary Apocalypse," *Journal of Religion,* 53 (January, 1973), 4. Subsequent references follow in parentheses.

[5] Nathan A. Scott, Jr., "History, Hope, and Literature," *Boundary 2,* 1 (Spring, 1973), 586. The Reninger Lecture, University of Northern Iowa, 1972. Subsequent references follow in parentheses.

which the multitudes yearn'' (p. 597). Scott would prefer a novelist such as Saul Bellow, whose writing ''after alienation'' (the phrase is Marcus Klein's, from the best book on that period in fiction) works instead toward an accommodation. But the age of the literary disruptionists is an age *after accommodation*. For twenty years Cold War America—the America in which Daniel Bell, Nathan Scott, Alfred Kazin, and Pearl Kazin Bell established themselves as critics—was taught to live under the bomb, in an eroding ecology, in deteriorating cities, while our cultural spokesmen made their persistent attempts to adjust, with the smoothness and coolness of reason, to the unbearable and even the unthinkable. What deviations we do find in the themes of Vonnegut and his contemporaries speak out against this smug accommodation. But Scott ignores their major innovations entirely, alluding to Gertrude Stein's comment on the decadence and pointlessness of ''diagramming sentences.''

The most superficial analysis of disruptive fiction—that it is simple aesthetic indulgence with no relevance to the world beyond—has done it the most damage. Alfred Kazin's commentary on Donald Barthelme shows the method in practice, even when it does not specifically consider linguistic play. Kazin calls it cultural play, which for him is just as bad:

> And Barthelme? Literature itself? This too has been denuded, stripped down to the absurd, reduced to its consumers. What is exotic in so much banality is the fact that we consumers of ''culture'' naturally stick our attentive inquisitive consciousness into everything. Nothing that will be put into a paperback is alien to us. The comic in Barthelme is this extreme unrelenting reference system— match us up with any subject!—without any free choice. We are computers.
>
> .   .   .   .
>
> Kenneth Burke says somewhere that ''we have been sentenced to the sentence,'' and Barthelme sentences us right back again to sentences constructed vindictively of American newspeak. Is Barthelme a ''novelist''? He is one of the few authentic examples of the ''antinovelist''—that is, he operates by countermeasures only, and the system that is his own joy to attack permits its lonely dissenters the sense of their own weakness. The almighty state is always in view. So Barthelme sentences us to the complicity with the system that he suffers from more than anyone. He is wearily attentive to every detail

of the sophistication, the lingo, the massively stultifying second-handedness of everything "we" say. Barthelme is outside everything he writes about in a way that a humorist like Perelman could never be. He is under the terrible discipline that the System inflicts on those who are most fascinated with its relentlessness. He is so smart, so biting, himself so unrelenting in finding far-flung material for his ridicule that his finished product comes out a joke about Hell. We go up sentence, down sentence, up and down. What severity we are sentenced to by this necessary satire! [6]

Robert Scholes, one of the most brilliant critics of the fictionists in John Barth's generation, tries his hand on Barthelme in an essay titled "Metafiction," but the result is an analysis almost identical to that of the most conservative of critics, Alfred Kazin: "This snow-like fallout of brain damage is not just a reminder of the pollution of our physical atmosphere, it is the crust of phenomenal existence which has covered our mental landscape, cutting us off from the essence of our being, afflicting even the artists. For Barthelme man has become a phenomenon among phenomena." [7] Metafiction, Scholes claims, attempts "to assault or transcend the laws of fiction—an undertaking which can only be achieved from within fictional form." [8] But that is John Barth's territory, and the failure to make the great leap from Barth to Barthelme has left much of contemporary criticism lost in the funhouse as well. About all of this, Charles Newman, editor of *Tri-Quarterly* and a disruptive fictionist himself, is the most bitter: "If we have changed so much, then never has a major mutation been absorbed so quickly or described so sloppily." [9]

Barth's "Literature of Exhaustion" essay, and even more the spirit in which it was understood, contributed to the confusion over disruptivist fiction. But comparisons with the New Novel did almost as much to block the appreciation of new works by Vonnegut, Barthelme, and their colleagues. Robbe-Grillet, Le Clezio, Sollers, Ricardou—here indeed was the linguistic play which Scott and others thought constituted the new American fiction as well. Ray-

[6] Alfred Kazin, *Bright Book of Life: American Novelists and Storytellers from Hemingway to Mailer* (Boston: Atlantic–Little, Brown, 1973), pp. 272–273.

[7] Robert Scholes, "Metafiction," *Iowa Review*, 1 (Fall, 1970), 109.

[8] Ibid., p. 106.

[9] Newman, "The Uses and Abuses of Death," p. 40.

mond Federman describes the French innovations: "Though these fictitious beings succeed in creating an illusion of progress, both for themselves and for the reader, they merely occupy time and space—the time it takes for a story to be read, and the space it requires for the story to be told. Ultimately their actions, motions, and reflections are mere verbal contortions. But this seemingly gratuitous verbalism is the most important aspect of the [French] fiction. . . . The characters very often do not exist in themselves. They are only what they say. They are a discourse; they are made of words; they are the movement (often contradictory) of their discourse," where things are done "strictly for a linguistic reason." [10] Therefore "writing is no longer an effort to communicate a pre-existent meaning, but a means of exploring language itself which is viewed in a particular space, *'le lien du language,'* and which has its own spatial and temporal conditions, and dimensions" (p. 6). In French fiction, therefore, one is correct in feeling that "This somewhat narcissistic activity of the writer results from the fact that now the only possible subject for fiction is fiction itself" (p. 7).

American disruptivist fiction is not like this. Barthelme himself has faulted the French for having "succeeded in making objects of their books without reaping any of the strategic benefits of their maneuver—a triumph of misplaced intelligence. Their work seems leaden, selfconscious in the wrong way. Painfully slow-paced, with no leaps of the imagination, concentrating on the minutiae of consciousness, these novels scrupulously, in deadly earnest, parse out what can safely be said. In an effort to avoid psychologism and unwarranted assumptions they arrive at inconsequence." [11] This is what Rust Hills takes to be American fiction when he condemns it in the pages of *Esquire:* "To say, 'Oh, boy, we've got a whole new "kind" of fiction, the idea of it is *nothing happens,'* is to deny fiction its own meaning. It's like saying, 'We've got this neat new shade of red—*green!'* Why call it fiction at all? Call it something else. 'Green writing,' say. Or 'faip,' short for 'Fooling Around in Prose.' Or 'spinach.' " [12] The more intelligent view is presented by

[10] Raymond Federman, *Cinq Nouvelles Nouvelles* (New York: Appleton-Century-Crofts, 1970), p. 5. Subsequent references follow in parentheses.

[11] Donald Barthelme, "After Joyce," *Location,* 1 (Summer, 1964), 16.

[12] Rust Hills, "Fiction," *Esquire,* 80 (August, 1973), 50.

Gilbert Sorrentino, Raymond Federman (in his American works), or Ronald Sukenick; they establish their books not just as linguistic games but as imaginatively created objects in the world, where fiction can have the same appreciated existence as painting, sculpture, music, or any of the arts. As Sukenick argues in his published correspondence with Federman:

> Rather than serving as a mirror or redoubling on itself, fiction adds itself to the world, creating a meaningful "reality" that did not previously exist. Fiction is artifice but not artificial. It seems as pointless to call the creative powers of the mind "fraudulent" as it would be to call the procreative powers of the body such. What we bring into the world is *per se* beyond language, and at that point language is of course left behind—but it is the function of creative language to be left behind, to leave itself behind, in just that way. The word is unnecessary once it is spoken, but it has to be spoken. Meaning does not pre-exist creation, and afterwards it may be superfluous.[13]

There is a generational gap, as well, between Barth and Barthelme, and in many senses this has obstructed the critical understanding of new fiction. When queried by John O'Brien about the difficult reception of his innovative novel *The Catacombs* (1965), black author William Demby said that it was less a matter of race than of age. "There might be a problem—not between black and white, but between the middle-aged and the young. Some critics, I am sure, just aren't with it. That's all. And maybe some black critics are like that, too, but that wouldn't have anything to do with being a black critic or not being a black critic." [14] Demby's caution is borne out by Nathan Scott in his attack on disruptive fiction's new aesthetic: "On the most strident and most obvious level, it is, of course, the belief which is declared today by the hordes of those young long-haired, jean-clad, pot-smoking bohemians who have entered the world of psychedelia." [15]

But race, and the whole cultural contrast between black and white, or between Western and non-Western traditions, can become

---

[13] Quoted in *Surfiction*, ed. Raymond Federman (Chicago: Swallow Press, 1974), p. 5.
[14] John O'Brien, *Interviews with Black Writers* (New York: Liveright, 1973), p. 51.
[15] Scott, " 'New Heav'ns, New Earth,' " pp. 12–13.

an issue for disruptivist fiction, as it has been in the works of Ishmael Reed. "I think that the Western novel is tied to Western epistemology, the way people in the West look at the world," Reed told John O'Brien. On the contrary, he sees his own books "as amulets, and in ancient African cultures words were considered in this way. Words were considered to have magical meanings and were considered to be charms." [16] But Reed does not carry this Africanism beyond the scope of general literary innovation; he is preeminently an American writer, and it is by purely American criteria that he wishes to be judged. To L. E. Sissman, who measured his novels as short of Emily Brontë's, Reed replies, "This is the kind of confusion and ignorance that you have prevailing in the American critical establishment. A man comparing my work—I grew up in Buffalo, New York, an American town—comparing it with a woman writer of nineteenth-century England who was involved with different problems and a different culture" (pp. 172–173). He reveals that his first novel, *The Free-Lance Pallbearers* (1967), "actually started out as a political satire on Newark. It was going to be a naturalistic, journalistic, political novel. But as it went through draft after draft, the style I thought was mine came back and I developed it" (p. 170). That personal style is the result of studying Americana in the Bancroft Library, but also from the native absorption of vaudeville, comic strips, and TV: "I've watched television all my life and I think my way of editing, the speed I bring to my books, is based upon some of the television shows and cartoons I've seen, the way they edit. Look at a late movie that was made in 1947—people become bored because there was a slower tempo in those times" (pp. 175–176). Most of all, Ishmael Reed sees himself as a modern American conjure man, whose new aesthetic matches so closely the work of other American disruptionists that his arguments against European determinations (like LeRoi Jones's theories on the blues) apply for all American, non-colonial work. "What it comes down to is that you let the social realists go after the flatfoots out there on the beat and we'll go after the Pope and see which action causes a revolution. We are mystical detectives about to make an arrest" (p. 179).

[16] O'Brien, *Interviews with Black Writers*, p. 172. This interview originally appeared in *Fiction International* #1 (Fall, 1973). Subsequent references follow in parentheses.

During the 1967–68 publishing season, when so much new fiction was becoming fantastic and wildly imaginative, black literature gave the impression of going political. Eldridge Cleaver, Julius Lester, and Malcolm X were treated as the strongest new voices; even James Baldwin turned to the essay form, and publishers reprinted Richard Wright's nonfiction works, continuing to satisfy general expectations that black writers should write of their own social, political, and ethnic reality—in conventionally realistic terms. Most of the truly contemporary black fiction, by LeRoi Jones, Ishmael Reed, William Demby, Charles Wright, Clarence Major, and John Edgar Wideman, received less notice than was accorded to the political works. "When somebody like Peter Prescott comes out and says the most interesting writing from blacks are the autobiographies of Malcolm X and Eldridge Cleaver," Reed complained, "it's like saying the most interesting white literature is Richard Nixon's *Six Crises* and Dwight Eisenhower's *Stories I Tell My Friends*" (p. 175).

Of young black fictionists, Charles Wright was one of the first to shatter the old conventions, presenting the usual "search for meaning" theme in a radical new form: imaginative literature, and ultimately fantasy. His impetus for *The Messenger* (1963) is the black experience, but only as environment can provide stimulus to any artist. As his white contemporaries were discovering, the modern world was indeed a crazy place which it was up to man to figure out:

> Here in this semi-dark room, I become frightened. Am I in America? The objects, chairs, tables, sofa are not specifically American. They, this room, have no recognizable country. I have always liked to believe that I am not too far removed from the heart of America (I have a twenty-five dollar U.S. Savings Bond) and I am proud of almost everything American. Yet I'm drowning in this green cornfield. The acres stretch to infinity. I dare not move. This country has split open my head with a golden eagle's beak. Regardless of how I try, the parts won't come together. And this old midtown brownstone is waiting mutely for the demolition crew, these two-and-a-half rooms which have sheltered me for two years. A room with a view: the magical Manhattan skyline, and all for five dollars a week because I have connections.[17]

---

[17] Charles Wright, *The Messenger* (New York: Farrar, Straus, 1963), pp. 4–5.

Wright's protagonist, Charles Stevenson, must forge more connections. His job as messenger makes him the link between disparate elements of New York City; he sees the full range of experience (stockbrokers, famous actors, and dead Puerto Rican babies), but he seems hopelessly estranged from what's really happening. " 'We're making history,' " confides a Wall Street broker to whom the messenger is delivering stocks; but Charles is not part of the "we," not part of the reality being measured by the Dow Jones ticker. From the raw materials of experience he would make something for himself: a better life, a piece of the American dream, but his story is that "I have moved like an uncertain ghost through the white world." Not simply because he is black; rather, his spirit will not accept the living death of such conformity. His single intellectual and moral equal in the book, the little girl Maxine, suggests what can be done. " 'I like clay. But I don't like to make boys and girls and dogs and houses. I like to make fantastic things.' " So Charles seeks imaginative space, a better world to make than simply the banal American quest. That allegedly real world is quite madly unreal; a Dow Jones average is only one arbitrary synthesis, basically no better (and practically much worse) than the satisfaction Charles can get from drinking, jazz, or even prayer. "I had a feeling that all was not lost," he discovers. "Somewhere there was such a thing as peace of mind and goodness." The hassles of his world, of his crazy friends Laura, Mitch, Jelly, and Lena, are not his problems. "None of them. Not a fucking one of them. You are your own problem, I said." So he clears his apartment, sells everything, and has a farewell party for his characters. " 'I am the future,' " he recalls from a grade school essay. "Fitzgerald and his green light!" He strips down to his integral self, for it is only from there that the making can begin. "There was horror in the knowledge that nothing was going to happen to me, that I was stoned on that frightening, cold level where everything is crystal clear. It was like looking at yourself too closely in a magnifying mirror." While his friends party on, "searching for that crazy kick that would still the fears, confusion, and the pain of being alive on this early August morning," Charles has come down to a true platonic conception of himself, pure self, for which a more substantial existence can be imaginatively created.

Wright's subsequent novel, *The Wig* (1966), is the very creation
Charles Stevenson, as pure imagining self, might make. Stripped to
nothing, his hero Lester Jefferson must become something. "Be-
wigged I am. Brave, an idealist. But what can I do with a good family name, a sponsor, a solid connection?" [18] What can he make of
himself? He faces the same social problem of *The Messenger:* "I
was destined for a higher calling. Perhaps not Madison Avenue or
Wall Street. No. A real man-sized job. A porter, a bus boy, a
shoeshine boy, the twenty-watt bulb. Sweating, toiling, studying
the map of the Great Society. Hadn't the drugstore prophet said,
'You may become whatever you desire?' " (p. 86). Clairol, Dale
Carnegie, a nose job—Lester takes society at its word, and sets out
to create a better self. An idealist creates as he sees, but the particular rose-colored glasses Wright's hero wears show us a world more
real for its very craziness. Human hair rugs, "clipped from live
Negro traitors," ancient rock and roll in plastic cases from "the
Parke-Bernet galleries," poisoned arrows wrapped in old *National
Reviews,* "Good Humor men equipped with transistor laughing
machines" hawking "extrasensory and paranoiac ice-cream bars,"
the "League of Nations Pill Building," "Happy Days Are Here
Again" played as a mambo: unreal, but in its very absurdity a marvelous clarification of the world we actually live in. *The Wig*
presents the same social obstructions as *The Messenger,* but
Wright's story goes far beyond the realities of job discrimination
into a hilarious and terrifying surreality when, with his employment
directory thrown out the window, Lester makes his career as a
chicken man, feathers electrified, crawling through the streets of
Harlem squawking "Eat me. Eat me. All over town" (p. 141).

In a world which denies the possibility of heroism, Lester must
create his own arena. "Rats. *Rats!* The Magic Word." Rats allow
space for heroism, and also a sense of superiority. "White folks can
call you people coons, but never rat, 'cause that's *them.*" They can
be killed with great bravado and imagination ("Call him Rasputin.
They love that"). But best of all is the situation Lester has created.
"Bare-chested, barefooted, I was sort of an urban Tarzan, a knight
without a charger," who, amidst the debilitating and demoralizing

---

[18] Charles Wright, *The Wig* (New York: Farrar, Straus & Giroux, 1966), pp. 27–28.
Subsequent references follow in parentheses.

Great Society, suddenly has the chance to yell, ''All right, ya rats!''
(p. 121). The transformed world becomes a better reality. But for
that very reason, because it is more real than the sham phoniness
masking the actual horror beneath, Wright's imaginative creation
becomes a Frankenstein. The fantastic scene of a little boy beaten to
death by his mother for not wanting to attend a segregated school is
too pathetically real, a reality Lester finally cannot bear. ''And one
fine morning,'' taking Nick Carraway's epigraph for Gatsby as his
own, Lester wills himself the end of all idealists: castration and
imaginative death. Escaping and transcending the hostile world has
been a comic delight, but his final peace is tragic.

Lester's death is a death of the imagination, more terrifying and
consequential than simple physical death. In Wright's third book,
Absolutely Nothing to Get Alarmed About (1973), he turns from
Charles Stevenson and Lester Jefferson to the actual Charles Stevenson Wright himself: serving time in the American 1970's, a lifer
in search of life. Death is everywhere, for the volume is dedicated to
deceased persons, the journals from which these pieces were collected are all but one defunct, and the whole project closes with a
letter to Nathanael West, c/o Purgatorial Heights. But its epigraph,
also from West, promises ''Life's worthwhile, for it is full of
dreams and peace, gentleness and ecstasy, and faith that burns like a
clear white flame on a grim dark altar.'' How, but by a fantastic
stretch of the imagination? This is America of 1967–72, five years
of assassinations, riots, war, decay, and national malaise. If there
can be such a place, Wright is living at the still point of this turned-
down world, in New York City, the Bowery, the Chinese Gardens.
Long departed from the East Village, Wright has headed south, on
the leading edge of the blight. Poverty boondoggles, panhandling
hippies, venereal disease: Wright is at the source of it all, the cold
turning of the earth.

He survives once again as an idealist, but as one coming to closer
terms with what's going on. Who he is makes him an imaginary
traveler on a very real voyage, an indicator who will show by his
presence the deeper truths of our lives. ''Afroed, slender, Levi bell-
bottoms, striped mock turtleneck shirt, and perhaps a couple of
books under my arm, I am always the intruder, the rapist, the

mugger.'' [19] Wright is privileged to see things differently, and can
sometimes be the catalyst to make things happen. He is favored with
a writer's perspective, but resists the bait of a residency ''at a small
black college in the South.'' Instead, he'll ''knock down more wine
and go out on the fifth-floor fire escape of the Kenton Hotel,'' where
the view is glorious:

> The pollution screen even filters the burning afternoon sun. There is
> no breeze. A sort of suspended quiet, although I can see traffic mov-
> ing down Chrystie Street; children playing ball in the park; drunks in
> twos and threes, supporting buddies like wounded soldiers after the
> battle of defeat. Toward the east, a row of decayed buildings has the
> decadent beauty of Roman ruins. But only at a distance. Trained
> pigeons, chickens, and junkies inhabit those rooftops. Taking another
> drink, I think: I wish I could fly, fly far away. (pp. 192–193)

He moves to the bottom of New York, to cheap hotels just off the financial district, where ''The streets are always jammed. Jammed to
the point of being stationary like a motion-picture still. Then, as if a
powerful switch had clicked, the crowd becomes animated, moves
on, goes through the repertoire of living, boogalooing between gray
inertia and the red-hot scream of progress'' (p. 58). But also mor-
ally, to the depths of the Chinese Gardens (Manhattan Bridge Park)
and a neighborhood where he can make his daily field trip and
junkie count (''two hours netted eighty-seven in a limited area, and
I wasn't trying very hard''). ''Like an addicted entomologist,''
Wright confesses, ''I am drawn to people.'' But everyone around is
sick, even unto death.

Worst of all, there is ''absolutely nothing to get alarmed about,''
Wright advises. ''Just another domestic scene in current American
life.'' But digesting these bizarre experiences finally does the same
thing for the reader that Wright's exotic drugs do for him, and that
the experience of absolute selfhood did for the protagonist of
Wright's first novel, *The Messenger,* in the same words. ''I always
get stoned on that frightening, cold level where everything is crystal
clear. It's like looking at yourself too closely in a magnifying mir-

[19] Charles Wright, *Absolutely Nothing to Get Alarmed About* (New York: Farrar, Straus &
Giroux, 1973), p. 132. Subsequent references follow in parentheses.

ror.'' The author's mirror is distortive, in a sense, for it sends back pictures that aren't exactly there. But what is out there is mad, chaotic, incapable of being understood, while Wright's translation clarifies as only the magic of an apt comparison (be it simile, image, or metaphor) can, and by using our wider powers of imaginative vision we get at least a sense of what's truly happening ''before our eyes.''

Ultimately, Charles Wright would like to straighten things out. ''Why can't we redesign the lifeboats, take a good hard look at our male and female relationships? Perhaps redefine sin, morality, and corruption for our time on this earth'' (p. 113). What passes for good now is often bad, and certainly vice versa. Wright examines the reality of our culture and carefully sorts out the unreal, be it the engineered irrelevancy of an anti-poverty program or the inappropriate panhandling of a white hippie. ''This one wanted fifteen cents. 'Motherfucker,' I screamed, 'I need $5,000.' '' At times he may want to die, but only ''in a country where rioting will produce emotion other than boredom.'' No matter what happens, nothing has the legitimacy to excite us, since it is imaginatively dead. Throughout this book we get the sense that Charles Wright is the only person who *sees* what's happening, who looks past the sham reality of our lives toward what is really going on. ''What would have been marvelous is that the ugly old city should have burned to the ground. This shock and a minor little civil war would perhaps force us to face the cold cunt of reality. Blacks would lose the war. But we have nothing to lose but our lives, and that doesn't seem very important in the present climate'' (p. 55).

Wright's collection was first called *Black Studies: A Journal,* but the title was scrapped for fear it would lead booksellers to shelve the work in the section which so facilely accommodates every genre from Eldridge Cleaver to Charles Chesnutt and Ishmael Reed. Wright's ''blackness'' is closer to the hue of Nathaniel Hawthorne, Franz Kafka, and the other great artists who looked past the reality of our lives toward what was really going on. His novels and essays try all aspects of that reality, from the Great Society ambitions to the dead end of the last, drug-spent frontier. ''At fourteen,'' Wright confides, ''I had written: 'I am the future.' Twenty-six years later—

all I want to do is excrete the past and share with you a few Black Studies.'' And that's what follows.

Clarence Major continues in the tradition established by Charles Wright. Eli Bolton, the hero of his first novel, *All-Night Visitors* (1969), makes the same imaginative leap from death, and then turns back to life all the better for the trip. He has faced experience—in Chicago slums and in Vietnam—and found it too horrible to accept. ''I can't believe the world is real—that I'm real—that incidents are ferocious, that love is possible—suddenly—I know! I swear I know! Nothing real! Nothing has any meaning! What have we done to each other?'' [20] Instead of a social examination, Eli undertakes an imaginative study of his origin and existence—not as a rejected orphan and hassled young man, but instead the mystery of the vagina and the spirit of his erect penis. Being fellated, he controls his being: ''I want to *stay* right here, with her, focused on every protrusion, every cord, abstract circle of myself, of her every 'feeling,' every hurling, every fleshy spit-rich convexity, mentally centered in all the invisible 'constructs' of myself, right here, where she and I now form, perform an orchestra she is conducting in juicy floodtides.'' He is ''percolating, oozing, dribbling at the dick like a river, but a slow river, being tapped by the mysterious rainfalls of Mother, voids, secrets, wet holes of the flesh world, carried on an expedition to the ends of my psychophysical reality; at the floodgates of emergency, my dark, fleshy Anita, love, a gateway into which I exist, and erupt, enter'' (p. 107). The imaginative is total freedom, where Eli is ''like a nightmare patriarch responsible to no one but myself.'' Time and space can freeze for his ideal constructions, concretized in sex; the rape of his departing mistress is a ''present urgent act to preserve her,'' an imaginative omnipotence which, as with Wright, can be killed only by castration. The imaginative is also more real, showing the truth not in social reportage but in total visions, as for a rude and hostile maitre d':

> As the old man comes toward us, the evil in his encroached face causes him to suddenly blow up with the kind of force behind an earthquake. The vast immodest sound, the liquids of his body, the

[20] Clarence Major, *All-Night Visitors* (New York: Olympia Press, 1969), p. 92. Subsequent references follow in parentheses.

spermy-substance of his brains shoot out, his eyeballs, rebellious question-marks, hang down suspended on long slimy patheticus strings from his sockets; Eunice's hand, inside mine, tightens; "Oh damn—look at that! That poor man—He's having a heart attack!" The gooey stuff splashes in nearby plates of food, customers jump back in their chairs, an old woman with a bust as big as a bathtub drops her monocle, falls over backwards in her chair, her floor-length gown flying over her head, her broom-stick size legs, juggling frantically for some balance, her rich, pink Playtex girdle is even drenched with the juices from the explosion—I wonder why some of the folks are beginning to hold their noses: then it hits me, the odor of the substance from the waiter's skull smells like shit. He is a lump of slimy flesh and starched garments, on the floor. Eunice is pulling at my sleeve; "Please, let's go, I'm getting sick. I can't eat here." Eunice, even before we reach the street, is gagging. (p. 43)

There is a purgation in such scenes as these. By pushing things to their imaginative limits, Eli has cut through the world's *dreck* to truth itself, which allows him to be, or even create himself as, a better human being. From his imaginary voyage Eli is returned to life, where he meets a deserted Puerto Rican mother (similar to the figure in Wright's *The Messenger*) and can admit "the tangible reality of herself simply in the world. *Her* dispossession was my responsibility, despite her husband. Who he was socially" (p. 200). Simple reality would rationalize a way out, but imaginative truth helps keep Eli real.

For his second novel Clarence Major chooses a modular approach. In *No* (1973) two voices pass the action back and forth, and the entire narrative is structured by a new metaphor for the black experience. The narrator observes of himself and his wife, "I have the trustworthy feeling that Oni are definitely on the way down, over, and out! Which, of course, implies that we were at one time in my opinion *up* from somewhere. Up from slavery?" [21] Major uses instead the metaphor of prison; penal psychology and the image of life imprisonment hold the work together—that and a carefully controlled manner of running parts of the action backward. A scene begins with a penultimate moment, a jump back to the moment just

[21] Clarence Major, *No* (New York: Emerson Hall, 1973), p. 193. Subsequent references follow in parentheses.

before, then to a sequence of events just before *that,* until by the end of the chapter narrative time has backtracked to the very beginning, when we are suddenly confronted with the end. This dramatic method is played against the quiet counterpoint of Major's two voices, following the action "as time took up space just happening." His hero would be an "escapee," but finds freedom only when he is no longer "a victim." The climax to his largely imaginative tale, and journey, comes in a dream, where he vaults into a bullring to touch the bull's head "and in a strange and beautiful way that single act became for me a living symbol of my own human freedom" (p. 204).

Among black authors Ishmael Reed remains the leading spokesman for the radical aesthetic of disruptivist fiction; as discussed earlier, his arguments are not limited to black fiction alone. "I was to learn," he says about his early teaching experiences, "that White authors, as well as Afro-American authors, are neglected by the American university. Before I arrived at Berkeley, there was no room in the curriculum for detective novels or Western fiction, even though some of the best contributions to American literature occur in these genres. At another major university, the library did not carry books by William Burroughs, who at least manages to get it up beyond the common, simple, routine narratives that critics become so thrilled about." [22] The narrative of Reed's first novel, *The Free-Lance Pallbearers* (1967), is everything but routine. In fact, there is little narrative at all; rather, the lyrical exploration of what Reed said in his interview was originally a political exposé of Newark. It is not called Newark: "I live in HARRY SAM. HARRY SAM is something else. A big not-to-be-believed out-of-sight, sometimes referred to as O-BOP-SHE-BANG or KLANG-A-LANG-A-DING-DONG. SAM has not been seen since the day thirty years ago when he disappeared into the John with a weird ravaging illness." [23]

For his description of the new American city, Reed has assembled a heap of adjectives and then deftly removed the nouns

[22] Ishmael Reed, *19 Necromancers from Now* (Garden City, N.Y.: Doubleday, 1970), pp. xiii–xiv.
[23] Ishmael Reed, *The Free-Lance Pallbearers* (Garden City, N.Y.: Doubleday, 1967), p. 1. Subsequent references follow in parentheses.

which they modify. The result is a hideously appropriate surreal real, an accurate portrait of what happens when our daily world loses its common sense. Bukka Doopeyduk is the protagonist, a "Nazarene apprentice" who, under the "Mojo Retraining Act," is about to become "the first bacteriological warfare expert of the colored race." His world presents a day-to-day challenge ("When I opened the frig, *something grabbed at me.* I shut it quickly"). On TV he can watch "the Art Linkletter show where a life supply of pigeons had been awarded to four cripples and some parents of children with a harelip," or pick up an issue of the *Reader's Digest* "(stars, snow, and reindeer on a blue cover). The lead article is 'Should Dolphins Go Steady—33 Parents Reply.' " Or he can go on a talk show himself: " 'Mr. Doopeyduk,' the Hangup said, 'we've had some weird customers up here on the show. Richard Nixon was on once discussing federal dog-napping legislation and so was a man who thought he had visited Mars. But you, Mr. Doopeyduk, by far are the most bizarre.' " He leaves the studio as "a commercial for Radio Free Europe was quickly put on. Two minutes of barbed wire and Spike Jones playing, 'Ave Maria' " (p. 115).

Yellow Back Radio Broke-Down (1969) encloses this wild lyricism within an appropriate, organic, and facilitating form: that of a modern hoodoo Western, Reed's completely native form which combines Negro conjurism with an American cowboy story. The result is much like Donald Barthelme's deft fracturing of familiar forms. The frontier town is Yellow Back Radio, which you can pass through as quickly as a station break; it shares the territory with another small hamlet, Video Junction, and the social action can be found at Big Lizzy's Rabid Black Cougar Saloon. There has been a children's revolt, with the adults sent into exile: "We chased them out of town. We were tired of them ordering us around. They worked us day and night in the mines, made us herd animals, harvest the crops and for three hours a day we went to school to hear teachers praise the old. Made us learn facts by rote. Lies really bent upon making us behave. We decided to create our own fiction." [24]

But the kids are routed by Bo Shmo and his neo-social-realist gang. The conjure cowboy Loop Garoo and the militant Indian poet

---

[24] Ishmael Reed, *Yellow Back Radio Broke-Down* (Garden City, N.Y.: Doubleday, 1969), p. 16. Subsequent references follow in parentheses.

Chief Showcase come to their rescue, working magic so potent that Pope Innocent must be called in to restore metaphysical order. Reed is the equal of Richard Brautigan in choosing magically apt metaphors for his action: when Loop Garoo is stranded in the desert, "In the distance large birds with buzzard coupons could be seen lining up for mess" (p. 33), or when a rancher looks around for help, his "cowpokes were pretending to be in a dentist office of the mind. They had their heads buried in Magazines" (p. 117). Reed's lyricism extends beyond the single shots of his first novel, and in *Yellow Back Radio* pervades the entire landscape which is the novel's structure: "Man, pass me another whiskey. This place is really getting eerie, never seed no town like this; all the planks holding up the buildings seem to lean, like tilt over, and there's a disproportionate amount of shadows in reference to the sun we get—it's like a pen and ink drawing by Edward Munch or one of them Expressionist fellows" (p. 97).

The Pope, as the figurehead of European reason, spirit, and culture, would oppose Loop's conjure magic: "Well we've figured it to be the Hoo-Doo, an American version of the Ju-Ju religion that originated in Africa—you know, that strange continent which serves as the subconscious of our planet" (p. 152), but the "mumbo jumbo" is too much for him or the others who would obstruct Loop's magic or Reed's native form.

In *Mumbo Jumbo* (1972) itself, Reed's third novel, he moves from the nineteenth-century popular form of the yellow back Western novel to the contemporary mode of the cinema. Before the book's "credits" (title, copyright, etc.) runs a scene in New Orleans: the mayor is taken ill with an epidemic which is ravaging his city, the symptoms being "stupid sensual things" such as wiggling uncontrollably to such music as the Eagle Rock and the Sassy Bump. "Don't you understand," he is told, "if this Jes Grew becomes pandemic it will mean the end of Civilization As We Know It?" [25] After a collage of modern rock dancing and a quote from Louis Armstrong about how a Dixieland band will march the streets, "The spirit hits them and they follow" (p. 7). Reed rolls the title and credits for his novel about the black conjure spirit, which,

[25] Ishmael Reed, *Mumbo Jumbo* (Garden City, N.Y.: Doubleday, 1972), p. 4. Subsequent references follow in parentheses.

starting with ragtime and then jazz, "just grew" to become an alternative culture threatening to take over America: "1920. Charlie Parker, the houngan (a word derived from *n'gana gana*) for whom there was no master adept enough to award him the Asson, is born. 1920–1930. That 1 decade which doesn't seem so much a part of American history as the hidden After-Hours of America Struggling to jam. To get through" (p. 16). Resisting the movement is the Wallflower Order, descendants of the Teutonic Knights, since "Only they could defend the cherished traditions of the West against Jes Grew." But the ultimate enemies of the new culture are the Atonists, the cult which opposed the Egyptian god Osiris with their own repressive religion, defusing Jes Grew for a time with Christ. "The Atonists got rid of their spirit 1000s of years ago with Him. The flesh is next. Plastic will soon prevail over flesh and bones. Death will have taken over" (p. 62).

Since 1967, the year of literary disruption, Ishmael Reed's fiction has come increasingly to resemble the thematics of *Mumbo Jumbo*. This novel itself is a conjure book of sorts, and in formalistic terms is a concrete attempt to capture the essence of an entire cultural transformation. In more immediate terms Reed has waged a one-man war against the New York publishing establishment; the dust jacket of *Mumbo Jumbo* boasts that he has in fact united that establishment in opposition to himself. In Berkeley he has operated a national communications center for black artists, and is the center of the movement to bring wider recognition to writers such as Charles Wright, Clarence Major, and himself. Reed's anthology of 1970, *19 Necromancers from Now,* was the first form of wide distribution many of these writers had, but by the summer of 1973 the *New York Times Book Review* not only featured Clarence Major's *No,* a novel which two years earlier they would never have noticed, but let a black author, George Davis, do the reviewing, while the paperback of *Mumbo Jumbo* was placed on their recommended list. His experience, seen in perspective with the wide popularity of Kurt Vonnegut, Jr., the steady achievement of Donald Barthelme, the national and international awards for Jerzy Kosinski, and the wider exposure of Ronald Sukenick, Raymond Federman, and Gilbert Sorrentino (who among them produced seven major works of fiction from 1971 to 1973), suggested that while the season of 1967–68 was the break-in of their work, 1973 was its break-*through*. The public was now ready, and only the publishers were left to discover that their industry and its leading genre were at the point not of death, but of a rebirth of formal achievement.

Before 1967 it was extremely difficult to publish innovative or disruptive fiction in America. For some reason endings were particularly objectionable, and major houses such as Houghton Mifflin, Appleton-Century-Crofts, Norton, and Random House performed corruption of texts unheard of for earlier writers of similar stature. Jerzy Kosinski describes the fate of his first novel, *The Painted Bird* (1965):

> The postscript resulted from a mistake. Initially in my correspondence with the publisher I often defended the idea of the book. In one letter I speculated about the "future" of the novel's protagonist, about the fate of the Boy "after the War." I wrote this letter from Europe where I was traveling. The editor at Houghton Mifflin thought that this was a "very telling letter," and she also thought that it could—indeed, should—become a postscript to *The Painted Bird,* and apparently she cabled to me about it; since the final galleys were just about to be sent to the printers, she rushed and used the negative option; if I would not reply she would assume that I agreed. Well, I was in France, staying in a large, disorganized hotel, and I never received that cable. Sometime later the book was published with that italicized ending. Unlike this unintended "epilogue" there were, however, many well-intended passages, paragraphs, and phrases of the original manuscript which did not make their way to Houghton's edition of *The Painted Bird;* even though they appeared in the final corrected galley proofs they were dropped "in the last minute"; we had an argument about it. All omitted parts were reintroduced in the Pocket Book edition (1966), to the revised Modern Library edition (1970), and to the forthcoming Bantam Book 1972 edition.[26]

The most celebrated cases of altered endings concern John Barth and Anthony Burgess. In the crucial year of 1967, when Barth's complete works were republished in a uniform edition by Double-

[26] Jerome Klinkowitz, "Jerzy Kosinski: An Interview," *Fiction International* #1 (Fall, 1973), p. 33. Reprinted in Joe David Bellamy, *The New Fiction: Interviews with Innovative American Writers* (Urbana: University of Illinois Press, 1974).

day, the author took the occasion to restore the original text of his first novel, *The Floating Opera* (1956). At the time "I was twenty-four," recalls Barth, "had been writing fiction industriously for five years, and had had—deservedly—no success whatever with the publishers. One finally agreed to launch the *Opera,* but on condition that the builder make certain major changes in its construction, notably about the stern. I did, the novel was published, critics criticized the ending in particular, and I learned a boatwright little lesson." [27] In the corrupted version published by Appleton-Century-Crofts, Todd Andrews is dissuaded from his suicide attempt by the sound of a little girl's voice, which allows him a rather sudden change toward affirmation and at least "relative" value. The restored ending is far more nihilistic: Todd's intended suicide will in fact destroy the whole boat and all its passengers, including the sentimental little girl, and his change in plans is far more gratuitous and chilling.

In 1963, when Norton published the American edition of *A Clockwork Orange* by Anthony Burgess, the last several pages of the original British version were simply dropped. This change may have worked to Burgess's advantage, but another case of an American publisher changing the ending of a British edition was not so fortuitous. American author Terry Southern began his career abroad, with *Candy* (1958) published in Paris, then *Flash and Filigree* (1958) and *The Magic Christian* (1959) in Great Britain. Because it was so outrageous that only an under-the-counter publisher would handle it, *Candy* made it to America intact and established Southern as a writer of some disruptive promise. But *The Magic Christian,* his best work, was reprinted by Random House in a drastically altered edition. The original English text, published by Andre Deutsch, told the story of Guy Grand, the magic Christian who uses his millions to catalyze the absurdity of America and the American people. He plays an accelerating series of jokes, fixing individuals and groups in their gullibility and greed. As his disruptions grow in intensity, he strikes closer and closer to society's ills. At first he simply does things on the order of purchasing a famous advertising agency and installing an illiterate, uncivilized Bantu

[27] John Barth, "Prefatory Note to the Revised Edition," *The Floating Opera* (Garden City, N.Y.: Doubleday, 1967), p. v.

tribesman as its president; the fun comes in watching the other exec-
utives and account men grovel and toady to him for their jobs.
Grand purchases a busy corner in Chicago's Loop, constructs a
huge vat which he stocks with blood, urine, and defecation from the
stockyards, and then—a few minutes before the morning rush
hour—dumps a briefcase of $100 bills into the stewing mess. He
charters a boat, *The SS Magic Christian,* for a high-society cruise
which culminates in high lunacy. But in Chapter Thirteen, the texts
diverge. In the 1959 Andre Deutsch original edition, Grand's project comes to a climax:

> Grand received the greatest setback of his career in 1953 when he was
> undone through a combination of madness and treachery by a key
> employee in his big project of that year.
>
> It all began about the time some Broadway wag put forward the
> slogan—*Nobody Ever Went Broke Underestimating The Intelligence
> of The American Public;* a slogan which enjoyed a certain watchword
> vogue among the cognoscenti of midtown commerce. Well, it rubbed
> Grand the wrong way, and got his dander up.[28]

Grand notices an American congressman who has been elected on
the slogan, *"the threat of American Communism,"* when, in fact,
"all that remained of the Communist movement was a sorrowful
rag—dead bones displayed with a sorrowful pathos once a Mayday
in the slum square of a few large cities, by a handful of poor old gaf-
fers and crones as nutty as the Senator himself. But he had *been
elected"* (p. 135). Grand's plan is his coup de grace: he will pay his
senator to accuse the most unlikely people of being Communists, to
appear with a secret list of hundreds of them, which will in fact be a
blank sheet of paper—and see how far the American public will take
the whole joke. Grand's setback comes when the people accept it
entirely; in horror he engineers a series of public hearings for the
senator and his committee, with the accuser behaving like a raving
madman. "But the men with the jacket never came. And, in fact, no
one raised a finger—a finger to topple the rotten egg from the wall;
no one" (p. 143).

This chapter is missing from the Random House edition pub-

---

[28] Terry Southern, *The Magic Christian* (London: Andre Deutsch, 1959), p. 134. Subsequent references follow in parentheses.

lished in February, 1960, and from all subsequent paperback editions (even the British Penguin reprinting). Instead, we read that "Grand had a bit of fun when he engaged a man to smash crackers with a sledgehammer in Times Square." [29] Obviously rewritten as filler (as Frank Norris rewrote, in the same number of words, a scene with McTeague looking for his hat to replace the "objectionable" narrative of Little August wetting his pants), it is one of the weakest sections in the book, and is particularly destructive coming just at the climax. That Terry Southern never developed into a major fictionist, and that the black humor movement itself never rose above its own sick jokes, perhaps may be ascribed to this castration of the movement's major text.

By 1974 Barth, Pynchon, Barthelme, and Kosinski had won National Book Awards for their fiction, and Kurt Vonnegut, Jr., was rumored to be a leading candidate for the Nobel Prize. Although writers were complaining that the fiction market had dried up, a wider range and style of work was being published than ever before. Imagination was no longer an evil word in fiction, and its engagement liberated the techniques of a whole generation of novelists, from the conservative use of social materials in John Edgar Wideman's *The Lynchers* (1973), where the theme concerns a group of blacks who would imaginatively unite their community through the symbolic lynching of a white policeman (and where the technique often consists of orchestrating thoughts and intentions as if they were dialogue upon the page), to the massively experimental collage of life and art in William Demby's novel, *The Catacombs* (1965, 1970), where the author feeds us daily accounts from the newspapers he reads (the Cuban missile crisis, the Kennedy assassination, the Pope's visit to America) and organizes his own fictional narrative around these incoming events (and imaginatively through them).

Undeterred by the fate of so many New Novel experiments, younger American authors were working with the sounds and forms and shapes of language itself, as Carl Krampf explored in his story, "The Creation of Condriction":

[29] Terry Southern, *The Magic Christian* (New York: Random House, 1960), p. 106.

I have just created a blurst condriction. I have no idea what *exactly* it is, but then I'm not the first creator who has done this. One day the idea just came to me. You are walking along, and then suddenly WHAM! it hits you, and you are surprised that you didn't think it sooner. So I got married. But getting back to my condriction. It was a moving thought. Its idea was motion. There was so much of it and nobody did anything about it. But what was the function, the "it" of the blurst condriction? Well (and good too) it was very much ahead of its time. After all, I invented it in the early 50's and even then it did its "own thing" (and very well too I might add and just did). Now in the early 50's nobody had even heard of doing your "own thing". . . .[30]

At the other extreme, William H. Gass expanded the figures of language into larger, encompassing images, and in block paragraph style used them to capture the process of reality. "In the Heart of the Heart of the Country" from his collection of the same name (1968) draws upon the "People," the "Politics," the "Weather," and even the telephone "Wires" of a small midwestern town to explain its essence. "I keep wondering," he concludes a section about "That Same Person," "whether, given time, I might not someday find a figure in our language which would serve him faithfully, and furnish his poverty and loneliness richly out." [31] "Imagination," he argues in his second novel, *Willie Masters' Lonesome Wife* (1968), "is the unifying power, and the acts of the imagination are our most free and natural; they represent us at our best." [32] Gass is one of the many literary disruptionists who first established himself in an academic career, beginning with his doctoral dissertation in philosophy at Cornell in 1954. But his subject was literary ("A Philosophical Investigation of Metaphor"), and the theories he developed there have served him well in his subsequent fiction. "Metaphors propose a new way of looking at or considering things," he argued, and emphasized that the metaphor itself "preserves itself as

[30] Carl Krampf, "The Creation of Condriction," *Mandala* #5 (1969), pp. 80–81. Reprinted in *Innovative Fiction,* ed. Jerome Klinkowitz and John Somer (New York: Dell, 1972), pp. 215–216.

[31] William H. Gass, *In the Heart of the Heart of the Country* (New York: Harper & Row, 1968), p. 190.

[32] William H. Gass, *Willie Masters' Lonesome Wife, Tri-Quarterly* Supplement #2, 1968, p. 27.

process.'' [33] What metaphors actually do is ''exhibit the process of abstraction. They do not produce abstractions. Rather, they indicate how certain abstractions may be made'' (p. xiv). Above all, ''Metaphors always present a process of abstraction. They never represent it'' (p. xvii). Raymond Federman, Ronald Sukenick, and Gilbert Sorrentino all have argued in their criticism and through their fiction that the novels should do the same—not represent life, but present the *process* of capturing and expressing it—and in his dissertation Gass provides the philosophical foundation for such a theory. It is the ''process of discovery'' which is metaphor's chief value (p. 204); rather than simply itemizing the new experience of life and providing a sense of discrimination, ''The metaphor presents its going-on'' (p. 235). In its fullest extension, the result is fiction.

The greatest ''disruption'' of fiction's tradition practiced by the innovators of 1967–68 and after was the return of the genre to a more purely aesthetic realm. The fictionist, according to Gass, ''must show or exhibit his world,'' of course; no major American writer was about to argue that the novel should completely abandon the world for self-contained linguistic play. But ''to do this,'' Gass emphasized, ''he must actually make something, not merely describe something that might be made.'' [34] He creates a world, and ''his world displays that form of embodied thought which is imagination'' (p. 10). There are no descriptions in fiction, Gass argues: ''there are only constructions'' (p. 17). Fiction's liability is that these constructions are such close impersonators of life: ''It seems incredible, the ease with which we sink through books quite out of sight, pass clamorous pages into soundless dreams. That novels should be made of words, and merely words, is shocking, really. It's as though you had discovered that your wife were made of rubber: the bliss of all those years, the fears . . . from sponge'' (p. 27).

Because for fiction's entire history such easy identifications have been its stock in trade, Raymond Federman has proposed a new name for the genre that describes disruptivist fiction: surfiction. He

---

[33] William H. Gass, ''A Philosophical Investigation of Metaphor,'' Ph.D. dissertation, Cornell University, 1954, p. xv. Subsequent references follow in parentheses.

[34] William H. Gass, *Fiction and the Figures of Life* (New York: Knopf, 1970), p. 8. Subsequent references follow in parentheses.

claims a greater vitality for this new genre because it reflects man's imagination, and not an illusory, allegedly real world which is in fact twice removed from reality. "The experience of life," Federman argues, "can only be meaningful in its recounted form." [35] To write fiction, therefore, is to produce meaning, not to reproduce it. "Consequently, fiction will no longer be regarded as a mirror of life, as a pseudo-realistic document, nor judged on the basis of its social, moral, psychological, metaphysical, commercial value, or whatever, but for what it is and what it does as an art form in its own right." [36]

The literary disruption witnessed in American fiction, beginning in force with the season of 1967–68 and continuing through the 1970's, signals not only a major development in the genre, but also its rebirth. The shock is not how far the disruptionists have gone, but how far we had let conventional fictionists desert the true ideals of artistic construction in favor of some wholly inappropriate documentation which was never really fiction at all.

[35] Raymond Federman, "Surfiction—Four Propositions in Form of an Introduction," in *Surfiction,* p. 8.
[36] Ibid., pp. 8–9.

Postface: 1980

"Let others bring order to chaos," Kurt Vonnegut announced as the self-consciously present author of *Breakfast of Champions*; "I would bring chaos to order, instead, which I think I have done."[1] Writing in 1972, Vonnegut was facing his first novel since *Slaughterhouse-Five*, which had been the book to make him at once almost ludicrously wealthy and famous, after a professional lifetime of penury. But *Slaughterhouse-Five* had been the benchmark for other equally momentous achievements. As Chapter One indicated, it synthesized the rough energies of Vonnegut's earlier novels and articulated the previously unspeakable truths which underlay Vonnegut's vision: the matters of Dresden and "what do you say about a massacre?" The new social realities created by World War II demanded new imaginative form, and only with *Slaughterhouse-Five* was Vonnegut to perfect the fictional technique for expressing them.

Interestingly enough, he drew all his materials from the American middle class: Billy Pilgrim's character and attitudes, the war as experienced by common infantry GI's, and the social values of the postwar suburbs. Explicitly literary techniques came from the same lowbrow sources, including science fiction pulp novels, television, and the comics. More speculative notions (for example, existence in the fourth dimension) were presented in comically familiar circumstances, such as the drunken Billy Pilgrim frantically searching for the steering wheel in the back seat of his car. Befitting its popular heritage, Vonnegut's Dresden novel became the first consistently innovative work of fiction in the new disruptive style to be embraced by large numbers of American readers. Always the ironist, Vonnegut later pondered what the firebombing had meant. "The raid didn't shorten the war by half a second, didn't weaken a German defense or attack anywhere, didn't free a single person from a death camp. Only

[1]Kurt Vonnegut, Jr., *Breakfast of Champions* (New York: Delacorte Press/Seymour Lawrence, 1973), p. 210. Subsequent references in parentheses.

one person benefited—not two or five or ten. Just one. . . . Me. I got three dollars for each person killed. Imagine that."[2]

What is also remarkable is that such a structurally inventive novel should be composed of such thoroughly middle-class materials. The academic argument (advanced by Leslie Fiedler and others) that "experimental" fiction had refined itself beyond the appreciation of popular readers is confounded at each turn by Vonnegut's commercial success. Unlike John Barth and Thomas Pynchon, who have drawn their models from classical literature and theoretical physics, Vonnegut simply stayed with the common fantasies he had exploited for fifteen years, during the heyday of such family magazines as *Collier's, The Saturday Evening Post,* and even such adult fare as *Argosy, Redbook,* and *Ladies' Home Journal.* Conventional literature remained just as distant from him as Barth's regressive parody and Pynchon's esoteric theory. "When people ask me who my culture heroes are," Vonnegut admitted earlier in 1972, "I express pious gratitude for Mark Twain and James Joyce and so on. But the truth is that I am a barbarian, whose deepest cultural debts are to Laurel and Hardy, Stoopnagel and Bud, Buster Keaton, Fred Allen, Jack Benny, Charlie Chaplin, Easy Aces, Henry Morgan, and on and on." These popular comedians, Vonnegut insisted, "have probably done more to shape my thinking than any writer."[3]

Breakfast of Champions invokes these Depression-era comics in its own Preface. And inside the book Vonnegut takes further exception to the traditions of mainstream, bookish literature. Despairing the "idiot decisions" made by his countrymen, Vonnegut realizes that it's not their fault: "They were doing their best to live like people invented in story books. This was the reason Americans shot each other so often: It was a convenient literary device for ending short stories and books" (pp. 209–210).

And so Vonnegut abandons orderly plot development, thematic selection, and all the other techniques of a fraudulent mimesis. Instead, he stands honestly at the head of his own story as it begins, and then drops back in whenever the book's action calls for his presence. Although the characters may not know about this playful

[2] David Hayman et al., "The Art of Fiction LXIV: Kurt Vonnegut," *Paris Review* #69 (Spring, 1977), p. 71.

[3] Kurt Vonnegut, Jr., "Preface," *Between Time and Timbuktu* (New York: Delacorte Press/Seymour Lawrence, 1972), p. xvii.

manipulation, the reader does; most of the reader's fun in *Breakfast of Champions* is in seeing Kurt Vonnegut, that shambling bear of a man, lope in and out of his story like a clumsy window dresser anxious to have everything right. Hence the most radical of disruptive literary techniques, the presence of a self-conscious writer within his story, is transformed by Vonnegut into simple popular comedy.

Before 1969 and the publication of *Slaughterhouse-Five,* Kurt Vonnegut was not thought of as an innovatively disruptive writer. Indeed, he was scarcely thought of at all. But in the writing of *Breakfast of Champions* he quickly adopted virtually all the disruptive techniques of his younger and more innovative colleagues, to produce a novel at once supremely experimental and doggedly bourgeois. His pose was one of utter simplicity and detachment; he wrote about the history of America on Planet Earth as if no one had encountered it before. His innocence, expressed by deadpan prose and childish line drawings of the simple objects he described, revealed much of the absurdity that our more knowing eyes screen out. He found that America, for example, was the only country "with a national anthem which was gibberish sprinkled with question marks" (p. 8). The graphic designs on our currency were just as silly. And our grand national history? "The sea pirates were white. The people who were already on the continent when the pirates arrived were copper-colored. When slavery was introduced onto the continent, the slaves were black. Color was everything" (p. 11). One of Vonnegut's tricks had been to undercut a supposedly awesome truth by using children's literature to describe it: *A Child's Cyclopedia of Wonders and Things to Do* for the time-warps in *The Sirens of Titan,* or *The Look-It-Up Book of the Stars and Planets* for deflating the space program in his essay, "Excelsior! We're Going to the Moon! Excelsior!" In *Breakfast of Champions* he expands this technique, born of his efforts in pulp science fiction and Sunday supplement journalism, to provide a perspective for his entire narrative.

Thematically, Vonnegut capped his lifelong interest in the imaginative transformation of reality by awarding to his science fiction writer Kilgore Trout the Nobel Prize—not for Literature, but for Medicine, for demonstrating the physiological effectiveness of ideas. Trout's epitaph reads, "We are healthy only to the extent that our ideas are humane" (p. 16). One of Trout's stories shows how ideas function less as carriers of concepts than as badges of Friendship;

another explains how they are essentially music to our ears. Above all, they are arbitrary and conventional—*made up,* in other words, and hence easy to reinvent for our changing needs. Eliot Rosewater had known this in *God Bless You, Mr. Rosewater* and in *Slaughter-house-Five. Breakfast of Champions* would teach this lesson to the world.

In addition to its innovative structure and ideas, which represent the triumph of innovative fiction in America, *Breakfast of Champions* also suggests the path disruptive fiction would follow in the later 1970's. Of all of Vonnegut's novels, it became the most articulate in defining the nature of human worth. "What in the hell are people for?" asked a dying character in Vonnegut's short story, "Welcome to the Monkey House," and *Breakfast of Champions* rises to great eloquence in answering that question. Vonnegut's spokesman is the Minimalist painter Rabo Karabekian, whose portraits leave out everything except "the immaterial core of every animal—the 'I am' to which all messages are sent. It is all that is alive in any of us." Karabekian's depiction of this quality is a single unwavering band of light, representing *awareness*. "Our awareness is all that is alive and maybe sacred in any of us," he says. "Everything else about us is dead machinery" (p. 221). It is the presence of this awareness, Vonnegut insists, which makes living beings inherently valuable. Only by concentrating on the "dead machinery" of our lives are they cheapened and made expendable; awareness is all. "What is the purpose of life?" Kilgore Trout has basically the same answer: "To be the eyes and ears and conscience of the Creator of the Universe" (p. 67).

Karabekian's theory is a restatement of the color-field aesthetic of Mark Rothko and the Minimalist canvases of Barnett Newman, both of whom painted in this manner in order to make deeply metaphysical statements. Such color-field paintings added a spiritual dimension to Abstract Expressionism, replacing the wild action of line with color's floating, illuminating presence. Rothko and Newman contributed a moral dimension to Abstract Expressionism in its later phase; Vonnegut's concerns in *Breakfast of Champions* pursue the same interest. What is significant is that Vonnegut pushes disruptive fiction toward moral statement, while adopting virtually all of its other "action writing" techniques.

Slapstick, published in 1976, is even more explicitly moral in its intention. Following the practice he inaugurated in *Slaughterhouse-Five* and continued in *Breakfast of Champions,* Vonnegut begins the book with an autobiographical Prologue relating the book's action to concerns in his personal life. For *Slaughterhouse-Five* it had been the experience of Dresden; with *Breakfast of Champions* it had been the task of staying cheerful during the Great Depression; now, in *Slapstick,* the autobiographical concern was with the death of his "ideal reader"—his sister Alice—and the devastating sense of loneliness which overtook him when his last connections with home disappeared.

Part of Vonnegut's disappointment was with human relations themselves. Love, as defined by one's predictable answer to the statement "I love you," seemed a sham. Common decency appeared more authentic, and also more useful to the human good. "I wish that people who are conventionally supposed to love each other would say to each other, when they fight, 'Please—a little less love, and a little more common decency,'" Vonnegut suggests.[4] Common decency had been the style of Vonnegut's family life as a child in Indianapolis—with his brother, with his beloved sister, and with his huge extended family of grandparents, uncles, aunts, and cousins which formed a sympathetic world where the youngster could feel secure. By the time of *Slapstick,* all of them were gone; there was no longer a bed for Kurt Vonnegut in Indianapolis, which now became as anonymous to him as any other faceless American city, and he felt achingly lonely. This is evident in the book's Prologue. In the novel itself Vonnegut transfers this idea to society at large, by detailing a future presidential campaign based on the creation of large artificial extended families so that each citizen can exclaim, "Lonesome no more!"

Trained as an anthropologist at the University of Chicago (1946–47) and awarded a M.A. by that institution in 1971, after many delays and rejections (with the novel *Cat's Cradle* finally accepted as his thesis), Vonnegut applies his professional discipline throughout *Slapstick.* Human beings seem to him like great, simple apes (the theory taught at Chicago in the 1940's), who can be prevented from doing mischief if provided with "a dozen or so rituals to be repeated

---

[4] Kurt Vonnegut, *Slapstick* (New York: Delacorte Press/Seymour Lawrence, 1976), p. 3. Subsequent references in parentheses.

simply endlessly" (p. 44). The extended family basis of society was drawn in like manner from "The Folk Society," the seminal essay by Robert Redfield published in the *American Journal of Sociology* in 1947, Vonnegut's last year at Chicago. Life itself was an imaginative invention, to be perfected when the two halves of human intelligence—intuition and logical habit—were united. The monstrous twins, Wilbur and Eliza, are Vonnegut's characterization of this dichotomy: united they form a single genius, but apart they are nothing. Personal dignity and meaning is the goal throughout *Slapstick*—which is indeed quite a test, given the slapstick world we inhabit. The ultimate models are the film comedians Laurel and Hardy, for in a booby-trapped world, and with no great intelligence, "They never failed to bargain in good faith with their destinies, and were screamingly adorable and funny on that account" (p. 1). As Robert Scholes said of the Bronx cheer that ends *Cat's Cradle,* the triumph for man caught in a divine practical joke is to "turn the humor back upon the joker." Vonnegut's earlier novels were good examples of such comic revenge, but *Slapstick* speaks more formally and more anthropologically of human potential.

Although *Slapstick* is written in Vonnegut's familiar style of short sentences, paragraphs, and chapters, with the action continually jumping back and forth between past and present (with at times a reference to the future), the book's effect is one of a firmly stated moral, as opposed to the great structural innovation which was employed in *Slaughterhouse-Five*. The destructive testing of *Breakfast of Champions,* modeled on the collision experiments carried out by engineers in Detroit to literally test the limits of their cars' endurance, is in *Slapstick* elevated to the saintly rituals of Stan Laurel and Oliver Hardy, "two angels of mine" as Vonnegut describes them in his dedication, whose films became "grotesque, situational poetry"—certainly a more elegant mode than the shenanigans of the previous novel. *Slapstick* "is about what life *feels* like to me," Vonnegut announces at the start, changing the activist mode of *Breakfast* to a more passive style of suffering and endurance. "There are all these tests of my limited agility and intelligence," Vonnegut complains. "They go on and on" (p. 1).

The innovative structure of the book may be more a product of habit than of design, since at times the "zip" of the story lags in favor of moral statement. That moral statement itself was foremost on Vonnegut's mind is indicated by the treatment he wrote for the potential producers of a film version. This twenty-two-page adaptation, sketching out the film scene by scene, reorganizes the story according to strictly chronological lines. Interplay of past and present is less important, Vonnegut seems to be saying, than the ultimate moral conclusion toward which every scene moves. Written and delivered to the producers in November, 1976, just two months after the novel was published and within the year in which Vonnegut wrote it, the screen treatment brings the moral to even greater prominence and underscores the path Vonnegut's art was taking.

Even more self-consciously moral is Kurt Vonnegut's novel completed and published in 1979, *Jailbird*.[5] It is in part a prison narrative, which expands to become a commentary on social good and evil in America since the days of Roosevelt. There is, of course, a tradition for such narratives—Eldridge Cleaver's *Soul on Ice,* parts of Malcolm X's *Autobiography*—but Vonnegut had to reinvent the form for the new realities of the 1970's. The reason? Watergate. As his fictional narrator, Walter F. Starbuck (Harvard '35), explains from his cell at Finletter Penitentiary:

> Was I shown no special respect as a Harvard Man? It was no distinction, actually. I met or heard of at least seven others. And no sooner would I leave than my cot would be taken by Virgil Greathouse, former Secretary of Health, Education and Welfare, who was also a Harvard man. I was quite low on the educational ladder at Finletter, with nothing but a poor bachelor's degree. I was not even Phi Beta Kappa. We must have had twenty or more Phi Beta Kappas, a dozen or more medical doctors, an equal number of dentists, a veterinarian, a Doctor of Divinity, a Doctor of Economics, and Doctor of Philosophy in Chemistry, and simply shoals of disbarred lawyers. Lawyers were so common that we had a joke for newcomers which went like this: "If you find yourself talking to somebody who hasn't been to Law School, watch your step. He's either the warden or a guard."

Vonnegut humanizes the narrative by having Starbuck tell stories, and tell them well, with the exquisite timing which has distinguished Vonnegut's own narratives. Contexts are invented for the springing

[5] Kurt Vonnegut, *Jailbird*. In manuscript at this reading. Published in September, 1979, by Delacorte Press/Seymour Lawrence (New York).

of slapstick jokes right out of the 1930's (Starbuck and an old girlfriend share them on the telephone), and as he prowls about New York on his first day of freedom, situations ranging from the mildly comic to the outrageously ludicrous pop up on every page. Governing it all is Starbuck's sense of himself as a self-effacing clown, involuntarily caught up by the wheels of history:

> I would soon be reminded of how much I used to smoke, for the gray, pin-stripe, three-piece Brooks Brothers suit awaiting me over in the supply room would be riddled with cigarette burns. There was a hole the size of a dime in the crotch, I remembered. A newspaper photograph was taken of me as I sat in the back of a Federal Marshal's green sedan, right after I was sentenced to prison. It was widely interpreted as showing how ashamed I was, haggard, horrified, unable to look anyone in the eye. It was in fact a photograph of a man who had just set his pants on fire.

Jailbird's by now traditional Prologue talks about Powers Hapgood, an actual Harvard man who impressed Vonnegut. Hapgood's family business, a canning operation, had been organized on altruistic principles which gave the workers a share in profits and a measure of control over how they performed their jobs. Hapgood himself was a champion of organized labor, and was jailed many times for leading illegal strikes. At one of his trials the judge asked him, "Why would a man from such a distinguished family and with such a fine education choose to live as you do?" Hapgood's reply: "Why? Because of the Sermon on the Mount, sir."

That sermon's devotion to an ideal of selfless charity is the moral which runs through *Jailbird,* from Prologue to Epilogue. Vonnegut's quaint and somewhat naive midwestern admiration for the promise of "Harvard Men" is part of his dream for America: from the best families, with the best of educations, and enjoying a legitimate position of power in American society, Harvard men like Walter F. Starbuck and his hero Kenneth Whistler would help all citizens share in the better life. Vonnegut even concocts a labor tragedy,. "The Cuyahoga Massacre," to traumatize Starbuck's patron so that the young man is sent to Harvard almost as an act of expiation. There was great beauty in the situation, Vonnegut shows us, when innocent and defenseless immigrants such as Nicola Sacco and Bartolomeo Vanzetti would draw to their defense such noblemen as the real Powers

Hapgood and the fictional Kenneth Whistler. Conventional wisdom of the day, from lawyers to judges and review panels, had no sympathy for the Italian-American anarchists. Only the saintly Harvard Men could see the truth, for they were the best and the brightest.

Walter Starbuck's post-Watergate world of 1979 lacks the noble edge which made possible the great labor and libertarian struggles of the 1920's and '30's. But that makes it all the easier to find moments of true grace and blessedness among the poeple. As he wanders about New York City during his first full day of freedom, Starbuck notes little bits of saintliness here and there, from a sympathetic room clerk to the archetypical coffee-ham-and-eggs waitress, whose uncritical cheer and love—everyone is "honeybunch" and "dear"—makes a welcome refuge from the holocaust of daily life. "My goodness," Starbuck reflects, "these waitresses and cooks are as unjudgmental as the birds and lizards on the Galapagos Islands, off Ecuador. . . . I had the feeling that if Frankenstein's monster crashed into the coffee shop through a brick wall, all anybody would say to him was, 'You sit down here, Lambchop, and I'll bring you your coffee right away.'"

The plot of *Jailbird,* a plot not even known to Walter Starbuck until near the end, is to take such random bits of holiness and organize them into a discipleship. One of his encounters has been with Mary Kathleen O'Looney, his old girlfriend from his days of Harvard radicalism. Ostensibly a poor shopping-bag lady, Mary is actually the widow and heir of Jack Graham, owner of the massive RAMJAC Corporation. Once she learns from Walter that a dozen or so people have blessed him with acts of kindness, she gathers them together almost as Christ gathered his Apostles. For RAMJAC they fill the roles of Vice-Presidents, also happening to fulfill America's middle-class dream of success. The VP's are rewarded in their own lives, while at her death Mary Kathleen has willed the fortunes of RAMJAC back to their rightful owners: the American people. Starbuck, chided for being born without a heart and for having set back humanitarianism one hundred years, is thus given a chance to redeem himself and all America in the process. "Acquire, acquire, acquire," Mary Kathleen urges her business directors, all so that the great corporate wealth of the country can be dispensed to the ultimate owners of all wealth —the humble, the meek, and the poor in spirit, to whom Christ dedicated the Sermon on the Mount.

Mary Kathleen O'Looney, with the Harvard man Walter F. Starbuck as her agent, would transform the economics of American life (another of *Jailbird*'s subjects), according to very sound business practice. The notion of acquiring and then dispersing a great fortune brings to mind Hawthorne's theme in *The House of the Seven Gables*. Vonnegut augments his moral theme with a bit of allegory; yet the allegory works in perfectly logical fashion, just like Eliot Rosewater's exemplary trick of writing out $300 checks to the science fiction writers at Milford. Both demonstrate the arbitrary nature of social reality, a reality which (as Starbuck and O'Looney knew as young Communists in the '30's) can be transformed.

Vonnegut, through his protagonist, would transform the work-a-day world of economic America into the Sermon on the Mount's Kingdom of the Blessed. To prove the feasibility of this change, he introduces another allegory, this time drawn from language (and language, we are told, is the substructure of perceived reality). Near the end of *Jailbird* Walter Starbuck meets two Pakistani ambulance attendants. They speak little English, but enough to explain the evolution of their own language, Urdu. "It had begun as a spare and ugly artificial language invented in the court of Genghis Khan. Its purpose in the beginning was military. It allowed his captains to give orders that were understood in every part of the Mongol Empire. Poets would later make it beautiful." In like manner, capitalism, the crudely practical economic system of the United States, would be made beautiful and humane by social poets of the type that Walter Starbuck and Mary Kathleen O'Looney had once hoped to be.

Jailbird ends with a recording of Starbuck's 1949 testimony to the infamous House Un-American Activities Committee. No greater champion of American capitalism than Richard Nixon is heard to ask Starbuck, "Why, as the son of immigrants who had been treated so well by Americans, as a man who had been treated like a son and been sent to Harvard by an American capitalist, had I been so ungrateful to the American economic system."

"Why?" Starbuck ponders. "The Sermon on the Mount, sir."

If Kurt Vonnegut's fiction of the 1970's adopted a self-consciously moral stance, Donald Barthelme's work of the same period showed that great technical innovation was still possible. Following the successes of his first three collections, Barthelme was chided for not extending his fictional art. *Sadness* (1972) and *Amateurs* (1976) were considered "soft" works, with few of the linguistic tricks demonstrated in his earlier volumes. On the other hand, *Guilty Pleasures* (1974) was nothing but play with language, since it collected his parodies and satires dating. back to 1963 (see Chapter Two, pp. 64–65). If Barthelme's art was to progress, there would have to develop a form particularly suited to the needs of his story.

In his novel *The Dead Father* (1975) and the collection *Great Days* (1979) Barthelme provides just such formal innovation. Large sections of the former plus seven complete stories in the latter are written in a "dash-dialogue" style. That is, there is no narration, no description, no externally present action; the presence of the author is not at all evident, for his managing hand is never seen. Instead, the entire fiction consists of dialogue lines—set off with dashes in the European manner, instead of with quotation marks—which rebound off one another with more effect, because there is no distracting material in between. Over half of *The Dead Father* is written in this manner, and the absence of the narrator is rarely a liability. Instead, the action advances more definitely because elemental sentences spoken by undescribed characters (rather than for them, by a storyteller) move things along.

Those sentences in *The Dead Father* which are not given over to dialogue are simple declarative affairs, instructing the reader in the universal qualities of fatherhood. The father's rugged features, his lordly language, and his generally impressive stature are proclaimed here and in the interpolated "Manual for Sons." Similar sentences denigrated the son—all sons, for that matter. "A son can never, in the fullest sense, become a father," we are told. "Some amount of amateur effort is possible. A son may after honest endeavor produce what some people might call, technically, children. But he remains a son. In the fullest sense."[6]

The real story of *The Dead Father* is told in the disembodied sections of dialogue—disembodied because they often lack immediate pertinence to the narrative, and also because each speaker's identity is lost after the first few exchanges. Barthelme's model for

[6] Donald Barthelme, *The Dead Father* (New York: Farrar, Straus & Giroux, 1975), p. 33. Subsequent references in parentheses.

these conversations is simple table talk (even a seating diagram is presented). A sense of the emerging action, such as the characters' discontent, evolves from simple comments on the food:

> Give you a shirtful of sore tit.
> Give you a fret in the gizzard.
> I tried to tell you but you wouldn't listen.
> Think I'm getting a nosebleed.
> Ways of dealing with them when they don't want you.
> Friendship is difficult at best.
> People are frightened.
> They disagree with me regularly but are not disloyal to me.
> Said there were various ways of handling it but I thought I could keep
> the lid on.
> Wake up one dark night with a thumb in your eye.
> Strung out like that along the hedges.
> Colder weather coming and then warmer.
> Since you have not as yet responded to my suggestion.
> Matter of paring down to a supportable minimum.
> Throw a little shit into the game.
> Always darkest just before the dawn.
> Take it any way you like it. (p. 60)

Such conversations begin as random grumblings, lack any real sense of direction, and soon deteriorate into fragments. But they do carry meaning, even as Barthelme moves them toward the abstract qualities of words alone. At times even silence speaks (as when Emma carries on a painfully one-sided conversation with an ape). By the end, we have an even deeper sense of the father's eminence and of the son's vulnerability and diminished stature, all thanks to the bits of conversation tossed out by Thomas, Julie, Emma, and the Dead Father himself, as the latter is hauled to his grave.

The more traditional sections of *The Dead Father* capitalize on Barthelme's favorite subject, the quality of the human voice. Examples given in the "Manual" portray the all-too-familiar rant characteristic of fathers everywhere:

> Hey son. Hey boy. Let's you and me go out and throw the ball around. Throw the ball around. You don't want to go out and throw the ball around? . . . Well, let's see, you don't want to go out and throw the ball around, you can help me work on the patio. You want to help

me work on the patio? Sure you do. Sure you do. . . . . C'mon kid, I'll
let you hold the level. And this time I want you to hold the fucking
thing straight. (p. 125)

Of course, the son can't hold the level straight. No son ever can. But
then there is the universal indictment sons deliver up against their
fathers, from which there is also no escape:

> He is mad about being small when you were big, but no, that's not it,
> he is mad about being helpless when you were powerful, but no, not
> that either, he is mad about being contingent when you were neces-
> sary, not quite it, he is insane because when he loved you, you didn't
> notice. (p. 143)

Great Days is the type of work that Robert Scholes and William H.
Gass call "metafictional," since its main endeavor is to study the ways
in which fiction is made. But Donald Barthelme is an old hand at
metafiction, and this later collection shows how deft he has become at
the business. *City Life* (1970) was almost purely metafiction, with
stories talking self-consciously about themselves ("Sentence") or
adding up to nothing more than random assemblages of words ("Bone
Bubbles"). The stories collected in *Sadness* (1972) seemed just the
reverse: with few technical remarks in evidence, they parsed out the
realistic details of contemporary urban life with much more fidelity
than those in the earlier volume (see, for example, "Critique de la Vie
Quotidienne"). *Great Days* is at once more metafictional and more
easily readable than either earlier volume, for Barthelme has found
the way to let fictions explore themselves at the same time they present an entertaining divertissement to the reader.

One of Barthelme's familiar devices is the set-piece narrative,
often contained in a paragraph or two (as in the miniature chapters of
Snow White), which explores the linguistic surfaces of life. In "The
Crisis" we read about a group of revolutionists who spend their first
day on a golf course, bereft of clubs and ball, wandering about the
fairways in utter disregard of the game and how it is played. Their
own innocence reflects the naïveté of the sentences themselves,
which, in simple declarative fashion, skirt the surface of the scene,
never getting down to essentials. "Yes, an afternoon on the links!"
the characters exclaim. "So green and full of holes and flags!"[7] In

---

[7] Donald Barthelme, *Great Days* (New York: Farrar, Straus & Giroux, 1979), p. 5.
Subsequent references in parentheses.

another story, "The Apology," a girlfriend begs her absent lover's forgiveness—but her entreaties work as offensive challenges which drive away another, unwanted suitor. Her sentences are thus filled with content, but are effective as simple forms. The prize of Barthelme's collection is "The New Music," in which characters use language to run through musical routines almost like vaudeville turns. Trading disembodied dialogue back and forth, one speaker tells of how he "went Xeroxing," copying "a box of English muffins, two pounds of ground veal and an apple. In flagrant violation of the Copyright Act" (p. 21). The other confesses that he was distracted by the approaches of a lovely young woman who "was looking at me quite seductively, very seductively, *smoldering* a bit," until he realized that "she was just practicing" (p. 22). Later they run through another routine which Barthelme had earlier published as a separate story, "Momma":

> —Momma didn't 'low no clarinet played in here. Unfortunately.
> —Momma.
> —Momma didn't 'low no clarinet played in here. Made me sad.
> —Momma was outside.
> —Momma was *very* outside.
> —Sitting there 'lowing and not-'lowing. In her old rocking chair.
> —'Lowing this, not-'lowing that.
> —Didn't 'low oboe.
> —Didn't 'low gitfiddle. Vibes.
> —Rock over your damn foot and bust it, you didn't pop to when she was 'lowing and not-'lowing.
> —Right. 'Course, she had all the grease.
> —True.
> —You wanted a little grease, like to buy a damn comic book or something, you had to go to Momma.
> —Sometimes yes, sometimes no. Her variously colored moods.
> —Mauve. Warm gold. Citizen's blue. (p. 29)

The conversation ranges over various topics and, as in *The Dead Father,* starts to deteriorate into grace notes and trills, one of which is "Daddy." But the partner objects. "We said we weren't going to do Daddy." So the subject of Momma is put back on the conversation's track, just as jazz musicians would agree which tune would be the subject of their improvisations. Improvisational jazz, improvisational comedy, and improvised conversations—Barthelme uses these models to get down to pure writing, without losing the sense of where the mimetic elements of his story are leading. The play of elements, both linguistic and contextual, reminds us that ours is an age of performance. The stories of *Great Days* play out these routines to the fullest.

After beginning with three stories crafted in his new style, *Great Days* moves on to a centerpiece of nine fictions in which the dialogue is filled out. Contexts are fashioned for the previously dangling conversations, but the emphasis is still upon verbal exchange. "Cortés and Montezuma" expands to the paragraph form; each separate paragraph (reminiscent of "Robert Kennedy Saved from Drowning") presents a brief discussion between the two leaders, with occasional sections reserved for listings of the new European words and concepts which, in the company of the Spanish conquerors, are infiltrating the Aztec domain. In "The Question Party" Barthelme moves to another time and culture, and to another highly artificial way of exchanging sentences. The characters here are engaged in a Victorian parlor game in which persons are challenged to supply a question matching each proposed answer. Throughout, language itself takes the most prominent part, as the gentlemen and ladies vie to outstyle each other with their intricate *bon mots*. Language itself finally disrupts the party—one rogue introduces some blatantly sexual terminology into this hothouse of restrained innuendo and unleashes pure pandemonium, climaxing with his own violent murder. The lesson is clear: once the language is exhausted, reality itself collapses. Other stories from this center section explore the ins and outs of voice; for example, the yammering of senior citizens in "Belief," and the reorchestration of "The Abduction from the Seraglio" in a South Texas country and western drawl. In "The Zombies" language deconstructs into simple rhythm. "The zombies say: 'Wonderful time! Beautiful day! Marvelous singing! Excellent beer! Would that lady marry me? I don't know!' In a high wind the leaves fall from the trees, from the trees" (pp. 116–117).

The volume concludes with four more stories in the dash-dialogue mode—this time a bit more adventuresome, because the reader has been shown how central dialogue must be to any of Barthelme's fictions. Conversations fade away into rhythmic exchanges, musical duets. The last piece ends with the archetypal form of all dialogue, in the form of a child's knock-knock joke which the adult speaker here unwittingly falls for:

> —There's a thing the children say.
> —They say: Will you always love me.
> —Always.
> —Will you always remember me?
> —Always.
> —Will you love me a year from now?
> —Yes, I will.
> —Will you remember me two years from now?
> —Yes, I will.
> —Will you remember me five years from now?
> —Yes, I will.
> —Knock knock.
> —Who's there?
> —You see? (pp. 171–172)

The work of virtually every major literary disruptionist underwent major change in the 1970's, but that change was neither random nor happenstance. In each case the modification of technique served to strengthen the respective writer's most personal talent. In Vonnegut's case, it involved including himself as a self-conscious creator throughout his book (*Breakfast of Champions*), and the result was, by the time of *Jailbird,* a great moral eloquence which had been struggling to find its voice all through his cataclysmic fiction of the '60's. Barthelme's transformation was just the opposite: by removing himself completely from the story, leaving no trace of the author/creator, he managed to focus attention on the linguistic and even musical properties of his fiction without resorting to the Dadaistic games of *City Life*. Other writers such as Ronald Sukenick, Raymond Federman, Gilbert Sorrentino, Clarence Major, Steve Katz, and Michael Stephens found ways of better expressing their own fictional strategies, as we shall see. But it was Jerzy Kosinski, the most consciously thematic of all the disruptionists, who undertook the most decided change in ideological posture. Changing times and Kosinski's own maturity and experience had much to do with this transformation, but the real reason was the existence of his previous books themselves.

Kosinski admitted to interviewer Daniel Cahill in 1975 that, in the years since its first publication, *The Painted Bird* had taken on a life of its own. The subject of political debate in Eastern Europe and of censorship campaigns in the United States, the book eclipsed its author's own life—a life that Kosinski had endeavored from the start to keep independent of the book. As the real-life Jerzy Kosinski and his fictional protagonists grew in age and experience, the Boy of *The Painted Bird* retained his own identity and language—a "new language of brutality and its consequent counter-language of anguish and despair," which Kosinski had created to explore the already historically effaced reality of World War II.[8] Increasing his distance from the novel, Kosinski confessed that, ten years later, he could not picture himself writing it again. Unlike the conditions portrayed in his other works, the imaginative condition of childhood central to *The Painted Bird* was "inverifiable."

Instead, he undertook a campaign to place the novel in the perspective of his own personal life and his career as a fictionist. The original Houghton Mifflin edition had been problematic, with much of Kosinski's more brutal descriptions removed and with an unintended epilogue added without his permission. After restoring the original text in its first paperback edition and then making further stylistic changes in its Modern Library edition,[9] Kosinski returned the book to its original publisher in 1975 for an "anniversary edition" (intended for the tenth, but actually appearing early in the eleventh year after first publication), from which all new paperback editions would derive.

Beginning with the dust jacket, the new edition spoke more directly of Kosinski's personal concern. The jacket was designed by Roy R. Behrens, and in his early versions the composite face of a deformed man stood out from a background of smaller characters in the style of Dürer or Bosch (a Boschean detail had been Kosinski's choice for both the Pocket Book and Bantam editions). But Kosinski objected that the facial deformations appeared syphilitic, and instead made a surprising counterproposal: he would give Behrens a photo of himself as a five-year-old child, handsome and innocent, with soft lips and wide, dark eyes, to be placed among the Dürer grotesqueries.

[8] Jerzy Kosinski, "Afterward" [*sic*], *The Painted Bird* (Boston: Houghton Mifflin, 1976), p. xii.

[9] Detailed by Philip R. Rider in "The Three States of the Text of Kosinski's *The Painted Bird*," *Papers of the Bibliographical Society of America*, 72 (3rd quarter, 1978), 361–384.

Kosinski had now turned practically 180 degrees from the anonymity and autobiographical disclaimers of the first edition, and was publishing the Boy's story with his own youthful photograph on the cover. Within, a detailed seventeen-page "Afterward" prefaced the novel, not only telling how Kosinski came to write the book but also offering information about his own experiences during the war, which now seemed closer than ever to the Boy's supposedly fictional tale. Interviews during the period displayed the same candor. Kosinski was now more closely identified with his book than a reader of the original edition might suspect.

This closeness served an important purpose as the author contemplated more novels. *The Painted Bird,* he now saw, was the commencement of a five-book cycle, each subsequent volume to "contain" all the previous works, climaxing with *Cockpit* (1975). *Blind Date* (1977), which revealed even more of Kosinski's personal experiences, would comment on the cycle as a whole. With references to both the author's life and the scenes in his earlier novels, and often mixing historical and fictional references in the same sentence, *Blind Date* became something quite new: an "auto-bibliography," the furthest extreme from Kosinski's careful self-detachment from the subjects in *The Painted Bird* of 1965.

In the novels since *The Painted Bird* Kosinski's protagonists have gradually matured, their experiences following Kosinski's own since his childhood during the war. *Steps* took the young man from Eastern Europe to America. *Being There* reflected the suddenness of attention, much as Kosinski himself must have experienced it with the success of his collective behavior books, his introduction to jet-set society through his marriage to Mary Weir, and the notoriety earned by *The Painted Bird.* His next novel, *The Devil Tree,* featured a younger protagonist—but drawn from the ranks of the bright and privileged students whom Kosinski had been teaching at Wesleyan, Princeton, and Yale. *Cockpit*[10] signals the cycle's end, if only in the age and physical condition of its protagonist, a man named Tarden who has retired from "the service" and whose health is marginal at best.

Tarden's character shows that the author's concerns (and manner of treating them) have also come full circle. The Boy was naive; Tarden is experienced. Society, which was in the beginning virtually

[10] Jerzy Kosinski, *Cockpit* (Boston: Houghton Mifflin, 1975).

omnipotent, is here manipulated by a man of power beyond the Boy's most eager fantasies. And Tarden himself is the supreme rationalist, the self-confident man grown from the Boy's first attempts to reason out his existence in a world which at the time resisted such investigation. But for all the advantages Tarden enjoys, there is a greater sense of loss. His ultimate security has sentenced him to utter loneliness in his living, his lovemaking, and especially his anticipated death. Innumerable stories restate this theme: of a bosom friend becoming a psychotic enemy, of lovers who betray, of one's own body decaying into a prison. The longer one lives, the more likely one is to end one's days as a helpless vegetable. "For me," Kosinski told Daniel Cahill just before the novel's publication, "what Tarden is terrified of is the indifference to life. He activates others and he activates therefore himself."[11] As in *Blind Date,* activation often takes the form of revenge against dishonest lovers, persecutors of the innocent, and enemies of the human spirit. But revenge is little consolation for the isolation Tarden suffers. The dedications of *The Painted Bird* and *Cockpit* set the limits of Kosinski's personal values, which in both cases depend upon life shared with a loved one. The first novel was dedicated "To my wife Mary, without whom even the past would lose its meaning." In *Cockpit,* with its protagonist pushed against the wall of alienation and indifference, Kosinski's dedication is more personal still: "For Katherina, the sound and touch of my life." Without such sound and touch, Tarden's life is a wasteland.

The five-book cycle from *The Painted Bird* to *Cockpit* has explored the relative values of personal security and power, from the orphan Boy cast loose upon the battlefield of World War II to the supremely confident agent controlling life from his self-contained cockpit. Kosinski's subsequent novel, *Blind Date,*[12] is closest in spirit to *Cockpit,* for it details the similar adventures of another mature protagonist—this time named George Levanter. However, Kosinski has made this newer novel the closest record to his own experiences since *The Painted Bird.* Levanter travels the world for "Investors International," which by several innuendoes becomes a fiction for the organization Kosinski led during these same years, the PEN/American Center. A visiting African dignitary mistakes Levanter for a bellboy, just

[11] Unpublished interview with Daniel Cahill, New York, June 17–18, 1975.
[12] Jerzy Kosinski, *Blind Date* (Boston: Houghton Mifflin, 1977).

as Kosinski was mistaken for a waiter during a PEN banquet for President Senghor. Levanter helps free an imprisoned writer, just as Kosinski wrote letters of protest for the Iranian writer Reza Baraheni.[13] Dozens of other stories connect: the Russian language episode in a Paris café, Kosinski's prank of squirting a garden hose from his high-rise apartment on West 57th Street, his trick of speeding letters through the mail by benefit of a dozen or so high-priority rubber stamps, his learning of English because his native Slavic tongues lacked the proper words for romantic seductions. Many of these autobiographical episodes were first recounted by Kosinski on talk shows—"to try them out on an audience," as he now explains. Others have been told by him and about him among friends; indeed, over the past ten years they have developed into an ongoing Kosinski legend which the author cultivates as his own life of fiction, another protective device.

But for those who know the entire Kosinski legend, *Blind Date* presents some real challenges. Just when we think we have tracked Kosinski down, he adds a coda designed to repel the autobiographical seeker. To the well-known story of his mother's death Levanter adds a startling revelation: he and his mother had been incestuous lovers since his adolescence. When Levanter and his companion are kidnapped by a maniacal taxidriver (a story Kosinski told in 1975), the presumed Kosinski stand-in murders the kidnapper in a scene of unmatched brutality. The more intimately one knows the real author, the more horrid are the scenes which follow each supposedly familiar story.

The novel's climax calls upon the most well-known Kosinski association, his narrow escape from the Charles Manson murders. In 1969 Kosinski, as a recent winner of the National Book Award and jet-set companion of the Roman Polanski/Sharon Tate/Abigail Folger group, became part of the lurid news story when only his misplaced luggage caused him to miss his scheduled flight to the fatal party. Indeed, the first police investigators suspected Kosinski himself might have been the murderer, since telegrams were found promising his arrival. As publicized by the media at the time, documented by Vincent Bugliosi in *Helter Skelter*[14] and by Ed Sanders in *The*

---

[13] Reza Baraheni, *The Crowned Cannibals* (New York: Vintage, 1977), pp. 202–206.

[14] Vincent Bugliosi, *Helter Skelter* (New York: Norton, 1974), pp. 31–33, 144, 178–180.

Family,[15] and discussed by talk show interviewers later, Kosinski's involvement would certainly be known to the more interested readers of *Blind Date.* For this most widely shared of his fictionalized experiences, Kosinski reserves his most calculatingly brutal writing. Having mastered this style in *The Painted Bird,* he uses it to detail the minute-by-minute experiences of some of his very closest friends. The writing is strongest because Levanter, and Kosinski, must imagine the scene. As in *The Great Gatsby,* the narrator has not been present at the killings, and so must reconstruct the happening in his mind. In Levanter's (and, again, Kosinski's) case, this reconstruction is fraught with personal responsibility, for the narrator was the one who introduced two of the principals on the book's archetypal blind date. Responsibility extends as far as the human imagination will allow it; guilt and anxiety know few limits, and this very energy informs the passage's style. The episode becomes the novel's heart.

But, as in *Cockpit,* revenge becomes an impersonal and depersonalizing affair, outweighing the moments of sympathy in Levanter's life and finally isolating him from humankind. For him, sexuality is particularly grotesque; he seems satisfied only with malformed creatures or anonymous rapes, and his flattering affair with the "Foxy Lady" turns out to be a sham, for her sex is artificial. His death at the novel's end is solitary and cold, a metaphor for the spiritual end man creates for himself by such willful isolation.

The themes of Kosinski's novels, then, have shifted since *The Painted Bird.* In the social context of that novel, personal self-sufficiency was the goal. *Steps* tested this goal against the social union of two persons, who could best meet as equals within their own selves. But with *Being There* the problematics of life—especially life in America—began to assert themselves, and Kosinski's next three novels present a series of protagonists each more calculating and austere than the last, from Jonathan Whalen through Tarden to George Levanter. Yet the development was not entirely negative, for in *Blind Date* a new philosophy was offered. The French biologist Jacques Monod appears in this novel, corresponding to the stories Kosinski has told, and bringing with him quotations from his book

---

[15] Ed Sanders, *The Family* (New York: Dutton, 1971), pp. 134–135, 263.

Chance and Necessity.[16] Monod's actual death figures as an episode
in the novel, but together with Levanter's death the emphasis is on the
hope for freedom within life.

Monod's argument in *Chance and Necessity,* which Kosinski's
protagonist rehearses in *Blind Date* (solving, in the process, Jonathan
Whalen's problem of family determinacy in *The Devil Tree*), is that
scientific interpretations of life which assume an "ascending, constructive, creative intent" or "purpose" in life are in fact "animist
projections," as cruelly misleading as they are fraudulent (p. 39).
Life instead is a machine, locked into its own order and impervious to
outside "hints" (p. 110); we live and we die simply as if "Our number
came up in the Monte Carlo game" (p. 146). As Vonnegut suggests in
more metaphorical terms, there is no free will when it comes to our
physical destiny, and it is horribly unfair to insist that there is human
responsibility in this regard.

To realize this condition, Monod insists, leads to a greater freedom. "All the traditional systems have placed ethics and values
beyond man's reach. Values did not belong to him; he belonged to
them. He now knows that they are his and his alone." (p. 173).
Kosinski repeats this quote in *Blind Date,* following Monod's thesis
that man should be happier without the need for false and domineer-
ing explanations. Our tragedy, as Vonnegut has agreed, is not our
biological determination, but what runs counter to it: "our need for an
explanation, the profound disquiet which goads us to search out the
meaning of existence. That same disquiet has created all the myths,
all the religions, all the philosophies, and science itself" (p. 167).

"With a true sense of the randomness of life's moments, man is at
peace with himself—and that peace is happiness."[17] Such is Kosinski's judgment of Monod's work, which in turn informs *Blind Date.*
And with this insight the initial five-book cycle is brought into view.
"In *The Painted Bird,*" Kosinski indicates, "society refuses the
individual (the Boy) a place within itself by waging a war against
him; in *Cockpit,* it is the individual (Tarden) who, refusing the place

[16] Jacques Monod, *Chance and Necessity* (New York: Alfred A. Knopf, 1971). References
in parentheses.

[17] Daniel Cahill, "An Interview with Jerzy Kosinski on *Blind Date,*" *Contemporary
Literature,* 19 (Spring, 1978), 142. Subsequent references in parentheses.

society insists he occupy, wages a war against the institutions of society." *Blind Date* "redirects these concerns" toward the duty of an individual "to examine and assume responsibility for *one's own* actions regardless of the societal framework in which they occur" (pp. 133–134). Destiny is not determinism, for it is written concurrently with the event, not prior to it.

The most radical innovators of the late 1960's and early '70's were Ronald Sukenick, Raymond Federman, and Gilbert Sorrentino. Their respective major novels—*Up, Double or Nothing,* and *Imaginative Qualities of Actual Things*—represented disruptive fiction in its ascendancy and set the goal of fiction as pure writing, to which other novelists would aspire. In particular, each of these novels was blatantly self-reflexive: in all cases the writer was present as the creator of his own story, taking pleasure in the act of creation which the reader was meant to share. For all three novels the major effect was comedy and, in a narrow sense, parody of the ways in which traditional novels are written. And like all works of parody, they shone brightest only by reflecting the object of their scorn.

Could these same techniques transcend parody and become liberating conventions in themselves? For fiction to be pure writing, they would have to—and in 1979 each of these authors produced a notable work with this in mind. Ronald Sukenick's fiction, which heretofore had carried a heavy critical and theoretical burden,[18] now distilled itself into pure writing as the author redirected his more critical thinking into several major essays on the subject of writing itself.[19] Free to write pure fiction, he quickly produced three novels: an exuberantly comic work entitled *The Fortune Teller,* a more arcane fiction based on mathematical permutations, and an energetic, breathless novel consisting of one 142-page sentence, *Long Talking Bad Condition Blues.*[20]

---

[18] *Up* contained reviews and critiques of itself by the author and by some of his characters; "The Death of the Novel" included a lecture on that subject; *Out* self-consciously deconstructed itself as a novel; the last section of *98.6* reads as a utopian essay on art and life.

[19] Ronald Sukenick, "Twelve Digressions Toward a Theory of Composition," *New Literary History,* 6 (Winter, 1974–75), 429–437; "Thirteen Digressions," *Partisan Review,* 43, #1 (1976), 90–101; "Fiction in the Seventies: Ten Digressions on Ten Digressions," *Studies in American Fiction,* 5 (Spring, 1977), 99–108.

[20] A section of *The Fortune Teller* appeared in *Trema* (Paris), #2 (1977), pp. 143–146; part of the numerological novel was printed as "The Endless Short Story: Five and Ten," in *Criss-Cross Art Communications,* 6 (March, 1978), 36–41; *Long Talking Bad Conditions Blues* was in manuscript at this writing, for Fall 1979 publication by the Fiction Collective, New York.

Sukenick's critical essays constitute the best aesthetic justification for the disruptive fiction that he and his colleagues have been writing. For him, the chief culprit had been Modernism, and particularly the critical establishment called into being by Modernism. The critical doctrines of T. S. Eliot, for example, reflected the reductivism of the day's positivistic science and philosophy, with disastrous consequences for literature. "The hermeneutics of the New Criticism was, in part, a prophylaxis designed to protect life from the disruptive energy of art," Sukenick proposed. Think of the horrified reaction to Charles Olson and Allen Ginsberg, and of how William Carlos Williams had been relegated to secondary status behind the high modernists, who devalued the poets following Walt Whitman. The most striking example was Henry Miller:

> Henry Miller is for American novelists what Whitman is for American poets. The source of his vitality is the current which began flowing when he reconnected our art with our experience. Experience begins with the self and Miller put the self back into fiction. For a writer the whole point of literary technique is the fullest possible release of the energy of his personality into his work, and when one comes into contact with that force, the whole superstructure that one had assumed to be the point of literature begins to burn away.[21]

Hence the vitalistic fiction of Miller, the conversational "I do this/I do that" poetry of Frank O'Hara, and the action painting of Hans Hofmann, Jackson Pollock, Franz Kline, and Willem de Kooning. The latter had been "the triumph of American painting"—like jazz, our country's original contribution to world art. Only in fiction did similar creativity lag behind, because of the systematic strictures imposed by the Modernist critics, who kept insisting that fiction must refer to a higher world of morals, myth, and order, rather than—like those other forms of art—to itself.

Fiction is no more about a "subject" than jazz is about a melody or abstract painting is about an object. Moreover, talking about the supposed fictional subject removes one from participation in the work itself, just as a coldly analytical survey of an action painting's images destroys the effective sense of composition in the work. The canvas is not a plane on which to represent, but an arena in which to act (Harold Rosenberg); in like manner, the novel is a field in which the novelist exercises his or her energies, and the proper appreciation is for the

[21] Sukenick, "Thirteen Digressions," p. 96.

reader to reenact that energy, to follow the lines of composition, just as the viewer sweeps and dances through a Pollock or de Kooning painting. Words are no more pledged to an exterior, conceptual reality than daubs of paint or notes of music, as any critic should know:

> The words used meditatively in a literary work are not the same words used instrumentally in the world of action. Words in dreams do not mean the same thing as words in the newspaper. The word *fog* in *Bleak House* does not mean the same thing as the word *fog* in the dictionary, though its meaning in *Bleak House,* once developed, could be, probably has been, added to the general sense—one sees this process on any page of the OED. What language signifies in a literary work is different from what it signifies in its general sense, but then may be added to that sense.[22]

Long Talking Bad Conditions Blues derives its form from Sukenick's earlier works—its quaintly coined terminology from *98.6,* its restless characters from *Up,* and its relentless forward movement from "Momentum." Behind it all is the author's radical theory of composition. The book has no subject other than itself, but for once there is no need for a self-conscious author at center stage. Instead, the movement of the writing codifies the energetic life being lived. Movement is indicated by syntax: "basically she didn't like Drecker, Drecker treated her like a piece of shit something about her liked being treated like a piece of shit that's why she liked him." The world in which *Blues* takes place is governed by the same wacky grammar. "Everything was breaking up and going to pieces," we are told, and the inclination is "the hell with it let it go." But the narrator is drawn by this energy, and tries to define it in two ways: by serving as a witness to its flow, and by coining names for its behavior. Hence characters slip into the "verbal holes" which correspond to the similarly vacuous "carnal wholes" of their bodies; fragmentation proceeds according to "shatter patterns"; the corollary to "flow" is "blockage," and a "lack of synchronic rhythms" can lead to "the sexual impasse" that all of Sukenick's characters seem to suffer. A sense of change, of a transformation of human values, appears imminent, and a language is invented to describe it: "loose tongues

22 Sukenick, "Twelve Digressions," p. 434.

would uncode the vatic structures of desire exposing the orgasm behind the orgasm and release seething fructive centers that would burn through the complacency of innuendo astonish the heavy stasis lassitude and pass on in hissing dimenuendos trascending disgust and exposing the nameless abyss."

Pseudo-language is, however, just a by-product of the energy itself. The narrator's chief role is to be its witness, just as Sukenick himself spent half a year observing life in Paris while thinking back to Brooklyn Dodgers' baseball. "That was how he thought about his function in this place," we learn, "that of keeping everything company . . . thinking who if not he would attend the petty iconography of the quotidian the texture of our days which is their meaning if any which unattended grows so lonely so forlorn." Such are the "obligations of observation," except that "it was never observation but always invention and even prophecy." As in *Out*, "his only model was clouds their resolution in the sky their subtle transitions from nothing to something in the empty air."

More than anything else, *Long Talking Bad Conditions Blues* reads as a testimony to living in the world. The author remains so open to experience that experience is finally all we have, no more or less valuable than the record of a Charlie Parker solo or a Jackson Pollock drip painting. Words refer to the author's experience in the world only as he commits it to the page, and even then, as in the book's conclusion, their syntactic function refers more closely to the act of fiction itself:

> while the day petered peacefully out in the gray afternoon drizzle smudging the outlines of the ancient city as he went walking off down The Walker noting moisture beading on black umbrellas the overhead fillagree of trees starting to leaf the muffled roar of distant motors the hiss of a bicycle the click of a boot the sway of a haunch the rose of a cheek the clunk of a car door closing a pigeon flopping gracelessly by the sculpted hairdo of a demoiselle the texture of a pastry tart in a store window the feel of a city street in the rain and all the other cheap thrills of the afternoon but wishing they hadn't demolished the old public toilets because he had to piss a fact more fundamental than a fund of ephemeral epiphanies but reflecting that all things come to an end at the same time recognizing there was no point imposing a sense of tragedy on old public toilets and that things didn't have beginnings and endings in that sense they just start and then they stop

The flow of writing, as expressing the energetic flow of experience, is the quality Sukenick seeks in his own writing and admires in
the work of others. Reviewing George Chambers's novel *The Bonny-
Clabber* for the *New York Times,* he praised its projective strength, its
quality of "going and going."[23] This same relentless forward motion
was what drew him to Raymond Federman's *Double or Nothing.*
Ostensibly a novel about a man sitting down to write a novel, its
proposed subject is an utter vacancy: the deaths of Federman's family
in a concentration camp during the war which, like Vonnegut's
Dresden massacre, is an atrocity answerable only by silence. At the
heart of *Double or Nothing* lies an "evasion . . . urgent and obsessive" which Sukenick found to be the enabling power of Federman's
work.[24] To cover up the nightmare is Federman's impetus for writing;
and like the sneaky thief he must be, Federman invents game upon
game to evade the awful truth. But once started, he must go on, for to
stop is to call forth the image he cannot face.

The Voice in the Closet[25] is Federman's third treatment of his
central theme. Because it is the closest so far to the central event, it is
the shortest and most intense. From *Double or Nothing* through *Take
It or Leave It* to this newest, smallest work, Federman's art has
followed the distillation of Sukenick's writing but is also compress-
ing itself to a central core. Because of the unspeakable nature of that
core, the surrounding writing is all the more highly charged. As
Charles Caramello notes:

> Federman inscribes his central event within an aesthetic of fiction that
> proscribes both centrality and event as possibilities. The central event
> in Federman's fiction is not the extermination of his family but the
> erasure of that extermination as a central event. It is, I believe,
> Federman's ambivalence toward this erasure that charges his work
> emotionally and that informs its risks.[26]

Hence Federman's fiction escapes the burden of content by its very
indirection; because of the vacant center, he must proceed by elabo-

---

[23] Ronald Sukenick, Review of *The Bonny-Clabber* by George Chambers, *New York Times
Book Review,* March 3, 1973, pp. 32–33.

[24] Ronald Sukenick, "Refugee from the Holocaust" [review of *Double or Nothing* by
Raymond Federman], *New York Times Book Review,* October 1, 1972, p. 40.

[25] Raymond Federman, *The Voice in the Closet:* in manuscript at this writing, published in
July, 1979, by the Coda Press (Madison, Wisconsin).

[26] Charles Caramello, "Flushing Out 'The Voice in the Closet,'" *Sub-Stance* #20 (1978),
101–113.

rate digression, one of the strategies Ronald Sukenick prefers to the dishonestly arrow-straight progress in so-called mimetic fiction.[27] That the digression becomes the story itself is preferrable as a sustaining convention to the artificial and awkward device of having the author self-consciously present within the work.

Writers grow beyond this technique in a variety of ways: Federman by digression, Sukenick by a distillation of experience reflected in the energy of writing, Barthelme by reducing his fictions to simple exchanges of sentences. Gilbert Sorrentino, in *Imaginative Qualities of Actual Things,* was the most intrusively present of authors, as he ran his disliked characters through scores of humiliations and then footnoted their complaints with amusing disclaimers of his own. But following the trend of literary disruption into the 1970's, Sorrentino found a way to efface himself from the novel without losing control of its self-apparent artifice. His own triumph in this method is *Mulligan Stew,*[28] a massive novel which sought a publisher for nearly five years before it was eventually released by Grove Press in May, 1979. Sorrentino's only presence in this novel is at the very start, in eleven pages distinctively printed on light blue paper. Here Sorrentino retaliates against five years of inept consideration by offering sample rejection letters and reader's reports. With this understandable rancor out of the way, *Mulligan Stew* proceeds as a marvelously self-contained novel.

Sorrentino's method is drawn from Flann O'Brien's *At Swim-Two-Birds* (1939), a comic masterpiece in which a book's characters revolt and lay their own designs against its tyrannical and inept author. But in Sorrentino's hand the "living novel" is expanded to allow the full range of writing techniques—narrative, notebooks, source material, author's letters, character's complaints and all. An unbelievably bad novel called *Guinea Red* is being written by a paranoiac failure named Anthony Lamont. His scenes are characterized by inflatedly bad writing and inept plotting (the book is a murder mystery, but Lamont keeps moving the corpse and changing its fatal wound). Between chapters we read letters to his sister, brother-in-law (O'Brien's sham novelist Dermot Trellis), and a midwestern college professor who may teach Lamont's work "in a surfiction course." Complementing the chapters are Lamont's working notes, his scrap-

---

[27] Sukenick, "Thirteen Digressions," p. 93.
[28] Gilbert Sorrentino, *Mulligan Stew* (New York: Grove Press, 1979).

books, and a curious series of notebooks which reveal the man's utter banality of spirit ("In Jellos we uncover one of the Great Yankee dishes. Try them with tuna and noodles in a casserole. Dalicious!"; "Pitchers are bad hitters because they think of the ball as their friend"). Often Sorrentino takes the initiative and uses these notebooks to list 1940's songs, slang expressions, and other popular culture effluvia in a catechism of question and response and finally a cacophony of pure linguistics—but even then stray words and phrases from this *mélange* pop up in Lamont's narrative. Finally, in Flann O'Brien fashion, Lamont's narrator slips away from the story and makes entries in his own notebook, denigrating Lamont's abilities as a fictionist and yearning for better employment.

Bad writing by Lamont is of course an excuse for comic writing by Sorrentino. Every element of the book being made is an invitation for Sorrentino to display all the excitement his pen can command. But unlike *Imaginative Qualities,* the proposition of *Mulligan Stew* lets the techniques, *as techniques,* be self-effacing. What remains is, as Sukenick and Federman would agree, pure writing.

Just as "the death of the novel" fueled the efforts of the literature of exhaustion group in the early 1960's, the infinitive "to write" suggests the primary urge felt by the disruptivists as their revolt entered its second decade. Strategies to free fiction from the representational story had been central since disruptivism's inception, and as its masters matured into the later '70's, *pure writing* became a more attainable goal. Younger writers, as yet unpublished when disruptive fiction made its great and spontaneous breakthrough in 1967, have revealed the great promise of "pure writing" by the variety of their works. Clarence Major, for example, has modeled his novel *Reflex and Bone Structure* on the classic form of the detective novel—only here the ratiocination takes place in the very writing of the book. Characters blend in and out of the music they listen to and the television shows they watch. Indeed, they are even formed by the very syntax of their author's writing:

> I am standing behind Cora. She is wearing a thin black nightgown. The backs of her legs are lovely. I love her. The word standing allows me to watch like this. The word nightgown is what she is wearing. The nightgown itself is in her drawer with her panties. The word Cora is

wearing the word nightgown. I watch the sentence: The back of her
legs are lovely.[29]

In *Emergency Exit* Major moves more aggressively toward pure
writing by making the words of his story refer inward to his own
creative act, rather than outward toward the great conceptual
beyond.[30] His tactic is a simple matter of structure. His novel consists
of the elementary units of discourse: words, sentences, paragraphs,
vignettes, and serial narratives. *Emergency Exit* is formed by equal
blocks of each, spread out and mixed among the others. At first,
simple sentences are presented to the reader. Then elements from
these same sentences reoccur in paragraphs, but still without a narrative reference. The strategy is to fix the word, as word, in the reader's
mind, apart from any exterior conceptual reference (much as an
abstract painter will present a line, or swatch of color, without any
corresponding image). Then come a number of narratives, coalescing
into a story of lovers and family. When enough sections of the serial
narrative accumulate to form a recognizable story, we find that the
independent and fragmentary scenes of the sentences and paragraphs
have been animated by characters with whom we can now identify.
Forestalling any attempt to rush off the page into incidental gossip is
the memory and further repetition of these words—whether they be
black mythology, snatches of popular song, or simply brilliant writing—within Major's arresting sentences and paragraphs. A word,
image, or scene which occurs within the narrative leads the reader
directly back to the substance of Major's own writing. All attention is
confined within the pages of the book.

In *Moving Parts* Steve Katz addresses himself to the obsessive
concern of readers and writers alike: the correspondence between
fiction and its source in real life. The opening story, "Female Skin,"
addresses this issue on several levels. For one, it presents a narrative
situation demanding pure imagination. The male narrator slips into
the skin of his friend Wendy Appel and ventures out into New York
City. The demands are obvious: the situation is medically impossible
and sexually adverse, and once this Frankensteinian creature is

[29] Clarence Major, *Reflex and Bone Structure* (New York: Fiction Collective, 1975), p. 74.

[30] Clarence Major, *Emergency Exit;* in manuscript at this writing, published in Fall 1979
by the Fiction Collective, New York; see the more complete analysis of this novel in the special
Clarence Major issue of *Black American Literature Forum* (Summer, 1979).

turned loose, even more improbable events transpire. But to make the experiment complete, Katz interpolates passages from his *Grasslands* journal, a diary kept on location when he was writing the script for a film which also employed the real Wendy Appel as video technician. Hence reality and fantasy are brought head to head, and the reader is left to examine the fallout in Katz's story.

Testing fantasy against reality is the point of the book's center pieces, the complementary "Parcel of Wrists" and "Trip." The former is an explicitly fantastic fiction, in which the author receives an unsolicited package of human wrists from "Irondale, Tennessee." After an eventful fiction with the wrists, the real Steve Katz buys a bus ticket to Nashville, rents a car, and follows Highway 43 (his favorite number) to the actual city of Irondale, Tennessee. But "Trip" fails to equal the fantasy of "Parcel of Wrists." How, indeed, can any part of the mundane world hope to rival the products of the human imagination?

The reason why imaginative fancies outscore realistic experience is made clear in "43," the numerological investigation which concludes *Moving Parts*. After running through his store of anecdotes about the marvelous recurrences of the number 43 in his life, Katz speculates on the appeal of systems and pseudo-systems in our otherwise rational lives. "The most informed and exhilarating moments occur when quotidian reality and my inventions intersect or have a mutual resonance," Katz admits.[31] Of course we agree, for here is the author's fancy corresponding (however coincidentally) with what seems the pattern of the universe. What of such familiar, middle-class pseudo-systems as astrology, biorhythms, and the sort, which now and then connect with the historically inevitable? Vonnegut has celebrated them as simple devices guaranteed to give everyone a humble, universal celebrity. Katz is more precise: "These systems are tools useful to help you yourself arrive at a description of reality, but as soon as you depend upon the system itself for the answers, start looking *at* it rather than *through* it, there begins to form a cataract of dogma over your perception of things as they are" (p. *43*–22) System as system becomes the equivalent of writing as writing: neither claims authority beyond itself. Once we participate in the process itself, there is no danger of being distracted:

---

[31] Steve Katz, *Moving Parts* (New York: Fiction Collective, 1977), p. *43*–45. Subsequent references in parentheses. Pagination includes italicized title.

Unless we can use any of these systems for our own benefit, rather than submitting to the rule of the system, we become victims of the system's dogma, and of those who profit by perpetuating that dogma. It does seem relaxing to find that one of these systems works for us, because suddenly certain of our responsibilities for ourselves are taken off our heads for the moment, and we can give up some anxieties and get high. The guru has done this for us. The practice is working, and it's great. But that feeling easily deteriorates into complacency. We keep defending the system even after its affect has disappeared, and we're worse off than at the outset. If we don't keep honing the freshness of our response to everything that's happening to us, we lose the sense of where we started from, become deluded about our gains and blind to our losses. (p. *43–23*)

The perfect role as writer is to craft one's existence into a life of fiction, to have one's life become the writing itself, and vice versa. Through three major works of fiction Michael Stephens has shown how this discipline carries both ethical and aesthetic weight. A child of poverty who at age eighteen had to decide whether to become a writer or to be a hoodlum like his brothers, Stephens determined to become a writer who would lyricize his impoverished upbringing and find within it the making of song—for what else, at base, should pure writing be? His first novel, *Season at Coole* (1972), takes his family background and fashions it into poetic myth, with the narrator—Mickey Mack Coole, a stand-in for Michael Gregory Stephens—its maker. This first novel was followed by *Paragraphs* (1974), twenty disparate passages that each take a minute or two to read, which tested his language against the full range of human sympathies. But how pure writing itself could answer to the human predicament was answered in Stephens's third prose work, *Still Life*. "Life is a farrago,"[32] its narrator, Buster Shigh, keeps saying as he shimmies up the drainpipe, drunk and locked out of his room. Still narrating his every act, Buster shimmies up and slides down, cascading into pools of splintered glass, wine, and vomit, all the while singing to us of hopeless pratfalls. Buster's language can make art of anything, and even as he flounders about, he improvises an essentially verbal experience:

The day before I had seen an afghan leap from a fifth floor window

[32] Michael Stephens, *Still Life* (New York: Kroesen Books, 1977), p. 1. Subsequent references in parentheses.

around the corner. It was pure grace, as though its ears were deseutudi-
nous wings that were about to come back to life. The afghan bounds to
the next building; no, it splattered over the concrete below, yelping in
utter pain, within minutes dying, it was dead. I neither yelped nor died
from my fall. I learned one thing, and that was to be circumspect upon
my next ascent up the side of the building to the room in which I slept. I
shimmied up the drainpipe, I spoke to myself, I said:

Steady Martin.

Or I said: Easy does it.

Or: You've got it now, Buster.

Watch your step, Mr. Shigh.

(That's prounounced "Shee," like the good people.) (p.3)

On the third try up he makes it, after his pants get stuck on the
drainpipe and he hangs, "legs dangling, thrashing in the ozone, arms
waving for help. Life is a farrago, I scream." But no sooner is he
reaching through the window for his keys than he slips and tumbles
backward, "landing on the concrete, mumbling to myself amid the
street rubble; bleeding, aching, pained, silent, and disfigured. I
whispered: O for a divine place that is not heaven!"

Such divine places, Michael Stephens knows, are made of art, and
not heavenly graces. There's a humor to Buster Shigh's action: when
his ex-wife's dog urinates on him, he pisses back; and his affair with
the dreamlike Lady Hand is slapstick love, a courtship conducted
with seltzer bottles and custard pies. Buster Shigh is the soul of
Buster Keaton, and twenty photos from Keaton's films illustrate (or
rather complement) the text. In addition, a cutout figure of Keaton,
striding from one misadventure to another, appears at the bottom
right on each set of pages not otherwise illustrated; the effect is to
impel the reader through the text like the frantic action of a Sennett,
Chaplin, or Keaton comedy.

The beauty of *Still Life* is not just its comedy. Pure physical sense is
its real story, as Buster—deprived but not depraved—thinks of things
he appreciates but so tragically lacks. "The male seduction of the
bouillabaisse, vichysoisse, the turnip," he ponders. "Food cakes that
looked like women dressed as angel food entered the room; food was
good to eat I was told, I sipped on a can of beer, sipped the gravy in
the bean can." He savors words most of all, for words he can create
and control—unlike the physical realities of this world, which elude
him and mock him. At one point Lady Hand entrusts him with

$3,000, which he uses to finance a riot of haute cuisine, the description of which is as savory as the meals themselves. When it's all over, he can't even tell the truth:

> The money was spent. I called her Ladyship, I decided to tell her I spent the money on heroin. It had more poet worrisome truth, more artist decay and fashionability.
> All in blood went his love riding . . .
> Imagine saying, I spent your dough on food. (p. 53)

The relationship ends, and Buster is once more flat on his ass ("I speak to you now from a gray damp place") in the gutter outside his flophouse hotel; dogshit or gum has welded the seat of his pants to the curb. Anything for a laugh, and once they laugh, you've got them. . . . And still life goes on. All is not then yet quite irrevocably lost.

Still Life was written when its author was variously Michael Gregory Stephens, M. G. Stephens, Machine Gun Stephens, Mickey Mack, MacCool, Mad Dog Michael, looney and boozy, all as therapy to hold off the pain, in such circumstances, of being a man. But Stephens is remarkably sympathetic to whatever environment he's writing in. Even during the East Village/*Gulfweed Voices* period of his early unpublished novel, he had chances to slip away to Provincetown and Wellfleet on the Cape, where artist friends would put him up, and from this wholly different context came his book of lyrical *Paragraphs*. Then in the summer of 1974 Stephens moved up to a borrowed apartment on Broadway, halfway between Needle Park and Spanish Harlem. Accustomed all his life to the street ambience, he picked up phrases of Spanish, wore Latino clothing, and in the second and third draftings of *Gulfweed Voices* transformed the narrator from Mickey Mack into Rico O'Reilly, Irish by birth but Spanish in temperament. The result was thoroughly convincing, and only from a six-month period in Stephens's life.

By 1975 Michael Stephens, incorrigible bachelor and despiser of family life, was married to a young Korean woman who had come to study classical music and voice; a year later they had a child. The final version of the Gulfweed novel, entitled *Shipping Out*,[33] reflects this maturity and distancing: Rico O'Reilly is now a character described

---

[33] Michael Stephens, *Shipping Out* (Cambridge: Apple-Wood Press, 1979).

by another, more stable narrator. But the true nature of Stephens's recent work is expressed in *Tangun Legend*,[34] the introduction to a booklength "translation from a text which does not exist, from a text for nothing." The writer has taken sentiments about Korea and Korean culture which "prevailing social customs" make inexpressible in that language, instead composing them in English. Ok Hee Yu-Stephens is hence a partner in the poems, just as she and Michael Stephens share a partnership in life. Yeats wrote Irish poems in English without knowing the original language, and—with Pound —began an unusual tradition of translation which Stephens here continues.

The Stephens sensibility responds well to Tangun, the Korean Bear Myth—of a national character which journeyed through time and space, through the various kingdoms and dynasties, and through the turmoil of Korea in the twentieth century. "Tangun was the king because of his patience," Stephens writes. "His hermit nation reflected this attitude." Korea, "the land of the morning calm," is forever threatened by the impatient tigers who cannot appreciate such treasures as "Lilac on mountain/ Lily Blossom on mountain/ Lotus flower bloom." Tangun's lesson to the people is the one Stephens has followed in his own life, credible because it has come from experience but useable as language.

> Tangun taught the Han people of the insane tongues
> Which conquerors made his tribe speak
> Or when mountain animals turned white with snow
> He spoke of blood spilled
> And blood running on mountain snow
> Of how Tangun's music was hushed
> Women given the conqueror for barter
> Children sent to the winds as soldiers
> Scholars delivered into early graves
> Of Japanese soldiers crushing ancient pottery
> Chinese soldiers rampaging on horses, Tangun learned
> Of the last Queen Min from Yi dynasty
> Assassinated by Japanese gangsters
> And of MacArthur and American tanks

Tangun's way finally triumphs, but only as does Buster Shigh's

[34] Michael Stephens, *Tangun Legend* (Iowa City: Seamark Press, 1978).

verbal craft. The Japanese rule like tigers, but the images of lilac, lily, and lotus are indestructible.

Expressing the inexpressible is the highest art for any writer. Whether for the Mineola Irish-American, for Bowery derelicts, or for present-day Koreans who have yet to fashion poetry continuing their high tradition, Michael Stephens has shown himself equal to the demands of his art.

The future of disruptive fiction is clear. Following the lead of Clarence Major, Steve Katz, and Michael Stephens, it must address the problems of contemporary life in its imaginative dimensions, far beyond the concerns of mimetic writing, and aspire to the highest call of literature. In the service of our highest hopes and greatest abilities, it must write poems that soar.

KURT VONNEGUT, JR. (b. 1922)

I. NOVELS

Player Piano
New York: Charles Scribner's Sons, 1952.
New York: Bantam Books, 1954 (retitled *Utopia 14*).
New York: Holt, Rinehart & Winston, 1966.
New York: Avon Books, 1967, 1970.
New York: Delacorte/Seymour Lawrence, 1971.
New York: Delta-Dell, 1972.
New York: Dell, 1974.

The Sirens of Titan
New York: Dell, 1959, 1966, 1970.
Boston: Houghton Mifflin, 1961.
New York: Delacorte/Seymour Lawrence, 1971.
New York: Delta-Dell, 1971.

Mother Night
Greenwich, Conn.: Fawcett, 1961 (printed February, 1962).
New York: Harper & Row, 1966 (including a new introduction by the author, incorporated into later editions).
New York: Avon Books, 1967, 1970.
New York: Delacorte/Seymour Lawrence, 1971.
New York: Delta-Dell, 1972.
New York: Dell, 1974.

Cat's Cradle
New York: Holt, Rinehart & Winston, 1963.
New York: Dell, 1965, 1970.
New York: Delta-Dell, 1965.
New York: Delacorte/Seymour Lawrence, 1971.

God Bless You, Mr. Rosewater
New York: Holt, Rinehart & Winston, 1965.
New York: Dell, 1966, 1970.
New York: Delta-Dell, 1968.
New York: Delacorte/Seymour Lawrence, 1971.

Slaughterhouse-Five
New York: Delacorte/Seymour Lawrence, 1969.
New York: Delta-Dell, 1970.
New York: Dell, 1972.

Breakfast of Champions
New York: Delacorte/Seymour Lawrence, 1973.
New York: Delta-Dell, 1974.
New York: Dell, 1975.

Slapstick
New York: Delacorte/Seymour Lawrence, 1976.
New York: Delta-Dell, 1977.
New York: Dell, 1978.

Jailbird
New York: Delacorte/Seymour Lawrence, 1979.

II. COLLECTIONS OF STORIES AND SHORT WORKS

Canary in a Cat House
Greenwich, Conn.: Fawcett, 1961.

Contents and original publication:
"Report on the Barnhouse Effect." *Collier's*, 125 (February 11, 1950), 18–19,
    63–65.
"All the King's Horses." *Collier's*, 127 (February 10, 1951), 14–15, 46–48, 50.
"D.P." *Ladies' Home Journal*, 70 (August, 1953), 42–43, 80–81, 84.
"The Manned Missiles." *Cosmopolitan*, 145 (July, 1958), 83–88.
"The Euphio Question." *Collier's*, 127 (May 12, 1951), 22–23, 52–54, 56.
"More Stately Mansions." *Collier's*, 128 (December 22, 1951), 24–25, 62–63.
"The Foster Portfolio." *Collier's*, 128 (September 8, 1951), 18–19, 72–73.
"Deer in the Works." *Esquire*, 43 (April, 1955), 78–79, 112, 114, 116, 118.
"Hal Irwin's Magic Lamp." *Cosmopolitan*, 142 (June, 1957), 92–95.
"Tom Edison's Shaggy Dog." *Collier's*, 131 (March 14, 1953), 46, 48–49.
"Unready to Wear." *Galaxy Science Fiction*, 6 (April, 1953), 98–111.
"Tomorrow and Tomorrow and Tomorrow" (originally "The Big Trip Up Yonder").
    Galaxy Science Fiction, (January, 1954), 100–110.

Welcome to the Monkey House
New York: Delacorte/Seymour Lawrence, 1968.
New York: Dell, 1970.
New York: Delta-Dell, 1970.

Contents and original publication:
"Preface." Not previously published.
"Where I Live" (originally "You've Never Been to Barnstable?"). *Venture-
    Traveler's World*, 1 (October, 1964), 145, 147–149.
"Harrison Bergeron." *Magazine of Fantasy and Science Fiction*, 21 (October,
    1961), 5–10.
"Who Am I This Time" (originally "My Name Is Everyone"). *Saturday Evening
    Post*, 234 (December 16, 1961), 20–21, 62, 64, 66–67.
"Welcome to the Monkey House." *Playboy*, 15 (January, 1968), 95, 156, 196, 198,
    200–201.
"Long Walk to Forever." *Ladies' Home Journal*, 77 (August, 1960), 42–43, 108.
"The Foster Portfolio." In *Canary in a Cat House* (*CCH*, above).
"Miss Temptation." *Saturday Evening Post*, 228 (April 21, 1956), 30, 57, 60, 62,
    64.
"All the King's Horses." In *CCH*.
"Tom Edison's Shaggy Dog." In *CCH*.
"New Dictionary" (originally "The Latest Word"). *New York Times Book Review*,
    October 30, 1966, pp. 1, 56.

"Next Door." *Cosmopolitan,* 138 (April, 1955), 80–85.
"More Stately Mansions." In *CCH.*
"The Hyannis Port Story." Written 1963, not previously published.
"D. P." In *CCH.*
"Report on the Barnhouse Effect." In *CCH.*
"The Euphio Question." In *CCH.*
"Go Back to Your Precious Wife and Son."*Ladies' Home Journal,* 79 (July, 1962), 54–55, 108, 110.
"Deer in the Works." In *CCH.*
"The Lie." *Saturday Evening Post,* 235 (February 24, 1962), 46–47, 51, 56.
"Unready to Wear." In *CCH.*
"The Kid Nobody Could Handle." *Saturday Evening Post,* 228 (September 24, 1955), 37, 136–137.
"The Manned Missiles." In *CCH.*
"Epicac." *Collier's,* 126 (November 25, 1950), 36–37.
"Adam." *Cosmopolitan,* 136 (April, 1954), 34–39.
"Tomorrow and Tomorrow and Tomorrow." In *CCH.*

III. PUBLISHED PLAYS

Between Time and Timbuktu, or Prometheus-5. New York: Delacorte/Seymour Lawrence, 1972; New York: Delta-Dell, 1972.
"Fortitude." *Playboy,* 15 (September, 1968), 99–100, 102, 106, 217–218.
Happy Birthday, Wanda June. New York: Delacorte/Seymour Lawrence, 1971; New York: Delta-Dell, 1971.
"The Very First Christmas Morning." *Better Homes and Gardens,* 40 (December, 1962), 14, 19–20, 24.

IV. UNCOLLECTED STORIES

"Ambitious Sophomore." *Saturday Evening Post,* 226 (May 1, 1954), 31, 88, 92, 94.
"Any Reasonable Offer." *Collier's,* 129 (January 19, 1952), 32, 46–47.
"Bagombo Snuff Box." *Cosmopolitan,* 137 (October, 1954), 34–39.
"The Big Space Fuck." *Again Dangerous Visions,* ed. Harlan Ellison, pp. 246–250. Garden City, N.Y.: Doubleday, 1972.
"The Boy Who Hated Girls." *Saturday Evening Post,* 228 (March 31, 1956), 28–29, 58, 60, 62.
"The Cruise of the Jolly Roger." *Cape Cod Compass,* 8 (April, 1953), 7–14.
"Custom-Made Bride." *Saturday Evening Post,* 226 (March 27, 1954), 30, 81–82, 86–87.
"Find Me a Dream." *Cosmopolitan,* 150 (February, 1961), 108–111.
"Hole Beautiful: Prospectus for a Magazine of Shelteredness." *Monocle,* 5, #1 (1962), pp. 45–51. With Karla Kuskin.
"Lovers Anonymous." *Redbook,* 121 (October, 1963), 70–71, 146–148.
"Mnemonics." *Collier's,* 127 (April 28, 1951), 38.
"A Night for Love." *Saturday Evening Post,* 230 (November 23, 1957), 40–41, 73, 76–77, 80–81, 84.
"The No-Talent Kid." *Saturday Evening Post,* 225 (October 25, 1952), 28, 109–110, 112, 114.
"The Package."' *Collier's,* 130 (July 26, 1952), 48–53.

"Poor Little Rich Town." *Collier's*, 130 (October 25, 1952), 90–95.
"The Powder Blue Dragon." *Cosmopolitan*, 137 (November, 1954), 46–48, 50–53.
"A Present for Big Nick." *Argosy*, December, 1954, pp. 42–45, 72–73.
"Runaways." *Saturday Evening Post*, 234 (April 15, 1961), 26–27, 52, 54, 56.
"Souvenir." *Argosy*, December, 1952, pp. 28, 76–79.
"Thanasphere." *Collier's*, 126 (September 2, 1950), 18–19, 60, 62.
"This Son of Mine. . . ." *Saturday Evening Post*, 229 (August 18, 1956), 24, 74, 76–78.
"2BR02B." *Worlds of If*, January, 1962, pp. 59–65.
"Unpaid Consultant." *Cosmopolitan*, 138 (March, 1955), 52–57.

V. POETRY

"Carols for Christmas 1969: Tonight If I Will Let Me." *New York Times Magazine*, December 21, 1969, p. 5.

VI. COLLECTION OF ESSAYS

Wampeters, Foma, & Granfalloons: Opinions
New York: Delacorte/Seymour Lawrence, 1974.
New York: Delta-Dell, 1975.
New York: Dell, 1976.
Contents and original publication:
"Preface." Not previously published.
"Science Fiction." *New York Times Book Review*, September 5, 1965, p. 2.
"Brief Encounters on the Inland Waterway." *Venture: Traveler's World*, 3 (October/November, 1966), 135–138, 140, 142.
"Hello, Star Vega." Review of *Intelligent Life in the Universe* by S. I. Shklovskii and Carl Sagan, *Life*, 61 (December 9, 1966), R3 (Regional).
"Teaching the Unteachable." *New York Times Book Review*, August 6, 1967, pp. 1, 20.
"Yes, We Have No Nirvanas." *Esquire*, 69 (June, 1968), 78–79, 176, 178–179, 182.
"Fortitude." *Playboy*, 15 (September, 1968), 99–100, 102, 106, 217–218.
"'There's a Maniac Loose Out There.'" *Life*, 67 (July 25, 1969), 53–56.
"Excelsior! We're Going to the Moon! Excelsior!" *New York Times Magazine*, July 13, 1969, pp. 9–11.
"Address to the American Physical Society." *Chicago Tribune Magazine*, June 22, 1969, pp. 44, 48–50, 52, 56 (as "Physicist, Purge Thyself").
"Good Missiles, Good Manners, Good Night." *New York Times*, September 13, 1969, p. 26.
"Why They Read Hesse." *Horizon*, 12 (Spring, 1970), 28–31.
"Oversexed in Indianapolis." Review of *Going All the Way* by Dan Wakefield, *Life*, 69 (July 17, 1970), 10.
"The Mysterious Madame Blavatsky." *McCall's*, 97 (March, 1970), 66–67, 142–144.
"Biafra: A People Betrayed." *McCall's*, 97 (April, 1970), 68–69, 134–138.
"Address to Graduating Class at Bennington College, 1970." *Vogue*, 156 (August 1, 1970), 54, 144–145 (as "Up Is Better Than Down").
"Torture and Blubber." *New York Times*, June 30, 1971, p. 41.

"Address to the National Institute of Arts and Letters, 1971." Published in *Proceedings* as "The Happiest Day in the Life of My Father." *Vogue,* 160 (August 15, 1972), 56–57, 93 (as "What Women Really Want Is . . .").

"Reflections on My Own Death." *Rotarian,* May, 1972, p. 24.

"In a Manner That Must Shame God Himself." *Harper's,* 245 (November, 1972), 60–68.

"Thinking Unthinkable, Speaking Unspeakable." *New York Times,* January 13, 1973, p. 31.

"Address at Rededication of Wheaton College Library." *Vogue,* 162 (July, 1973), 62–64 (as "America: What's Good, What's Bad?").

"Invite Rita Rait to America!" *New York Times Book Review,* January 28, 1973, p. 47.

"Address to P.E.N. Conference in Stockholm, 1973." Not previously published.

"A Political Disease." Review of *Fear and Loathing on the Campaign Trail '72* by Hunter S. Thompson, *Harper's,* 246 (July, 1973), 92, 94.

"Playboy Interview." *Playboy,* 20 (July, 1973), 57–60, 62, 66, 68, 70, 72, 74, 214, 216.

VII. UNCOLLECTED ARTICLES AND REVIEWS

"Closed Season on the Kids." Review of *Don't Shoot—We Are Your Children* by J. Anthony Lukas, *Life,* 70 (April 9, 1971), 14.

"Deadhead among the Diplomats." Review of *The Triumph* by J. Kenneth Galbraith, *Life,* 64 (May 3, 1968), 14.

"Der Arme Dolmetscher." *Atlantic Monthly,* 196 (July, 1955), 86–88.

"Don't Take It Too Seriously." Review of *Prize Stories 1966: The O Henry Awards,* ed. Richard Poirier and William Abrahams, *New York Times Book Review,* March 20, 1966, pp. 1, 39.

"Everything Goes Like Clockwork." Review of *Once a Greek . . .* by Friedrich Dürrenmatt, *New York Times Book Review,* June 13, 1964, p. 4.

"The Fall of a Climber." Review of *Any God Will Do* by Richard Condon, *New York Times Book Review,* September 25, 1966, pp. 5, 42.

"Foreword." *Transformations* by Anne Sexton. Boston: Houghton Mifflin, 1971, pp. vii–x.

"Foreword." *Write If You Get Work: The Best of Bob & Ray* by Bob Elliott and Ray Goulding. New York: Random House, 1975, pp. v–vii.

"General Electric News Bureau Release, January 3, 1950." In "Truth, Beauty, and The Wolf at the Door." *Playboy,* 20 (December, 1973), 229.

"The Happy Conservative." Review of *A Hymnal* by William F. Buckley, Jr. *Politics Today,* January/February, 1979, p. 60.

"He Comes to Us One by One and Asks What the Rules Are" [on Ross MacDonald]. *Chicago Tribune Book World,* July 15, 1973, p. 3.

"Headshrinker's Hoyle on Games We Play." Review of *Games People Play* by Eric Berne, *Life,* 58 (June 11, 1965), 15, 17.

"The High Cost of Fame." *Playboy,* 18 (January, 1971), 124.

"Infarcted! Tabescent!" Review of *The Kandy-Colored Tangerine-Flake Streamline Baby* by Tom Wolfe, *New York Times Book Review,* June 27, 1965, p. 4.

"Introduction." *Our Time Is Now: Notes from the High School Underground,* ed. John Birmingham, pp. vii–x. New York: Praeger, 1970. (Expanded from "Times Change," below.)

"Introduction." *Rigadoon* by Louis-Ferdinand Céline. New York: Penguin Books, 1975, pp. xii–xx. (Same introduction used for other Céline novels in Penguin editions.)

"Joseph Heller's Extraordinary Novel about an Ordinary Man." Review of *Something Happened* by Joseph Heller, *New York Times Book Review,* October 6, 1974, pp. 1–2. (Reprinted as an advertising brochure by Ballantine Books in 1975.)

Kurt Vonnegut, Jr., Reads Slaughterhouse-Five. Liner notes by Vonnegut signed "Philboyd Sludge." New York: Caedmon Records, 1973.

"Let the Killing Stop." *The Register* (Yarmouth Port, Mass.), October 23, 1969. (Speech at Barnstable High School on Cape Cod.)

"Message of the Leaked Minutes." *The Nation,* 227 (September 30, 1978), 307–308.

"Money Talks to the New Man." Review of *The Boss* by Goffredo Parise, *New York Times Book Review,* October 2, 1966, p. 4.

"Nashville." Review of the film by Robert Altman, *Vogue,* 166 (June, 1975), 103.

"The Necessary Miracle" [on Mark Twain]. *The Nation,* 229 (July 7, 1979) 21–22.

"New York: Who Needs It." *Harper's* 257 (August, 1975), 3.

"Nixon's the One." *Earth Day—The Beginning* (New York: Bantam, 1970), pp. 64–65.

"The Noodle Factory." *Connecticut College Alumni Magazine,* 54 (Fall, 1976), 3–5, 42–43. Reprinted as "On Reading/Writing/Freedom," *Mademoiselle,* August, 1977, pp. 96, 104–105.

"Only Kidding, Folks?" Review of seven novels by Stanislaw Lem, *The Nation,* 226 (May 13, 1978), 575.

"Opening Remarks." *The Unabridged Mark Twain,* ed. Lawrence Teacher, pp. xi–xv. Philadelphia: Running Press, 1976.

"Reading Your Own." *New York Times Book Review,* June 4, 1967, p. 6.

Response to questions in John Stafford's essay. *Aspen Leaves,* 2, #1 (1975), pp. 69–76.

"The Scientific Goblins Are Gonna Git Us." Review of *Unless Peace Comes,* ed. Nigel Calder, *Life,* 65 (July 16, 1968), 8.

"Second Thoughts on Teacher's Scrapbook." Review of *Up the Down Staircase* by Bel Kaufman, *Life,* 59 (September 3, 1965), 9–10.

"Times Change." *Esquire,* 73 (February, 1970), 60.

"Tom Wicker Signifying." Review of *A Time to Die* by Tom Wicker, *New York Times Book Review,* March 9, 1975, pp. 2–3.

"The Unsaid Says Much." Review of *Absent Without Leave* by Heinrich Böll, *New York Times Book Review,* September 12, 1965, pp. 4, 54.

"Vonnegut on Trout." *Fantasy & Science Fiction,* 48 (April, 1975), 158.

"War as a Series of Collisions." Review of *Bomber* by Len Deighton, *Life,* 69 (October 2, 1970), 10.

"Well All Right." *Cornell Daily Sun,* November 4, 1971, p. 4. (Reprints two samples of Vonnegut's student writing.)

"Writers, Vonnegut, and the USSR." *P.E.N. Newsletter* #17 (November, 1974), pp. 1–2.

VIII. INTERVIEWS AND RECORDED REMARKS

Abramson, Marcia. "Vonnegut: Humor with Suffering." *The Michigan Daily* (Ann Arbor), January 22, 1969, p. 2.

"Ask Them Yourself." *Family Week,* October 28, 1973, p. 2.

Banks, Ann. "Symposium Sidelights." *Novel,* 3 (Spring, 1970), 208–211.

Bellamy, Joe David, and John Casey. "Kurt Vonnegut, Jr." In *The New Fiction: Interviews with Innovative American Writers,* pp. 194–207. Urbana: University of Illinois Press, 1974. (Incorporates Casey's interview, below.)

Blumenfeld, Ralph. "Novelist into Playwright." *New York Post,* November 11, 1970, p. 38.

Bosworth, Patricia. "To Vonnegut, the Hero Is the Man Who Refuses to Kill." *New York Times,* October 25, 1970, sec. 2, p. 5.

Broun, Heywood Hale. "Conversation with Kurt Vonnegut." Prentice-Hall Audio Library #79. (From a "Literary Guild First Editions" radio broadcast, 1973.)

Bryan, C. D. B. "Kurt Vonnegut, Head Bokononist." *New York Times Book Review,* April 6, 1969, pp. 2, 25.

"Can Merlin Save the Whales?" *Boston Sunday Herald Traveler Book Guide,* March 29, 1970, pp. 9–10.

Cargas, Harry James. "Are There Things a Novelist Shouldn't Joke About?" *Christian Century,* 93 (November 24, 1976), 1048–1050.

Casey, John. "Kurt Vonnegut, Jr.: A Subterranean Conversation." *Confluence,* 2 (Spring, 1969), 3–5. Reprinted in Bellamy and Casey, above.

Clancy, L. J. "Running Experiments Off: An Interview." *Meanjin Quarterly,* 30 (Autumn, 1971), 46–54.

"Commencement Speaker Vonnegut Joins College's 'Extended Family.'" *The Pulteney St. Survey* (Hobart & Smith College), June, 1974, p. 1.

Connors, Caryl. "There's a New Artistic Team in Town: The Vonnegut's, Dad and Daughter." *People,* 12 (October 15, 1979), 36–39.

"The Conscience of the Writer." *Publishers Weekly,* 199 (March 22, 1971), 26–27.

Cousins, Norman. "Outlooks: When American and Soviet Writers Meet." *Saturday Review,* June 24, 1978, pp. 42–45.

Dunlap, Frank. "God and Kurt Vonnegut, Jr., at Iowa City." *Chicago Tribune Magazine,* May 7, 1967, pp. 48, 84, 86, 88.

Eckholt, Larry. "Vonnegut Vows to Survive Critics." *Des Moines Register,* April 2, 1977, p. 1B.

Engle, Paul. "A Point That Must Be Raised: The Equalization of Fiction." *Chicago Tribune Book World,* June 10, 1973, p. 1.

Freund, Betsy L. "Who's on Top?" *Harper's Bazaar,* 105 (July, 1972), 52–53.

Friedenreich, Kenneth. "Kurt Vonnegut: The PR Man Turned Novelist." *Newsday,* August 11, 1975, magazine section, p. 12.

Friedrich, Otto. "Ultra Vonnegut." *Time,* May 7, 1973, pp. 65–69.

Gehman, Richard. "Nobody Quite Like Him." *Chicago Tribune Books Today,* April 2, 1967, pp. 13–14.

Gussow, Mel. "Vonnegut Is Having Fun Doing a Play." *New York Times,* October 6, 1970, p. 56.

Hayman, David, David Michaelis, George Plimpton, and Richard L. Rhodes. "The Art of Fiction LXIV." *Paris Review* #69 (Spring, 1977), pp. 55–103.

Heffernan, Harold. "Vonnegut Likes a Change of Scenery." *Star-Ledger* (Trenton, N.J.) June 8, 1971, p. 26.

Henkle, Roger. "Wrestling (American Style) with Proteus." *Novel: A Forum on Fiction,* 3, #3 (Spring, 1970), pp. 197–207.

Hickey, Neil. "'Between Time and Timbuktu.'" *TV Guide,* 20 (March 11, 1972), 24–26.

Horwitz, Carey. "An Interview with Kurt Vonnegut, Jr." *Library Journal,* 98 (April 15, 1973), 1311.

"In Vonnegut's View, Life Is Absurd but Not Worth Leaving."*Chicago Tribune,* June 14, 1976, p. 5.

Johnson, A. "Authors and Editors." *Publishers Weekly,* 195 (April 21, 1969), 20–21.

Kisor, Henry. "Live and Learn: A Chat with Kurt Vonnegut." *Chicago Sun-Times Book Week,* September 16, 1979, pp. 10–11.

Klinkowitz, Jerome. "Lonesome No More: Interview with Kurt Vonnegut." *Washington Post Book World,* September 2, 1979, p. 7.

Kramer, Carol. "Kurt's College Cult Adopts Him as Literary Guru at 48." *Chicago Tribune,* November 15, 1970, sec. 5, p. 1.

Krementz, Jill. "The Inquiring Photographer." *New York,* September 18, 1978, p. 10.

Lingeman, Richard. "God Bless You, Mr. Mihajlov." *New York Times Book Review,* July 2, 1978, p. 23.

McCabe, Loretta. "An Exclusive Interview with Kurt Vonnegut, Jr." *Writers Yearbook—1970,* pp. 92–95, 100–101, 103–105.

McLaughlin, Frank. "An Interview with Kurt Vonnegut, Jr." *Media & Methods,* May, 1973, pp. 38–41, 45–46.

Mahoney, Lawrence. "'Poison Their Minds with Humanity.'" *Tropic: The Miami Herald Sunday Magazine,* January 24, 1971, pp. 8–10, 13, 44.

Mantell, Harold, producer and director. *Kurt Vonnegut: A Self Portrait.* Princeton, N.J.: Films for the Humanities, 1975. (29-minute 16-mm color film.)

Mitchell, Greg. "Meeting My Maker: A Visit with Kurt Vonnegut, Jr., by Kilgore Trout." *Crawdaddy,* April 1, 1974, pp. 42–51.

Mitgang, Herbert. "That's Life, And So On." *New York Times Book Review,* September 9, 1979, p. 55.

Moravec, Jeff, and Dan Rank. "The Iowan Interview: Kurt Vonnegut, Jr." *The Northern Iowan,* April 5, 1977, pp. 6–7.

Navasky, Victor. "In Cold Print: Copyrights." *New York Times Book Review,* July 20, 1975, p. 22.

———. "In Cold Print: When Editors and Salesmen Meet." *New York Times Book Review,* January 20, 1974, p. 2.

Noble, William T. "'Unstuck in Time' . . .a Real Kurt Vonnegut: The Reluctant Guru of Searching Youth." *Detroit Sunday News Magazine,* June 18, 1972, pp. 14–15, 18, 20, 22–24.

Okrent, Daniel. "A Very New Kind of WIR." *The Michigan Daily* (Ann Arbor), January 21, 1969, pp. 1–2.

———. "The Short, Sad Stay of Kurt Vonnegut, Jr." *The Michigan Daily* (Ann Arbor), January 25, 1969, p. 2.

"People." *Sports Illustrated,* February 19, 1973, p. 52.

Rank, Dan. "Vonnegut's Trip to Iowa a 'Sentimental Journey.'" *The Northern Iowan,* April 5, 1977, p. 1.

Reasoner, Harry. "Man on the Moon: The Epic Journey of Apollo XI." CBS News transcript, July 20, 1969, pp. 1–4.

———. *Sixty Minutes.* CBS News transcript, September 15, 1970, pp. 14–17.

Reel, Guy. "Kurt Vonnegut's Letters Recount His Days at UT." *University of Tennessee Daily Beacon,* November 29, 1978, pp. 1, 6. Supplemented by a letter to the editor from Donald Fiene, December 1, 1978, p. 3.

Reilly, Charles. "An Interview with Kurt Vonnegut, Jr." *Delaware Literary Review* (University of Delaware), Spring, 1976, pp. 20–27.

Reinhold, Robert. "Vonnegut Has 15 Nuggets of Talent in Harvard Class." *New York Times,* November 18, 1970, pp. 49, 77.

Robertson, Nan. "The Vonneguts: Dialogue on a Son's Insanity." *New York Times,* October 23, 1970, p. 45.

Romine, Dannye. "Listening to Kurt Vonnegut, Higgledy-Piggledy." *Charlotte* (N.C.) *Observer-Sun,* February 18, 1979, pp. 1F, 8F.

Saal, Rollene W. "Pick of the Paperbacks." *Saturday Review,* 53 (March 28, 1970), 34.

Scholes, Robert. "A Talk with Kurt Vonnegut, Jr." In *The Vonnegut Statement,* ed. Jerome Klinkowitz and John Somer. New York: Delacorte/Seymour Lawrence, 1973, pp. 90–118.

"'71." *University of Chicago Alumni Magazine,* May–June, 1971, p. 43.

Sheed, Wilfrid. "The Now Generation Knew Him When." *Life,* 67 (September 12, 1969), 64–66, 69.

———. "The Good Word: Writer as Something Else." *New York Times Book Review,* March 4, 1973, p. 2.

Shenker, Israel. "Kurt Vonnegut, Jr., Lights Comic Path of Despair." *New York Times,* March 21, 1969, sec. 1, p. 41.

Standish, David. *"Playboy* Interview." *Playboy,* 20 (July, 1973), 57–60, 62, 66, 68, 70, 72, 74, 214, 216. Reprinted in *Wampeters, Foma & Granfalloons.*

Stein, Howard. "Making Contact with Kurt Vonnegut, Jr." In *A Time to Speak,* pp. 29–41. New York: Harcourt Brace Jovanovich, 1974.

Taylor, Robert. "Kurt Vonnegut." *Boston Globe Sunday Magazine,* July 20, 1969, pp. 10–12, 14–15.

Thomas, Phil. "Growing Sales Puzzle Writer." *Ann Arbor News,* December 12, 1971, p. 41.

Todd, Richard. "The Masks of Kurt Vonnegut, Jr." *New York Times Magazine,* January 24, 1971, pp. 16–17, 19, 22, 24, 26, 30–31.

Troy, Carol. "Carol Troy Interviews Kurt Vonnegut." *Rags,* March, 1971, pp. 24–26.

Unger, Art. "Kurt Vonnegut, Jr.: Class of 71." *Ingenue,* December, 1971, pp. 14–18.

"Vonnegut Likes." *Yale Daily News,* April 6, 1971, p. 1.

"Vonnegut's Gospel." *Time,* 95 (June 29, 1970), 8.

"We Talk to. . .Kurt Vonnegut." *Mademoiselle,* August, 1970, p. 296.

Wolf, William. "Kurt Vonnegut: Still Dreaming of Imaginary Worlds." *Insight: Sunday Magazine of the Milwaukee Journal,* February 27, 1972, pp. 15–18.

IX. SPECIAL NUMBERS OF SCHOLARY JOURNALS

"Kurt Vonnegut; Jr.: A Symposium," *Summary,* 1, #2 (1971). Contents cited below.

"Vonnegut." *Critique,* 12, #3 (1971), Contents cited below.

X. CRITICAL ESSAYS AND BOOKS ABOUT VONNEGUT

Abádi-Nagy, Zoltán. "'The Skillful Seducer': Of Vonnegut's Brand of Comedy." *Hungarian Studies in English,* 8 (1974), 45–56.

"An Account of the Ancestry of Kurt Vonnegut, Jr., by an Ancient Friend of His Family." *Summary*, 1, #2 (1971), pp. 76–118.

Adams, Marion. "You've Come a Long Way Since Shortridge High, Kurt Vonnegut, Jr." *Indianapolis*, October, 1976, pp. 27–33.

Aichinger, Peter. *The American Soldier in Fiction, 1880–1963*, pp. 76, 81, 86, 87, 92–94, 98, 102, 112. Ames: Iowa State University Press, 1975.

Aldiss, Brian. *Billion Year Spree*, pp. 258, 313–316. Garden City, N.Y.: Doubleday, 1973.

————. "Guru Number Four." *Summary*, 1, #2 (1971), pp. 63–68.

Anastasyev, N. "Hope and False Hopes." In *Twentieth Century American Literature: A Soviet View*, pp. 92–95, 99. Moscow: Progress Publishers, 1976.

"The Banning of Billy Pilgrim." *Christian Century*, 88 (June, 1971), 681.

Bell, Pearl K. "American Fiction: Forgetting Ordinary Truths." *Dissent*, Winter, 1973, pp. 26–34.

Bellamy, Joe David. "Kurt Vonnegut for President: The Making of an Academic Reputation." In *The Vonnegut Statement*, ed. Jerome Klinkowitz and John Somer, pp. 71–89. New York: Delacorte/Seymour Lawrence, 1973.

Benfey, Theodor. "Seeds and the Vonneguts." *Chemistry*, 45 (November, 1972), 2.

Berger, Harold L. *Science Fiction and the New Dark Age*, pp. ix, 9, 17–19, 20, 22, 25, 37, 65, 69, 77, 123, 124, 215n. Bowling Green, Ohio: Bowling Green University Popular Press, 1976.

Bestuzhev-Lada, I. "Kogda lishim stanovitsya chelovechestvo" [When Mankind Becomes Superfluous], foreword to *Utopija 14* (*Utopia 14*, trans. M. Bruhnov from the retitled Bantam ed. of *Player Piano*), pp.5–24. Moscow: Molodaya gvardiya, 1967.

Bodtke, Richard. "Great Sorrows, Small Joys: The World of Kurt Vonnegut, Jr." *Cross Currents*, 20 (Winter, 1970), 120–125.

Boni, John. "Analogous Form: Black Comedy and Some Jacobean Plays." *Western Humanities Review*, 28 (Summer, 1974), 201–215.

Bourjaily, Vance. "What Vonnegut Is and Isn't." *New York Times Book Review*, August 13, 1972, pp. 3, 10. Reprinted as introduction to *Kurt Vonnegut, Jr.: A Checklist*, comp. Betty L. Hudgens, pp. xi–xvi (as "Kurt"). Detroit: Gale Research, 1972.

Brier, Peter A. "Caliban Reigns: Romantic Theory and Some Contemporary Fantasists." *Denver Quarterly*, 13 (Summer, 1978), 38–51.

Brown, G. "*Happy Birthday, Wanda June*." *Plays & Players*, 25 (October, 1977), 32.

Bryan, C. D. B. "Kurt Vonnegut on Target." *New Republic*, 155 (October 8, 1966), 21–22, 24–26.

Bryant, Jerry H. *The Open Decision*, pp. 303–324. New York: Free Press, 1970.

Buck, Lynn. "Vonnegut's World of Comic Futility." *Studies in American Fiction*, 3 (Autumn, 1975), 181–198.

Burhans, Clinton S. "Hemingway and Vonnegut: Diminishing Vision in a Dying Age." *Modern Fiction Studies*, 21 (Summer, 1975), 173–191.

Carson, Ronald. "Kurt Vonnegut: Matter-of-Fact Moralist." *Listening*, 6 (Autumn, 1971), 182–195.

Ciardi, John. "Manner of Speaking." *Saturday Review*, 50 (September 30, 1967), 16, 18.

Clancy, L. J. "'If the Accident Will': The Novels of Kurt Vonnegut." *Meanjin Quarterly*, 30 (Autumn, 1971), 37–45.

Coale, Sam. "Vonnegut: The Single Artificer of His World." *Wheaton College Alumni Magazine,* 60 (February, 1973), 18–20.

Cook, Bruce. "When Kurt Vonnegut Talks—and He Does—the Young All Tune In." *National Observer,* October 12, 1970, p. 21.

Crump, G. B. "D. H. Lawrence and the Immediate Present: Kurt Vonnegut, Jr., Ken Kesey, and Wright Morris." *D. H. Lawrence Review,* 10 (Summer, 1977), 103–141.

Dahiya, Bhim. "Structural Patterns in the Novels of Barth, Vonnegut, and Pynchon." *Indian Journal of American Studies,* 5, #1–2 (1976), pp. 53–68.

DeMott, Benjamin. "Vonnegut's Otherworldly Laughter." *Saturday Review,* 54 (May 1, 1971), 29–32, 38.

Dickstein, Morris. *Gates of Eden: American Culture in the Sixties,* pp. 13, 14, 97–99, 100, 103, 108–112, 218, 222, 233, 244, 286. New York: Basic Books, 1977. Revised and expanded from "Black Humor and History: Fiction in the Sixties," *Partisan Review,* 43, #2 (1976), pp. 185–211.

Diehl, Digby. "And Now the Movies." *Showcase/Chicago Sun-Times,* February 28, 1971, p. 2.

Edelstein, Arnold. *"Slaughterhouse-Five:* Time Out of Joint." *College Literature,* 1 (1974), 128–139.

Ellison, Harlan. "Introduction" to *The Big Space Fuck.* In *Again, Dangerous Visions,* pp. 242–245. Garden City, N.Y.: Doubleday, 1972.

Engel, David. "On the Question of Foma: A Study of the Novels of Kurt Vonnegut, Jr." *Riverside Quarterly,* 5 (February, 1972), 119–128.

Engel, Wilson F., III. "Pilgrim as Prisoner: Cummings and Vonnegut." *Notes on Contemporary Literature,* 7, #1 (1977), pp. 13–14.

Farmer, Philip Jose. "The Obscure Life and Hard Times of Kilgore Trout." In *The Book of Philip Jose Farmer,* pp. 218–231. New York: Daw Books, 1973.

Festa, Conrad. "Vonnegut's Satire." In *Vonnegut in America,* ed. Jerome Klinkowitz and Donald L. Lawler, pp. 133–149. New York: Delacorte Press/Seymour Lawrence, 1977.

Fiedler, Leslie A. "The Divine Stupidity of Kurt Vonnegut." *Esquire,* 74 (September, 1970), 195–197, 199–200, 202–204.

Fiene, Donald M. "Kurt Vonnegut as an American Dissident: His Popularity in the Soviet Union and His Affinities with Russian Literature." In *Vonnegut in America,* ed. Jerome Klinkowitz and Donald L. Lawler, pp. 258–293. New York: Delacorte Press/Seymour Lawrence, 1977.

———. "Vonnegut—Big in Russia." *New York Times Book Review,* April 3, 1977, pp. 3, 46–47.

———. "Vonnegut's Quotations from Dostoevsky." *Notes on Modern American Literature,* 1 (Fall, 1977), Item 29.

———. "Vonnegut's *The Sirens of Titan." Explicator,* 34 (December, 1975), Item 27.

Flora, Joseph M. "Cabell as Precursor." *Kalki,* 6 (1975), 118–137.

"Forty-six and Trusted." *Newsweek,* March 3, 1969, p. 79.

Frank, Armin Paul. "Where Laughing Is the Only Way to Stop It from Hurting." *Summary,* 1, #2 (1971), pp. 51–62.

Fussell, Paul. *The Great War and Modern Memory,* pp. 143–144, 246. New York: Oxford University Press, 1975.

Gardner, John. *On Moral Fiction,* p. 87. New York: Basic Books, 1978.

Giannone, Richard. *Vonnegut: A Preface to His Novels*. Port Washington, N.Y.: Kennikat Press, 1977.

Godshalk, William. "Kurt Vonnegut's Renaissance Hero." *Clifton: Magazine of the University of Cincinnati*, 1 (1973), 41–45.

––––––. "The Recurring Characters of Kurt Vonnegut, Jr." *Notes on Contemporary Literature*, 3, #1 (1973), pp. 2–3.

––––––. "Vonnegut and Shakespeare: Rosewater at Elsinore." *Critique*, 15, #2 (1973), pp. 37–48.

Goldsmith, David. *Kurt Vonnegut: Fantasist of Fire and Ice*. Popular Writers Series Pamphlet #2. Bowling Green, Ohio: Bowling Green University Popular Press, 1972.

Goss, Gary L. "The Selfless Billy Pilgrim." *Buffalo Spree*, 5 (Fall, 1971), 34–35, 44–45, 47, 52–53, 60–61.

Greiner, Donald J. "Vonnegut's *Slaughterhouse-Five* and the Fiction of Atrocity." *Critique*, 14, #3 (1973), pp. 38–51.

Gros-Louis, Dolores K. "*Slaughterhouse-Five:* Pacifism versus Passiveness." *Ball State University Forum*, 18, #2 (1977), pp. 3–8.

Grossman, Edward. "Vonnegut and His Audience." *Commentary*, 58 (July 19, 1976), 40–46.

Haden-Guest, Anthony. "Out Here in the Hamptons: Snapshots of the Literary Life." *New York*, September 1, 1975, pp. 43–47.

Hansen, Arlen J. "The Celebration of Solipsism: A New Trend in American Fiction." *Modern Fiction Studies*, 19 (Spring, 1973), 5–15.

Harris, Charles B. *Contemporary American Novelists of the Absurd*, pp. 51–75. New Haven: College & University Press, 1971.

––––––. "Time, Uncertainty and Kurt Vonnegut, Jr.: A Reading of *Slaughterhouse-Five*." *Centennial Review*, 20 (Spring, 1976), 228–243.

Haskell, John D., Jr. "Addendum to Pieratt & Klinkowitz: *Kurt Vonnegut, Jr.*" *Papers of the Bibliographical Society of America*, 70 (1st Quarter, 1976), 122.

Hassan, Ihab. "Fiction and Future: An Extravaganza for Voice and Tape." *Liberations*, pp. 193–194. Middletown, Conn.: Wesleyan University Press, 1971. Reprinted in *Paracriticisms*, pp. 113–114. Urbana: University of Illinois Press, 1975.

––––––. *Contemporary American Literature, 1945–1972*, pp. 45–47, 65, 86. New York: Frederick Ungar, 1973.

Hauck, Richard Boyd. *A Cheerful Nihilism*, pp. 193–194. Bloomington: Indiana University Press, 1971.

Hayman, David. "The Jolly Mix: Notes on Techniques, Style and Decorum in *Slaughterhouse-Five*." *Summary*, 1, #2 (1971), pp. 44–50.

Hendin, Josephine. *Vulnerable People: A View of American Fiction Since 1945*, pp. 4, 5, 9, 20, 23, 30–40, 44, 49–51, 213, 216, 217. New York: Oxford University Press, 1978. Expanded from "The Writer as Culture Hero, the Father as Son." *Harper's*, 249 (July, 1974), 82–87.

Hildebrand, Tim. "Two or Three Things I Know about Kurt Vonnegut's Imagination." In *The Vonnegut Statement*, ed. Jerome Klinkowitz and John Somer, pp. 121–132. New York: Delacorte/Seymour Lawrence, 1973.

Hillegas, Mark. "Dystopian Science Fiction: New Index to the Human Situation." *New Mexico Quarterly*, 31 (1961), 238–249.

Hillman, Tony. "Hooked." *Summary*, 1, #2 (1971), pp. 69–72.

Irving, John. "Kurt Vonnegut and his Critics." *New Republic*, 181 (September 22, 1979), 41–49.

Isaacs, Neil D. "Unstuck in Time: *Clockwork Orange* and *Slaughterhouse-Five*." *Literature/Film Quarterly*, 1 (1973), 122–131.

Iwamoto, Iwao. "A Clown's Say—A Study of Kurt Vonnegut, Jr.'s *Slaughterhouse-Five*." *Studies in English Literature* (Tokyo), 1975, pp. 21–23.

Jones, Peter G. *War and the Novelist*, pp. 2, 204–229, 234–235. Columbia: University of Missouri Press, 1976.

Kael, Pauline. "Current Cinema." *New Yorker*, 46 (January 23, 1971), 76–78.

Kateb, George. *Utopia and Its Enemies*, pp. 187–188. Glencoe, Ill.: Free Press, 1963.

Kazin, Alfred. "The War Novel: From Mailer to Vonnegut." *Saturday Review*, 54 (February 6, 1971), 13–15, 36. Reprinted in *Bright Book of Life*, pp. 82–83, 86–90, 258n, 289. Boston: Atlantic/Little, Brown, 1973.

Kenedy, R. C. "Kurt Vonnegut, Jr." *Art International*, 15 (May, 1971), 20–25.

Kennard, Jean. *Number and Nightmare: Forms of Fantasy in Contemporary Literature*, pp. 11, 12, 19, 23, 28, 29, 33, 61, 75, 79, 101–128, 131–133, 166, 193, 203–204. Hamden, Conn.: Shoestring Press, 1975.

Keogh, J. G., and Edward Kislaitis. "*Slaughterhouse-Five* and the Future of Science Fiction." *Media & Methods*, January, 1971, pp. 38–39, 48.

Ketterer, David. *New Worlds for Old: The Apocalyptic Imagination, Science Fiction, and American Literature*, pp. ix, 19, 36, 39, 125, 206, 242n, 263, 270, 272, 296–333. Bloomington: Indiana University Press, 1974.

Kiely, Robert. "Satire as Fantasy" *Summary*, 1, #2 (1971), pp. 41–43.

Klawans, Stuart. "Vonnegut, Bradbury, and the Fantastic Company They Keep." *Chicago Tribune Book World*, May 19, 1974, p. 4.

Klinkowitz, Jerome. "Kurt Vonnegut, Jr., and the Crime of His Times." *Critique*, 12, #3 (1971), pp. 38–53.

———. "The Dramatization of Kurt Vonnegut, Jr." *Players*, 50 (February-March, 1975), 62–64.

———. "Kurt Vonnegut: A Chronology"; "Vonnegut in America"; "A Do-It-Yourself Story Collection By Kurt Vonnegut"; "The Vonnegut Bibliography"; "A Note on Vonnegut in Europe." In *Vonnegut in America*, ed. Jerome Klinkowitz and Donald L. Lawler, pp. 3–6, 7–36, 53–60, 217–252, 255–257. New York: Delacorte Press/Seymour Lawrence, 1977.

———. "Kurt Vonnegut Jr.'s SuperFiction." *Revue Francaise d'Etudes Américaines* (Sorbonne), #1 (April, 1976), pp. 115–124. Expanded in Klinkowitz and Roy R. Behrens, *The Life of Fiction*, pp. 85–93. Urbana: University of Illinois Press, 1977.

———. "Kurt Vonnegut, Jr.: The Canary in a Cathouse"; "*Mother Night, Cat's Cradle*, and the Crimes of Our Time"; "Why They Read Vonnegut." In *The Vonnegut Statement*, ed. Jerome Klinkowitz and John Somer, pp. 7–17, 18–30, 158–177. New York: Delacorte/Seymour Lawrence, 1973.

———. "The Literary Career of Kurt Vonnegut, Jr." *Modern Fiction Studies*, 19 (Spring, 1973), 57–67.

———. "Lost in the Cat House." *The Falcon*, #5 (December, 1972), pp. 110–113.

———. "Vonnegut at Midpoint." *Seems* #2 (Winter, 1972–73), pp. 27–34.

———, and Somer, John. "The Vonnegut Statement." In *The Vonnegut Statement*, ed. Jerome Klinkowitz and John Somer, pp. 1–3. New York: Delacorte/Seymour Lawrence, 1973.

Knight, Damon. *In Search of Wonder,* pp. 166–167, 236–237. Chicago: Advent Publishers, 1967.

Kopper, Edward A., Jr. "Color Symbolism in Vonnegut's *Slaughterhouse-Five.*" *Notes on Modern American Literature,* 1 (1977), Item 17.

———. "Operation Gomorrah in *Slaughterhouse-Five.*" *Notes on Contemporary Literature,* 8 (September, 1978), 6.

Korenva, M. "The Contemporary War Novel." In *Twentieth Century American Literature: A Soviet View,* pp. 61, 63, 64, 69. Moscow: Progress Publishers, 1976.

Krementz, Jill. "Pictorial." *Summary,* 1, #2 (1971), between pp. 34–35.

Lawing, John V., Jr. "Kurt Vonnegut: Charming Nihilist." *Christianity Today,* 19 (February 14, 1975), 17–20, 22.

Lawler, Donald L. "Vonnegut in Academe"; "*The Sirens of Titan:* Vonnegut's Shaggy Dog Story." In *Vonnegut in America,* ed. Jerome Klinkowitz and Donald L. Lawler, pp. 51–52, 61–86, 187–214. New York: Delacorte Press/Seymour Lawrence, 1977.

Lawrence, Seymour. "A Publisher's Dream." *Summary,* 1, #2 (1971), pp. 73–75.

LeClair, Thomas. "Death and Black Humor." *Critique,* 17, #1 (1975), pp. 5–46.

Leff, Leonard. "Science and Destruction in Vonnegut's *Cat's Cradle.*" *Rectangle,* 46 (Spring, 1971), 28–32.

———. "Utopia Reconstructed: Alienation in Vonnegut's *God Bless You, Mr. Rosewater.*" *Critique,* 12, #3, (1971), pp. 29–37.

Leonard, John. "Why Vonnegut Smiles." *New York Times,* syndicated May 9, 1976.

Lessing, Doris. "Vonnegut's Responsibility." *New York Times Book Review,* February 4, 1973, p. 35.

Leverence, W. John. "*Cat's Cradle* and Traditional American Humor." *Journal of Popular Culture,* 5 (1972), 955–963.

Lewis, Flora. "A Writer of and for the Times." *Chicago Sun-Times,* January 5, 1971, p. 22.

Lifton, Robert Jay. "Kurt Vonnegut's Duty-Dance with Death." *American Poetry Review,* 1 (January/February, 1973), 41.

Lodge, David. *The Modes of Modern Writing,* pp. 229, 232, 242–243, 272–273. Ithaca: Cornell University Press, 1977.

Lundquist, James. *Kurt Vonnegut.* New York: Frederick Ungar, 1976.

McConnell, Frank D. *Four Postwar American Novelists: Bellow, Mailer, Barth and Pynchon,* pp. xxiii, 57, 93, 182–183. Chicago: University of Chicago Press, 1977.

McGinnis, Wayne. "The Ambiguities of Bokononism." *Iowa English Yearbook,* 26 (Spring, 1977), 21–23.

———. "The Arbitrary Cycle of *Slaughterhouse-Five:* A Relation of Form to Theme." *Critique,* 17, #1 (1975), pp. 55–68.

———. "Names in Vonnegut's Fiction." *Notes on Contemporary Literature,* 3, #3 (1973), pp. 7–9.

———. "The Source and Implications of *Ice-Nine* in Vonnegut's *Cat's Cradle.*" *American Notes & Queries,* 13 (1974), 40–41.

———. "Vonnegut's *Breakfast of Champions:* A Reductive Success." *Notes on Contemporary Literature,* 5 (1974), 6–9.

MacGregor, James. "Sampling Vonnegut's Black Humor." *Wall Street Journal,* March 12, 1972, p. 12.

McInerny, John M. "Children for Vonnegut." *Notes on Modern American Literature,* 3 (1978), Item 4.

McNelly, Willis E. "Kurt Vonnegut as Science Fiction Writer." In *Vonnegut in America,* ed. Jerome Klinkowitz and Donald L. Lawler, pp. 87–96. New York: Delacorte Press/Seymour Lawrence, 1977.

———. "Science Fiction: The Modern Mythology." *America,* September 5, 1970, pp. 125–127.

May, John R. "Vonnegut's Humor and the Limits of Hope." *Twentieth Century Literature,* 18 (January, 1972), 25–36. Reprinted in *Toward a New Earth,* pp. 191–200. Notre Dame, Ind.: University of Notre Dame Press, 1972.

Mayo, Clark. *Kurt Vonnegut: The Gospel from Outer Space.* San Bernardino, Calif.: R. Reginald/Borgo Press, 1977.

Meades, Jonathan. "Kurt Vonnegut: Fantasist." *Books & Bookmen,* February, 1973, pp. 34–37.

Meeter, Glenn. "Vonnegut's Formal and Moral Otherworldiness: *Cat's Cradle* and *Slaughterhouse-Five.*" In *The Vonnegut Statement,* ed. Jerome Klinkowitz and John Somer, pp. 204–220. New York: Delacorte/Seymour Lawrence, 1973.

Mellard, James J. "The Modes of Vonnegut's Fiction: Or, *Player Piano* Ousts *Mechanical Bride* and *The Sirens of Titan* invade *The Gutenberg Galaxy.*" In *The Vonnegut Statement,* ed. Jerome Klinkowitz and John Somer, pp. 178–203. New York: Delacorte/Seymour Lawrence, 1973.

Meredith, William. "Meredith on Vonnegut." *Connecticut College Alumni Magazine,* 54 (Fall, 1976), 2.

Merrill, Robert. "Vonnegut's *Breakfast of Champions:* The Conversion of Heliogabalus." *Critique,* 18, #3 (1977), pp. 99–108.

———, and Peter A. Scholl. "Vonnegut's *Slaughterhouse-Five:* The Requirements of Chaos." *Studies in American Fiction,* 6 (1978), 65–76.

Messent, Peter B. "*Breakfast of Champions:* The Direction of Vonnegut's Fiction." *Journal of American Studies,* 8 (1st Quarter, 1974), 101–114.

Morrow, Patrick D. "The Womb Image in Vonnegut's *Cat's Cradle.*" *Notes on Contemporary Literature,* 6 (1976), 11–13.

Myers, David. "Kurt Vonnegut, Jr.: Morality-Myth in the Antinovel." *International Fiction Review,* 3 (1976), 52–56.

Nelson, Gerald B. "Eliot Rosewater." In *Ten Versions of America,* pp. 61–76. New York: Alfred A. Knopf, 1972.

Nelson, Jon Eric. "Yeats and Vonnegut: The Artist as Mythmaker." *Lutheran Quarterly,* Summer, 1973, pp. 124–135.

Nelson, Joyce. "*Slaughterhouse-Five:* Novel and Film." *Literature/Film Quarterly,* 1 (1973), 149–153.

———. "Vonnegut and 'Bugs in Amber.'" *Journal of Popular Culture,* 7 (1973), 551–558.

"New Creative Writers." *Library Journal,* June 1, 1952, p. 1007.

O'Connor, Gerald W. "The Function of Time Travel in Vonnegut's *Slaughterhouse-Five.*" *Riverside Quarterly,* 5 (1972), 206–207.

Olderman, Raymond M. *Beyond the Waste Land,* pp. 187–219. New Haven: Yale University Press, 1972.

Orlova, R. "O romane Kurta Vonneguta" [On Kurt Vonnegut's Novel], afterword to *Boinya nomer pyat', ili krestovyi pokhod detei,* trans. by Rita Rait-Kovalyova from *Slaughterhouse-Five. Novyi Mir,* 4 (1970), 179–180.

O'Sullivan, Maurice J., Jr. "*Slaughterhouse-Five:* Kurt Vonnegut's Anti-Memoirs." *Essays in Literature,* 3 (1976), 44–50.

Pagetti, Carlo. "Kurt Vonnegut, tra fantascienza e utopia." *Studi Americani* (Roma), 12 (1966), 301–322.

Palmer, Raymond C. "Vonnegut's Major Concerns." *Iowa English Yearbook* #14 (Fall, 1969), pp. 3–10.

"Paperback Talk." *New York Times Book Review,* July 18, 1976, p. 27.

Pauley, Rebecca M. "The Moral Stance of Kurt Vonnegut." *Extrapolation,* 15 (December, 1973), 66–71.

Peterson, Clarence. "Who Is the People's Choice?" *Chicago Tribune Book World,* June 10, 1973, p. 2.

"Playboy Advisor." *Playboy,* 22 (December, 1975), 56–57.

Prioli, Carmine A. "Kurt Vonnegut's Duty-Dance." *Essays in English Literature,* 1, #3 (1973), pp. 44–50.

Puetz, Manfred. "Imagination and Self-Definition." *Partisan Review,* 44, #3 (1977), pp. 235–244.

———. "Who Am I This Time: Die Romane von Kurt Vonnegut."' *Jarbuch für Amerikanstudien,* 19 (1974), 111–125.

Purdy, Strother B. *The Hole in the Fabric: Science, Contemporary Literature, and Henry James,* pp. 12, 18–20, 27, 37, 61, 63, 79, 93, 130, 171–172. Pittsburgh: University of Pittsburgh Press, 1977.

Ranley, Ernest W. "What Are People For?" *Commonweal,* 94 (May 7, 1971), 207–211.

Reed, Peter J. "The Later Vonnegut." In *Vonnegut in America,* ed. Jerome Klinkowitz and Donald L. Lawler, pp. 150–186. New York: Delacorte Press/Seymour Lawrence, 1977.

———. "Kurt Vonnegut, Jr." In *Dictionary of Literary Biography,* ed. Jeffery Helterman and Richard Layman, I, 493–508. Detroit: Gale Research, 1978.

———. *Writers for the 70's: Kurt Vonnegut, Jr.* New York: Warner Paperback Library, 1972.

Rhodes, Carolyn. "Tyranny by Computer: Automated Data Processing and Oppressive Government in Science Fiction." In *Many Futures, Many Worlds,* ed. Thomas D. Clareson, pp. 66–93. Kent, Ohio: Kent State University Press, 1977.

Rice, Susan. "*Slaughterhouse-Five:* A Viewer's Guide." *Media & Methods,* October, 1972, pp. 27–33.

Ritter, Jess. "Teaching Kurt Vonnegut on the Firing Line." In *The Vonnegut Statement,* ed. Jerome Klinkowitz and John Somer, pp. 31–42. New York: Delacorte Press/Seymour Lawrence, 1973.

Rottensteiner, Franz. *The Science Fiction Book: An Illustrated History,* p. 147. New York: Seabury Press 1975.

Rubens, Philip M. "Names in Vonneguts *Cat's Cradle.*" *Notes on Contemporary Literature,* 8 (January, 1978), 7.

St. Germain, Amos. "*Breakfast of Champions:* Kurt Vonnegut, Jr., Is Still on the Case." In *Proceedings of the Fifth National Convention of the Popular Culture Association* (microfilm), ed. Michael Marsden, pp. 233–243. Bowling Green, Ohio: Bowling Green University Popular Press, 1975.

Samuels, Charles Thomas. "Age of Vonnegut." *New Republic,* 164 (June 12, 1971), 30–32.

Schatt, Stanley. *Kurt Vonnegut, Jr.* Boston: Twayne, 1976.

———. "The Whale and the Cross: Vonnegut's Jonah and Christ Figures." *Southwest Quarterly,* Winter, 1971, pp. 29–42.

Scholes, Robert. "Afterword." In *The Sounder Few,* ed. R. H. W. Dillard et al., pp. 186–191. Athens, Ga.: University of Georgia Press, 1971.

————. "Chasing a Lone Eagle." *Summary*, 1, #2 (1971), pp. 35–40. Reprinted in *The Vonnegut Statement*, ed. Jerome Klinkowitz and John Somer, pp. 45–54. New York: Delacorte/Seymour Lawrence, 1973. Reprinted in *Fabulation and Metafiction*, pp. 150–155. Urbana: University of Illinois Press, 1979.

————. "Fabulation and Satire." In *The Fabulators*, pp. 35–55. New York: Oxford University Press, 1967. Reprinted in *Fabulation and Metafiction*, pp. 156–162. Urbana: University of Illinois Press, 1979.

————. "History as Fabulation: Malamud and Vonnegut." In *Fabulation and Metafiction*, pp. 200–205. Urbana: University of Illinois Press, 1979.

————. "'Mithridates, He Died Old': Black Humor and Kurt Vonnegut, Jr." *Hollins Critic*, 3 (October, 1966), 1–12. Reprinted in *The Sounder Few*, ed. R. H. W. Dillard et al., pp. 173–185. Athens: University of Georgia Press, 1971.

————, and Eric Rabkin. *Science Fiction*, pp. 28, 29, 31, 67, 93, 97–98, 99, 104, 109, 129, 132, 182. New York: Oxford University Press, 1977.

Scholl, Peter A. "Vonnegut's Attack upon Christendom." *Newsletter of the Conference on Christianity and Literature*, 22 (Fall, 1972), 5–11.

Schriber, Mary Sue. "Bringing Chaos to Order: The Novel Tradition and Kurt Vonnegut, Jr." *Genre*, 10 (1977), 283–297.

————. "You've Come a Long Way, Babbitt! From Zenith to Ilium." *Twentieth Century Literature*, 17 (April, 1971), 101–106.

Schulz, Max. "The Unconfirmed Thesis: Kurt Vonnegut, Black Humor, and Contemporary Art." *Critique*, 12, #3 (1971), pp. 5–28. Reprinted in *Black Humor Fiction of the Sixties*, pp. 43–65. Athens: Ohio University Press, 1973.

Schwartz, Sheila. "Science Fiction: Bridge Between the Two Cultures." *English Journal*, 60 (November, 1971), 1043–1051.

Scully, Malcolm G. "Books." *Chronicle of Higher Education*, 7 (December 18, 1972), 5.

Seelye, John. "What the Kids Are Reading." *New Republic*, 163 (October 17, 1970), 23–26.

Shaw, Patrick W. "The Excrement Festival: Vonnegut's *Slaughterhouse-Five*." *Scholia Satyrica*, 2, #3 (1976), pp. 3–11.

Shipler, David K. "Vonnegut's *Slaughterhouse-Five* Staged in Moscow." *New York Times*, January 13, 1976, p. 40.

Skorodenko, V. "O bezumnom mire; puzitsii khudozhnika" [On the Irrational World and the Position of the Artist], afterword to *Kulybel' dyla Koshki*, trans. by Rita Rait-Kovalyova from *Cat's Cradle*, pp. 212–233. Moscow: Molodaya gvardiya, 1970.

Somer, John, "Geodesic Vonnegut; Or, If Buckminster Fuller Wrote Novels." In *The Vonnegut Statement*, ed. Jerome Klinkowitz and John Somer, pp. 221–253. New York: Delacorte/Seymour Lawrence, 1973.

Springer, Mary Doyle. *Forms of the Modern Novella*, pp. 12, 78–81, 84, 89, 91, 92, 94. Chicago: University of Chicago Press, 1975.

Stafford, John. "Alligators Are Free: A Note on the Work of Kurt Vonnegut, Jr." *Aspen Leaves*, 2, #1 (1975), pp. 69–76.

Tanner, Tony. "The Uncertain Messenger: A Study of the Novels of Kurt Vonnegut, Jr." *Critical Quarterly*, 11 (Winter, 1969), 297–315. Reprinted in *City of Words*, pp. 181–201. New York: Harper & Row, 1971.

Tilton, John W. *Cosmic Satire in the Contemporary Novel*, pp. 69–103. Lewisburg, Pa.: Bucknell University Press, 1977.

Trachtenberg, Stanley. "Vonnegut's Cradle: The Erosion of Comedy." *Michigan Quarterly Review*, 12 (1973), 66–71.

Tunnell, James. "Kesey and Vonnegut: Preachers of Redemption." *Christian Century*, 89 (November 22, 1972), 1180–1183.

Turner, Susan M. "Life Is Sure Funny Sometimes. . .and Sometimes It Isn't. . .A Guide to Understanding Kurt Vonnegut, Jr., *or* The Fool's Guide to Confusion *or* A Shot in the Dark *or* What Vonnegut Means to Me (This Week Anyway)." *The Thoroughbred* (University of Louisville), 2 (Spring, 1971), 43–46.

Uphaus, Robert W. "Expected Meaning in Vonnegut's Dead-End Fiction." *Novel*, 8 (Winter, 1975), 164–175.

Vanderwerken, David L. "Pilgrim's Dilemma: *Slaughterhouse-Five.*" *Research Studies*, 42 (1974), 147–152.

Vasbinder, Sam. "The Meaning of Foma in *Cat's Cradle.*" *Riverside Quarterly*, 5 (1973), 300–302.

Veeder, William. "Technique as Recovery: *Lolita* and *Mother Night.*" In *Vonnegut in America*, ed. Jerome Klinkowitz and Donald L. Lawler, pp. 97–132. New York: Delacorte Press/Seymour Lawrence, 1977.

Vinograde, Ann C. "A Soviet Translation of *Slaughterhouse-Five.*" *Russian Language Journal*, 93 (1972), 14–18.

Vitiello, Greg. "Time and Timbuktu." *Image*, 9 (March, 1972), 6–9.

Vonnegut, Bernard, Loree Rackstraw, and Jill Krementz. "A Vonnegut Album" (photographs). In *Vonnegut in America*, ed. Jerome Klinkowitz and Donald L. Lawler, pp. 37–48. New York: Delacorte Press/Seymour Lawrence, 1977.

Vonnegut, Mark. *The Eden Express,* pp. 28–29, 46, 57, 58, 70, 89, 93, 112, 120–124, 129, 160, 176–177. New York: Praeger, 1975.

Wakefield, Dan. "In Vonnegut's *Karass.*" In *The Vonnegut Statement*, ed. Jerome Klinkowitz and John Somer, pp. 55–70. New York: Delacorte/Seymour Lawrence, 1973.

Walsh, Chad. *From Utopia to Nightmare,* pp. 85–88. New York: Harper & Row, 1962.

Weales, Gerald. "What Ever Happened to Tugboat Annie?" *The Reporter*, 35 (December 1, 1966), 50, 52–56.

Wilson, Loree. "Fiction's Wild Wizard." *Iowa Alumni Review*, 19 (June, 1966), 10–12.

Wolheim, David. *The Universe Makers,* pp. 70–71. New York: Harper & Row, 1971.

Wood, Karen, and Wood, Charles. "The Vonnegut Effect: Science Fiction and Beyond." In *The Vonnegut Statement*, ed. Jerome Klinkowitz and John Somer, pp. 133–157. New York: Delacorte/Seymour Lawrence, 1973.

Wood, Michael. "Dancing in the Dark." *New York Review of Books*, 20 (May 31, 1973), 23–25.

Wymer, Thomas L. "The Swiftian Satire of Kurt Vonnegut, Jr." In *Voices for the Future*, ed. Thomas D. Clareson, pp. 238–262, 280–281. Bowling Green, Ohio: Bowling Green University Popular Press, 1976.

Zielinski, Mary. "Polish Readers Like Vonnegut and Science Fiction." *Cedar Rapids Gazette*, November 19, 1978, pp. 1B, 3B.

XI. Doctoral Dissertations

Austin, Marvin Fraley, Jr. "The Novels of Kurt Vonnegut, Jr.: A Confrontation with the Modern World." University of Tennessee, 1975.

Baker, Marilyn Joyce. "Against Humanism: Alienation in the Works of Elie Wiesel, Günter Grass, and Kurt Vonnegut." University of Southern California, 1977.

Camara, George C. "War and the Literary Extremist: The American War Novel, 1945–1970." University of Massachusetts, 1974.

Fitzgerald, Sister Ellen. "World War II and the American Novel: Hawkes, Heller, Kosinski, and Vonnegut." University of Notre Dame, 1974.

Gerson, Steven Marc. "Paradise Sought: Adamic Images in Selected Novels by Saul Bellow and Kurt Vonnegut." Texas Technical University, 1977.

Goldsmith, David Hersh. "The Novels of Kurt Vonnegut, Jr." Bowling Green State University, 1970.

Goshorn, James William. "The Queasy World of Kurt Vonnegut, Jr.: Satire in the Novels." University of New Mexico, 1971.

Group, Robert James. "Familiar Novelties: Kurt Vonnegut's Comic Epics in Prose." University of South Carolina, 1978.

Hancock, Joyce Ann. "Kurt Vonnegut and the Folk Society." University of Kentucky, 1978.

Hearron, William Thomas. "New Approaches in the Post-Modern American Novel: Joseph Heller, Kurt Vonnegut, and Richard Brautigan." State University of New York at Buffalo, 1973.

Hoffman, Thomas. "The Theme of Loneliness in Vonnegut's First Four Novels." University of Oklahoma, 1978.

Keogh, William Richard. "Violence and American Humor." University of Massachusetts, 1976.

LeClair, Thomas Edmund. "Final Words: Death and Comedy in the Fiction of Donleavy, Hawkes, Barth, Vonnegut, and Percy." Duke University, 1972.

Lonie, Charles Anthony. "Accumulations of Silence: Survivor Psychology in Vonnegut, Twain, and Hemingway." University of Minnesota, 1974.

McGinnis, Wayne Douglas. "Kurt Vonnegut, Jr.'s Confrontation with Meaninglessness." University of Arkansas, 1974.

Marino, Vincent. "Creating Conscience through Black Humor: A Study of Kurt Vonnegut's Novels." University of Southwest Louisiana, 1978.

Olderman, Raymond Michael. "Beyond the Waste Land: A Study of the American Novel in the Nineteen-Sixties." Indiana University, 1969.

Pavich, Paul Nicholas. "Kurt Vonnegut, Jr.: Apostle to the Disillusioned." University of New Mexico, 1974.

Rice, Elaine Fritz. "The Satire of John Barth and Kurt Vonnegut, Jr.: The Menippean Tradition in the 1960's in America." Arizona State University, 1974.

St. Germain, Amos Joseph. "Religious Interpretation and Contemporary Literature: Kurt Vonnegut, Jr., Robert Coover, and John Barth." University of Iowa, 1974.

Schatt, Stanley. "The World Picture of Kurt Vonnegut, Jr." University of Southern California, 1970.

Shaw, William Gray. "Comic Absurdity and the Novels of Kurt Vonnegut, Jr." Oklahoma State University, 1975.

Shor, Ira Neil. "Vonnegut's Art of Inquiry." University of Wisconsin, 1971.

Somer, John. "Quick-Stasis: The Rite of Initiation in the Novels of Kurt Vonnegut, Jr." Northern Illinois University, 1971.

Waxman, Robert Ernest. "Updike, Gass and Vonnegut: Studies in Contemporary American Fiction." Yale University, 1977.

Weinstein, Sharon Rosenbaum. "Comedy and Nightmare: The Fiction of John Hawkes, Kurt Vonnegut, Jr., Jerzy Kosinski, and Ralph Ellison." University of Utah, 1971.

XII. BIBLIOGRAPHIES

Burns, Mildred Blair. "Books by Kurt Vonnegut." *Hollins Critic*, 3 (October, 1966), 7. Updated in *The Sounder Few: Selected Essays from The Hollins Critic*, ed. R. H. W. Dillard et al., pp. 192–193. Athens: University of Georgia Press, 1971.

Fiene, Donald M. "Kurt Vonnegut and the Soviet Union: An Annotated Bibliography." In *Vonnegut in America*, ed. Jerome Klinkowitz and Donald L. Lawler, pp. 284–293. New York: Delacorte Press/Seymour Lawrence, 1977.

Hudgens, Betty L. *Kurt Vonnegut, Jr.: A Checklist*. Detroit: Gale Research, 1972.

Klinkowitz, Jerome. "The Vonnegut Bibliography." In *Vonnegut in America*, ed. Jerome Klinkowitz and Donald L. Lawler, pp. 217–252. New York: Delacorte Press/Seymour Lawrence, 1977.

———, and Asa B. Pieratt, Jr. *Kurt Vonnegut, Jr.: A Descriptive Bibliography and Annotated Secondary Checklist*. Hamden, Conn.: Shoe String Press/Archon Books, 1974.

———, and Stanley Schatt. "The Vonnegut Bibliography." In *The Vonnegut Statement*, ed. Jerome Klinkowitz and John Somer, pp. 255–277. New York: Delacorte/Seymour Lawrence, 1973.

Schatt, Stanley, and Jerome Klinkowitz. "A Kurt Vonnegut Checklist." *Critique*, 12, #3 (1971), pp. 70–76.

DONALD BARTHELME (b. 1931)

I. NOVELS

Snow White
New York: Atheneum, 1967. Slightly revised in *New Yorker,* 42 (February 18, 1967). Also incorporates "The Affront," *Harper's Bazaar,* 94 (November, 1965), 169, 229–230, and "Several Garlic Tales," *Paris Review* #37 (Spring, 1966), pp. 62–67.
New York: Bantam, 1968.
New York: Atheneum, 1972.

The Slightly Irregular Fire Engine (for children)
New York: Farrar, Straus & Giroux, 1971.

The Dead Father. New York: Farrar, Straus & Giroux, 1975. Incorporates "Manual for Sons," *New Yorker,* 51 (May 12, 1975), 40–50.
New York: Pocket Books, 1976.

II. COLLECTIONS OF STORIES AND SHORT WORKS

Come Back, Dr. Caligari
Boston: Little, Brown, 1964.
Garden City, N.Y.: Doubleday/Anchor, 1965.
Boston: Little, Brown, 1972.

Contents and original publication:
"Florence Green Is 81." *Harper's Bazaar,* 92 (September, 1963), 90–95.
"The Piano Player." *New Yorker,* 39 (August 31, 1963), 24.
"Hiding Man." *First Person,* 1 (Spring-Summer, 1961), 65–75.
"Will You Tell Me?" *Art and Literature* #1 (March, 1964), pp. 68–76.
"For I'm the Boy Whose Only Joy Is Loving You," *Location,* 1 (Summer, 1964), 91–93 (as "For I'm the Boy").
"The Big Broadcast of 1938." *New World Writing* #20 (1962), pp. 108–120.
"The Viennese Opera Ball." *Contact* #10 (June, 1962), pp. 40, 42–44.
"Me and Miss Mandible." *Contact* #7 (February, 1961), pp. 17–28 (as "The Darling Duckling at School").
"Marie, Marie, Hold on Tight." *New Yorker,* 39 (October 12, 1963), 49–51.
"Up, Aloft in the Air." Not previously published.
"Margins." *New Yorker,* 40 (February 22, 1964), 33–34.
"The Joker's Greatest Triumph." Not previously published.
"To London and Rome." *Genesis West,* 2 (Fall, 1963), 33–38.
"A Shower of Gold." *New Yorker,* 39 (December 28, 1963), 33–37.

Unspeakable Practices, Unnatural Acts
New York: Farrar, Straus & Giroux, 1968.
New York: Bantam, 1969.
New York: Pocket Books, 1976.

Contents and original publication:
"The Indian Uprising." *New Yorker,* 41 (March 6, 1965), 34–37.
"The Balloon." *New Yorker,* 42 (April 16, 1966), 46–48.

"This Newspaper Here." *New Yorker*, 41 (February 12, 1966), 28–29.
"Robert Kennedy Saved from Drowning." *New American Review* #3 (April, 1968),
   pp. 107–116.
"Report." *New Yorker*, 43 (June 10, 1967), 34–35.
"The Dolt." *New Yorker*, 43 (November 11, 1967), 56–58.
"The Police Band." *New Yorker*, 40 (August 22, 1964), 28.
"Edward and Pia." *New Yorker*, 41 (September 25, 1965), 46–49.
"A Few Moments of Sleeping and Waking." *New Yorker*, 43 (August 5, 1967),
   24–26.
"Can We Talk." *Art and Literature* #5 (Summer, 1965), pp. 148–150.
"Game." *New Yorker*, 41 (July 31, 1965), 29–30.
"Alice." *Paris Review* #43 (Summer, 1968), pp. 25–31.
"A Picture History of the War." *New Yorker*, 40 (June 20, 1964), 28–31.
"The President." *New Yorker*, 40 (September 5, 1964), 26–27.
"See the Moon?" *New Yorker*, 42 (March 12, 1966), 46–50.

City Life
New York: Farrar, Straus & Giroux, 1970.
New York: Bantam, 1971.
New York: Pocket Books, 1976.

Contents and original publication:
"Views of My Father Weeping." *New Yorker*, 45 (December 6, 1969), 56–60.
"Paraguay." *New Yorker*, 45 (September 6, 1969), 32–34.
"The Falling Dog." *New Yorker*, 44 (August 3; 1968), 28–29.
"At the Tolstoy Museum." *New Yorker*, 45 (May 24, 1969), 32–37.
"The Policemen's Ball." *New Yorker*, 44 (June 8, 1968), 31.
"The Glass Mountain." Not previously published.
"The Explanation." *New Yorker*, 44 (May 4, 1968), 44–46.
"Kierkegaard Unfair to Schlegel." *New Yorker*, 44 (October 12, 1968), 53–55.
"The Phantom of the Opera's Friend." *New Yorker*, 45 (February 7, 1970), 26–27.
"Sentence." *New Yorker*, 45 (March 7, 1970), 34–36.
"Bone Bubbles." *Paris Review* #48 (Fall, 1969), pp. 189–202 (as "Mouth").
"On Angels." *New Yorker*, 45 (August 9, 1969), 29.
"Brain Damage." *New Yorker*, 46 (February 21, 1970), 42–43.
"City Life." *New Yorker*, 44 (January 18, 1969), 31–32. (Combined with "City Life
   II," *New Yorker*, 45 [June 21, 1969], 32–37.)

Sadness
New York: Farrar, Straus & Giroux, 1972.
New York: Bantam, 1974.

Contents and original publication:
"Critique de la Vie Quotidienne." *New Yorker*, 47 (July 17, 1971), 26–29.
"Traumerei." Not previously published.
"The Genius." *New Yorker*, 47 (February 20, 1971), 38–40.
"Perpetua." *New Yorker*, 47 (June 12, 1971), 40–42.
"A City of Churches." *New Yorker*, 48 (April 22, 1972), 38–39.
"The Party." *New Yorker*, 48 (February 26, 1972), 30–31.
"Engineer-Private Paul Klee Misplaces an Aircraft between Milbertshofen and
   Cambrai, March 1916." *New Yorker*, 47 (April 3, 1971), 33–34.
"A Film." *New Yorker*, 46 (September 26, 1970), 31. (Combined with "Flying to
   America," *New Yorker*, 47 [December 4, 1971], 50–58, and untitled, unsigned
   "Notes and Comment" column, *New Yorker*, 46 [June 13, 1970], 25).
"The Sandman." *Atlantic Monthly*, 230 (September, 1972), 62–65.

"Departures." *New Yorker,* 47 (October 9, 1971), 42–44.

"Subpoena." *New Yorker,* 47 (May 29, 1971), 33.

"The Catechist." *New Yorker,* 47 (November 13, 1971), 49–51.

"The Flight of Pigeons from the Palace." *New Yorker,* 46 (August 8, 1970), 26–29 (as "The Show").

"The Rise of Capitalism." *New Yorker,* 46 (December 12, 1970), 45–47.

"The Temptation of St. Anthony." *New Yorker,* 48 (June 3, 1972), 34–36.

"Daumier." *New Yorker,* 48 (April 1, 1972), 31–36.

Guilty Pleasures
New York: Farrar, Straus & Giroux, 1974.
New York: Delta-Dell, 1976.

Contents and original publication:
"Down the Line with the Annual." *New Yorker,* 40 (March 21, 1964), 34–35.

"Letters to the Editore." *New Yorker,* 50 (February 25, 1974), 34–35.

"That Cosmopolitan Girl." *New Yorker,* 49 (July 16, 1973), 26–27. (Signed "Lily McNeil.")

"Eugénie Grandet." *New Yorker,* 44 (August 17, 1968), 24–25.

"Snap Snap." *New Yorker,* 41 (August 28, 1965), 108–111.

"The Angry Young Man." *Fiction,* 2, #2 (1973), p. 7.

"L'Lapse." *New Yorker,* 39 (March 2, 1963), 29–31.

"The Teachings of Don B.: A Yankee Way of Knowledge." *New York Times Magazine,* February 11, 1973, pp. 14–15, 66–67.

"Swallowing." *New York Times,* November 4, 1972, p. 33.

"The Young Visitirs." *New Yorker,* 48 (February 10, 1973), 27–28. (As "A Made Up Story," unsigned.)

"The Palace." *New Yorker,* 49 (December 24, 1973), 29–30. (Untitled and unsigned.)

"The Dragon." *New Yorker,* 48 (February 26, 1972), 25–26. (Untitled and unsigned.)

"An Hesitation on the Banks of the Delaware." *New Yorker,* 49 (September 3, 1973), 25. (As "A Dream," signed "Lily McNeil.")

"The Royal Treatment." *New York Times,* November 3, 1973, p. 29. (Signed "Lily McNeil.")

"Mr. Foolfarm's Journal." *Village Voice,* 19 (May 16, 1974), 1, 54.

"Heliotrope." *New Yorker,* 50 (April 1, 1974), 27. (Untitled and unsigned.)

"And Now Let's Hear It for the Ed Sullivan Show!" *Esquire,* 71 (April, 1969), 126–127, 54, 56.

"Bunny Image, Loss Of: The Case of Bitsy S." Not previously published.

"The Expedition." *Audience,* 2 (July/August, 1972), 56–60.

"Games Are the Enemies of Beauty, Truth and Sleep, Amanda Said." *Mademoiselle,* 64 (November, 1966), 212–213.

"A Nation of Wheels." *New Yorker,* 46 (June 13, 1970), 36–39.

"Two Hours to Curtain." Not previously published, except for sections from "Flying to America," *New Yorker,* 47 (December 4, 1971), 50–58.

"The Photographs." *New Yorker,* 49 (January 28, 1974), 32–33.

"Nothing: A Preliminary Account." *New Yorker,* 49 (December 31, 1973), 26–27.

Amateurs
New York: Farrar, Straus & Giroux, 1976.
New York: Pocket Books, 1977.

Contents and original publication:
"Our Work and Why We Do It." *New Yorker*, 49 (May 5, 1973), 39–41.
"The Wound." *New Yorker*, 49 (October 15, 1973), 36–37.
"110 West Sixty-First Street." *New Yorker*, 49 (September 24, 1973), 33–34.
"Some of Us Had Been Threatening Our Friend Colby." *New Yorker*, 49 (May 26, 1973), 39–40.
"The School." *New Yorker*, 50 (June 17, 1974), 28.
"The Great Hug." *Atlantic*, 235 (June, 1975), 44–45.
"I Bought a Little City." *New Yorker*, 50 (November 11, 1974), 42–44.
"The Agreement." *New Yorker*, 50 (October 14, 1974), 44–45.
"The Sergeant." *Fiction*, 3, #2/3 (1975), pp. 24–25.
"What to Do Next." *New Yorker*, 49 (March 24, 1973), 35–37.
"The Captured Woman." *New Yorker*, 52 (June 28, 1976), 22–25.
"And Then." *Harper's*, 247 (December, 1973), 87–89.
"Porcupines at the University." *New Yorker*, 46 (April 25, 1970), 32–33.
"The Educational Experience." *Harper's*, 246 (June, 1973), 62–65.
"The Discovery." *New Yorker*, 49 (August 20, 1973), 26–27.
"Rebecca." *New Yorker*, 51 (February 24, 1975), 44–45.
"The Reference." *Playboy*, 21 (April, 1974), 163, 186–187.
"The New Member." *New Yorker*, 50 (July 15, 1974), 28–30.
"You Are As Brave As Vincent Van Gogh." *New Yorker*, 50 (March 18, 1974), 34.
"At the End of the Mechanical Age." *Atlantic*, 231 (June, 1973), 52–55.

Great Days
New York: Farrar, Straus & Giroux, 1979.

Contents and original publication:
"The Crisis." *New Yorker*, 53 (October 24, 1977), 42–43.
"The Apology." *New Yorker*, 54 (February 20, 1978), 35–37.
"The New Music." *New Yorker*, 54 (June 19, 1978), 29–30. (Also incorporates "Momma," *New Yorker*, 54 [October 2, 1978], 32–33.
"Cortés and Montezuma." *New Yorker*, 53 (August 22, 1977), 25–26.
"The King of Jazz." *New Yorker*, 52 (February 7, 1977), 31–32.
"The Question Party." *New Yorker*, 52 (January 17, 1977), 32–34.
"Belief." *University of Houston Forum*, 13 (Winter, 1976), 47–49.
"Tales of the Swedish Army." *New Yorker*, 53 (December 26, 1977), 23–24.
"The Abduction from the Seraglio." *New Yorker*, 53 (January 30, 1978), 30–31.
"The Death of Edward Lear." *New Yorker*, 46 (January 2, 1971), 21.
"Concerning the Bodyguard." *New Yorker*, 54 (October 16, 1978), 36–37.
"The Zombies." *New Yorker*, 53 (April 25, 1977), 35.
"Morning." *New Yorker*, 54 (May 1, 1978), 36–37.
"On the Steps of the Conservatory." *New Yorker*, 53 (February 21, 1977), 33–35.
"The Leap." *New Yorker*, 54 (July 31, 1978), 27–29.
"Great Days." *Partisan Review*, 44, #3, (1977), pp. 501–511.

III. UNCOLLECTED STORIES

"Adventure." *Harper's Bazaar*, 104 (December, 1970), 92–95.
"Alexandria and Henrietta." *New American Review* #12 (1971), pp. 82–87.
"Aria." *New Yorker*, 55 (March 12, 1979), 37.
"The Bed." *Viva*, 1 (March, 1974), 68–70.

"The Bill." *Viva*, 1 (November, 1973), n.p.

"Captain Blood." *New Yorker*, 54 (January 1, 1979), 26–27.

"Cornell." Joseph Cornell Exhibition Catalogue, Leo Castelli Gallery, New York, February-March, 1976, unpaged. Reprinted in *Ontario Review #5* (Fall/Winter, 1976), p. 50.

"The Dassaud Prize." *New Yorker*, 51 (January 12, 1976), 26–29.

"Edwards, Amelia." *New Yorker*, 48 (September 9, 1972), 34–36.

"Grandmother." *New Yorker*, 55 (September 3, 1979), 26–28.

"The Great Debate." *New Yorker*, 52 (May 3, 1976), 34–35.

"How I Write My Songs, by Bill B. White." *New Yorker*, 54 (November 27, 1978), 36–37.

"The Inauguration." *Harper's*, 246 (January, 1973), 86–87.

"A Man." *New Yorker*, 48 (December 30, 1972), 26–27.

"Man's Face." *New Yorker*, 40 (May 30, 1964), 29.

"Manfred" (with Karen Snow). *New York Times Magazine*, April 18, 1976, p. 87.

"Monumental Folly." *Atlantic*, 237 (February, 1976), 33–40.

"The Mothball Fleet." *New Yorker*, 47 (September 11, 1971), 34–35.

"Natural History." *Harper's*, 243 (August, 1971), 44–45.

"Newsletter." *New Yorker*, 46 (July 11, 1970), 23.

"Over the Sea of Hesitation." *New Yorker*, 48 (November 11, 1972), 40–43.

"Philadelphia." *New Yorker*, 44 (November 30, 1968), 56–58.

"Presents." *Penthouse*, 9 (December, 1977), 106–110.

"The Short Story Contest." *New York Times Magazine*, February 1, 1976, p. 79.

"The Story Thus Far:". *New Yorker*, 47 (May 1, 1971), 42–45.

"Then." *Mother #3* (November/December, 1964), pp. 22–23.

"Three." *Fiction*, 1, #1 (1972), p. 13.

"The Willie and Wade Park." *Harper's*, 258 (June, 1979), 75–77.

"Wrack." *New Yorker*, 48 (October 21, 1972), 36–37.

IV. ARTICLES AND REVIEWS

"After Joyce." *Location*, 1 (Summer, 1964), 13–16.

"As Grace Paley Faces Jail with 3 Other Writers." *New York Times* (Op-Ed page), February 2, 1979, p. 25.

"The Case of the Vanishing Product." *Harper's*, 223 (October, 1961), 30–32.

Contemporary Arts Museum. Houston, 1961. Unsigned pamphlet.

"Contemporary Arts Museum Annual Report, 1961–1962." Unsigned.

"Culture, Etc." *Texas Observer*, 51 (March 25, 1960), 7.

"Dead Men Comin' Through/The Current Cinema." Review of *The Onion Field*. *New Yorker*, 55 (October 1, 1979), 103–105.

"The Earth As an Overturned Bowl/The Current Cinema." Review of *Woyzeck*. *New Yorker*, 55 (September 10, 1979), 120–122.

"Elaine de Kooning Paints a Picture." Unsigned broadside, June, 1962.

"The Elegance Is Under Control." Review of *The Triumph* by John Kenneth Galbraith, *New York Times Book Review*, April 21, 1968, pp. 4–5.

"The Emerging Figure." Exhibition catalogue, Contemporary Arts Museum, Houston, May-June, 1961. Text reprinted in *University of Houston Forum*, 3 (Summer, 1961), 23–24.

"Introduction." *Architectural Graphics*. Exhibition catalogue, Contemporary Arts Museum, Houston, April 8–29, 1960.

"Mr. Hunt's Wooly Utopia." Review of *Alpaca* by H. L. Hunt, *The Reporter*, 22 (April 14, 1960), 44–46.

"A Note on Elia Kazan." *University of Houston Forum,* 1 (September, 1956), 19–22.

"Parachutes in the Trees/The Current Cinema." Review of *Soldier of Orange. New Yorker,* 55 (September 17, 1979), 132, 134–135.

"Peculiar Influences/The Current Cinema." Reviews of *The Europeans* and *Nosferatu, the Vampyre. New Yorker,* 55 (October 15, 1979), 182–184.

Untitled commentary on "Paraguay." In *Writer's Choice,* ed. Rust Hills, pp. 25–26. New York: David McKay. 1974.

"Reiner, David," and "Pages from the Annual Report." *University of Houston Forum,* 3 (March, 1959), 13–18. Unsigned.

"Robert Morris." Exhibition catalogue, Washburn Galleries, New York, February 1-March 6, 1976, pp. 3–4.

"she." Preface to an exhibition catalogue of women in art. Cordier & Ekstorm, New York, December 3, 1970-January 16, 1971. Unpaged.

"Special Devotions/The Current Cinema." Reviews of *The Green Room* and *Love and Bullets. New Yorker,* 55 (September 24, 1979), 132–133.

"Survival of the Writer: Support by Organizations and Foundations." In *The Publication of Poetry and Fiction: A Conference* (Library of Congress, October 20–21, 1975), pp. 126–129, 154–155. Washington, D.C.: Library of Congress, 1977.

"A Symposium on Fiction" (with William H. Gass, Grace Paley, and Walker Percy). *Shenandoah,* 27 (Winter, 1976), 3–31.

"Three Festivals/The Current Cinema." *New Yorker,* 55 (October 8, 1979), 164, 167–168.

"The Tired Terror of Graham Greene." Review of *The Comedians* by Graham Greene. *Holiday,* 39 (April, 1966), 146, 148–149.

Ways and Means. Contemporary Arts Museum, Houston, October/November, 1961.

V. INTERVIEWS AND RECORDED REMARKS

Baker, John F. "PW Interviews Donald Barthelme." *Publishers Weekly,* 206 (November 11, 1974), 6–7.

Cross, Leslie. "Down in the Village with Donald Barthelme." *Milwaukee Journal,* February 4, 1973, sec. 4, p. 4.

Donald Barthelme, I, II, III, and IV. Los Angeles: Pacifica Tape Library, 1976.

Klinkowitz, Jerome. "Donald Barthelme." In *The New Fiction: Interviews with Innovative American Writers,* ed. Joe David Bellamy, pp. 45–54. Urbana: University of Illinois Press, 1974.

Lish, Gordon. *New Sounds in American Fiction.* Cummings LP 51612, 1969.

Schickel, Richard. "Freaked Out on Barthelme." *New York Times Magazine,* August 16, 1970, pp. 14–15, 42.

Simon, Jeff. "Donald Barthelme." *Buffalo Evening News,* July 28, 1978, pp. 1, 24 ("Gusto" section).

Wood, Susan. "High Priest of Trash and Flash." *Houston City Magazine,* 3 (February, 1979), 31–34, 36.

VI. UNTITLED, UNSIGNED "COMMENT" PIECES BY BARTHELME IN *The New Yorker*

Note: 11 columns, plus "she" (see IV, above), are reprinted in a limited edition, *Here in the Village* (Northridge, Calif.: Lord John Press, 1978), indicated by *HV* below. Certain others appear in *Sadness* (*S*) and *Guilty Pleasures* (*GP*).

New Yorker, 46 (June 13, 1970), 25. *S* and *GP*.
New Yorker, 47 (January 29, 1972), 28.
New Yorker, 48 (February 26, 1972), 25. *GP*.
New Yorker, 48 (February 10, 1973), 27. *GP*.
New Yorker, 49 (December 24, 1973), 29. *GP*.
New Yorker, 49 (December 31, 1973), 17.
New Yorker, 50 (April 1, 1974), 27. *GP*.
New Yorker, 50 (November 11, 1974), 37. *HV*.
New Yorker, 50 (November 18, 1974), 43.
New Yorker, 51 (June 23, 1975), 29–30. *HV*.
New Yorker, 51 (August 11, 1975), 19. *HV*.
New Yorker, 51 (September 29, 1975), 27. *HV*.
New Yorker, 51 (October 20, 1975), 31. *HV*.
New Yorker, 51 (November 24, 1975), 39. *HV*.
New Yorker, 51 (January 19, 1976), 21.
New Yorker, 52 (June 14, 1976), 23. *HV*.
New Yorker, 52 (July 12, 1976), 25–26.
New Yorker, 52 (October 11, 1976), 31. *HV*.
New Yorker, 53 (October 10, 1977), 35.
New Yorker, 53 (October 24, 1977), 33. *HV*.
New Yorker, 54 (June 26, 1978), 21. *HV*.
New Yorker, 54 (August 28, 1978), 19. *HV*.
New Yorker, 54 (November 27, 1978), 32.
New Yorker, 54 (December 4, 1978), 39.
New Yorker, 54 (December 25, 1978), 21.
New Yorker, 55 (July 30, 1979), 19.

VII. Special Issue of a Scholarly Journal Devoted to Barthelme
Critique, 16, #3 (1975). Contents listed below.

VIII. Critical Essays and Books about Barthelme

Aldridge, John W. "Donald Barthelme and the Doggy Life." *Atlantic*, 222 (July, 1968), 89–91. Reprinted in *The Devil and the Fire*, pp. 216–266. New York: Harper's Magazine Press, 1972.

Bellamy, Joe David. "Introduction." *SuperFiction*, pp. 317. New York: Vintage Books/Random House, 1975.

Bocock, Maclin. "'The Indian Uprising'; Or, Donald Barthelme's Strange Object Covered with Fur." *Fiction International* #4/5 (1975), pp. 134–146.

Conroy, Frank. "An Explorer's Notes: Donald Barthelme Does It Again." *New York Times Book Review*, June 6, 1971, pp. 4–5.

Davis, Robert Murray. "Donald Barthelme's Textual Revisions." *Resources for American Literary Study*, 7 (1977), 182–191.

Dervin, Daniel A. "Breast Fantasy in Barthelme, Swift, and Philip Roth: Creativity and Psychoanalytic Structure." *American Imago*, 33 (1976), 102–122.

Dickstein, Morris. *Gates of Eden: American Culture in the Sixties*, pp. 14, 103, 127, 218–219, 231–232, 234, 236, 238, 242–246, 290–291. New York: Basic Books, 1977. Revised and expanded from "Fiction Hot and Kool: Dilemmas of the Experimental Writer," *TriQuarterly* #33 (Spring, 1975), pp. 257–272.

Ditsky, John M. "The Man on the Quaker Oats Box: Characteristics of Recent Experimental Fiction." *Georgia Review*, 26 (Fall, 1972), 297–313.

————. "'With Ingenuity and Hardwork, Distracted': The Narrative Style of Donald Barthelme." *Style*, 9 (Summer, 1975). 388–400.

Doxey, W. S. "Donald Barthelme's 'Views of My Father Weeping': A Modern View of Oedipus." *Notes on Contemporary Literature*, 3, #2 (1973), pp. 14–15.

Flowers, Betty. "Barthelme's *Snow White:* The Reader-Patient Relationship." *Critique*, 16, #3 (1975), pp. 33–43.

Gardner, John. *On Moral Fiction*, pp. 79–81. New York: Basic Books, 1978.

Gass, William H. "The Leading Edge of the Trash Phenomenon." *New York Review of Books*, 10 (April 25, 1968), 5–6. Reprinted in *Fiction and the Figures of Life*, pp. 97–103. New York: Alfred A. Knopf, 1970.

Gates, David. "A Highly Irregular Children's Story: *The Slightly Irregular Fire Engine*." *Virginia Quarterly Review*, 52 (Spring, 1976), 298–308.

Giles, James R. "The "Marivaudian Being' Drowns His Children: Dehumanization in Donald Barthelme's 'Robert Kennedy Saved From Drowning' and Joyce Carol Oates' *Wonderland*." *Southern Humanities Review*, 9 (Winter, 1975), 63–75.

Gillen, Francis. "Donald Barthelme's City: A Guide." *Twentieth Century Literature*, 18 (January, 1972), 37–44.

Gilman, Richard. "Fiction: Donald Barthelme." In *The Confusion of Realms*, pp. 42–51. New York: Random House, 1969. Reprinted from *The New Republic*, 156 (June 3, 1967), 27–29.

Glicksberg, Charles I. "Experimental Fiction: Innovation versus Form." *Centennial Review*, 18 (Spring, 1974), 127–150.

Graff, Gerald. "Babbitt at the Abyss: The Social Context of PostModern American Fiction." *TriQuarterly* #33 (Spring, 1975), pp. 305–337. Revised and expanded in *Literature Against Itself*, pp. 33, 52–53, 57, 76, 220, 224–230, 236–238. Chicago: University of Chicago Press, 1979.

————. "The Myth of the Post Modernist Breakthrough." *TriQuarterly* #26 (Winter, 1973), pp. 383–417.

Guerard, Albert J. "Notes on the Rhetoric of Anti-Realistic Fiction." *TriQuarterly* #30 (Spring, 1974), pp. 3–50.

Harris, Charles B. *Contemporary American Novelists of the Absurd*, pp. 24, 124–127. New Haven: College & University Press, 1971.

Hassan, Ihab. *Contemporary American Literature, 1945–1972*, pp. 56, 64, 82, 84, 171. New York: Frederick Ungar, 1973.

————. *Paracriticisms*, pp. 44, 58, 82–83, 87, 101, 109, 141. Urbana: University of Illinois Press, 1975.

Hendin, Josephine. *Vulnerable People: A View of American Fiction Since 1945*, pp. 61–63, 71. Reprinted from "Angries: S–M as a Literary Style," *Harper's*, 248 (February, 1974), 87–93.

Johnson, R. E. "'Bees Barking in the Night': The End and Beginning of Donald Barthelme's Narrative." *Boundary 2*, #5 (Fall, 1976), pp. 71–92.

————. "Structuralism and the Reading of Contemporary Fiction." *Soundings*, 58 (1974), 281–306.

Kazin, Alfred. *Bright Book of Life: American Novelists and Storytellers from Hemingway to Mailer*, pp. 38, 183, 271–274. Boston: Atlantic/Little, Brown, 1973.

Klinkowitz, Jerome. "Donald Barthelme." *Dictionary of Literary Biography*, ed. Jeffery Helterman and Richard Layman, I, 34–39. Detroit: Gale Research, 1978.

————. "Donald Barthelme's SuperFiction." *Critique*, 16, #3 (1975), pp. 5–18. Revised and expanded in Klinkowitz and Roy R. Behrens, *The Life of Fiction*, pp.

72–84. Urbana: University of Illinois Press, 1977.

———. "Innovative Short Fiction: 'Vile and Imaginative Things.'" In *Innovative Fiction*, ed. Klinkowitz and John Somer, pp. xv–xxvii. New York: Dell, 1972.

———. "Literary Disruptions; Or, What's Become of American Fiction?" *Partisan Review*, 40, #3 (1973), pp. 433–444. Revised and expanded in *Surfiction*, ed. Raymond Federman, pp. 165–179. Chicago: Swallow Press, 1975.

Kramer, Hilton. "Barthelme's Comedy of Patricide." *Commentary*, 62 (August, 1976), 56–59.

Krupnick, Mark C. "Notes from the Funhouse." *Modern Occasions*, 1 (Fall, 1970), 108–112.

Leland, John. "Remarks Re-marked." *Boundary 2*, 5 (Spring, 1977), 795–811.

LeVot, André. "Disjunctive and Conjunctive Modes in Contemporary American Fiction." *University of Houston Forum*, 13, #3 (1976), pp. 44–45.

Lingeman, Richard. "Steal My Name and You Got Trash." *New York Times Book Review*, February 3, 1974, p. 39. (Satirical reply to Barthelme's letter of December 23, 1973, p. 17.)

Lodge, David. *The Modes of Modern Writing*, pp. 226, 232, 234–235, 236, 271–272. Ithaca: Cornell University Press, 1977.

Longleigh, Peter L., Jr. "Donald Barthelme's *Snow White*." *Critique*, 11, #3 (1969), pp. 30–34.

McCaffery, Larry. "Barthelme's *Snow White:* The Aesthetics of Trash." *Critique*, 16, #3 (1975), pp. 19–32.

———. "Meaning and Non-Meaning in Barthelme's Fictions." *Journal of Aesthetic Education*, 13 (January, 1979), 69–80.

McConnell, Frank D. *Four Postwar American Novelists: Bellow, Mailer, Barth, and Pynchon*, pp. xxvi, 57, 93. Chicago: University of Chicago Press, 1977.

McNall, Sally Allen. "'But Why Am I Troubling Myself about Language?' Style, Reaction, and Lack of Reaction in Barthelme's *Snow White*." *Language & Style*, 8 (1974), 81–94.

Maloy, Barbara. "Barthelme's *The Dead Father:* Analysis of an Allegory." *Linguistics in Literature*, 2, #2 (1977), pp. 43–119.

Moran, Charles. "Barthelme the Trash-Man: The Uses of Junk." *CEA Critic*, 36 (May, 1974), 32–33.

Nicol, Charles. "I Am Donald Barthelme." *Harper's Bookletter*, March 3, 1975.

"Notes of Concern Mark Book Award Ceremony." *New York Times*, April 14, 1972, p. 21.

Oates, Joyce Carol. "Whose Side Are You On?" *New York Times Book Review*, June 4, 1972, p. 63.

Olderman, Raymond. *Beyond the Waste Land: The American Novel in the Nineteen-Sixties*, pp. 20, 24. New Haven: Yale University Press, 1972.

Peden, William. *The American Short Story*, pp. 12, 19, 27, 177–179, 183, 185, 188. Boston: Houghton Mifflin, 1975.

Pomaska, Anna. "The Teachings of Don Juan." *New York Times Magazine*, March 11, 1972, pp. 98–99.

Prescott, Peter S. "The Writer's Lot." *Newsweek*, 82 (December 24, 1973), 83–85.

Puetz, Manfred. "Imagination and Self-Definition." *Partisan Review*, 44, #2 (1977), pp. 235–244.

Rother, James. "Parafiction: The Adjacent Universe of Barth, Barthelme, Pynchon, and Nabokov." *Boundary 2*, 5 (Fall, 1976), 21–44.

Samuels, Charles Thomas. "Moving Through 'The Indian Uprising.'" In *The*

Process of Fiction, 2nd ed., ed. Barbara McKenzie, pp. 529–537. New York: Harcourt Brace Jovanovich, 1974.

Schmitz, Neil. "Donald Barthelme and the Emergence of Modern Satire." *Minnesota Review*, 1 #4 (1972), pp. 109–118.

———. "What Irony Unravels." *Partisan Review*, 40, #3 (1973), pp. 482–490.

Scholes, Robert. "Metafiction." *Iowa Review*, 1 (Fall, 1970), 100–115. Reprinted in *Fabulation and Metafiction*, pp. 105, 114–119, 122, 131. Urbana: University of Illinois Press, 1979.

Shadoian, Jack. "Notes on Donald Barthelme's *Snow White*." *Western Humanities Review*, 24 (Winter, 1970), 73–75.

Shelton, Frank W. "Barthelme's Western Tall Tale: Porcupines at the University." *Notes on Contemporary Literature*, 9 (January, 1979), 2–3.

Shorris, Earl. "Donald Barthelme's Illustrated Wordy-Gurdy." *Harper's*, 246 (January, 1973), 92–94, 96.

Stern, Daniel. "The Mysterious New Novel." In *Liberations*, ed. Ihab Hassan, pp. 31–32. Middletown, Conn.: Wesleyan University Press, 1971.

Stevick, Philip. "Scherezade Runs Out of Plots, Goes on Talking; The King, Puzzled, Listens: An Essay on the New Fiction." *TriQuarterly* #26 (Winter, 1973), pp. 332–362.

———. "Lies, Fictions, and Mock Facts." *Western Humanities Review*, 30 (Winter, 1976), 1–12.

Stott, William. "Donald Barthelme and the Death of Fiction." *Prospects* #1 (1975), pp. 369–386.

Tanner, Tony. *City of Words: American Fiction 1950–1970*, pp. 141, 393, 400–406. New York: Harper & Row, 1971.

Vidal, Gore. *Matters of Fact and Fiction*, pp. 99, 102–107. New York: Random House, 1977.

Waldron, Ann. "Barthelme Bit His Lip, Clutched His Scotch, and Answered On." *Houston Chronicle/Zest Magazine*, April 23, 1972, p. 14.

———. "Barthelme Meets the Penwomen." *Houston Chronicle/Zest Magazine*, August 12, 1973, p. 16.

———. "Ex-Houstonian's Children's Book Wins Award." *Houston Chronicle*, April 12, 1972, p. 24.

Weixlmann, Joe and Sher. "Barth and Barthelme Recycle the Perseus Myth." *Modern Fiction Studies*, 25 (Summer, 1979), 191–207.

Whalen, Tom. "Wonderful Elegance: Barthelme's 'The Party.'" *Critique*, 16, #3 (1975), pp. 45–48.

Wickes, George. "From Breton to Barthelme: Westward the Course of Surrealism." *Proceedings: Pacific NW Conference on Foreign Languages*, 22 (1971), 208–214.

Wilde, Alan. "Barthelme Unfair to Kierkegaard: Some Thoughts on Modern and Postmodern Irony." *Boundary 2*, 5 (Fall, 1976), 45–70.

IX. DOCTORAL DISSERTATIONS

Costello, Thomas Leonard. "Parody and Social Satire in the Fiction of Donald Barthelme." Michigan State University, 1976.

Hoekzema, Loren Lee. "Two Readings of Lyrical Space: William H. Gass's *In the Heart of the Heart of the Country* and Donald Barthelme's *City Life*." Ohio University, 1976.

McNall, Sally Allen. "Order as Surprise: A Stylistic Comparison of Experimental Fiction." Arizona State University, 1975.

Press, David Paul. "New Forms of Short Fiction in America." University of Oklahoma, 1978.

Taylor, David Michael. "Donald Barthelme: An Approach to Contemporary Fiction." Florida State University, 1977.

X. PUBLIC DISAVOWED FORGERIES OF STORIES ALLEGEDLY WRITTEN BY BARTHELME

"Divorce." *Carolina Quarterly,* 25 (Fall, 1973), 52–59.

"Cannon!" *Voyages,* 5 (1973), 62–67.

"Cannon!" *Georgia Review,* 27 (Winter, 1973), 566–572. (Text differs.)

"Cannon!" *Ann Arbor Review* #17 (1973), pp. 65–71. (Text differs.)

"Sentence Passed on the Show of a Nation's Brain Damage, etc. Or, The Autobiography of a Crime." *December,* 15, #1–2 (1973), pp. 83–94.

XI. BIBLIOGRAPHIES

Klinkowitz, Jerome. "Donald Barthelme: A Checklist, 1957–1974." *Critique,* 16, #3 (1975), pp. 49–58.

Klinkowitz, Jerome, Asa Pieratt, and Robert Murray Davis. *Donald Barthelme: A Comprehensive Bibliography and Annotated Secondary Checklist.* Hamden, Conn.: Shoe String Press/Archon Books, 1977.

McCaffery, Larry. "Donald Barthelme, Robert Coover, and William H. Gass: Three Checklists." *Bulletin of Bibliography,* 31 (1974), 101–106.

JERZY KOSINSKI (b. 1933)

I. NOVELS

The Painted Bird
Boston: Houghton Mifflin, 1965 (a heavily corrupted edition, with an epilogue added without the author's permission).
New York: Pocket Books, 1966 (a restoration of Kosinski's text).
New York: Modern Library, 1970 (with new revisions by Kosinski).
New York: Bantam, 1972 (reprints Pocket Books text).
Boston: Houghton Mifflin, 1976 (reprints Modern Library text, with author's new "Afterward" as introduction).
New York: Bantam, 1978 (reprints Modern Library text with 1976 "Afterward" as postscript).

Steps
New York: Random House, 1968.
New York: Bantam, 1969.

Being There
New York: Harcourt Brace Jovanovich, 1971.
New York: Bantam, 1972.

The Devil Tree
New York: Harcourt Brace Jovanovich, 1973.
New York: Bantam, 1974.

Cockpit
Boston: Houghton Mifflin, 1975.
New York: Bantam, 1976.

Blind Date
Boston: Houghton Mifflin, 1977.
New York: Bantam, 1978.

Passion Play
New York: St. Martin's Press, 1979.

II. SCHOLARSHIP AND CRITICISM

Dokumenty walki o Czlowieka: Wspomnienia Proletariatczykow [Documents Concerning the Struggle of Man: Reminiscences of the Members of "The Proletariat"], *Przeglad Nauk Historycznych i Spolecznych* [The Review of Social and Historical Sciences], 4 (1954), 411–432. Published separately as a booklet by Lodzkie Towarzystwo Naukowe [Scientific Society of Lodz, Poland], 1955.
Program Rewolucji Ludowej Jakoba Jaworskiego [The Program of the People's Revolution of Jakob Jaworski], *Przeglad Nauk Historycznychi Spolecznych [The Review of Social and Historical Sciences], 5 (1954), 207–236. Published separately as a booklet by Lodzkie Towarzystwo Naukowe [Scientific Society of Lodz, Poland], 1955.*

The Future Is Ours, Comrade (pseud.: Joseph Novak)
Garden City, N.Y.: Doubleday, 1960.
New York: E. P. Dutton, 1964.

No Third Path (pseud.: Joseph Novak)
Garden City, N.Y.: Doubleday, 1962.

Socjologia Amerykánska (editor)
New York: Polski Instytut Naukowy w Ameryce, 1962.

Notes of the Author
New York: Scientia-Factum, 1965.

The Art of the Self
New York: Scientia-Factum, 1968. (Parts reprinted from *New York Times Book Review*, October 20, 1968, and *The Tin Drum* [Wesleyan University], December 18, 1968; complete text reprinted in *Exile*, 1, #1, [1972], 48–67).

Tijd van leven—tijd van kunst [The time of life—the time of art]. Amsterdam: Uitgeverij de Bezige Bij, 1970. (Expanded versions, restoring the original text, of *Notes of the Author* and *The Art of the Self*).

American P.E.N. Newsletter, Summer, 1973—. Regular comments by Kosinski as president and later vice-president.

"Against Book Censorship." *Media & Methods*, 12 (January, 1976), 20–24.
"'The Banned Book' as Psychological Drug—a Parody." *Media & Methods*, 13 (January, 1977), 18–19.
"Dead Souls on Campus." *New York Times*, October 13, 1970, p. 20.
"Hiram Haydn: 1907–1973." *American Scholar*, 43 (Summer, 1974), 376–377.
"Is Solzhenitsyn Right?" *Time*, 111 (June 26, 1978), 22.
Jerzy Kosinski on Fiction. Audio cassette. North Hollywood: Center for Cassette Studies, 1973. (Withdrawn at author's insistence by Court Order).
"The Lone Wolf." *American Scholar*, 41 (Fall, 1972), 513–519.
"Maxims of Jerzy Kosinski." *Confrontation*, 3 (Winter/Spring, 1970), 75.
"Our 'Predigested, Prepackaged Popular Culture.'" *US News & World Report*, January 8, 1979, pp. 52–53.
"Packaged Passion." *American Scholar*, 42 (Spring, 1973), 193–204.
"The Reality Behind Words." *New York Times*, October 3, 1971, p. 23.
"The Secret Life of Our Times." Review of *New Fiction from Esquire*, ed. Gordon Lish, *New York Times Book Review*, January 13, 1974, pp. 26, 28, 30.
"'Seven Beauties': A Cartoon Trying to Be a Tragedy." *New York Times/Arts & Leisure*, March 7, 1976, pp. 2, 15.
"Telling Ourselves Tales to Make It through the Night." Review of *The White Album* by Joan Didion. *Los Angeles Times Book Review*, May 27, 1979, pp. 1, 29.
"Time to Spare." *New York Times*, May 21, 1979, p. A19.
"To Hold a Pen." *American Scholar*, 42 (Fall, 1973), 555–567.
"The Writer's Dilemma." Sound Seminar Audio Tape. New York: McGraw-Hill, 1970.

III. Interviews and Recorded Remarks

Allen, Henry. "A Painted Bird, A Painted World." *Style/Washington Post*, August 30, 1971, pp. B1, B6.

Amory, Cleveland. "Trade Winds." *Saturday Review*, 54 (April 17, 1971), 16–17.

"The Books That Shaped Lives." *Christian Century*, 93 (November 24, 1976), 1052.

Cahill, Daniel J. "*The Devil Tree:* An Interview with Jerzy Kosinski." *North American Review*, 258 (Spring, 1973), 56–66.

———. "An Interview with Jerzy Kosinski on *Blind Date.*" *Contemporary Literature*, 19 (Spring, 1978), 133–142.

———. "Life at a Gallop: Interview with Jerzy Kosinski." *Washington Post Book World*, September 16, 1979, p. 10.

"The Conscience of the Writer." *Publishers Weekly*, 199 (March 22, 1971), 26–28.

Diehl, Digby. "Author's Put-on in a No-death Land." *Showcase/Chicago Sun-Times*, June 13, 1971, p. 11.

Fischer, Mary A. "Peter Sellers' Chance of a Lifetime." *Rolling Stone*, April 19, 1979, pp. 63–64.

"Flogging It." *Time*, 107 (April 5, 1976), 76–77.

Fosburgh, Carey. "Why More Top Novelists Don't Go to Hollywood." *New York Times/Arts and Leisure*, November 21, 1976, pp. 1, 13–14.

Frymer, Frank. "Novelist Kosinski Is Afraid Television Is 'Castrating Our Children.'" *Newsday*, July 1, 1971, pp. 14–17.

Gallo, William. "Jerzy Kosinski: Writing by Chance and Necessity." *Rocky Mountain News* (Denver), November 30, 1977.

Gardner, Raymond. "Painted Bird of Youth." *The Guardian* (London), June 25, 1973, p. 10.

Griffin, Patricia. "Conversation with Jerzy Kosinski." *Texas Arts Journal*, 1977, pp. 5–11.

Haydn, Hiram. *Words and Faces*, pp. 215–222. New York: Harcourt Brace Jovanovich, 1974.

"Jerzy Kosinski's Seventh Novel Goes to St. Martin's." *Publishers Weekly*, 213 (April 9, 1979), 89.

Kane, John. "Jerzy Kosinski." *Yale Lit*, 141 (August, 1972), 12–16.

Kettner, Linda. "Novelist Kosinski Tells What It's Like 'Being There.'" *Cedar Falls Record*, September 16, 1975, p. 3.

Kisor, Henry. "One-on-one with Kosinski." *Chicago Sun-Times Book Week*, September 9, 1979, pp. 11–12.

Klinkowitz, Jerome. "Jerzy Kosinski: An Interview." *Fiction International* #1 (Fall, 1973), pp. 30–48. Reprinted in *The New Fiction: Interviews with Innovative American Writers*, ed. Joe David Bellamy, pp. 142–168. Urbana: University of Illinois Press, 1974.

———. "Jerzy Kosinski: Puppetmaster." *Panorama/Chicago Daily News*, October 22, 1977, pp. 16, 22.

"Kosinski: Most Obsessive." *New York Post*, February 7, 1979, p. 6.

"Kosinski Named New P.E.N. President." *Publishers Weekly*, 203 (May 21, 1973), 28.

Lawson, Carol. "Behind the Best Sellers." *New York Times Book Review*, October 21, 1979, p. 58.

Melton, William. "*I Get My Best Ideas In Bed.*" Los Angeles: Nash, 1971.

Mount, Douglas N. "Authors & Editors." *Publishers Weekly*, 199 (April 26, 1971), 13–16.

Movius, Geoffrey. "A Conversation with Jerzy Kosinski." *New Boston Review*, 1 (Winter, 1975), 3–6.

Nathan, Paul S. "Multiple Kosinskis." *Publishers Weekly*, 203 (April 30, 1973), 48.

———. "Surreptitious Tapes." *Publishers Weekly*, 214 (October 23, 1978), 85.

Newman, Edwin. *Comment!* (NBC News transcript), 1 (February 28, 1971), 6–8.
———. *Comment!* (NBC News transcript), 2 (September 3, 1972), 1–2.
Nichols, Lewis. "Author." *New York Times Book Review*, October 31, 1965, p. 8.
Nowicki, R. E. "Interview with Jerzy Kosinski." *San Francisco Review of Books*, March, 1978, pp. 10–13.
Plimpton, George, and Rocco Landesman. "The Art of Fiction LXVI."*Paris Review* #54 (Summer, 1972), pp. 183–207.
"Polish Joke." *Time*, 113 (February 19, 1979), 94, 96.
Quigley, Kathleen. *"The Painted Bird's* Author Turns to Polo for Novel." *Palm Beach Daily News*, n.d. (ca. March 1979), p. 1.
Raymont, Henry. "National Book Awards: The Winners." *New York Times*, March 11, 1969, p. 42.
———. "Writer Fearful of Nuclear Peril." *New York Times*, March 13, 1969, p. 44.
Ross, Chuck. "Rejected." *New West*, 4 (February 12, 1979), 39–42.
Schapp, Dick. "Stepmother Tongue." *Book Week*, 14 (November, 1965), p. 6.
Sheehy, Gail. "The Psychological Novelist as Portable Man." *Psychology Today*, 11 (December, 1977), 52–56, 126, 128, 130.
Sheppard, R. Z. "Playing It by Eye." *Time*, 97 (April 26, 1971), 93.
Silverman, A., et al. "Jerzy Kosinski Interview." *Berkeley Barb* #641 (November 25-December 1, 1977).
Sohn, David. "A Nation of Videots." *Media & Methods*, 11 (April, 1975), 24–26, 28, 30–31, 52, 54, 56–57.
Spring, Michael. "Kosinski on TV." *Literary Cavalcade*, December, 1978, p. 19.
Sweeney, Louise. "Jerzy Kosinski and the 9 Million Dollar Glass of Water." *Christian Science Monitor*, March 1, 1979, pp. B4–B6.
Tartikoff, Brandon. "Exclusive Interview with Jerzy Kosinski." *Metropolitan Review*, 2 (October 26, 1971), 3, 14–15.
Teicholz, Tom. "A Blind Date with Jerzy Kosinski." *East Side Express*, February 2, 1978, pp. 1, 13–17.
Varro, Barbara. "Jerzy Kosinski." *Chicago Sun-Times*, November 24, 1976, pp. 27, 45.
Walter, John. "The Anguish of Jerzy Kosinski and His Film." *Washington Star*, February 13, 1979, p. D2.
Warga, Wayne. "Jerzy Kosinski Reaches Down into Life and Writes." *Calendar/Los Angeles Times*, April 22, 1973, pp. 1, 54.
Wetzsteon, Ross. "Jerzy Kosinski: Existential Cowboy." *Village Voice*, August 11, 1975, pp. 39, 37.
Zito, Tom. "Sellers and Kosinski—Alliance for the Absurd." *Washington Post*, February 2, 1979, pp. D1, D5.
[Comment on his fiction.] *1979 Bantam College Catalogue*, Literature, p. 4.

IV. Critical Essays About Kosinski

Aldridge, John W. "The Fabrication of a Culture Hero." *Saturday Review*, 54 (April 24, 1971), 25–27. Reprinted in *The Devil and the Fire*, pp. 267–273. New York: Harper's Magazine Press, 1972.
Anderson, Don. "The End of Humanism: A Study of Kosinski." *Quadrant*, 113 (1976), 73–77.
Bolling, Douglass. "The Precarious Self in Jerzy Kosinski's *Being There.*" *Greyfriar*, 16 (1975), 41–46.

Boyers, Robert. "Language and Reality in Kosinski's *Steps*." *Centennial Review*, 16 (Winter, 1972), 41–61.

Brantlinger, Patrick. "McLuhan's 'Global Village' or Kosinski's 'Village Videot.'" *Media & Methods*, 14 (April, 1978), 36–41.

Bugliosi, Vincent. *Helter Skleter: The True Story of the Manson Murders*, pp. 31–33, 144, 178–180. New York: Norton, 1974.

Cahill, Daniel J. "Jerzy Kosinski: Retreat from Violence." *Twentieth Century Literature*, 18 (April, 1972), 121–132.

Carter, Nancy Corson. "1970 Images of the Machine and the Garden: Kosinski, Crews, and Pirsig." *Soundings*, 61 (1978), 105–122.

Centing, Richard. "Jerzy Kosinski." *Under the Sign of Pisces: Anaïs Nin and Her Circle*, 1 (Winter, 1976), 9–11.

Coale, Samuel. "The Quest for the Elusive Self: The Fiction of Jerzy Kosinski." *Critique*, 14, #3 (1973), pp. 25–37.

———. "The Cinematic Self of Jerzy Kosinski." *Modern Fiction Studies*, 20 (Autumn, 1974), 359–370.

Cooley, Margaret T. "National Book Awards—The Winners." *Library Journal*, 94 (April 1, 1969), 1476–1477.

Corngold, Stanley. "Jerzy Kosinski's *The Painted Bird*: Language Lost and Regained." *Mosaic*, 4 (Summer, 1973), 153–168.

Cunningham, Lawrence S. "The Moral Universe of Jerzy Kosinski." *America*, 139 (November 11, 1978), 327–329.

Daler, John Kent von. "An Introduction to Jerzy Kosinski's *Steps*." *Language & Literature*, 1, #1 (1971), pp. 43–49.

Elmenpor, P. "Jerzy Kosinski and the Uses of Evil." *Christian Century*, 95 (May 17, 1978), 530–532.

"England's Loss." *Times* (London), May 5, 1969, p. 10.

Gardner, John. "The Way We Write Now." *New York Times Book Review*, July 9, 1972, pp. 32–33.

Gogal, John M. "Kosinski's Chance: McLuhan Age Narcissus." *Notes on Contemporary Literature*, 1, #4 (1971), pp. 8–10.

Greenstone, Maryann D. "Jerzy Kosinski: Chronicler of the Jewish Experience." *Studies in Bibliography & Booklore*, 10 (Winter, 1971–72), 53–56.

Hazlett, Bill. "Writer Nearly Shared Fate." *Los Angeles Times*, August 12, 1969, pp. 3, 18.

Hirschberg, Stuart. "Becoming an Object: The Function of Mirrors and Photographs in Kosinski's *The Devil Tree*." *Notes on Contemporary Literature*, 4, #3 (1973), pp. 14–15.

Howe, Irving. "From the Other Side of the Moon." *Harper's*, 238 (March, 1969), 102–105.

Hutchinson, James D. "Authentic Existence and the Puritan Ethic." *Denver Quarterly*, 7 (Winter, 1973), 106–114.

———. "The Invisible Man as Anti-Hero." *Denver Quarterly*, 6 (Spring, 1971), 186–192.

———. "Retrospect: Judging a Book Award." *Denver Quarterly*, 4 (Autumn, 1969), 128–135.

Kamm, Henry. "Poles Are Bitter about Novel Published Abroad." *New York Times*, December 12, 1966, p. 2.

Kaufmann, Stanley. "A Double View." *World*, February 27, 1973, pp. 42–46.

Kennedy, William. "Who Here Doesn't Know How Good Kosinski Is?" *Look*, 35

(April 20, 1971), 12.

Kleiner, Dick. "Butchered Reputations Live on After Dead." NEA Syndicate, December 18, 1969.

Klinkowitz, Jerome. "Being Here." *Falcon* #4 (Spring, 1972), pp. 122–125.

———. "Insatiable Art and the Great American Quotidian." *Chicago Review*, 25 (Summer, 1973), 172–177.

Knight, Anne. "Jerzy Kosinski: Self-Searching." *Horizon*, 20 (November, 1977), 96.

Lane, Meta, and John Williams. "The Narrator of *The Painted Bird*: A Case Study." *Renascence*, 24 (Summer, 1972), 198–206.

Langer, Lawrence L. *The Holocaust and the Literary Imagination*, pp. 61, 167–191, 200, 249, 250, 287. New Haven: Yale University Press, 1975.

Loukides, Paul. "The Radical Vision." *Michigan Academician*, 5 (1973), 497–503.

Lustig, Arnost. "Love and Death in New Jerzy." *Washington Post*, November 11, 1977.

Mortimer, Gail L. "'Fear Death by Water': The Boundaries of Self in Jerzy Kosinski's *The Painted Bird*." *Psychoanalytic Review*, 63 (1976–77), 511–528.

Mudrick, Marvin. "Must We Burn Mme. de Beauvoir?" *Hudson Review*, 21 (Winter 1968–69), 751–763.

Northouse, Cameron. "Jerzy Kosinski." *Dictionary of Literary Biography*, ed. Jeffery Helterman and Richard Layman, I, 266–275. Detroit: Gale Research, 1978.

Prendowska, Krystyna. "Jerzy Kosinski: A Literature of Contortions." *Journal of Narrative Technique*, 8 (1978), 11–25.

Reza, Baraheni. *The Crowned Cannibals*, pp. 202–206. New York: Vintage Books/ Random House, 1977.

Richey, Clarence W. *"Being There* and *Dasein."* *Notes on Contemporary Literature*, 2 (September, 1972), 3–15.

Richter, David H. "The Three Denouements of Jerzy Kosinski's *The Painted Bird*." *Contemporary Literature*, 15 (Summer, 1974), 370–385. See also commentary by Jerome Klinkowitz, and Richter's reply, in "Two Bibliographical Questions on Kosinski's *The Painted Bird*," *Contemporary Literature*, 16 (Winter, 1975), 126–128.

Rider, Philip R. "The Three States of the Text of Kosinski's *The Painted Bird*." *Papers of the Bibliographical Society of America*, 72 (3rd Quarter, 1978), 361–384.

Rosenbaum, L. P. "Jerzy Kosinski: The Writer's Focus." *Index*, 5 (Spring, 1976).

Sanders, Ed. *The Family*, pp. 134–135, 263. New York: E. P. Dutton, 1971.

Sanders, Ivan. "The Gifts of Strangeness: Alienation and Creation in Jerzy Kosinski's Fiction." *Polish Review*, 19, #3–4 (1974), pp. 171–189.

Sewell, Ernestine. "The Jungian Process of Individuation as Structure in *The Painted Bird*." *South Central Bulletin*, 38 (1978), 160–163.

Sloan, James Park. "Literary Debunking, Or How to Roast Your 'Favorite' Author." *Third Press Review*, 1 (September/October, 1975), 10–11.

———. "On Kosinski." *University Review* #18 (Summer, 1971), p. 3.

Spendal, R. J. "The Structure of *The Painted Bird*." *Journal of Narrative Technique*, 6 (1976), 132–136.

Stade, George. "The Realities of Fiction and the Fiction of Reality." *Harper's*, 245 (May, 1973), 90–94.

Stone, Elizabeth. "Horatio Algers of the Nightmare." *Psychology Today*, 11 (December, 1977), 59–60, 63–64.

Tepa, Barbara J. "Jerzy Kosinski's Polish Contexts: A Study of *Being There*." *Polish Review*, 22, #2 (1977), pp. 52–61.

———. "Kosinski Takes Another Chance." *Polish Review*, 23, #3 (1978), pp. 104–108.

Tucker, Martin. "Leading the Life of Chance." *Commonwealth*, 94 (May 5, 1971), 221–222.

Weales, Gerald. "Jerzy Kosinski: The Painted Bird and Other Disguises." *Hollins Critic*, 9 (October, 1972), 1–12.

Young, Tracy. "On Jerzy Kosinski." *Mademoiselle*, 77 (August, 1973), 68, 77.

V. DOCTORAL DISSERTATIONS

Bloomfield, Mitchell Bernard. "The Fiction of Jerzy Kosinski: The Perverse in the Modern Imagination." Michigan State University, 1975.

Fitzgerald, Sister Ellen. "World War II in the American Novel: Hawkes, Heller, Kosinski, and Vonnegut." University of Notre Dame, 1974.

Golden, Robert Edward. "Violence and Art in Postwar American Literature: A Study of O'Connor, Kosinski, Hawkes, and Pynchon." University of Rochester, 1972.

Hutchinson, James D. "The Art of the Self: The Quest for Authenticity in the Novels of Jerzy Kosinski." University of Denver, 1974.

Lipani, David Joseph. "Jerzy Kosinski: A Study of His Novels." Bowling Green State University, 1973.

Tepa, Barbara Jane. "Inside the Kaleidoscope: Jerzy Kosinski's Polish and American Contexts." St. John's University, 1975.

Weinstein, Sharon Rosenbaum. "Comedy and Nightmare: The Fiction of John Hawkes, Kurt Vonnegut, Jr., Jerzy Kosinski, and Ralph Ellison." University of Utah, 1971.

VI. BIBLIOGRAPHIES

Rusch, Frederick E. "Jerzy Kosinski: A Checklist." *Bulletin of Bibliography*, 31 (January/March, 1974), 6–9.

Walsh, Thomas P., and Cameron Northouse. *John Barth, Jerzy Kosinski, and Thomas Pynchon: A Reference Guide*. Boston: G. K. Hall, 1978.

LEROI JONES (IMAMU AMIRI BARAKA) (b. 1934)

I. NOVEL

The System of Dante's Hell
New York: Grove Press, 1965.
New York: Grove Press/Black Cat Edition, 1966.
New York: Grove Press/Evergreen Edition, 1975 (as *Three Books by Imamu Amiri Baraka*).

II. COLLECTION OF SHORT FICTION

Tales
New York: Grove Press, 1967.
New York: Grove Press/Evergreen Edition, 1968
New York: Grove Press/Black Cat Edition, 1969.
New York: Grove Press/Evergreen Edition, 1975 (as *Three Books by Imamu Amiri Baraka*).

Contents and Original Publication:
"A Chase (Alighieri's Dream.)" *Pa'Lante,* 1 (May 19, 1962), 91–93.
"The Alternative." *Transatlantic Review,* 18 (Spring, 1965), 46–60.
"The Largest Ocean in the World." *Yugen,* 8 (December 2, 1962), 58–59.
"Uncle Tom's Cabin: Alternate Ending." Not previously published.
"The Death of Horatio Alger." *Evergreen Review,* 9, #36 (June, 1965), pp. 28–29, 92–93.
"Going Down Slow." *Evergreen Review,* 10, #43 (October, 1966), pp. 41–43, 93–96.
"Heroes Are Gang Leaders." Not previously published.
"The Screamers." *Genesis West,* 2 (Fall, 1963), 81–86.
"Salute." Not previously published.
"Words." Not previously published.
"New-Sense." Not previously published.
"Unfinished." Not previously published.
"New Spirit." Not previously published.
"No Body No Place." Not previously published.
"Now and Then." Not previously published.
"Answers in Progress." *Umbra Anthology,* 3 (Winter, 1967), 37–39.

III. POETRY BOOKS

Preface to a Twenty Volume Suicide Note
New York: Totem Press, 1961.

The Dead Lecturer
New York: Grove Press, 1964.
New York: Grove Press/Evergreen Editions, 1965.

New York: Grove Press/Evergreen Edition, 1975 (as *Three Books by Imamu Amiri Baraka*).

Black Art
Newark: Jihad Productions, 1966.

Black Magic Poetry 1961–1967
Indianapolis: Bobbs-Merrill, 1969.

In Our Terribleness
Indianapolis: Bobbs-Merrill, 1970.

IV. DRAMA

Dutchman and the Slave
New York: William Morrow, 1964
New York: Apollo Editions, 1966.

Slave Ship
Newark: Jihad Productions, 1967

The Baptism and the Toilet
New York: Grove Press, 1967.

Four Black Revolutionary Plays
Indianapolis: Bobbs-Merrill, 1969.

Jello
Chicago: Third World Press, 1970.

The Motion of History and Other Plays
New York: William Morrow, 1978.

V. SCHOLARSHIP AND CRITICISM IN BOOK FORM

Cuba Libre
New York: Fair Play for Cuba Committee, 1961

Blues People
New York: William Morrow, 1963.
New York: Apollo Editions, 1963.

Home: Social Essays
New York: William Morrow, 1966.
New York: Apollo Editions, 1967

Black Music
New York: William Morrow, 1967.
New York: Apollo Editions, 1968.

Raise Race Rays Raze
New York: Random House, 1971.
New York: Vintage, 1972

[Political pamphlets.] *Toward Ideological Clarity; New Era in Our Politics: The Revolutionary Answer to Neo-Colonialism in Newark Politics; Revolutionary*

Culture and the Future of Pan-Afrikan Culture; Creating a Unified Consciousness; National Liberation and Politics. Newark: Congress of African People, 1974.

VI. SPECIAL NUMBER OF A SCHOLARLY JOURNAL

Boundary 2, 6 (Winter, 1978). Contents listed below.

VII. INTERVIEWS AND RECORDED REMARKS

Baraka, Imamu Amiri. "'Why I Changed My Ideology': Black Nationalism and the Socialist Revolution." *Black World,* 24, #4 (1975), pp. 30–42.
Benston, Kimberly W. "Amiri Baraka: An Interview." *Boundary 2,* 6 (Winter, 1978), 303–316.
Bernard, Sidney. "An Interview with LeRoi Jones." *Literary Times,* May/June, 1967, p. 19.
Brown, Lloyd. "Jones (Baraka) and His Literary Heritage in *The System of Dante's Hell.*" *Obsidian,* 1, #1 (1975), pp. 5–17.
Gotleib, Saul. "An Interview with LeRoi Jones after the Newark Riots." *Evergreen Review,* 11 (December, 1967), 50–53, 96–97.
"Jazz and Revolutionary Black Nationalism." *Jazz,* 5 (April, 1966–June, 1967).
"Jones Explains New Tactic for Power in Newark." *Washington Post,* April 21, 1968, sec. A., p. 7
"Like LeRoi Says, It Doesn't Mean We're Going to Be Working Hand in Hand, but It's a Start." *East Village Other,* May 10, 1968, pp. 3, 17.
Ossman, David. *The Sullen Art: Interviews with Modern American Poets,* pp. 77–81. New York: Corinth, 1963.
"The Roots of Violence." *Negro Digest,* 13 (August, 1964), 16–26.
Susskind, David. "Black Revolution and White Backlash." *National Guardian,* July 4, 1964, pp. 5–9.
X, Marvin. "Everything's Cool: An Interview." *Black Theatre,* 1 (1968), 16–23.
———. "God Is Black! Islam and Black Art." *Black Theatre,* 2 (1969), 11–19.
———. "Islam and Black Art: An Interview with LeRoi Jones." *Negro Digest,* 18 (January, 1969), 4–10, 77–80.

VII. CRITICAL BOOKS AND ESSAYS ABOUT JONES

Baker, Houston. "'These Are the Songs If You Have the Music': An Essay on Imamu Baraka." *Minority Voices,* 1, #1 (1977), pp. 1–18.
Benston, Kimberly W. *Baraka: The Renegade and the Mask.* New Haven: Yale University Press, 1976.
———. "Ellison, Baraka, and the Faces of Tradition." *Boundary 2,* 6 (Winter, 1978), 333–354.
Brown, Cecil. "About LeRoi Jones." *Evergreen Review,* 14 (February, 1970), 65–70.
———. "The Apotheosis of a Prodigal Son." *Kenyon Review,* 30 (November, 1968), 654–661.
Brown, Lloyd W. "LeRoi Jones as Novelist: Theme and Structure in *The System of Dante's Hell.*" *Negro American Literature Forum,* 7 (Winter, 1974), 132–142.

Fischer, William C. "The Pre-Revolutionary Writings of Imamu Amiri Baraka." *Massachusetts Review*, 14 (Spring, 1973), 259–305.

Fuller, Hoyt. "Contemporary Negro Fiction." *Southwest Review*, 50 (Autumn, 1965), 321–335.

———. "The Negro Writer in the United States." *Ebony*, 20 (November, 1964), 126–128, 130–132, 134.

———. "Perspectives." *Negro Digest*, 13 (July, 1964), 49–50, 87–92.

Hagopian, John V. "Another Ride on Jones's Subway." *CLA Journal*, 21 (1977), 269–274.

Hammill, Pete. "Harlem Encounter." *New York Post*, October 12, 1965, p. 44.

Hentoff, Nat. "Uninventing the Negro." *Evergreen Review*, 9 (November, 1965), 34–36, 66–69.

Hudson, Theodore M. *From LeRoi Jones to Amiri Baraka*. Durham: Duke University Press, 1973.

Joye, Barbara. "From Stereotype to Archetype." *Phylon*, 28 (Spring, 1967), 109–111.

Kauffmann, Stanley. "LeRoi Jones and the Tradition of the Fake." *Dissent*, 12 (Spring, 1965), 207–212.

Klinkowitz, Jerome. "LeRoi Jones: *Dutchman* as Drama." *Negro American Literature Forum*, 7 (Winter, 1974), 123–126.

"LeRoi Jones: A Fierce and Blazing Talent." *New York Herald Tribune*, April 12, 1964, p. 26.

Lhamon, W. T. "Baraka and the Bourgeoise Figure." *Studies in Black Literature*, 6, #1 (1975), pp. 18–21.

Littlejohn, David. *Black on White*, pp. 4–5, 68–70, 74–79, 94–100. New York: Grossman, 1966.

Mackey, Nathaniel. "The Changing Same: Black Music in the Poetry of Amiri Baraka." *Boundary 2*, 6 (Winter, 1978), 355–386.

Margolies, Edward. *Native Sons*, pp. 190–199. Philadelphia: Lippincott, 1968.

Menchise, Don N. "LeRoi Jones and a Case of Shifting Identities." *CLA Journal*, 20 (1976), 232–234.

Newfield, Jack. "LeRoi Jones at Arms." *Village Voice*, 9 (December 17, 1964), 1, 12.

Phelps, Donald. "LeRoi Jones, Discovered Alone." *For Now* #2 (1967), pp. 9–11, 14–16.

Redding, J. Saunders. "The Problems of the Negro Writer." *Massachusetts Review*, 6 (Autumn/Winter, 1964–1965), 57–70.

Richardson, Jack. "Blues for Mr. Jones." *Esquire*, 65 (June, 1966), 106–108, 138.

Schneck, Stephen. "LeRoi Jones, or, Poetics and Policemen, or, Trying Hearts, Bleeding Hearts." *Ramparts*, 6 (June 29, 1968), 14–19.

Sollors, Werner. *Amiri Baraka/Le Roi Jones: The Quest for a 'Populist Moderism.'* New York: Columbia University Press, 1978.

———. "Does Axel's Castle Have a Street Address, or, What's New? Tendencies in the Poetry of Amiri Baraka (LeRoi Jones)." *Boundary 2*, 6 (Winter, 1978), 387–414.

Sorrentino, Gilbert. "For the *Floating Bear:* Prose of Our Time." *Floating Bear* #30 (1964), pp. 11–13.

Taylor, Willene P. "The Fall of Man in Imamu Amiri Baraka's *Dutchman.*" *Negro American Literature Forum*, 7 (Winter, 1974), 127–131.

Wakefield, John. "Amiri Baraka (LeRoi Jones): 'The Alternative,'" pp. 187–204. In *The Black American Short Story in the 20th Century,* edited by Peter Bruck. Amsterdam: Grüner, 1977.

Williams, John A. "The Negro in Literature Today." *Ebony,* 18 (September, 1963), 73–76.

Williams, Sherley Anne. "Anonymous in America." *Boundary 2,* 6 (Winter, 1978), 435–442.

———. *Give Birth to Brightness.* New York: Dial Press, 1972.

Wright, Jay. "Love's Emblem Lost: LeRoi Jones' 'Hymn for Lanie Poo." *Boundary 2,* 6 (Winter, 1978), 415–434.

Zatlin, Linda G. "Paying His Dues: Ritual in LeRoi Jones' Early Dramas." *Obsidian,* 2, #1, (1976), pp. 21–31.

VIII. DISSERTATIONS

Fox, Robert Elliott. "The Mirrors of Caliban: A Study of the Fiction of LeRoi Jones (Imamu Amiri Baraka), Ishmael Reed, and Samuel R. Delany." State University of New York at Buffalo, 1977.

Harris, William Joseph. "Jones/Baraka: The Evolution of a Black Poet." Stanford University, 1974.

Hudson, Theodore R. "From LeRoi Jones to Amiri Baraka: The Literary Works." Howard University, 1971.

Lacey, Henry Clark. "A Study of the Poetry, Drama, and Fiction of Imamu Amiri Baraka (LeRoi Jones)." State University of New York at Binghamton, 1975.

Reed, Roland Lee. "Form and Meaning in Some Plays of Imamu Amiri Baraka (LeRoi Jones)." University of Nebraska, 1972.

IX. BIBLIOGRAPHIES

Benston, Kimberly W. *Baraka: The Renegade and the Mask,* pp. 278–283. New Haven: Yale University Press, 1976.

Dace, Letitia. *LeRoi Jones (Imamu Amiri Baraka): A Checklist of Works by and about Him.* London: Nether Press, 1971. (Most complete primary and secondary record.)

Hudson, Theodore M. "Bibliography." *From LeRoi Jones to Amiri Baraka,* pp. 198–209. Durham: Duke University Press, 1973.

Sollers, Werner. *Amiri Baraka/Le Roi Jones: The Quest for a 'Populist Moderism,'* pp. 301–328. New York: Columbia University Press, 1978.

JAMES PARK SLOAN (b. 1944)

I. Novels

War Games
Boston: Houghton Mifflin, 1971
New York: Avon, 1974.

The Case History of Comrade V
Boston: Houghton Mifflin, 1972.
New York: Avon, 1973.

II. Short Fiction

"Bird Sanctuary." *Story Quarterly* #5/6 (1977), pp. 77–84.
"Raskolnikov, Creator of Dostoevsky." *Modern Occasions* #2 (1974), pp. 105–110.

III. Scholarship and Criticism

"Nixon and the Liberals: The Response of the Liberal Intellectuals to the Career of Richard M. Nixon, 1946–1962." B.A. Honors Thesis in History, Harvard College, Cambridge, Mass., March 19, 1968.

"Literary Debunking, Or How to Roast Your 'Favorite' Author." *Third Press Review,* 1 (September/October, 1975), 10–11.
"Mark Van Doren." *Showcase/Chicago Sun-Times,* December 24, 1972, p. 3.
"On Kosinski," *University Review* #18 (Spring, 1971), p. 3.
"On Writing a First Novel." *The Writer,* November, 1971, pp. 20–23.
"Rejected! Your Masterpiece Does Not Meet Our Standards" (with Jeanette Pasin Sloan). *Midwest Magazine/Chicago Sun-Times,* January 12, 1975, pp. 16–17, 21, 23.
Review of *Spring Snow* by Yukio Mishima, *Chicago Sun-Times Book Week,* July 2, 1972, p. 17.
Review of *Marriages and Infidelities* by Joyce Carol Oates, *Chicago-Sun Times Book Week,* September 10, 1972, p. 18.
Review of *Gravity's Rainbow* by Thomas Pynchon, *Chicago Sun-Times Book Week,* March 18, 1973, p. 19.
Review of *The Hippodrome* by Cyrus Colter, *Chicago Sun-Times Book Week,* April 22, 1973, p. 13.
Review of *Dog Tags* by Stephen Becker, *Chicago Sun-Times Book Week,* September 16, 1973, p. 14.
Review of *My Petition for More Space* by John Hersey, *Chicago Tribune Book World,* September 15, 1974, p. 3.
Review of *In Their Wisdom* by C. P. Snow, *Chicago Tribune Book World,* November 11, 1974, p. 3.
Review of *Billion Dollar Baby* by Bob Greene, *Chicago Journalism Review,* 7 (December, 1974), 30–31.

Review of *Sneaky People* by Thomas Berger, *Chicago Tribune Book World*, April 20, 1975, p. 3.

Review of *Interview with the Vampire* by Anne Rice, *Chicago Tribune Book World*, May 9, 1976, p. 1.

Review of *A Rumor of War* by Philip Caputo, *Chicago Tribune Book World*, May 29, 1977, p. 1.

Review of *The Last Best Hope* by Peter Tauber, *Chicago Tribune Book World*, August 8, 1977, p. 4.

Review of *Natural Shocks* by Richard Stern, *Chicago Tribune Book World*, December 25, 1977, p. 1.

Review of *The Human Factor* by Graham Greene, Chicago Tribune Book World, March 5, 1978, p. 1.

Review of *Altered States* by Paddy Chayefsky, *Chicago Tribune Book World*, July 9, 1978, p. 5.

Review of *Sex Life* by Bruce Cook, *Chicago Tribune Book World*, January 4, 1979, p. 3.

Review of *Good as Gold* by Joseph Heller, *Chicago Tribune Book World*, March 18, 1979, p. 1.

"Saying the Unsayable: A Problem in Narrative Conventions." *Harvard Advocate*, Spring, 1971, pp. 8–17.

"An Unhappy Little Mess" [on Wilbur Mills]. *Chicago Journalism Review*, 7 (October, 1974), 20–22.

IV. INTERVIEWS

Colwell, Carolyn K. "A Close Look at James Park Sloan." *Suburban Week* (Elk Grove Village, Ill.), January 24–25, 1973, p. 3.

Fortun, Judy. "We Label That Which We Don't Understand." *This Week at K & B* (Krock's & Brentano's Bookstores, Chicago), 3 (June 2, 1972), 1.

Gerson, Ed. "James Park Sloan." *The Hyde Parker*, Summer, 1973, pp. 19–22, 48.

Gordon, Robert. "Illini Interview: James Park Sloan." *Chicago Illini*, 14 (October 15, 1973), 7, 11.

RONALD SUKENICK (b. 1932)

I. NOVELS

Up
New York: Dial Press, 1968.
New York: Delta Editions/Dell Publishing, 1970.
Paris: Editions Champ Libre, 1973.
Part of *Up* appearing in a magazine:
"The Kite." *New American Review,* #1 (September, 1967), pp. 200–211.

Out
Chicago: Swallow Press, 1973.
Parts of *Out* appearing in magazines:
"The Key." *Fiction,* 1, #3 (1972), pp. 2–3.
"From *Out.*" *Partisan Review,* 39 (Spring, 1972), 238–254.
"From His Upcoming Novel *Out.*" *Northwest Review,* 13, #1 (1973), pp. 93–105.
"From *Out.*" *Massachusetts Review,* 14 (Spring, 1973), 352–363.
"On the Wing." *North American Review,* 258 (Summer, 1973), 29–48.
"From *Out.*" *Fiction International* #1 (Fall, 1973), pp. 54–59.
"From *Out.*" *Chicago Review,* 23 (Winter, 1973), 16–58.

98.6
New York: Fiction Collective, 1975.
Parts of *98.6* appearing in magazines:
"From *98.6.*" *Barataria Review,* 1, #1 (1974), pp. 21–40.
"From *98.6.*" *Seems* #4 (Autumn, 1974), pp. 14–33.
"Palestine." *Partisan Review,* 42, #1 (1975), pp. 23–29.
"From *98.6.*" *Big Moon,* 1, #1, (1975), pp. 78–89.
"From *98.6.*" *Center* #7 (April, 1975), p. 61.
"The Children of Frankenstein." *TriQuarterly* #34 (Fall, 1975), pp. 87–100.
"The Monster." *Iowa Review,* 6 (Winter, 1975), 33–46.

Long Talking Bad Conditions Blues
New York: Fiction Collective, 1979.

II. COLLECTION OF SHORT FICTION

The Death of the Novel and Other Stories
New York: Dial Press, 1969 (redistributed by Serendipity Books, Berkeley, Calif.).

Contents and original publication:
"The Permanent Crisis." *Epoch,* 10 (Fall, 1960), 211–217.
"Momentum." Not previously published.
"The Death of the Novel." Not previously published.
"Roast Beef: A Slice of Life." Not previously published.
"What's Your Story." *Paris Review,* #44 (Fall, 1968), pp. 33–51.
"The Birds." Not previously published.

III. Uncollected Short Fiction

"The Endless Short Story (Aziff)." *TriQuarterly* #35 (Winter, 1976), I, 42.
"The Endless Short Story: Bush Fever." *Substance,* Fall, 1979.
"The Endless Short Story: Dong Wanq." *Statements 2* (New York: Fiction Collective, 1977), pp. 212–217.
"The Endless Short Story: Five & Ten." *Criss-Cross Art Communications,* 6 (March, 1978), 36–41.
"The Endless Short Story: Gorganzola." *Departures,* #2 (Fall, 1979).
"The Endless Short Story: Verticals and Horizontals." *Statements: New Fiction from the Fiction Collective* (New York: Braziller, 1975), pp. 184–188.
"The Endless Short Story: What's Watts." *New Letters,* Spring, 1979.
"Extract from *The Fortune Teller.*" *Trema* (Paris), #2 (1977), pp. 143–146.
"From 'The Endless Short Story.'" *Lillabulero* #14 (Spring, 1974), pp. 109–118.
"A Long Way from Nowhere." *Epoch,* 14 (Fall, 1964), 69–77.
"One Every Minute." *Carolina Quarterly,* 13 (Spring, 1961), 57–64.
"A Postcard from *The Endless Short Story.*" Austin, Texas: Cold Mountain Press Poetry Post Card Series Two, 1974.

IV. Scholarship and Criticism

"A Wallace Stevens Handbook: A Reading of His Major Poems and an Exposition of His Theory and Practice." Ph.D. dissertation, Brandeis University, 1962.
Wallace Stevens: Musing the Obscure. New York: New York University Press, 1967; Gotham Library paperback edition, 1968.

"Author as Editor and Publisher." *New York Times Book Review,* September 15, 1974, p. 55.
Commentary on "The Birds." In *Cutting Edges,* ed. Jack Hicks, pp. 547–548. New York: Holt, Rinehart & Winston, 1973.
Commentary on *98.6. Barataria Review,* 1, #1 (1974), p. 21.
Commentary on *Out. Massachusetts Review,* 14 (Spring, 1973), 93.
"The Ecology of Literature." *Village Voice,* 18 (April 5, 1973), 26–28.
"Eight Digressions on the Politics of Language." *New Literary History,* 11 (Spring, 1979), 467–477.
"The Endless Short Story." *Village Voice,* 18 (September 6, 1973), 13–14, 34. Continued as "The Next Part of the Story," *Village Voice,* 18 (September 13, 1973), 15–16.
"The Fiction Collective." *New York Times Book Review,* December 22, 1974, p. 16.
"Fiction in the Seventies: Ten Digressions on Ten Digressions." *Studies in American Fiction,* 5 (Spring, 1977), 99–108. Reprinted in *American Fiction,* ed. James Nagel, pp. 99–108. Boston: Northeastern University Press, 1977.
"Innovative Fiction/Innovative Criteria: On Reinventing the Novel." *Fiction International,* #2/3 (1976), pp. 133–134.
"L'experience artistique du suject (table ronde)" (with Noelle Batt, et al.) *Revue Française d'Etudes Americaines* #7 (Avril, 1979), pp. 41–50. (Sukenick's statement is in English.)
"Live & Let Alone on the Lower East Side." *Village Voice,* 13 (June 13, 1968), 6–7, 17–18.
"Millicent Versus Sex." Review of *Thy Daughter's Nakedness* by Myron S. Kaufman, *New York Times Book Review,* October 27, 1968, p. 66.

"Misreading Bloom." Review of *Wallace Stevens: The Poems of Our Climate* by Harold Bloom, *Partisan Review*, 45, #4 (1978), pp. 634–636.

"The New Innovative Fiction" (with Raymond Federman). *Antaeus* #20 (Winter, 1976), pp. 138–149.

"The New Tradition." *Partisan Review*, 39 (Fall, 1972), 580–588. Reprinted as "The New Tradition in Fiction" in *Surfiction*, ed. Raymond Federman, pp. 35–45. Chicago: Swallow Press, 1975.

"News from Utopia." *Harper's Bookletter*, 2 (August 18, 1975), 1.

"Not My Bag." Review of *The Bag* by Sol Yurik and *The Universal Baseball Association* by Robert Coover, *New York Review of Books*, 12 (March 13, 1969), 40–41.

"On Paul Metcalf." *Lillabulero* #12 (Winter, 1973), pp. 49–50.

"On the New Cultural Conservativism." *Partisan Review*, 39 (Summer, 1972), 448–451.

"Rat-Race at Coney." Review of *Under the Boardwalk* by Norman Rosten, *New York Times Book Review*, September 14, 1968, p. 18.

"Refugee from the Holocaust." Review of *Double or Nothing* by Raymond Federman, *New York Times Book Review*, October 1, 1972, pp. 40–41.

Review of *Adventures of Mao on the Long March* by Frederic Tuten, *New York Times Book Review*, November 7, 1971, p. 40.

Review of *The Bonny-Clabber* by George Chambers, *New York Times Book Review*, March 3, 1973, pp. 32–33.

"Statement." In *Statements: New Fiction from the Fiction Collective*, ed. Jonathan Baumbach, pp. [7–8]. New York: Braziller, 1975.

"The S. S. Dictionary Is Going Down." *Village Voice*, 19 (February 21, 1974), 20.

"Taboo or Not Taboo." *Village Voice*, 19 (January 3, 1974), 4.

"Thirteen Digressions." *Partisan Review*, 43, #1 (1976), pp. 90–101.

"Twelve Digressions Toward a Theory of Composition." *New Literary History*, 6 (Winter, 1974–75), 429–437.

"Upward & Juanward: The Possible Dream" [on Carlos Castaneda]. *Village Voice*, 18 (January 25, 1973), 27–28, 30–31. Reprinted in *Seeing Castaneda*, ed. Daniel Noel, pp. 110–120. New York: Putnam's, 1976.

"Writers for Carter." *Partisan Review*, 44 (Spring, 1977), 108–109.

V. INTERVIEWS

Bellamy, Joe David. "The Tape Recorder Records." *Falcon* #2–3 (April, 1971), pp. 5–25.

———. "Imagination as Perception." *Chicago Review*, 23 (Winter, 1972), 59–72. Reprinted in Bellamy's *The New Fiction: Interviews with Innovative American Writers*, pp. 55–74. Urbana: University of Illinois Press, 1974.

Nagel, James. "A Conversation in Boston." In *American Fiction*, pp. 175–202. Boston: Northeastern University Press, 1977.

VI. CRITICAL ESSAYS ON SUKENICK

Adams, Timothy Dow. "Obscuring the Muse: The Mock-Autobiographies of Ronald Sukenick." *Critique*, 20, #1, (1978), pp. 27–39.

Beebe, Maurice. "Reflective and Reflexive Trends in Modern Fiction." *Bucknell Review*, 22 (Fall, 1976), 19–20.

Bell, Pearl Kazin. "American Fiction: Forgetting Ordinary Truths." *Dissent*, Winter, 1973, pp. 26–34.

Bolling, Doug. "Some Observations on Experimental Fiction: The Work of Sukenick, Gass, Wildman, and Federman." *Northeast Review*, Winter, 1975–76, pp. 1–18.

Bradbury, Malcolm. *The Novel Today*, p. 20. Manchester: Manchester University Press, 1977.

Broderick, Vincent A. "Disruptive Participants: Observations of Works by Sukenick and Sorrentino." *Kobe College Studies* (Japan), 1978, pp. 39–68.

Cheuse, Alan. "Way Out West: The Exploratory Fiction on Ronald Sukenick." In *Itinerary Criticism #7: Essays on California Writers*, ed. Charles Crow, pp. 115–121. Bowling Green, Ohio: Bowling Green State University Press, 1978.

Federman, Raymond. "In." *Partisan Review*, 41, #1 (1974), pp. 137–142.

Friedman, Melvin J. "Dislocations of Setting and Word: Notes on American Fiction Since 1950." *Studies in American Fiction*, 5 (Spring, 1977), 79–98.

―――. "To 'Make It New': The American Novel Since 1945." *Wilson Quarterly*, 2 (Winter, 1978), 133–142.

Hassan, Ihab. *The Dismemberment of Orpheus*, p. 254. New York: Oxford University Press, 1971.

―――. *Paracriticisms*, pp. 83, 87, 106–107, 141–142. Urbana: University of Illinois Press, 1975.

―――. "Reading *Out*." *Fiction International* #1 (Fall, 1973), pp. 108–109.

Klinkowitz, Jerome. "Getting Real: Making It (Up) with Ronald Sukenick." *Chicago Review*, 23 (Winter, 1972), 73–82.

―――. "Innovative Short Fiction: 'Vile and Imaginative Things.'" In *Innovative Fiction*, pp. xv–xxviii. New York: Dell, 1972.

―――. "Literary Disruptions; Or, What's Become of American Fiction?" *Partisan Review*, 40 (Fall, 1973), 433–444. Reprinted in expanded form in *Surfiction*, ed. Raymond Federman, pp. 165–179. Chicago: Swallow Press, 1975.

―――. "A Persuasive Account: Working It Out with Ronald Sukenick." *North American Review*, 258 (Summer, 1973), 48–52. Reprinted in *Seeing Castaneda*, ed. Daniel Noel, pp. 131–139. New York: Putnam's, 1976.

―――, and Roy R. Behrens. *The Life of Fiction*, pp. 18–30. Urbana: University of Illinois Press, 1977.

Lodge, David. *The Modes of Modern Writing*, pp. 232, 243, 272. Ithaca: Cornell University Press, 1977.

Martin, Jay, et al. "Composure and Decomposition: Three Pieces on the Fiction Collective." *Partisan Review*, 46, #2 (1979), pp. 280–297.

Noel, Daniel. "Tales of Fictive Power: Dreaming and Imagining in Ronald Sukenick's Postmodern Fiction." *Boundary 2*, 5 (Fall, 1976), 117–135.

Pütz, Manfred. *The Story of Identity: American Fiction of the Sixties*, pp. 176–193. Stuttgart: Metzler, 1979.

Wolfe, Tom. "Why They Aren't Writing the Great American Novel Anymore." *Esquire*, 78 (December, 1972), 152–158, 272–280.

Zavarzadeh, Mas'ud. *The Mythopoeic Reality*, pp. 33, 34, 37, 40. Urbana: University of Illinois Press, 1976.

RAYMOND FEDERMAN (b. 1928)

I. NOVELS

Double or Nothing
Chicago: Swallow Press, 1971.
Chicago: Swallow Press paperback, 1973.
Parts of *Double or Nothing* appearing in magazines:
"A Time for Noodles." In *Future's Fiction,* ed. Richard Kostelanetz, pp. 7–87.
  Princeton: Panache, 1971.
"Double or Nothing—Excerpts." *Panache* #8 (1972), pp. 2–30.
"The Toothbrush." *Panache* #11 (1973), pp. 44–51.

Amer Eldorado
Paris: Editions Stock, 1974.

Take It or Leave It
New York: Fiction Collective, 1976.
Parts of *Take It or Leave It* appearing in magazines:
"Dashing from DON to TIOLI." *Center* #4 (November, 1972), pp. 23–26.
"On Jazz." *Partisan Review,* 40 (Summer, 1973), 65–73.
"On Literature" and "On Politics." *Oyez Review,* 8 (Winter, 1973–74), 58–65.
"Buickspecial." *North American Review,* 259 (Summer, 1974), 29–34.
"Cyrano of the Regiment." *Partisan Review,* 42, #2 (1975), pp. 215–244.
"The Masturbatory Gesture." *Seems* #6/7 (Summer, 1975), pp. 22–29.

The Voice in the Closet
Madison: Coda Press, 1979.
Parts of *The Voice in the Closet* appearing in magazines:
"Vociferations and Further Vociferations." *Chicago Review,* 26 (Spring, 1975),
  133–150.
"Voicelessness." *Chicago Review,* 28 (Spring, 1977), 109–114.
"The Voice in the Closet." In *Statements 2,* ed. Jonathan Baumbach and Peter
  Spielberg, pp. 95–105. New York: Fiction Collective, 1977. Reprinted in *Tri-
  Quarterly* #38 (Winter, 1977), pp. 168–173.
"Voices Within Voices." In *Performance in Postmodern Culture,* ed. Michel Be-
  namou and Charles Caramello, pp. 159–198. Madison: Coda Press, 1977.
"La Voix dans le cabinet débarras." *Cahiers du Double* #2 (1978), pp. 206–218.
"The Voice in the Closet." *Paris Review,* #74 (Fall–Winter, 1978), pp. 12–141.
  (Includes historical preface not included in book version.)

II. BOOKS OF POETRY

Paysages Provisiores/Temporary Landscapes
Venice: Mica, 1965.

Parmi Les Monstres/Among the Beasts
Paris: Jose Millas-Martin, 1967.

Me Too
Reno: West Coast Poetry Review Editions, 1975.

III. Uncollected Short Fiction

"Au pied du livre." *Sub-stance* #5/6 (Summer, 1973), pp. 73–74.
"The Captain and the Kids." *Assembling* #1 (1970), n.p.
"D'une parenthese . . . a l'autre." *Et Maintenant,* 3 (Spring, 1973).
"False Evidence." *Kolokon* (Great Britain), 1 (Summer, 1966), 34–40.
"Hat Missive," "Questionnaire," and "HATS HATS HATS . . .," *Milk Quarterly*
    #11/12 (1978), pp. 16–17, 26–27, 80.
"Histoire du Ballon." *West Coast Review,* 4 (Fall, 1969), 34–40.
"An Impromptu Swim." *Out of Sight* #73 (April, 1974).
"Inside the Thing." *Oyez Review,* 8 (Fall, 1974), 88–91.
"The Man on the Bridge." *Mica,* 1, #1 (1960), pp. 18–22. As "Robin St. Gill."
"Premembrance." *Mississippi Review,* #21 (Fall, 1978), pp. 100–113.
"Rumor Transmissable in Either Direction Ad Infinitum." Supplement to *Assembling* #6 (1976), broadside.
"Self-Plagiaristic Autobiographical Poem in Form of a Letter from Here and Elsewhere." *Oyez Review* #5 [n.s.] (1977), pp. 50–55.
"Setting and Tripping." In *Statements: New Fiction from the Fiction Collective,* ed.
    Jonathan Baumbach, pp. 86–90. New York: Braziller, 1975.
"Suspension." *UCLAN Review Magazine,* 6 (Winter, 1970), 10–16.

IV. Scholarship and Criticism: Books

"Samuel Beckett's Early Novels: From Social Reality to Fictional Absurdity." Ph.D.
    dissertation, University of California–Los Angeles, 1965.
Journey to Chaos: Samuel Beckett's Early Fiction. Berkeley: University of California Press, 1965.
Samuel Beckett: His Works and His Critics. An Essay in Bibliography. With John
    Fletcher. Berkeley: University of California Press, 1970.
Cinq Nouvelles Nouvelles. New York: Appleton-Century-Crofts, 1970.
Surfiction: Fiction Now and Tomorrow. Chicago: Swallow Press, 1975.
Cahier de l'Herne: Samuel Beckett. Paris: Editions de l'Herne, 1975.
Samuel Beckett: The Critical Heritage. Ed. with Lawrence Graver. London: Routledge & Kegan Paul, 1979.

V. Uncollected Scholarship and Criticism

"Beckett and the Fiction of Mud." In *On Contemporary Literature,* ed. Richard
    Kostelanetz, pp. 255–261. New York: Avon, 1964.
"Beckett's Belaqua and the Inferno of Society." *Arizona Quarterly,* 20 (Autumn,
    1964), 231–241.
Commentary on Ihab Hassan's *Paracriticisms.* Reader's report reprinted on dustjacket. Urbana: University of Illinois Press, 1975.
"Fiction Today or the Pursuit of Non-Knowledge." *Humanities in Society,* 1 (Spring,
    1978), 115–131.
"Fiction: Problèmes de lecture et d'écriture." *Ethique et Esthétique dans la littérature du XXéme Siècle,* ed. Maurice Cagnon. Stanford: Stanford University Press,
    1978.

"Film: The Agony of Perceivedness." *Joyce Quarterly,* 8 (Summer, 1971), 363–371.

"Film." *Film Quarterly,* 20 (Winter, 1966–67), 46–51.

"*How It Is* with Beckett's Fiction." *French Review,* 38 (February, 1965), 459–468.

"Imagination as Plagiarism." *New Literary History,* 7 (Spring, 1976), 563–578.

"The Impossibility of Saying the Same Old Thing the Same Old Way—Samuel Beckett's Fiction Since *Comment c'est.*" *L'Esprit Créateur,* 11 (Fall, 1971), 21–43.

"In." Review of *Out,* by Ronald Sukenick. *Partisan Review,* 41, #1 (1974), pp. 137–142.

"Interview about the New Fiction in America." *Le Figaro Littéraire* (Paris), June 15, 1976.

"Jean Genet ou le théâtre de la haine." *Esprit* #39 (April, 1980), pp. 697–713.

"Jean-Luc Godard and Americanism." *Film Heritage,* 3 (Spring, 1968), 1–10, 48.

"The Language of Dada: Intermedia of Words." *Dada/Surrealism* #1 (Fall, 1972), pp. 19–23.

"Life in the Cylinder." *Fiction International* #1 (Fall, 1973), pp. 113–117.

"Michel Butor: Une Lecture de *Mobile.*" *Le Monde,* March 22, 1967, p. iv.

"The New Innovative Fiction" (with Ronald Sukenick). *Antaeus* #20 (Winter, 1976), pp. 138–149.

"The New Novel: Safety in Numbers." *Buffalo Evening News,* January 11, 1975, p. C12. Revised and expanded as "Death of the Novel or Another Alternative," *Revue Française d'Etudes Americaines* #3 (April, 1977), pp. 111–114.

"La Nouvelle poésie américaine." *Iô, Revue des Lettres et des Arts* #22 (June, 1959), pp. 9–31.

"Le Poete et les jouets." *French Review,* 39 (February, 1966), 567–576.

"Playgiarism: A Spatial Displacement of Words." *Eureka Review* #1 (1975), pp. 1–17. Revised and expanded in *Sub-stance* #16 (1977), pp. 107–112.

"Pour Maurice Roche." In *Maurice Roche par les Autres.* Paris: Editions Athanor, 1978.

Review of *Comment C'est* by Samuel Beckett, *French Review,* 34 (May, 1961), 594–595.

Review of *Samuel Beckett: The Comic Gamut* by Ruby Cohen, *French Review,* 38 (February, 1965), 577–579.

Review of *The Testament of Samuel Beckett* by Josephine Jacobsen and William R. Mueller, *French Review,* 38 (February, 1965), 579–580.

Review of *The Journal of Jean Cocteau,* ed. Wallace Fowlie, *Modern Language Journal,* 42 (March, 1965), 197–198.

Review of *Beckett and Behan* by Alan Simpson, *Modern Drama,* 8 (May, 1965), 123–124.

Review of *The Novels of Samuel Beckett* by John Fletcher, *L'Esprit Créateur,* 5 (Summer, 1965), 117–118.

Review of *Contemporary French Poetry* by Alexander Aspel and Donald Justice, *Romantic Review,* 57 (April, 1966), 154–155.

Review of *Deux films français* by Robert Hammond, *Modern Language Journal,* 50 (April, 1966), 236–237.

Review of *Configuration: critique de Samuel Beckett* by Melvin J. Friedman, *Modern Language Journal,* 50 (April, 1966), 241–242.

Review of *Jean Anouilh: A Study in Theatrics* by John Harvey, *Modern Drama,* 9

(Summer, 1966), 469–471.

Review of *Marcel Proust et les signes* by Gilles Deleuze, *French Review*, 40 (October, 1966), 151–153.

Review of *Réalité et imagination* by Maurice Lecuyer, *French Review*, 40 (November, 1966), 308–310.

Review of *Pour Samuel Beckett* by Ludovic Janvier, *Novel*, 2 (Winter, 1969), 191–192.

Review of *Selected Poems* by Guillevic, *French Review*, 44 (October, 1970), 178–179.

Review of *The Poetic Theory of Pierre Reverdy* by Robert Greene, *Comparative Literature*, 23 (Winter, 1971), 74–77.

Review of *La Mort de la littérature* by Jacques Ehrmann, *French Review*, 56 (February, 1973), 671–673.

"Samuel Beckett: The Liar's Paradox." In *Samuel Beckett: The Art of Rhetoric*, ed. Edouard Morot-Sir, pp. 119–141. Chapel Hill: University of North Carolina Press, 1976.

"Samuel Beckett ou le bonheur en Enfer." *Symposium*, 21 (Winter, 1967), 14–21. Reprinted in *Esprit* #363 (July/August, 1967), pp. 90–97, as "Le Bonheur chez Beckett."

"Samuel Beckett: une selection bibliographique." *Le Monde*, January 17, 1968, p. v.

"Surfiction: A Position." *Partisan Review*, 40 (Fall, 1973), pp. 113–117. Reprinted as "Introduction" to *Surfiction*. Chicago: Swallow Press, 1975.

"Sylvia Plath." *Esprit* #371 (May, 1968), pp. 825–832.

"Trylog." *Chicago Review*, 28 (Fall, 1976), 93–109 (conversation with Mas'ud Zavarzadeh and Joseph Hynes).

VI. Essays on Federman

Bolling, Doug. "Some Observations on Experimental Fiction: The Work of Sukenick, Gass, Wildman, and Federman." *Northeast Review*, Winter, 1975–76, pp. 1–18.

Bradbury, Malcolm. *The Novel Today*, p. 12. Manchester: Manchester University Press, 1977.

Caramello, Charles. "Flushing Out 'The Voice in the Closet.'" *Sub-stance* #20 (1978), pp. 101–113.

Dienstfry, Harris. "The Choice of Inventions." *Fiction International*, #2/3 (1974), pp. 147–150.

Eder, Doris L. "*Surfiction*: Plunging into the Surface." *Boundary 2*, 5 (Fall, 1976), 163–166.

Friedman, Melvin J. "Dislocations of Setting and Word: Notes on American Fiction Since 1950." *Studies in American Fiction*, 5 (Spring, 1977), 79–98.

———. "To 'Make It New': The American Novel Since 1945." *Wilson Quarterly*, 2 (Winter, 1978), 133–142.

Hassan, Ihab. *Paracriticisms*, pp. 87, 141. Urbana: University of Illinois Press, 1975.

Klinkowitz, Jerome. "Literary Disruptions; Or, What's Become of American Fiction?" *Partisan Review*, 40 (Fall, 1973), 433–444. Revised and expanded in *Surfiction*, ed. Raymond Federman, pp. 165–179. Chicago: Swallow Press, 1975.

————."Raymond Federman's Visual Fiction." *West Coast Poetry Review*, Spring, 1979, 123–124.

Lodge, David. *The Modes of Modern Writing*, pp. 230, 232, 272. Ithaca: Cornell University Press, 1977.

McCaffery, Larry. "The Fiction Collective, 1974–1978: An Innovative Alternative." *Chicago Review*, 30 (Autumn, 1978), 107–126.

————. "New Rules of the Game: *Take It or Leave It*." *Chicago Review*, 29 (Summer, 1977), 144–149.

Porush, David. "On *Take It or Leave It*." *Eureka Review* #2 (1977), pp. 85–88.

Scholes, Robert. *Fabulation and Metafiction*, pp. 136–138, 210, 214–215. Urbana: University of Illinois Press, 1979.

Sukenick, Ronald. "Refugee from the Holocaust." *New York Times Book Review*, October 1, 1972, pp. 40–41.

Tatham, Campbell. "Mythotherapy and Postmodern Fictions: Magic Is Afoot." In *Performance in Postmodern Culture*, ed. Michel Benamou and Charles Caramello, pp. 137–157. Madison: Coda Press, 1977.

————. "Correspondence/Notes/Etceteras." *Chicago Review*, 26 (Spring, 1975), 112–132.

Zavarzadeh, Mas'ud. *The Mythopoeic Reality*, pp. 40, 98. Urbana: University of Illinois Press, 1976.

VII. DOCTORAL DISSERTATIONS

Caramello, Charles. "Silverless Mirrors: On the Book in Postmodern American Fiction." University of Wisconsin–Milwaukee, 1978.

Karfiol, Judith. "New American Fiction and the Aesthetics of Albert Camus and Alain Robbe-Grillet." University of Southern California, 1978.

GILBERT SORRENTINO (b. 1929)

I. NOVELS

The Sky Changes
New York: Hill & Wang, 1966.

Steelwork
New York: Pantheon, 1970 (redistributed by Serendipity Books, Berkeley, Calif.).

Imaginative Qualities of Actual Things
New York: Pantheon, 1971 (redistributed by Serendipity Books, Berkeley, Calif.).

Splendide-Hotel
New York: New Directions, 1973.
New York: New Directions Paperbacks, 1973.

Flawless Play Restored; Or, the Masque of Fungo
Los Angeles: Black Sparrow, 1974.

Mulligan Stew
New York: Grove Press, 1979.
New York: Grove Press/Evergreen edition, 1979.
Parts of *Mulligan Stew* appearing in magazines:
"Catechism." *Chicago Review,* 25 (Winter, 1973), 19–31.
"Rayon Violet" and "A Library." *Vort* #6 (Fall, 1974), pp. 36–40.
"*Art Futures* Interview of the Month: Barnett Tete." *New Directions* #30 (1975), pp. 12–28.
"Anonymous Sketch of the Writer." *Partisan Review,* 41 (Spring, 1975), 24–29.
"Perfect Gifts." *Seems* #6/7 (Summer, 1975), pp. 94–101.
"The Notebooks of Anthony Lamont." *TriQuarterly* #34 (Fall, 1975), pp. 146–157.
"She Is the Queenly Pearl." *Partisan Review,* 42 (Winter, 1975), 535–549.
"A Garland of Impressions and Beliefs Culled from a Lifetime." *Chicago Review,* 27 (Winter, 1975), 25–29.
"O'Mara of No Fixed Abode." *TriQuarterly* #38 (Winter, 1977), pp. 179–190.
"Chats with the Real McCoy." *Atlantic,* 243 (March, 1979), 123–126.

II. POETRY BOOKS

The Darkness Surrounds Us
Highlands, N.C.: Jonathan Williams, 1960.

Black and White
New York: Totem Press, 1964.

The Perfect Fiction
New York: Norton, 1968.

Corrosive Sublimate
Los Angeles: Black Sparrow, 1971.

A Dozen Oranges
Los Angeles: Black Sparrow (Sparrow 46), 1976.

White Sail
Los Angeles: Black Sparrow, 1977.

Sulpiciae Elegidia/Elegiacs of Sulpicia
Mt. Horeb, Wis.: Perishable Press, 1977.

The Orangery
Austin: University of Texas Press, 1978.

III. UNCOLLECTED SHORT FICTION

"Decades." *Esquire,* 88 (August, 1977), 95–96, 138–140.
"Land of Cotton." *Harper's,* 255 (November, 1977), 73–76.
"The Moon in Its Flight." *New American Review* #13 (1971), pp. 153–163.

IV. CRITICISM

"Art Is A Country by Itself." *The Nation,* December 14, 1970, pp. 635–636.
"The Art of Hubert Selby." *Kulchur,* 4 (Spring, 1964), 27–43. Reprinted as a pamphet by Grove Press.
"Baseball Amouncers." *TV Guide,* 26 (May 6, 1978), 44.
"For the *Floating Bear*: Prose of Our Time." *Floating Bear* #30 (1964), pp. 11–13.
"Jack Spicer: Language as Image." *For Now* #5 (1966), pp. 28–36.
"Kitsch Into 'Art': The New Realism." *Kulchur,* 2 (Winter, 1962), 10–23.
"The Late Jack Spicer's Work Is a Miraculous Thing." *Village Voice,* 20 (October 13, 1975), 83–84.
"Louis Zukofsky." *Paideuma,* 7 (Winter, 1978), 401–402.
Letter to LeRoi Jones, *Floating Bear* #11 (1961), pp. 2–4.
Letter on Irwin Shaw and Ernest Hemingway, *New York Times Book Review,* December 17, 1978, p. 45.
"Neon, Kulchur, Etc." *TriQuarterly* #43 (Fall, 1978), pp. 298–316.
[On Donald Phelps.] *Vort* #6 (Fall, 1974), p. 157.
"Poetry Chronicle." *Kulchur,* 3 (Spring, 1963), 69–82.
"Reflections on 'Spring and All.'" *Kulchur,* 2 (Spring, 1962), 40–46.
"Remembrances of Bop in New York, 1945–1950." *Kulchur,* 3 (Summer, 1963), 70–82.
Review of *Watermelons* by Ron Loewinsohn, *Kulchur* #2 (1961), pp. 91–92.
Review of *Like I Say* and *Memoirs of an Interglacial Age* by Philip Whalen, *Kulchur* #3 (1961), pp. 79–81.
Review of *L'Avventura* Michelangelo Antonioni and *Rocco and His Brothers* by Luchino Visconti, *Kulchur* #4 (1961), pp. 90–93.
Review of *The Shell Game* by Joe Early, *Kulchur,* 2 (Autumn, 1962), 85–87.
Review of *Burning Conscience* by Claude Eatherly and Gunther Anders, *Kulchur,* 2 (Winter, 1962), 86–87.
Review of *The Lion's Tail and Eyes* by Robert Bly et al., *Kulchur,* 3 (Summer, 1963), 84–86.
Review of *The Wake* by Andrew Hoyem and *Residence on Earth* by Pablo Neruda, *Kulchur,* 3 (Winter, 1963), 88–92.

Review of *The Collected Later Poems* by William Carlos Williams, *Kulchur,* 3 (Autumn, 1963), 82–83.

Review of *The Moderns,* ed. LeRoi Jones, *Kulchur,* 4 (Summer, 1964), 81–86.

Review of *Because I Was Flesh* by Edward Dahlberg, *Kulchur,* 4 (Autumn, 1964), 88–89.

Review of *Flats* by Rudolph Wurlizter, *The Quest for Christa T* by Christa Wolf, and *Lame Duck* by E. M. Beekman, *Modern Occasion,* 1 (Fall, 1971), 618–622.

Review of *The Blood Oranges* by John Hawkes, *Modern Occasions,* 2 (Winter, 1972), 156–157.

Review of *Selected Poems* by John Weiners, *Parnassus,* 1 (Spring/Summer, 1973), 121–125.

Review of *William Carlos Williams* by Robert Coles, *Partisan Review,* 42, #3 (1975), pp. 462–467.

Review of *The Journals* by Paul Blackburn, *Parnassus,* 4 (Spring/Summer, 1976), 57–67.

Review of *A Month of Sundays* by John Updike, *Partisan Review,* 43, #1 (1976), pp. 119–121.

Review of *JR* by William Gaddis and *Beyond the Bedroom Wall* by Larry Woiwode, *Partisan Review,* 43, #4 (1976), pp. 613–618.

Review of *Blue Chicory* by Lorine Niedecker, *New York Times Book Review,* February 13, 1977, p. 27.

Review of *Too Much Flesh and Jabez* by Coleman Dowell, *New York Times Book Review,* January 1, 1978, p. 6.

"Rights: Some Personal Reactions." *Kulchur,* 3 (Winter, 1963), 19–21.

"Signal: A New Magazine." *Floating Bear* #29 (1964), pp, 15–16.

"Some Notes Toward a Paper on Prosody." *Yugen* #7 (1961), pp. 34–37.

"Ten Pamphlets." *Poetry,* 112 (April, 1968), 56–61.

"The Various Isolated: W. C. Williams' Prose." *New American Review* #15 (1972), pp. 192–207.

"Writer's Choice." *Partisan Review,* 42 (#3, 1975), 475; 43 (#1, 1976), 145.

V. SPECIAL NUMBERS OF SCHOLARLY JOURNALS ON SORRENTINO

Grosseteste Review (Great Britain), 6, #1/4 (1973).
Vort #6 (Fall, 1974).
Contents listed below.

VI. INTERVIEWS AND RECORDED REMARKS

Alpert, Barry. "Gilbert Sorrentino: An Interview." *Vort* #6 (Fall, 1974), pp. 3–30.
O'Brien, John. "Imaginative Qualities of Gilbert Sorrentino: An Interview." *Grosseteste Review,* 6, #1/4 (1973), pp. 69–84.
Ossman, David. *The Sullen Art,* pp. 46–55. New York: Corinth, 1963.
Sorrentino, Gilbert. "Biographical Note." In *The New American Poetry,* ed. Donald Allen, p. 444. New York: Grove Press, 1960.

VII. CRITICAL ESSAYS ON SORRENTINO

Alpert, Barry. "Local Turf." *Vort* #6 (Fall, 1974), pp. 59–61.

Armstrong, Peter. "Gilbert Sorrentino's *Imaginative Qualities of Actual Things.*" *Grosseteste Review,* 6, #1/4 (1973), pp. 65–68.

Broderick, Vincent A. "Disruptive Participants: Observations of Works by Sukenick and Sorrentino." *Kobe College Studies* (Japan), 1978, pp. 39–68.

Caserio, Robert L. "Gilbert Sorrentino's Prose Fiction." *Vort* #6 (Fall, 1974), pp. 63–69.

Emerson, Stephen. "*Imaginative Qualities of Acutal Things.*" *Vort* #6 (Fall, 1974), pp. 85–89.

Hannigan, Paul. "*Imaginative Qualities of Actual Things.*" *Plowshares,* 1 (Spring, 1973), 92–94.

Hornick, Lita. "*Kulchur:* A Memoir." *TriQuarterly* #43 (Fall, 1978), pp. 281–297.

Howard, Richard. "Interior Landscapes." *New Leader,* May 9, 1966, pp. 24–25.

Kenner, Hugh. "The Traffic in Words: No Place for the Avant-Garde." *Harper's,* 258 (June, 1979), 83–84, 88–90.

Klinkowitz, Jerome. "Gilbert Sorrentino's SuperFiction." *Chicago Review,* 25 (Spring, 1974), 77–89. Reprinted in *Vort* #6 (Fall, 1974), pp. 69–79. Revised and expanded in Klinkowitz and Roy R. Behrens, *The Life of Fiction,* pp. 7–15. Urbana: University of Illinois Press, 1977.

———. "Novels of Gilbert Sorrentino." *Village Voice,* 18 (November 22, 1973), 27–28.

Mottram, Eric. "The Black Polar Night: The Poetry of Gilbert Sorrentino." *Vort* #6 (Fall, 1974), pp. 43–59.

O'Brien, John. "Gilbert Sorrentino: Some Various Looks." *Vort* #6 (Fall, 1974), pp. 79–85.

Phelps, Donald. "Extra Space." *Vort* #6 (Fall, 1974), pp. 89–96.

Scholes, Robert. "*Imaginative Qualities of Actual Things.*" *Saturday Review,* October 23, 1971, p. 88.

Skodnick, Roy. "*Corrosive Sublimate*/Beauty is a Rare Thing." *Vort* #6 (Fall, 1974), pp. 42–43.

Weaver, Mike. *William Carlos Williams: The American Background,* p. 217. New York: Cambridge University Press, 1971.

Weinfield, Henry. "The Image in Time." *Vort* #6 (Fall, 1974), pp. 41–42.

———. "After the Deluge: An Essay on *Splendide-Hotel.*" *Vort* #6 (Fall, 1974), pp. 61–63.

Wright, Martin. "Gilbert Sorrentino's *Imaginative Qualities of Actual Things.*" *Grosseteste Review,* 6, #1/4 (1973), pp. 61–64.

Zinnes, Harriet. "Polar Night of America." *Parnassus,* 3, #1 (1974), pp. 204–209.

VIII. Doctoral Dissertation

Karfiol, Judith. "New American Fiction and the Aesthetics of Albert Camus and Alain Robbe-Grillet." University of Southern California, 1978.

Index